Language and Globalization

Series Editors: **Sue Wright**, University of Portsmouth, UK and **Helen Kelly-Holmes**, University of Limerick, Ireland.

In the context of current political and social developments, where the national group is not so clearly defined and delineated, the state language not so clearly dominant in every domain, and cross-border flows and transfers affect more than a small elite, new patterns of language use will develop. The series aims to provide a framework for reporting on and analysing the linguistic outcomes of globalization and localization.

Titles include:

David Block
MULTILINGUAL IDENTITIES IN A GLOBAL CITY
London Stories

Jenny Carl and Patrick Stevenson (*editors*)
LANGUAGE, DISCOURSE AND IDENTITY IN CENTRAL EUROPE
The German Language in a Multilingual Space

Diarmait Mac Giolla Chríost
LANGUAGE AND THE CITY

Julian Edge (*editor*)
(RE)LOCATING TESOL IN AN AGE OF EMPIRE

John Edwards
CHALLENGES IN THE SOCIAL LIFE OF LANGUAGE

Aleksandra Galasińska and Michał Krzyżanowski (*editors*)
DISCOURSE AND TRANSFORMATION IN CENTRAL AND EASTERN EUROPE

Roxy Harris
NEW ETHNICITIES AND LANGUAGE USE

Jane Jackson
INTERCULTURAL JOURNEYS
From Study to Residence Abroad

Helen Kelly-Holmes and Gerlinde Mautner (*editors*)
LANGUAGE AND THE MARKET

Clare Mar-Molinero and Patrick Stevenson (*editors*)
LANGUAGE IDEOLOGIES, POLICIES AND PRACTICES
Language and the Future of Europe

Clare Mar-Molinero and Miranda Stewart (*editors*)
GLOBALIZATION AND LANGUAGE IN THE SPANISH-SPEAKING WORLD
Macro and Micro Perspectives

Ulrike Hanna Meinhof and Dariusz Galasinski
THE LANGUAGE OF BELONGING

Richard C. M. Mole (*editor*)
DISCURSIVE CONSTRUCTIONS OF IDENTITY IN EUROPEAN POLITICS

Leigh Oakes and Jane Warren
LANGUAGE, CITIZENSHIP AND IDENTITY IN QUÉBEC

Mario Saraceni
THE RELOCATION OF ENGLISH

Christina Slade and Martina Mollering (*editors*)
FROM MIGRANT TO CITIZEN: TESTING LANGUAGE, TESTING CULTURE

Colin Williams
LINGUISTIC MINORITIES IN DEMOCRATIC CONTEXT

Forthcoming titles:

Robert Blackwood and Stefani Tufi
THE LINGUISTICS LANDSCAPE OF THE MEDITERRANEAN
A Study of French and Italian Coastal Cities

Grit Liebscher and Jennifer Dailey-O'Cain
LANGUAGE, SPACE AND IDENTITY IN MIGRATION

Language and Globalization
Series Standing Order ISBN 978-1-4039-9731-9 Hardback
978-1-4039-9732-6 Paperback
(*outside North America only*)

You can receive future titles in this series as they are published by placing a standing order. Please contact your bookseller or, in case of difficulty, write to us at the address below with your name and address, the title of the series and the ISBN quoted above.

Customer Services Department, Macmillan Distribution Ltd, Houndmills, Basingstoke, Hampshire RG21 6XS, England

---

Other books by John Edwards:

LANGUAGE AND DISADVANTAGE

THE IRISH LANGUAGE

LANGUAGE, SOCIETY AND IDENTITY

MULTILINGUALISM

LANGUAGE IN CANADA

UN MUNDO DE LENGUAS

LANGUAGE AND IDENTITY

LANGUAGE DIVERSITY IN THE CLASSROOM

MINORITY LANGUAGES AND GROUP IDENTITY

Challenges in the Social Life of Language

John Edwards
St Francis Xavier University, Nova Scotia, Canada

First published 2011 by
PALGRAVE MACMILLAN

Palgrave Macmillan in the UK is an imprint of Macmillan Publishers Limited, registered in England, company number 785998, of Houndmills, Basingstoke, Hampshire RG21 6XS.

Palgrave Macmillan in the US is a division of St Martin's Press LLC, 175 Fifth Avenue, New York, NY 10010.

Palgrave Macmillan is the global academic imprint of the above companies and has companies and representatives throughout the world.

Palgrave® and Macmillan® are registered trademarks in the United States, the United Kingdom, Europe and other countries.

ISBN 978-0-230-50031-0 hardback

This book is printed on paper suitable for recycling and made from fully managed and sustained forest sources. Logging, pulping and manufacturing processes are expected to conform to the environmental regulations of the country of origin.

A catalogue record for this book is available from the British Library.

A catalog record for this book is available from the Library of Congress.

10 9 8 7 6 5 4 3 2 1
20 19 18 17 16 15 14 13 12 11

Printed and bound in The United States of America

For
Bonnie and Michael Joyce
with appreciation for their hospitality
and assistance over many years

Contents

1
Introduction

General observations

My intention in this collection is to discuss some of the most important issues in the 'social life of language'. Many of these, perhaps in slightly different clothing, have been important before; some have *always* been important; but all have attracted considerable recent attention and will continue to do so as we move deeper into the new century. This is not a 'how-to' book: I offer no pat remedies for linguistic tensions and injustices, nor do I always make strongly pointed remarks about the relationships that link language with ethnicity, nationalism, religion and gender. Rather, I am concerned in this book to direct readers' attention to some of the most contentious and highly charged matters under these headings, to present what I take to be the most important evidence, facts and opinions bearing upon them, and to then leave readers to draw their conclusions. I do reserve the occasional right, however, to nudge a little in one direction or another.

Beyond highlighting topics of relevance under a broad language rubric, this book also emphasises their relationships to wider social and political issues, for it is a truism that linguistic perspectives can provide an important window into larger matters. So, as part of the discussion of aspects of the social life of language that are of intrinsic and independent interest, I also try to make a case for the interconnections among them, and for their collective contribution to our understanding of important phenomena and the social contexts which both produce and are influenced by them. It will be seen that the twin threads linking all the topics and contributing, therefore, to the fluency, interest and value of the overall discussion, are *power* and *identity*. The sources of power, its expression, and its impact upon social, cultural and linguistic life will be made clear throughout, and so will the motivating influence of what has come to be called 'identity politics'. The two forces sometimes act in harness as, for example, when power operates in the service of the maintenance of 'mainstream' identities and values – but they can also pull in opposition, as in situations where 'small' languages and cultures struggle to preserve ethnolinguistic continuity in the face of strong external pressures.

One of the important features of this book, often only implicitly touched upon, is a plea for triangulation of effort. Every aspect of the 'social life of language' is relevant for more than one discipline. Still, while the topic cries out for greater inter- and cross-disciplinary attention, many treatments make little or no reference to pertinent information from neighbouring scholarly domains. Worse, some of them seem entirely unaware of other information and other perspectives. No one can adequately walk all the pathways, of course, but if one's chosen topic is of both temporal and scholarly depth, then at least some acknowledgement of other tracks in the wood must be made, some familiarity demonstrated. Perhaps the most egregious failing is the lack of socio-historical contextualisation which is so evident in most contemporary social-science undertakings. In Paul's first letter to the Corinthians, we are told that, while faith, hope and charity are all abiding virtues, 'the greatest of these is charity', and I would like to suggest that, among the abiding virtues of best practice in social science, the greatest is historical awareness.

A recent example of good practice is found in Oakes's (2001) study of language attitudes and perceptions of group identity. Noting that most such investigations have not had particularly strong empirical underpinnings, he makes use here of the findings from a questionnaire survey of more than 400 student respondents. Surveys alone are not sufficient, of course, and so it is gratifying to find that the greater part of Oakes's book draws upon 'materials from a range of fields (e.g. the sociology of language, sociolinguistics, social psychology, political science, history, economics) for a comprehensive examination of the role of language in national identity' (p. vii). In fact, Oakes goes beyond the contextualisation encouraged above, exhibiting two further virtues: there is a highly desirable comparative emphasis, in a joint consideration of France and Sweden; relatedly, the book brings literature written in Swedish and French to a readership which we know is largely unable to navigate beyond English.

Current interest in the social life of language is largely contextualised in three great modern themes: the linkages between language and identity, the interactions among 'big' and 'small' varieties, and the 'new' ecology of language. These are closely intertwined in two important ways. First, matters of sociocultural maintenance and survival are at their heart: indeed, it would not be inaccurate to see specific questions of powerful and endangered languages, on the one hand, and broader matters of ecological interrelationships, on the other, as central constituents of the larger theme of language-and-identity. The themes (or sub-themes) are also closely related in that they focus attention upon the twin aspects, communicative and symbolic, of language itself. While linguistic instrumentality is usually the immediate or patent bone of contention in discussions of endangered languages or in assessments of ecological interplay – and while instrumentality may, in some instances, be the only such bone – the point at which people typically become most exercised over language matters occurs when they feel that *more* than instrumentality is at stake. People go to war over ideas more frequently than they do over tools. If groups go to the barricades over the language of school or of work, there usually exist more latent worries, too. And this is not particularly mysterious, because, while separable in some circumstances, the symbolic and the instrumental aspects of language often coexist. More importantly, in 'at-risk' settings in which such separation is seen to be in train, users desire that they *should* coexist, and this may well lead to actual or attempted interventions.

While it is undoubtedly true that the symbolic value of language can (and commonly does) outlast communicative language shift, and thus continue to provide a psychological and social anchor for groups and individuals (a typical context here involves old-world immigrants in new-world settings) and while, indeed, such continuity is a very common scenario in most situations in which minorities and majorities must rub along together, it should be remembered that, in a long-term historical sense, the communicative aspect is a prerequisite for the symbolic. And, since most psychological dynamics having to do with identity, whether or not these matters are consciously articulated, typically rest upon such a long-term perspective (as the use of words like 'heritage', 'tradition' and 'authenticity' makes clear), it is no wonder that linguistic instrumentality is seen as something to be buttressed wherever possible. It is unlikely that the symbolic half of the picture will persist forever without the reinforcement of ordinary usage.

Setting the stage for the social life of language

Born in 1895, Joyce Oramel Hertzler was a vice-president of the American Sociological Association, a long-serving faculty member and department chairman at the University of Nebraska, and a distinguished emeritus professor. A research award is named in his honour. He published widely, on themes ranging from utopianism, to humour, to institutions and societies, ancient and modern. In 1965, a book entitled *A Sociology of Language* built upon a 1953 article in which Hertzler argued that more attention should be paid to the interaction of language and situation. While acknowledging that recent scholarship in anthropology and psychology had dealt with language, Hertzler noted the rather specific approaches of each: the former was essentially interested in the relationship between languages (particularly 'primitive' varieties) and cultures; the latter was concerned primarily with developmental aspects of language learning. Within sociology, however, Hertzler found most treatments to be 'more or less superficial, unsystematic, or confined only to certain limited or special aspects of language in society. In the main, they have merely skirted the edges of a sociology of language' (p. 5). This is regrettable, Hertzler pointed out, because 'sociology has abundant reasons for examining [language] in its sociocultural context', the chief and most general one being simply that language has 'crucial significance in the operation of human society'. How surprising, then, that sociologists 'have paid so little attention to it' (p. 7).

In a note at the end of his introduction, Hertzler paid tribute to the 'comprehensive and systematic treatment' of Cohen (1956). This work is certainly an interesting one, but not of sufficient scope to invalidate Hertzler's later remark that 'the sociology of language is still in its rudimentary stage of development' (p. 6). Nor, indeed, does it seriously challenge the status of his own book as the earliest general treatment of the sociology of language. Not only does it range very widely across most of the important topics within the sociology of language, the book emphasises the need for cross- and inter-disciplinary attention: 'from non-sociological sources...the works of social linguists, historians of language, philosophers of language, folklorists...anthropologists...cultural history...the sociologies of knowledge, science and literature' (pp. 6–7). Given a continuing need for fuller embedding and for greater willingness to cross scholarly borders, we should be particularly grateful that this seminal work came from the pen of a wide-ranging scholar. I think that we should also, however, regret a little that Hertzler does not occupy a more central place in the scholarly pantheon. But the two points are related: where fragmented, decontextualised and historically naïve treatments abound, perhaps we should not expect much attention to broader scholarship.

Hertzler's reference to 'social linguists' is rather prescient: a year before his book appeared, a 'sociolinguistics' conference was held in California, the proceedings of which were edited by Bright (1966). Since then, there has been some debate over distinctions of emphasis between *sociolinguistics* and the *sociology of language*, as well as a great deal of overlap in the subjects commonly listed under each rubric. At the beginning of the next decade, for instance, Joshua Fishman published his *Sociolinguistics* (1970a); a revised edition two years later appeared as *The Sociology of Language* (1972). In the broadest terms, we might say that the latter term implies particular attention to social behaviour revealed and elucidated through the study of language, and that the former tends to stress the linguistic variation presented or encouraged in different contexts. Perhaps, then, the terms are best viewed as describing two sides of the one coin. However, the distinction just noted is not necessarily endorsed by all who use the terms, and some have alternated in their usage while carrying on with the same sort of work.

It has sometimes also been thought that 'sociolinguistics' may carry the seeds of its own demise, since it represents what many consider to be a necessary broadening of the larger field of linguistics. If it were to become generally accepted that there can be no meaningful linguistics without attention to context, then sociolinguistics could be absorbed. Fishman (1970b: 8–9) thus pointed out:

> the leading advocates and adherents of sociolinguistics are also commonly the ones that prophesy its earliest demise, not for lack of success but, on the contrary, as a result of hopefully [sic] carrying the day within the fold of linguistics proper.

As Fishman goes on to say, such a 'self-liquidation' does not apply to a field styled 'the sociology of language'. This may be viewed as a new, enduring and autonomous sub-topic of sociology, a relatively loose conception 'falling easily into the growing company of sociologies of this and that' (Edwards, 1976: 9).

In practice, the two terms are used loosely and sometimes interchangeably. In any event, given a mingling of context and language, it is possible that *both* might be more or less accurately used within the same investigation. One might, for example, use social-situational information to comment upon linguistic forms produced, while usage might be studied in order to better understand the context. This simply reflects the fact that context can influence linguistic choice, and linguistic choice can be an index to perceptions of context – may, indeed, even *alter* that context (as Herman noted in his classic 1961 paper). This, incidentally, may bring us more to a *social psychology of language*, a perspective whose most basic emphasis is upon perception, attitude, belief and individual action, than to a sociological approach with *its* traditional stress on group dynamics. Perhaps, then, we can justify *three* basic approaches to the social life of language, and perhaps in some instances one will seem more obviously apposite than the others.[1] We should always bear in mind, however, that we are not usually dealing with watertight and mutually exclusive categories.

Whatever terms are used, the common thread is a concern with the social life of language, not with the technicalities of language itself. Neither linguistics (with its traditional emphases upon structure, acquisition, use and history) then, nor psycholinguistics (language acquisition, language-and-thought relationships, and so on) reflect the primary thrust here. Rather, the emphasis is upon interactions among language, society and culture. The social life of language is a hybrid field of study and, as already implied, one that sometimes straddles or sits rather uncertainly on disciplinary fences.

Readers may find it interesting at this point to consider what Chomsky, the most prominent linguist of our time, has said about the social life of language or, more specifically, about sociolinguistics ('self-liquidating' or not). In a discussion of the relationship between linguistics and the 'human sciences', he has acknowledged that some descriptive work (the demonstration that Black English is a valid dialect, for example) may be useful for combatting educational prejudices. However, all such undertakings, he feels, are trivial on a scientific level, and he rejects their tendency to display 'theoretical pretensions'. More pointedly, Chomsky has claimed that 'the existence of a discipline called "sociolinguistics" remains for me an obscure matter', and that sociology lacks basic and explanatory principles (1979: 55–56). Indeed, work in these areas hardly qualifies as research at all, since it does not come to grips with underlying principles and structures. Chomsky's remarks about the work of two very well-known scholars are thus hardly surprising:

[Labov] is doing something very useful on the level of educational practice...but on the linguistic level, this matter is evident and banal...The work of Bernstein may very well be reactionary in its implications, and perhaps hardly worth discussing as a specimen of the rational study of language. I had believed it should no longer be necessary to say that the spoken language of an urban ghetto is a real language. (pp. 55–56)

Chomsky's sentiments are not unlike those of Lord Rutherford, who is reported to have said that 'all science is either physics or stamp collecting'

(Birks, 1962). Indeed, summarising his observations about the activities of Labov, Bernstein and applied linguistics generally, Chomsky remarks that 'You can...collect butterflies and make many observations. If you like butterflies, that's fine; but such work must not be confounded with research' (p. 57). An obvious counter-argument accuses Chomsky of rather restrictive practice here, particularly since it is possible to imagine that any *asocial* theorising in linguistics must be a 'rather sterile type of activity' (Wardhaugh, 2006: 10; see also Andersen, 1988).

Central to Chomsky's conception of 'research' and central, therefore, to his disdain for most elements of the social life of language, is the elevation of what Wardhaugh and others have seen as armchair theorising and asocial sterility into 'idealisation'. Chomsky insists that, in order to get at the core principles and structures (of language and, indeed, of all scientific subjects) that hold the promise of explanatory insight, one must pare a subject down to essentials:

> Opposition to idealization is simply objection to rationality; it amounts to nothing more than an insistence that we shall not have meaningful intellectual work...you *must* abstract some object of study, you must eliminate those factors which are not pertinent...When you work within some idealization, perhaps you overlook something which is terribly important. That is a contingency of rational inquiry that has always been understood. One must not be too worried about it. One has to face this problem and try to deal with it, to accommodate oneself to it. It is inevitable. (Chomsky, 1979: 57)

The general argument here is a strong one. It is a principle basic to the cumulative and building-block conception of science that, without the setting of limits, no meaningful activity is possible. The specific argument is that the most important job for students of language is the uncovering of fundamental principles; later, perhaps, this asocial linguistics might form the foundation of more broadly based enquiries which could extend outward from the 'idealised' speaker to the world in which he or she speaks.

There are several related strands in Chomsky's position in these matters. At the most general level, he is critical of the empirical underpinning of most 'human science', claiming (as we have seen) that it represents a trivialisation of true research. In linguistic matters, a concern for underlying structure will necessarily imply an abstraction of language from its socially chaotic expression. To use familiar and famous terms, this means that the study of linguistic *competence* is more pivotal and more scientific than are descriptions of actual *performance*; or, if you prefer Saussure, that delving into the philosophy of *langue* is an altogether deeper effort than studying *parole*.[2] These sorts of points are meant to distinguish the rational and intellectual pursuit of the elemental verities from fact-grubbing and ephemeral explanations in ever-changing social environments. It is of course quite clear that such distinctions have always been made. They are reflected, for instance, in the pecking orders found across (and within) academic disciplines.[3]

The arguments as they apply to *language* have a particular immediacy, and are particularly engaging, simply because everyone uses language. While both the pure and applied aspects of physics and chemistry are closed books to most people, everyone is familiar (and most are quite expert) with the applied nature of language. Furthermore, many feel that it is precisely *within* its applied context that language is most meaningful and most worthy of study. Add to this the view that a linguistic discipline which purposely ignores real-life variation is rather precious (or worse), and we arrive at an important parting of the ways. On the one hand, we find linguistic scholars who are convinced that theoretical and socially decontextualised work is the only worthwhile sort; on the other, we find critics who claim, in effect, that this neglects the human essence of language, an essence that evaporates under what they consider to be unnaturally disembodied enquiry. Readers will find the summary comments of Calvet (1987, 1999) useful here, as well as the rather more swingeing remarks of Williams (1992).

My own view is that both Chomsky and his critics are right, because they are concerned with different fields: areas and topics that are only *apparently* linked by a common linguistic element. Chomsky and his epigones are centrally interested in the way language 'works', and many of them are even more interested in what the workings of language may tell us about human mental functions. For them, linguistics is thus a part of psychology, and arguably the most important part. This approach to the study of language is clearly of very great importance, but it carries no implication that investigations of language-in-society must wait until more 'idealised' conceptions are solidified. Sociolinguists may reasonably carry on with work on language variation as it occurs in actual usage, and sociologists or social psychologists of language need not abandon their attention to language as the pillar of social communication and a prime marker of group identity.[4]

Topics

Part 1: Perceptual underpinnings

At a number of points throughout this book, I attempt to refocus our attention upon older work and to suggest why it may still have something important to say – particularly, of course, in the light of further developments. This is particularly clear in the second chapter, where I devote two sections and part of a third to studies by Richard LaPiere. The important generality is simply that the elucidation and the assessment of attitude remain highly relevant to our investigations of the social life of language. While there have been recent attempts to oust attitude from its traditionally central position within social study (see Chapter 2, note 5), I argue that these are misguided. I also point out, however, that we need to be a little more careful in our understanding of attitude.

Were they to provide nothing more than a glimpse of the investigative methods of early twentieth-century social enquiry, LaPiere's experiments would still make eminently worthwhile reading. They do more, however. They give us a fascinating historical snapshot of racial attitudes and the accepted descriptive vocabulary of the times, and they also highlight many of the continuingly important themes and pitfalls of attitudinal research. Putting to one side the obvious methodological flaws and inconsistencies that present themselves to modern eyes, we can easily isolate some of these. We see, for instance, the contortions through which American white soldiers attempted to understand French acceptance of their black counterparts: this worrying and puzzling situation found a cognitive solution, of course, and it is one that continues in use today. LaPiere also suggested that his 'more thoughtful' respondents found it less easy to make categorical judgements when asked their opinion of black people; firm and straightforward responses were more likely to come from those of lower social status. He also pointed out that prejudicial attitudes in French commercial life were most likely to emerge in a sort of sympathy with foreign (white) postures: the implication here is that people will very often fall in with the views of others, particularly when they stand to gain by it. LaPiere's travels also prompted him to make some remarks about the greater racial animosity on the English side of the Channel. I don't think we need pay too much attention to the particulars of the argument, although it is entirely possible that the French *were* less prejudiced than the English. More important is the simple exercise of making cross-cultural comparisons and trying to interpret the results. As part of this exercise, LaPiere expresses the forward-looking sentiment that there is nothing 'biological' or 'natural' in white prejudice towards blacks.

In the second and more famous of LaPiere's studies – the one that is still given a sentence or two in every social psychology textbook – we observe his clever demonstration that attitudes and behaviour need not go hand-in-hand. Why would a Chinese couple, travelling across the United States, be well received at all but one of 250 hotels, camps and restaurants when existing attitudinal work had revealed strong prejudices against 'Orientals'? And why would almost all of those 250 establishments answer a later letter of enquiry by saying that they would either refuse service to Chinese people outright, or that their feelings were 'uncertain'. There are, of course, a number of obvious reasons that could account for the discrepancy here: one might simply be less prejudiced when confronted with an actual group member who is so clearly not an abstract concept; one might put one's racist feelings aside in order to make money; one might not wish to *appear* prejudiced in a public setting; one might have no desire to embarrass another person, even if the latter were a member of a disliked group; one might be afraid; and so on.

The most important generality is simply that we have to be very careful indeed in measuring attitudes and in extrapolating from our findings. One of LaPiere's most astute observations was that we should not be seduced by the ease and apparent utility of the usual methods, notably questionnaires and other such self-report instruments. It is surely better (if, we might add, considerably more untidy) to make 'a shrewd guess' about something important than to take pains to measure accurately that which is not, a sentiment that many social scientists might do well to take to heart.

I conclude this second chapter with some further remarks about difficulties that often bedevil our attempts to come to grips with attitudes in general, and with language attitudes in particular. I mention the two most important here. The first is that our 'respondents', 'informants' or 'subjects' are typically extremely willing to do what we ask of them. Willingness, however, can often compromise both truth and accuracy. Relatedly, I also point out here the very great difficulties involves in knowing just how to differentially weight the answers we receive from informants. In fact, I suggest that in most investigations no weighting occurs (or *could* occur) at all. This is an egregious failing, and one that can severely compromise the interpretation of results.

The second problem is, again, an extremely common one, and it rests upon a simple confusion of 'attitude' with 'belief'. Strictly speaking, the latter is a component of the former; or, to put it the other way, 'attitude' means more than just 'belief'. The extra ingredient here is affect or emotion. While in some circumstances, this may seem a rather precious distinction, in many others it is most important. If I ask an informant, 'Would you like your child to learn German?', I cannot rationally interpret a 'yes' as reflecting a favourable attitude, or a 'no' as an unfavourable one. I have simply assessed a belief. To get closer to attitude, I would have to probe further, and ask my informant what he or she feels about the matter. Someone could agree with the statement, for instance, grudgingly accepting that German would be of considerable value, while wishing fervently that this were not true. On the other hand, and on the grounds of perceived non-utility, one could reply in the negative while feeling deeply and positively attached to the language, the culture, or both. Readers will see, then, that most 'attitude questionnaires' are nothing of the kind and, more importantly, that many of the discussions arising from the findings are inaccurate.

Chapter 3 continues the discussion of attitude, but turns it in a more specifically linguistic dimension. I begin with a consideration – perhaps a reconsideration – of whether we should bother very much about attitudes at all. There has never been, of course, the slightest shortage of opinions about language, particularly about its quality, the superiority of one variety to another, and so on. Furthermore, people from all parts of the social spectrum have participated: from kings and scholars, to statesmen and the perennially disgusted letter writers from Tunbridge Wells. Among other things, all such expressions have to do with identity, and with the writers' associations of something personal and valued with a particular language, dialect or accent. I suggest that it is unwise to be too dismissive of what are very often highly coloured and intemperate linguistic opinions. First, and most generally, these are the voices of 'the people'; second, and more specifically, these popular points of view both reflect and influence important social dynamics. In Chapter 4, for instance, I explain how attitudes that have currency in the real social world regularly transform linguistic difference into linguistic deficit.

Nonetheless, it has sometimes seemed reasonable to assume that, in that same social world, language attitudes (or, at least, some *types* of language attitude) are not very important after all. Macnamara (1973) made the cogent argument that, when it comes to large-scale language shift, attitudes are generally overpowered by necessity. This seems accurate, since it hard to imagine many instances of language shift occurring without people's hands being forced in some way or another. Nonetheless, I think that if we separate *instrumental* attitudes from *integrative* ones and if, as well, we accept a useful distinction between *positive* and *favourable* postures, we can clarify matters somewhat. The example I provide in Chapter 3 is of a nineteenth-century Irish speaker who realises that the linguistic wind is now blowing very much in the direction of English: such a person could very well be described as having a positive and instrumental attitude towards learning English, but not a favourable or integrative one.

I go on to suggest that, in terms of more formal contexts of language learning (most notably in the classroom), attitudes may come back into their own, as it were. If, as has been the case for millions of children, classroom activities are not driven by any intrinsic necessity, then – precisely because the learning of French or German or Spanish seems disconnected from events beyond the school gates, precisely because the classroom seems a very weak reflection of the wider world – children's attitudes may make a very real difference. It may seem curious, perhaps, to imagine that it is the essential artificiality of the classroom, and the classification of language lessons under the same general heading that covers all other school subjects, that bring attitudes and motivations more to the centre of things. Nonetheless, learning German in secondary-school classes in the middle of Alberta is importantly different than learning it as a consequence of having to make one's living in Bonn, and it is not unreasonable to think that personal attitudes and inclinations are going to have more of an impact in the former scenario than in the latter. (I am prescinding here from questions of variations in general intelligence and aptitude; these will make a difference in all contexts, including those in which all those other school subjects are presented, too.)

This part of the story is concerned with the circumstances in which attention to attitude is entirely justified, and I make reference to the very large literature that reflects the study of language attitudes and motivation and, more specifically, the ways in which favourable dispositions might be encouraged, supported and rewarded. I move on, then, to some general remarks about the centrality of *perception* in all aspects of social life and about the specific forms perceptions of language variation have regularly assumed. We know, for reasons that go well beyond actual language, of course, how different regional and status-laden dialects are evaluated – that is to say, how their *speakers* are assessed – and we know very well how perceptions are, in fact, social reality. In all societies that are at all linguistically stratified, we find strong perceptual variations. The implications for stereotyping, and for what may flow from it, are obvious. We typically think of people being unfairly evaluated here, of children's cognitive abilities being mis-evaluated on the basis of unfavourable assessments of their speech, and so on. But sometimes, too, people who have more socially approved attributes, including linguistic ones, may have their way through life made rather easier. There is another sizeable social-psychological literature showing very clearly how having the right speech styles, physical looks, height and weight, gender, clothing, names, address, antecedents, and so on can all be extremely influential; any social psychology textbook will provide numerous examples (see, for instance, Myers *et al.*, 2009).[5]

I also note in Chapter 3 that we need more detailed information about the specific linguistic cues that elicit stereotyped reactions, and I end with a brief section outlining the ways in which we manipulate our language in order to 'accommodate' to others. This may involve variations in dialect, accent, style and register, as well as in speech rate and pitch, message content, and many paralinguistic accompaniments. At the heart of this process is the desire to present ourselves in a certain light. The most frequent variant, perhaps, involves convergence towards others so as to heighten their favourable perceptions of us; on the other hand, we may also make *divergences*, in situations in which we wish to increase social distance, to dissociate ourselves from others, to make a provocative point, and so on.

Chapter 4 represents a third consideration of attitudes, focussing upon language attitudes in more specific contexts. I open with a discussion of standard and non-standard dialects. Linguistically, of course, all dialects are equally valid systems; socially, however, they rise or fall in status according to the fortunes of their speakers. Among other things, this relationship means that we can often gain useful insights into different corners of the social world via speech and language perceptions. This possibility is heightened when we realise that distinctions between standard and non-standard varieties occur along a number of evaluative dimensions. Furthermore, a large number of studies have revealed that, on some of these dimensions – notably, those having to do with the perceived warmth, friendliness and integrity of speakers – those standard-dialect users who are judged most favourably in terms of intelligence, ambition, competence and prestige tend *not* to receive the greatest approval ratings.

In this chapter I also point out, however, that there are some language varieties that may be termed 'regional standards', inasmuch as they evoke the most favourable perceptions in terms of *both* competence and prestige *and* friendliness and reliability. There is a great deal of revealing work to be conducted here: some will involve considering 'off-shore' accents and dialects that may, for historical reasons, still regularly attract certain evaluations, even within regions in which they are rarely or never used. This seems to me to be a particularly interesting avenue, given the global spread of English, the rise of many localised Englishes, and the continuing interplay of British versus American English in international affections. It is also of some relevance to the increasing number of choices that now must be made when teaching English (which English?) to schoolchildren.

The other sections of this chapter deal with the dynamics of language, making the general point that once-and-for-all assessments of beliefs, attitudes, stereotypes and prejudices are impossible. On the contrary, we need repeated enquiries here (as, indeed, we do in *all* societal investigations). In the first section, I simply point out that the Queen's English – even the idiolect of the monarch herself – is changing. In the second, I discuss some rather poignant features of dialect evaluation. We know, for instance, that the maternal varieties of socially disadvantaged groups are generally looked down upon and considered inaccurate or improper by others; but we also know that the speakers of those disdained varieties tend to accept, themselves, these stereotyped and linguistically unenlightened views. But it is in this very psychosocial area that we see the greatest dynamism.

For example, dialects that were once the poor relations can become reinvigorated as the social position of their speakers alters. The emergence or resurgence of black and Hispanic group 'pride' is a case in point here, casting dialect varieties in new and favourable lights, lights whose power is sufficient to attract people from outside the groups themselves. The phenomenon of 'covert prestige' is relevant here, of course: the directness, the vibrancy, the 'toughness' and even the (perceived) lack of subtlety and nuance that are seen to mark non-standard dialects have proved attractive to speakers whose normal and general usage is more standard. The study of non-standard dialects also reinforces our sense that *all* varieties, even those whose use may create difficulties for their speakers, can act as important and valued bearers of group identity and solidarity. Ryan's famous 1979 study suggested reasons for the persistence of 'low-prestige' forms, but this remains an understudied area: we would profit from further knowledge of the intertwinings among pride, solidarity and (lack of) prestige. Investigations in the area reveal the continuing belief in 'substandard' styles – a linguistically incorrect opinion, to be sure, but also a socially powerful one. This, in fact, leads directly to the final section of the chapter, in which I come to the regrettable conclusion that social attitudes and prejudices continue to turn dialect differences into deficiencies.

I also devote a section here to 'Ebonics', to the recent discussions surrounding the status, use and possible teaching of Black English. The intrinsic importance here is evident, given the very large numbers of Americans (and, indeed, others) who speak one form or another of Black

English. But there is also great illustrative and heuristic value to scholarship here. This is simply because any developments in our perceptions and understanding of dialects that have traditionally been placed on the lowest rungs of the status ladder must necessarily inform our sense of *all* non-standard varieties.

Part 2: Identity matters

Chapter 5 is the first of three in which I turn from attitudes to identity; of course, such a turn hardly means that we have left attitudes behind. It would be more accurate to say that, in considering matters of language and identity, we are considering the operation of beliefs and attitudes in a particular context. I begin with two general observations. The first is that the language–identity relationship is thrown into particular relief in times of change, tension, upheaval: transitional times. This being so, it is no wonder that close attention is often given to minority-group settings; after all, when small communities must coexist with large ones, some degree of tension is more or less always present. The other generality, to which I devote the second section of this chapter, has to do with the centrality of group membership for virtually all human beings. To paraphrase Maria's letter in *Twelfth Night*: sometimes we are born into groups, sometimes we join groups, and sometimes we have group membership thrust upon us. In this book I am of course more interested in those collectivities which have greater permanence, but group allegiances can be important even in transitory circumstances. I describe one or two 'classic' studies (including those of Muzafer Sherif and Henri Tajfel) that demonstrate how incredibly easy it is to create those allegiances. The famous experiments of Stanley Milgram and Philip Zimbardo are also relevant here, for they show how artificially contrived identities can have powerful effects. The overall point is, simply, that 'groupness' and feelings of 'belongingness' typically constitute extremely important parts of our identity. There is a third generality, too, and it comes in the final section of this chapter. I reiterate, with some further analysis, the point that all languages and dialects, even those of low standing within the community, are valid communicative systems; consequently, all varieties are perfectly adequate bearers of group identity.

One feature of groupness has to do with labels: how do we call ourselves, how do others name us, and how do we denominate them? At one level, group designations are simply shorthand labelling devices; at another, they can prove particularly revealing. What may we read into the social perceptions of communities whose name for themselves simply translates as 'the people' or 'the human beings'? What do names like 'the mutes', 'the stammerers' or 'the edible ones' tell us about prejudiced or dominant–subaltern relationships? Why do groups so deeply resent 'voice appropriation'? How can translators be considered as quislings? The answers to all these questions bring us squarely back to conceptions of identity, of belonging, of 'us-and-them' and, of course, of the central importance of language that runs through them.

It is this theme that animates the next section, the core concern of which is the importance of language as symbol. The communicative and symbolic aspects of language may coexist, often in a virtually seamless and hence unremarked way, for 'mainstream' speakers in mainstream settings. For minority-group members, however, the two facets are separable: practical or oppressive conditions may have brought about communicative language shift, but the symbolic associations of the original variety may remain of psychological importance to feelings of identity continuity. There are many interesting avenues to follow here. First and foremost, we would like to know more about the circumstances in which the two functions become separated. Second, we might reasonably ask (as many of those concerned with language revival do, for instance) if the linkage between them can be made strong again in settings where communicative shift has occurred. Third, since the symbolic features of language emerge from, and are ultimately dependent upon, the more instrumental ones, it would be of considerable use to know how long, and under what conditions, the former can be expected to continue to play a role in the absence of the latter. There are practical implications to be found in each of these approaches to the communicative-symbolic nexus: implications for patterns of assimilation and/or pluralism in immigrant and indigenous minorities; implications for programmes of language maintenance and revival; implications for fuller understanding of identity continuity in the presence and absence of the original language.

Chapters 6 and 7 bring specific contexts more directly into the language-and-identity story. In the first, I touch upon three of the broadest settings, beginning with some remarks on ethnic and national allegiances, but prefacing them with a word or two about social-psychological attempts to come to grips with the actual and perceived strength of group-language vitality. Language is hardly the only, or the only important, marker of group boundaries, but it is one of the most resilient. In terms of ethnicity and nationalism, it is a particularly important feature because – at least in its spoken garb – it can act as an immediately obvious border stone. It is also, of course, of the greatest symbolic importance, and rare indeed is the nationalist movement that has neglected language as (at least) a rallying-point.

I provide some historical background to the phenomenon of linguistic nationalism, touching upon an obvious consequence of its perceived importance: the desire to preserve, protect and purify language. This partly accounts for the rise and maintenance of the academies, councils and committees that are or have been found in virtually all countries of the world. I say 'partly' because, in their very earliest incarnations, language academies were often primarily charged with the categorisation and standardisation that printing and the growth of literacy made necessary – charged, that is to say, with language planning. Most of these institutions continue this sort of work but, in many instances, they have also taken on more overtly protective tasks. The attempts of the *Académie française* to keep English at bay, to make sure that borrowings are not used instead of new or existing French words, and to spearhead common linguistic activities across *la francophonie* are perfect examples of undertakings that may be linguistically naïve and, some might say, pointless, but which are at the same time extremely easy to understand in social and psychological terms. Language prescriptivism and purism are essentially in the service of identity and boundary maintenance. In anglophone contexts, for reasons that I lay out in Chapter 6, one-man academies in the shape of lexicographers have emerged: Samuel Johnson in England, and Noah Webster in the United States.

I am in the process of paying closer attention to the topic (see Edwards, in preparation-b), because it is clear that we need much more work on institutional language efforts. While there already exists a considerable language-planning literature, much of it is tied very closely to particular contexts and particular needs. As well, insufficient energy has been devoted to the specifically puristic and prescriptivist enterprise, to those elements of language planning that bear most immediately and most strongly upon our understanding of 'groupness' and identity.

If language is a central feature of group belonging, then religion has historically been at least equally salient. Furthermore, no one who has paid the slightest attention to the current events of the last few years could possibly believe that religion was fading from the scene, except perhaps within rational contexts which, more and more, are coming to resemble islands in a great swell of faith. The secular predictions of even a few years ago, even within the western world, appear increasingly inaccurate. Consequently, the third of those 'broad' settings noted above is the religious one. I try to point out here that, although there is a literature on 'religious language', part of a much larger one on the sociology of religion, there is relatively little on the intermingled contribution of religious and linguistic perceptions and markers to group identity.

The idea that languages, or certain forms of language, are themselves holy articles of faith is a very old one. The mystical connection between words and things was at the heart of that famous 'naming day' in the Garden of Eden, and the Christian concept of the *logos* involves an indissoluble link among God, thought, word and deed. Even at this most basic level, then, the centrality of language to religious identity is obvious. Furthermore, those sixteenth- and seventeenth-century enquiries to discover just what that first holy language was become more understandable when we see them, not as efforts at biblical exegesis but, rather, as attempts to stake cultural and linguistic claims. Was the Adamic variety Hebrew? Aramaic? Arabic? These were important undertakings that would, if verified, place one group and its language unassailably above all others. We may no longer see attempts to claim a language as the divine medium, the original *lingua humana*, but there has been no shortage of efforts to make special claims about certain languages, usually as part of nationalist rhetoric. The capacity for identity-bearing is clear but so, unfortunately, is that for antipathy towards 'inferior' languages – and peoples.

I also spend a little time in Chapter 6 on the modern and well-known 'cases' of Ireland and Israel, for each can illuminate our understanding. Israel is said to show us a uniquely successful example of language revival (or, at least, reinvigoration) in a context in which a lingua franca was desired and where an obvious one was ready in the wings. The rise of Hebrew in this setting also demonstrates an important linguistic home truth. We now understand all varieties to be adequate communicative systems, but we also accept that their expressive power is not the same across all social domains. There are perfectly good languages that make not the slightest mention of nuclear physics, an omission that does not compromise their essential validity. There are perfectly good languages whose vocabularies soar to scientific heights: *their* validity is not undermined by a pattern of verbal moods, voices and tenses that speakers of many American aboriginal languages would find laughably simple. Hebrew's contribution here is to remind us that a language (in this instance, an essentially religious medium) whose vocabulary was not well suited to modern secular expression – whose expressive power, that is to say, was markedly deficient in some domains – could quite easily be expanded to meet new requirements.

In Ireland, there are interesting connections among Catholicism, English and Irish. The fact that virtually all Irish speakers were once staunchly religious can be understood as a double-edged sword in terms of language maintenance. On the one hand, successful promulgation of the idea that Catholicism was uniquely expressible through Irish could obviously work to the benefit of the language. On the other, the very fact that Irish identity remained so strongly supported on religious pillars may have suggested to some that communicative language shift might be less of an assault on that identity, more readily and less painfully undergone. In fact, the story of Irish reveals that both of these scenarios played out, in different constituencies and at different times. Overlaying everything, of course, were imperatives from abroad that had both religious and linguistic impact.

The last 'religious' section here deals with the work of missionaries, another rich and important field that remains woefully understudied. In fact, with the rejuvenated work and influence of evangelical groups both at home and abroad we can readily understand that this ought to be more of a 'growth area' within the social life of language. Central to missionary zeal, after all, is communication. As in the Irish context, we see a variety of accommodations between religious and linguistic demands. Missionaries have often, for example, felt that the replacement of 'pagan' tongues with their own was something devoutly to be wished. Literacy in a 'developed' language, after all, opens many new doors. On the other hand, the use of indigenous vernaculars and the encouragement of local literacies have also recommended themselves. Perhaps the single most interesting aspect under the missionary rubric, however, and the one that best exemplifies the heart of most religion–language linkages, is the centrality of faith. The ultimate purpose is saving souls, and where spiritual push comes to secular shove there can be little doubt that languages are primarily means to ends.

I have skipped over another section, one that occurs about midway through Chapter 6. Current treatments of the 'ecology of language' are of great and ongoing importance and, as my discussion makes clear, I have very real reservations about many of them. In a general sense, language ecology might be thought of as a description applicable to any fully fleshed investigation into the social life of language. However, in its modern incarnation, language ecology is a term that has been narrowed and co-opted. Its animating impulse is the protection of linguistic diversity, and so its primary focus is on the plight of endangered languages. This largely translates into accounts of the depredations of English and how they might and ought to be resisted. While there is nothing wrong with this in itself, it is disingenuous to label something as 'ecology', a term suggesting breadth and comprehensiveness, and then restrict one's coverage on ideological grounds.

I suggest that, despite various postures and assertions, the case made for diversity under the rubric of 'language ecology' rests essentially upon moral foundations and that assumptions of 'language rights' lie at the core of these foundations. There are a number of interesting ancillary points made by proponents of this 'new' ecology which I also examine here. It is at its moral core, however, a core suffused with romanticism, that the topic requires closest attention. The unrealistic and potentially damaging dynamics of this 'new' but narrow perspective undoubtedly constitute one of the most pressing challenges in the social life.

In Chapter 7, I turn to the interplay of language and gender. As in the second chapter of the book, I pay some considerable attention to an older piece of work: in this case, Erving Goffman's insights into the presentation or 'display' of gender. As in the second chapter, I attempt to show the continuing usefulness of the work, its continuing relevance to current enquiries and challenges. As in the second chapter, I actually step back a little from considerations of language *per se*, so as to better contextualise the linguistic postures and attitudes that stem from deeper social stereotypes.

As a brief contextualisation of all that follows, I start the chapter with a short section showing how children learn and reproduce gender-trait stereotypes from a very early age, certainly before they first go to school. I then turn to the reconsideration of Goffman's important work on 'gender display', although I actually preface the discussion with some evidence of its continuing relevance, thirty years on. His own work, I suggest, is more referred to than closely studied (one of the reasons, of course, why I pay some attention to it here). It is undoubtedly true that some of his illustrations place men and women in contexts less likely to be depicted now, but the most remarkable feature of all those hundreds of pictures presented for analysis is the continuity over time of their stereotypic messages. And this, of course, clearly indicates one of the great and ongoing 'challenges' of our time: to better understand, analyse and perhaps interfere in one of the areas of social life where the power of traditional attitudes, stereotypes and prejudices has remained so robust.

With the work of Goffman and some of his intellectual descendants providing important background detail, I return specifically to language in the last third of Chapter 7. In some ways, the material is quite familiar, and the discussion ranges over the linguistic and paralinguistic usages generally put under the heading of 'women's language'. Interestingly enough, a little closer attention reveals that many of these usages may also be found in men's talk. When they are, however, they often assume different colouring and attract different interpretations. The underlying message, for example, in an (apparent) request like 'Is there any ketchup?', may vary according to circumstance. If a husband makes it to his wife, the message might actually be '(Please) bring me the ketchup', but this need not be the sub-text if it is a daughter speaking to her mother. If a woman uses a tag question ('She's very nice, isn't she') we may interpret this as a 'softening', or a mark of uncertainty, submissiveness or conversational facilitation. This is unlikely to be the gloss we apply when a man says 'You understand what I'm saying, don't you?' As Deborah Cameron carefully documents, language usage and, in particular, language interactions between men and women often have more to do with power than with gender.

I conclude by reminding readers that male speech has, for a very long time, been seen as the 'norm' against which female usage has been analysed. It is noteworthy that, in his famous book on language, Otto Jespersen devoted his thirteenth chapter to 'The Woman'. I need hardly say that no corresponding section was considered necessary for the other half of humanity. Apart from noting female linguistic conservatism and remarking upon some of the same language characteristics that Robin Lakoff and others described half a century later, Jespersen felt moved to write that 'the vocabulary of a woman as a rule is much less extensive than that of a man' (p. 248), that women were less likely to appreciate humour, that their work was often 'accompanied with a lively chatter' (p. 254), *og så videre*. It is only fair to say that Jespersen added that 'woman is linguistically quicker than man' (p. 249) and that social evolution might eventually 'modify *even* the linguistic relations of the two sexes' (p. 254; my italics). Now, one might reasonably point out that Jespersen's are the views of an earlier age; however, with due regard to the sturdiness of Goffman's observations, and with any sort of ear to the current social ground, readers may (preferably after reading Jespersen for themselves) wish to consider how much of what he wrote has, in fact, dated. They will then perhaps agree with me that much important work remains to be done under the heading of language and gender.

Part 3: Language contact and its consequences

In the final four chapters of this book, I turn to one of the most pressing issues of our time: the unprecedented ramifications of contact between 'bigger' and 'smaller' languages. In general terms, this means contact between the large European varieties and all the rest, as well as that between powerful regional lingua francas and their local neighbours. In more specific terms, it very often means contact between English and other languages. This last phenomenon, at least, throws into sharpest relief all the other contact settings, revealing virtually all the important details found elsewhere, and usually presenting those features in

their boldest and most heightened forms. It is for this reason that I have
focussed so closely upon it in this final third of the book. It is intrinsically interesting and important and, at the same time, illustrative of
tendencies of very long historical standing.

In Chapter 8, I begin with some fairly obvious remarks about the
dynamics of language spread. Only one or two introductory points need
be made here. First, it is clear that the initial reasons for the spread of language (conquest, trade and so on) are typically not those that continue to
maintain it. Second, any particularised concern for the vernaculars of the
masses is historically rare. Why, after all, should those in power care very
much, so long as their subjects did what they were told? And why indeed
should they bother very much about their own languages, since the clear
superiority of those varieties would quite naturally lead to their adoption by those others fortunate enough to learn them? Benign neglect,
then, accompanied by an unthinking linguistic superiority: these were
the rather latent linguistic concomitants of more obvious and immediate
forms of imperialism. (These are of course only general observations; my
later discussions, beginning in the final section of Chapter 8, reveal more
patent expressions of linguistic preferences and prejudices.)

Following a section providing some very cursory details of the contemporary scope of English (something to which I return in Chapter 9),
I discuss what I term the 'imperial thesis'. This, largely associated with
the writings of Robert Phillipson and other similarly minded activists,
has many intricate and interesting nuances at whose base, however, is
a remarkably simple argument. It is that the spread and the scope of
English, its juggernaut-like progress of destruction, and the manifest
unfairness of its global presence can only be fully understood via more
or less conscious policies of 'linguicism'. The hegemony of English is
seen to be constantly abetted by the co-opted peoples around the world
whose own 'agency' is sometimes absent, sometimes merely enervated.
There are, then, powerful pushes and pulls which, working in tandem,
have led to the present unbalanced and inequitable situation.

I examine these suggestions, comparing their force with the rather more
parsimonious explanations for the English presence in the world. The latter rest upon another simple thesis: unequal distributions of linguistic
dominance have little to do with official policies or conscious intentions.
Some have argued that these do not actually exist, although I think it is
easy enough to find all sorts of official and quasi-official pronouncements
praising English, hoping for its ever-increasing clout, and so on. There is,
rather, an important twofold point here. First, any conscious language
policies are, at best, minor instruments in the imperial orchestra. Second,

their presence would count as nothing in the absence of the real social and political movements which carry them along. Indeed, the potency of those movements could easily permit the disappearance of them altogether, with only the slightest of hiccups, remaining content in the knowledge – to the extent, that is, that such powerful waves notice their language passengers in any formal way at all – that desirable linguistic currents would continue to flow along many simultaneous channels.

In the closing section of the eighth chapter, I begin a discussion that continues in the next: a cursory documentation of the very gradual rise of English, the changing fortunes of which inexorably affected both the attitudes and the foreign-language-learning inclinations of anglophones. My general point is simply that the language which, today, is so dominant and whose speakers are so regularly criticised for their inability or unwillingness to learn other varieties was once, itself, in the position of a minor linguistic player.

Chapter 9 represents a broad revision and expansion of an earlier piece with the same title, and its opening point is exactly the one I have just made. For a long time, the English language was of very little use once 'passe Douer'. Consequently, the English of the day (or, at least, the educated amongst them) were keen language learners. They were motivated by immediate, practical and instrumental reasons having to do with travel and trade, but they were also attracted by continental cultures and treasures, full access to which required other languages. In other words, they were in exactly the same position as a great many non-anglophones today. There are differences, of course, and the single most important one is that, unlike lingua francas of the past, historical circumstance has given English an extended life. Its original imperial bearers faded from the scene, but their language did not, since the global torch then passed to the direct inheritors of that initial anglophone community. And now, while we may reasonably consider that the fortunes of those American inheritors will not prove everlasting, it is also entirely reasonable to consider that the next leading player(s) on the world stage will further extend the life of the language, so powerfully penetrating a lingua franca as it has become.

It is an interesting consequence of the power and the longevity of English as a world language that time and social circumstance have enabled the emergence of a host of localised Englishes. To say that following *their* fortunes will be both fascinating and of the greatest importance is something of an understatement. Similarly, and relatedly, the study of the ebb and flow of English loans and borrowings will continue to provide important insights into rather wider ebbs and flows.

And, as the final section of Chapter 9 suggests, the ramifications of world English in learning contexts, whether in school or in the street, are of the greatest moment.

I conclude this section with some remarks on Spanish in the United States, the growing force of which both stretches and strains the anglophone American fabric. First, and most obviously, the powerful *de facto* existence of Spanish necessitates all sorts of more or less immediate accommodations in commercial and official life. Secondly, unlike all other immigrant groups (with the exception of francophones in the northeast), Spanish speakers in America – particularly Mexican ones, of course – remain closely connected to their homelands; the possibilities here, both of continuous growth and of cross-cultural intertwinings, also command our closest attention. Third, however, the *specific* long-term meanings of the powerful and often concentrated Spanish presence remain unclear and, hence, require continued enquiry. Will the typical immigrant patterns of linguistic assimilation occur among Hispanic Americans, even if they take a little longer than the traditional three-generation span to unfold? Or are we at the beginning of a new and stable bilingualism, an American diglossia? And, if so, what will this mean for the learning of Spanish among anglophones? Whatever happens, we can be sure that the American story will continue to be of great importance well beyond its own shores.

In Chapter 10, I move towards some of the actual language-learning facts and figures that we need to understand, since they represent one of the most immediate reflections of large-scale linguistic tectonics. That might be said to represent the input dimension. What is the impact on the foreign-language classroom of a world made increasingly safe for anglophones? Of course, we are also very interested in the output side, in the mechanics of instruction and reception, in the scope and the depth of the language capabilities that are being acquired, in the trends in learning languages *vis-à-vis* other subjects. Additionally, we are interested to know if more and more of the future of language learning among anglophones is to be essentially an instrumental one. We probably cannot return to the golden days in which learning languages was inevitably accompanied by learning about cultures, but are to we believe those hard-minded commentators who tell us that, since English-speaking students no longer have the interest they once did in reading deeply their *own* literature, it is extremely unlikely that we can attract significant numbers of them to study other people's?

I open Chapter 10 with a short discussion of some 'popular' assessments of anglophone language-learning inclinations and abilities.

Readers may initially think this of purely historical and anecdotal interest but, as elsewhere in this book, I hope that I have in fact been able to suggest some continuingly important trends of opinion, trends that in this case may be taken as some sort of backdrop to the figures and statistics that follow. Of these, I need make little comment here: the numbers, as they say, speak for themselves. Across anglophone contexts, they reveal that learning foreign languages at school has declined in recent years, and they suggest that, today, those most concerned and worried can at best hope for some levelling off, some stability. There are, of course, nuances here. The declines are most notable in the 'traditional' languages, particularly French. The learning of Spanish is in the strongest position, not only in America but also in Canada and the United Kingdom, but the figures show that strength is a relative quantity here. There are signs of an increasing take-up of Chinese and Arabic, but the actual numbers remain quite low in most settings.

It is also very noteworthy that, in the new-world 'receiving' countries, a great deal of the learning of 'foreign' languages is, in fact, undertaken by immigrants from countries where those varieties are anything but foreign. This means that the figures, such as they are, are frequently further compromised by the presence of sizeable blocks of non-anglophone students. (I mean 'compromised' in the sense, of course, that the figures do not accurately reveal how many English speakers are learning new languages; and they are the most important constituency, for the purposes of the present argument.) It is equally, if not more, noteworthy that in some jurisdictions official postures towards language learning at school have taken strange shapes. In Britain, for example, secondary-school languages have been made optional for a great many pupils, with predictable results. At the same time, the government there intends to introduce (this year) more language-learning possibilities at the primary level. Even in the most optimistic construction this seems a rather back-to-front arrangement, and it is no wonder that many in the language-teaching community are talking of a 'lost generation', nor that the knock-on effects have reduced and, in some cases, eliminated language provisions at university level.

I conclude Chapter 10 with some brief notes on the growing presence of English at university level in non-anglophone countries, particularly in northern Europe. This reflects the obvious internal demand for more courses and, indeed, entire programmes in English. It also reflects, however, sufficient confidence in those quarters in offering some competition to universities in English-speaking countries in catering for the large and growing external demand. It also, incidentally, makes it even

easier for anglophone students to have their 'year abroad' without learning much, if anything, of another language.

Chapter 11 first presents some generalities about some possible
language-contact futures. One of these is that a considerable amount of
writing about language maintenance, shift and revival makes the mistake of considering these matters to be analysable and 'treatable' in relative isolation. (Much of the language-planning literature, for instance,
falls into this error.) In fact, of course, these phenomena are typically
symptoms of larger contact dynamics: the simple implication is that
nothing meaningful can be said or done about them in isolation from
the wide social currents that bear them along. This means, among other
things, that a great deal of research and writing – on matters that have,
after all, a real existence in the real world – will not have any impact
outside the academic cloisters. Another generality here is that the current unprecedented scope of language contact means that a great many
languages must deal with the onward march of English. Of course,
'small' and stateless varieties are often the most vulnerable to external influence, but even those of some strength, even those that have
a state behind them are not immune to such influence. A smaller and
more intensely interconnected world is one in which the border guards
of language – agencies, councils, academies, linguistic activists of all
stripes – find their jobs more and more difficult. This part of the chapter
ends with a plea for more and fuller disciplinary cross-fertilisation, and
a reminder that the language issues here derive most of their force and
emotional charge from the concerns surrounding group *identity* that
underpin them.

The tone of my discussion of the work of Abram de Swaan and
Phillipe van Parijs makes clear, I hope, my endorsement of their essential message. Although each of them has many interesting things to say,
that basic message is simply that English is now, and for the foreseeable
future, the global lingua franca, that academic mutterings about linguistic conspiracies rest upon mistaken and often quite authoritarian
stances, and that the single most important task in the contemporary
social life of language is to try and separate the clear instrumental value
of English from unwanted cultural accompaniments. This task, then, is
all about fairness and the levelling of various playing fields. The expansion of English and the spawning of localised varieties constitute the
single most obvious demonstration that such levelling can be done.
Whether it *will* always be done, and whether the timescale of developments is to everyone's taste are other (related) matters. Since there is
little or no chance, however, of going back, the practical posture of

these scholars makes eminently good sense. That it also recommends itself on the grounds of disinterested analysis is what elevates it above mere pragmatism.

This is not to say that all elements of that posture are equally compelling. (Van Parijs's ideas about a sort of compensatory 'free-riding' centred upon dubbing practices and 'web poaching' strike me as curiously 'micro' adjustments in very 'macro' contexts, for example.) In the final section of the chapter, then, I present some criticisms. Many of them are worth consideration, but I hope that most readers will agree with me that their chief effect is to highlight and not to eliminate the basic theses. Several commentators cast doubt on the notion that we need (or should have) one overarching lingua franca: at one level, this is simply flying in the face of a reality to which more and more people around the world subscribe; at another, it suggests a lack of historical awareness. When Réaume points to the 'hard and soft imperialism' without which English would not have achieved its current position, she is merely describing what has always been the case. It is a circular argument: were it not for the dominance of its speakers, the language would not be dominant!

Another critical theme has to do with the allegedly bloodless 'rational-choice' stance that de Swaan and van Parijs have adopted. It is patently clear, however, that it is precisely the *non*-instrumental aspects of the matter that occasion their research at all. If things could be entirely understood at the level of tools, we would need no discussion of 'compensation', of 'fairness', of some sort of redress for non-native speakers, of the possibility of maintaining a widely desirable, and desired, instrumentality without having to accept a particular set of cultural luggage. In other words, both authors are acutely aware of the powerful symbolic functions of language, and only a wilful or limited reading could support the idea that, just because they do not mention the word 'identity' very often, the concept is absent from their discussion.

Nonetheless, despite the fact that their arguments remain compelling on a number of important grounds, and despite the fact that current criticisms are not overly robust, I would be the last person to suggest that we ought not to pay close attention to those criticisms.

Coda

I hope that the rather extended summaries supplied above, together with the chapter material that follows, make clear what I consider to be some of the most pressing current issues in the social life of language.

For obvious reasons, many of the discussions have had to be abbreviated here and, indeed, there are important matters that I have not been able to take up at all in this book. I hope that the extensive list of references at the end will prove useful for those readers wishing to overcome these deficiencies. I need only reiterate here that the vital threads connecting all aspects of the social life of language, whether I have touched upon them or not, are those labelled 'power' and 'identity'.

My last task here is the agreeable one of thanking some friends and colleagues for their assistance. Among them are Yvon Grenier, Mehmet Ümit Necef, Howard Giles, Scott Reid, Steven Baldner and Christopher Byrne. As well, a great many scholars – most of whom I have never met – responded quickly and efficiently to my requests for information or reprints of their work. Finally, I would be remiss if I did not acknowledge the probing attention some of my work has received at conferences and speaking venues on both sides of the Atlantic.

Notes

1. Others are of course possible: anthropological linguistics, varieties of applied and educational linguistics, and so on.
2. I don't mean to suggest here that the competence/performance dichotomy can be exactly mapped onto the *langue/parole* one.
3. It is perhaps not unfair, as well, to see in Chomsky's posture the familiar disdain that 'pure' scientists have of 'applied' ones. University physics departments are more prestigious than are schools of education. There is physics, and then there is stamp-collecting and the netting of butterflies.
4. In view of Chomsky's rather dismissive attitude towards 'applied' study, it is interesting to read the blurb he supplied for the back cover of a recent book on African languages (including American Black English): 'This deeply informed and solidly grounded inquiry provides an illuminating perspective into the nature, variety, and social and cultural setting of languages of Africa and the diaspora, and implications for instruction and language policy. A very valuable contribution' (Chomsky, 2009).
5. Despite what the eminent literary critic, Hugh Kenner (1971: 26) referred to as the 'intolerably enigmatic' nature of that famous line at the end of Keats's *Ode on a Grecian Urn* ('beauty is truth, truth beauty'), and despite the scorn of those who have seen it as a trite conclusion to the poem, it seems clear enough that many have always felt that the two do, indeed, go hand in hand.

Part 1
Perceptual Underpinnings

2
The Study of Attitudes: *Reculer pour mieux sauter*

An introductory note

Before coming to grips with language attitudes in particular, it makes sense to pay a little attention to attitudes generally. There is a huge literature here and it lies at the very heart of the social-psychological enterprise; I shall return to the point. In its essentials, however, our approach to attitudes has remained both stable and robust. In a formal and 'non-popular' sense, attitude comprises three components: belief, emotion and a disposition to act (or, if you like, cognitive, affective and behavioural elements; see the further discussion, below). Teasing out the interconnections here has often proved difficult, however. All of this makes it both interesting and apposite to cast an eye back to some early work in the area, work that has been relatively neglected (at least in its detail), that illustrates the central features and problems of attitudinal research, and that – in the specific group boundaries that it focuses upon – touches on assessments very similar to those that under-pin language attitudes.

LaPiere I: 1928

Some of the most interesting work in attitude research has to do with preference and prejudice – the pervasive negative effects of racial preju-dice, for example, hardly need documenting – and a study by LaPiere (1934) is frequently cited as an early and classic demonstration of atti-tude–behaviour inconsistency. It is worth going into some detail here, however, since the citations are typically very cursory, and leave out the author's prescient observations. Furthermore, still earlier work by LaPiere (1928) is rarely mentioned at all: a pity, since it both sets the stage for the second enquiry and firmly embeds these social-scientific investigations in real-life contexts. To fully appreciate this, we need to consider some relevant racial history.[1]

During the first world war, American black troops serving in France often found an acceptance from their counterparts there, as well as from civilians, that they were denied at home. This, it was thought, could not be allowed to continue. So in August 1918, a French liaison officer with the Americans, one Colonel Linard, issued a statement entitled 'Secret Information Concerning the Black American Troops'. This was later published in *The Crisis*, a black civil-rights magazine founded in 1910 by William Du Bois (Linard, 1919). Linard's observations had the blessing of General John 'Black Jack' Pershing, the commander of the American Expeditionary Force (indeed, they have been mistakenly attributed to Pershing himself). Directed towards French officers, Linard's short statement pointed out that intimacy between the French and the black American troops must be prevented, the latter must not be commended too highly ('particularly in the presence of white Americans'), and the 'native population' must refrain from 'spoiling the Negroes'. Above all, Linard told his readers to remember that 'the black man is regarded by the white American as an inferior being'. The racist attitudes reflected here were of course kindled by black–white fraternisation in France, but they also aroused concerns about the consequences of social acceptance once the black soldiers returned home. After all, 'an experience of "undue social mixing" in France would undo the lifelong lessons inculcated by Jim Crow' (Slotkin, 2005: 255).

The observations that prompted Linard's cautionary tract were of course available to a great many people, and they led to LaPiere's initial investigation of prejudice in France and England. He opened the first article as follows:

> When, during 1918, many thousands of American Negro soldiers were sent to France they were surprised and delighted to find that the French people received them on a basis of equality with their white brothers...they could eat in any café, sit in any station, ride in any part of the train, and talk to the same girls who talked to the white soldiers. (1928: 102)

LaPiere goes on to note that these 'white brothers' were 'thoroughly disgusted' with these developments, and that they explained them in one of two ways: either the French were themselves 'of inferior caliber and flattered the Negro in order that they might more easily obtain his money', or they 'treated the Negroes as equals in order to show their great appreciation of America's aid in the war for democracy'. Since, however, African colonial troops were also given favourable treatment by the French, the second explanation typically gave way to the first. The overall conclusion, then, was that 'the French must be inferior to Americans who, to their minds, correctly recognize the Negro's real character' (p. 102).[2]

This was the context in which LaPiere's intriguing study is to be understood – intriguing because he seems to have combined extensive travel in France with a great number of 'casual conversations' (over 400, in fact, in more than three dozen locales), during the course of which he elicited French attitudes towards blacks. (In the interests of tapping the views of different social groups, the author mentions 'occasionally alternating while travelling by railway between first, second and third class accommodations. Similarly, a like procedure was followed in the choice of hotels, cafés and restaurants': pp. 103–104.) LaPiere reported that some 67% of his informants appeared to be without prejudice, about 11% responded 'with prejudice', and the remaining 22% gave answers that were 'doubtful' in one way or another. He notes that many of the 'doubtful' assessments came from 'the more thoughtful' of his respondents, those who resist simple and categorical judgements: 'with such people it is probable that the personality of the Negro would be the deciding factor in situations of actual contact' (p. 104).

LaPiere also broke the responses down by social class, gender and rurality. Given his methodology, the first of these dimensions was obviously the most difficult to accurately subdivide. Some 25% in his upper-status category presented themselves as 'doubtful', about 43% in the middle-status group, but only 10% in the lower ranks. The author himself remarks upon a 'general tendency towards a more rational attitude in the middle group' (p. 104). On the other hand, 86% of those in the 'lower ranks' were classified as being without prejudice, compared to 54% in the middle group and only 8% in the highest of the three categories. The gender breakdown revealed no significant variation, but, along the rural–urban distinction we find a similar pattern as that obtaining under the class rubric: while more rural residents (80%) than urban dwellers (53%) were returned as prejudice-free, more of the latter (29%) fell into that desirable 'doubtful' category of answers than did their rural cousins (17%). If we were to summarise matters here, we might say that members of the middle class seemed the most likely to discuss racial matters in a cautionary or circumspect way; for (possibly) less thoughtful but more immediately favourable (non-prejudiced) responses, however, we should look at lower-class and rural informants. LaPiere's own summary was that 'the French have little color antipathy' (p. 105), except where they have been contaminated by English and American tourists:

> The fact that, with the exception of tourist hotels whose policy is adjusted to foreign, not French, attitudes, French hotel proprietors do not object to colored guests certainly indicates that the French people as a whole are not adverse [sic] to associating, at least impersonally, with dark-skinned peoples. (p. 106)

Across the Channel, however, LaPiere found a very different picture. While his travels in Britain were more restricted (he visited London, Birmingham, Liverpool and North Wales), he nevertheless asked about 300 people for their views of 'good colored persons'. His findings there were massively different from those in France: overall, he reported that 80% of his 'English' respondents were prejudiced towards black people. Among his three class categories, the middle-class informants were, as in France, the most likely to give 'doubtful' responses, but here the proportion was only 18%.

Why, LaPiere asked himself, 'do the French lack this color prejudice which is so strong in England' (p. 108)? Neither country had large black populations, although he does touch upon the presence of black troops in France during the war, and the longstanding French contacts with North Africa. He also mentions 'the historical tendency of the "Latin Races" to look upon Africans with less racial antagonism than the "Nordics" do': this, it was apparently once suggested, implied 'a closer blood relationship with these blacks'. On further reflection, however, LaPiere believes it to be 'wholly deniable that [historical] contacts have led the French to consider themselves less white than do the English' (p. 110). And so, apart from suggesting that the French–English difference may stem from different colonial contacts that the two empires had with black populations, LaPiere remained uncertain about the meaning of his results. He does conclude, however, with the laudable note that French reactions, at least, demonstrate that there is no inherent, or 'biological', or 'natural' white prejudice towards 'dark or black skinned peoples' (p. 111).

I have gone into some detail here, and this for three reasons. First, LaPiere's 1928 study is hardly ever cited, even though it was the foundation for his more famous piece six years later; even Allport (1958 [1954]), in his classic work on prejudice, makes no mention of it. Second, it provides an excellent period 'flavour' of academic attitudes (which is why, of course, I have used so many of LaPiere's own words here). Third, it is one of the very earliest systematic studies in its area. It was not at all an acceptable study by modern standards, of course. For instance, the sampling technique, if we can call it that, was anecdotal at best. The actual question that LaPiere put to his many conversational partners varied according to context and circumstance: in France it was generally some variant of 'would you let a good Negro live at your home?' while in England (and Wales) the basic query was 'would you let [white] children...associate with those of good colored people?' Not only are these two 'basic' questions quite unalike, but the author went on to write that 'the particular questions asked depended...on the situation, for every effort was made to prevent any suspicion arising as to the purpose of the questioning' (p. 106).

Quite apart from the variant questions that were posed, LaPiere's rationale here seems rather naïve. Another obvious flaw in the study (of which he was quite aware) is the haphazard way in which informants were assigned to one of the three social-class categories: people he met in 'first-class' hotels and railway carriages were put in the upper group; 'travelling men, hotel and other business proprietors, French motorists, etc.' in the middle; and all the rest were 'lumped in the lower group' (p. 104). The very large reported difference in overall levels of prejudice on either side of the Channel is also a red flag to modern readers. And finally, some of LaPiere's own phrasing (his remarks about the 'good Negro', for example) falls oddly on contemporary ears.

On the plus side, of course, are the facts that LaPiere's work represents an early attempt in a field that was soon to become very crowded, and that it provides a snapshot at the beginning of more or less modern sociological enquiry. Remarks about 'good colored people' reveal what were acceptable postures at the time, even among educated commentators. It was an age, after all, in which politicians, journalists, novelists and others routinely made remarks about Jews, blacks and others that have since been ruled out of civilised discourse (but see note 2, and the remarks, below, about the 'bogus pipeline'). A further example is provided when LaPiere describes the situation of a black American soldier who remained in France, settled in a French village with a white wife and three children, and 'scoffed' at any suggestion that he might return to the United States: 'His attitude can best be summed up by his reply to that suggestion. "Boy," he said, "over here I's a man, over there I's a nigger [sic]"' (p. 108). The sentiment is not questionable nor, indeed, is it at all an unfamiliar one, and LaPiere acknowledges that it captures in 'a much less involved and far more vital' way the essence of his own investigations. Nonetheless, the choice or, at least, the reproduction of words might now be easily taken as a reinforcement, conscious or otherwise, of an unpleasant stereotype. Finally, I think we should acknowledge that LaPiere's imprecise but well-meaning study of attitudes has proved important for later work, both for highlighting areas for further study – and, occasionally, for making valuable and prescient remarks (about the social origins of prejudice, for instance) – and for illuminating pitfalls and shortcomings to be avoided.

LaPiere II: 1934

LaPiere's much more famous study (1934) – Linn (1965: 354) describes it as 'the first study which examined the relationship between human behavior and expressed attitudes', which may be a little strong – also departs from contemporary notions of research acceptability. LaPiere was again able to combine work and travel, but this study has many fewer obvious flaws than his enquiries in France and Britain. This is largely because of the simplicity of its comparison of stated attitudes and actual behaviour. He begins by referring to this very distinction, as it may have compromised his earlier findings concerning prejudice towards blacks, particularly that expressed by those in a position to profit by their custom. Thus, he writes, 'there need be no relationship between what the hotel proprietor says he will do and what he actually does when confronted with a colored patron. Yet there may be' (p. 231). As in the earlier work, LaPiere points out the interesting tension that may affect those who stand to profit from black patronage: their reactions may be greatly influenced by the antipathies of their overwhelmingly white clientele, but they may also be tempered by 'pecuniary motives'; see also below.

In this second study, LaPiere reports findings based upon 'ten thousand miles of motor travel, twice across the United States, up and down the Pacific Coast' (p. 232), with a young Chinese student and his wife. They went to 66 hotels, 'auto camps' and tourist homes, as well as 184 restaurants and cafés, and met with only one rejection – this, even though existing social-distance studies had revealed considerable American antipathy towards 'Orientals'. Then, about six months after the completion of the journeys, LaPiere wrote to all 250 board or lodging sites, asking if they would be prepared to 'accept members of the Chinese race as guests in your establishment' (p. 233). Of the 128 responses received, some 90% said no, and all but one of the rest stated that they were 'uncertain' and that acceptance or rejection would 'depend upon circumstances'.

There were, again, some methodological problems. The possible effects of a white member in the travelling party may have confounded some or all of the interactions, for instance, as might the fact that the Chinese couple spoke in 'unaccented English', were neat, well dressed, and arrived with baggage. Some of the post-journey questionnaires asked only the simple question just mentioned, while in others it was accompanied by similar questions about a number of groups (including Japanese, Armenians, Indians, Jews and Blacks).

Nonetheless, it has always been accepted that LaPiere's study clearly demonstrates that what people think and feel may not always be reflected in what they do. Commenting on the dangers involved in the usual questionnaire assessment of attitudes, La Piere notes:

> If Mr A adjusts himself to Mr B in a specified way we can deduce from his behavior that he has a certain 'attitude' towards Mr B and, perhaps, all of Mr B's class. But if no such overt adjustment is made it is impossible to discover what A's adjustment would be should the situation arise. (p. 236)

The findings from questionnaire studies reflect only what LaPiere called 'a verbal reaction to an entirely symbolic situation' and, while this *may* be indicative of actual behaviour, 'there is no assurance that it will' (p. 236). Here is his concluding paragraph, worth citing in full:

> The questionnaire is cheap, easy, and mechanical. The study of human behavior is time consuming, intellectually fatiguing, and depends for its success upon the ability of the investigator. The former method gives quantitative results, the latter mainly qualitative. Quantitative measurements are quantitatively accurate; qualitative evaluations are always subject to the errors of human judgment. *Yet it would seem far more worth while to make a shrewd guess regarding that which is essential than to accurately measure that which is likely to prove quite irrelevant.* (p. 237; my italics)

Beyond LaPiere

As noted at the outset here, there is a very large social-psychological literature on attitudes. In fact, the study of attitudes has historically been at the very centre of things, Allport (1954: 45) calling it the 'primary building stone in the edifice of social psychology'. The reason, of course, is the not unreasonable feeling that important links exist between attitudes and behaviour, between what we think and say, and what we do. Cohen (1964: 138) thus wrote of the assumption that attitudes are the 'precursors of behavior...determinants of how a person will actually behave in his [sic] daily affairs'. We have just been discussing, of course, a demonstration that the attitude–behaviour relationship is hardly a straightforward one, and LaPiere's work can be said to have set in motion more subtle enquiries. Early hopes that detailed knowledge of attitudes would allow accurate predictions of behaviour were soon dashed, then. By the time Festinger (1957) suggested that, not only did attitudes not predict behaviour very well, they often *followed* it, the need for more nuanced investigations of the attitude-belief-behaviour complex had become obvious. As Abelson (1972) later put it, people seem quite good at finding reasons for what they have done, but not so good at doing things which reason would seem to suggest. Indeed, some commentators, including Abelson, Wicker (1971) and others, were to argue that inconsistencies here were so great, and predictive power so minimal, that studying attitudes was in many ways a fruitless enterprise.[3]

In an important review of existing studies, Wicker (1969) takes LaPiere's title for his own ('Attitudes versus actions') and begins his article with a brief summary of that earlier study. His synthesis leads to one broad conclusion: behaviour cannot always – or even often – be accurately predicted on the basis of stated attitudes. In short, circumstances alter cases, or, as Wicker puts it: 'the *situational threshold* for expressing negative feelings toward an ethnic group on a questionnaire may be lower than the threshold...in a face-to-face situation' (p. 44; original italics). The studies that he surveyed involved a broad range of informant groups, and of attitude measures and topics. Overall, the studies 'suggest that it is considerably more likely that attitudes will be unrelated or only slightly related to overt behaviors than that attitudes will be closely related to actions' (p. 65). Wicker concludes with a useful overview of the personal and situational factors that typically influence the attitude–behaviour relationship.

It is of course my contention here that although LaPiere's work was undoubtedly flawed when considered through current social-scientific lenses, it nevertheless established benchmarks of interest that have remained central ever since. The seminal nature of his work, particularly the 1934 study, is demonstrated by the many citations it continues to receive. Of specific interest are the references made by Kutner *et al.* (1952), Allport (1958 [1954]) and Wicker (1969). I mention the first of these (an extremely brief report) only because it shows the continuing and direct influence of LaPiere's work. Here, a black girl joined two white friends at eleven restaurant tables in New York, and service was never refused. Follow-up enquiries took the form of requests for dinner reservations, with the note that some in the party would be 'colored'. When the restaurateurs were asked if they would have any objection, no replies were received. Telephone calls were then made, in the course of which most simply denied having received the enquiries, and all the restaurateurs hedged.

Allport (1958 [1954]: 55) refers to LaPiere's 'outstanding contribution', and goes on to provide his own summary:

> We may venture the following generalization: where clear conflict exists, with law and conscience on the one side, and with custom and prejudice on the other, discrimination is practiced chiefly in covert and indirect ways, and not primarily in face-to-face situations where embarrassment would result. (p. 56)

Allport's sentiments here recall the earlier notes about 'social desirability', as well as LaPiere's remarks about the 'pecuniary motives' that may block the expression of real attitudes and, more generally, his observation about the priority that careful speculations about what is essential should have over accurate measurements of what is irrelevant (or, we might add, skewed or incomplete).[4] It is appropriate, then, to end here with a brief discussion of the challenging problems that continue to beset the study of attitudes and beliefs.

A recent issue of *Canadian Psychology* was devoted to developments in psychological measurement (Hunsley, 2009a). Although the articles focus particularly upon the assessment of personality characteristics, both 'normal' and otherwise, there is also some attention given to measurement in the service of personnel selection (the contribution of Goffin and Boyd), as well as a brief but useful overview of intelligence testing (Gottfredson and Saklofske). The use of 'implicit' techniques is dealt with by Gawronski – that is, measures that try to infer psychological postures and attitudes from observable performance – but the real connecting thread here, one that is germane to my discussion, is the broad reliance upon self-reported data and the obvious pitfalls involved in this. Measurement in one form or another is, as the editor observes, 'the cornerstone of all forms of scientific inquiry in psychology' (Hunsley, 2009b: 117), and, as Holden and Troister point out in their paper, self-reported data are routinely solicited from virtually everyone in western society: schoolchildren, job applicants, psychiatric patients, prison inmates, survey informants of every description, and so on. And yet the difficulties involved in obtaining accurate and pertinent information can be enormous.[5]

It is clear that recent decades have seen considerable changes in conceptions of acceptable and unacceptable expressions and behaviour. The 'n-word', for instance, once so blithely and widely used across all social strata, is now subject to the greatest prohibitions and those who disregard them do so at considerable peril. Nonetheless, the altered face of public acceptability may have done little more than to drive racist attitudes underground and to make their expression less overt. In some important work on what they termed the 'bogus pipeline' effect, Jones and his colleagues (Jones and Sigall, 1971; Sigall and Page, 1971) led people to think that their attitudes could be accurately measured by machine. When they were asked to *verbally* express the opinions that they now believed were also being electronically monitored, some depressingly familiar perceptions were revealed. Indeed, there was a partial re-emergence of prejudices that had been expressed openly in attitude studies of the 1920s and 1930s, prejudices that had become anathematised since then. It would seem, then, that many stated opinions are crafted for public expression, are in fact what their authors consider to be 'socially desirable' observations. Since these may not accurately reflect *real* feelings, they are thus likely to disappear or become attenuated in settings where there seems to be no point in deception, where (for instance) people believe that there exists an electronic monitor that cannot be deceived or, more mundanely, in contexts in which people feel they are among like-minded individuals: a useful recent overview is that of Plant *et al.* (2003). We may not have moved as far along the path of civilised conduct as we may think (see note 2). Even within the most enlightened of circles, racism of various sorts – often more subtle than it once was and perhaps, therefore, even more disheartening – continues its baleful course; see the recent collection on prejudice in the university (Henry and Tator, 2009).

Beyond immediate (or 'pecuniary') self-interest, and beyond desires to avoid embarrassment or to appear in a 'socially desirable' light, there are other reasons for attitude–behaviour inconsistency. Fear, for instance, is a strong motivator. Differences between reactions to an abstract or hypothetical member of a given group and to an actual instance of one are also of interest. This is because it is not inevitably the case that a professed lack of prejudice breaks down in interactions with people from the relevant group. On the contrary: sometimes, in settings where one need not be on any politically correct guard, general racist feelings may be revealed. At the same time, genuine friendships can be maintained with individual members of the theoretically (or, indeed, actually) disliked group. Many readers will have encountered these apparently paradoxical circumstances, the most common explanation for which is that some 'special' category or 'allowance' has been made for selected individuals; and this is, of course, a specific illustration of the workings of cognitive dissonance reduction. Linn's (1965) study throws some further light on different reactions in 'symbolic' or hypothetical contexts and in actual or personal ones.

It is worth noting here that, even if reported attitudes do not always correspond to actual behaviour – even if, in some situations, they *rarely* do so – we ought not to assume that they are without value. Sometimes what people say is just as interesting and revealing as what they do. Discrepancies may provide some perspective on the intertwining of the individual with the social, rather than presenting disturbing or perplexing anomalies. Robert Merton (1940) pointed to the mistaken idea that verbal responses are only of minor importance, 'that in one sense or another overt behavior is "more real" than verbal behavior'. He goes on to illustrate why this assumption is 'both unwarranted and scientifically meaningless', reminding the reader that 'the expression of opinion is itself a recurrent phase of social activity' (p. 21). I should like to remind *my* readers that Merton's fuller discussion remains a clear and valuable treatment of the strengths and shortcomings of questionnaire enquiries, and of the assumptions that are inaccurately made about respondents and their responses. Well worth reading, seven decades on.

The willing worker

LaPiere's plea to pay more attention to what really counts remains a highly relevant matter for all those engaged in the assessment of attitudes (or beliefs). First, we know from long experience that most participants in social-scientific enquiries will do more or less anything that is asked of them. One doesn't have to think here of the egregious experiments of either Milgram (in which people were willing to give what they thought were electric shocks to others) or Zimbardo (who set up a mock prison in which volunteer participants fell all too readily into the roles of prisoners and guards); see Milgram (1963, 1974) and Zimbardo *et al.* (1973), further discussion of which will be found in Chapter 5. One need only bear in mind that the 'general attitude' of experimental subjects is one of 'ready complacency and cheerful willingness to assist the investigator in every possible way'. These are words written a century ago (Pierce, 1908: 267); they have been borne out ever since.

Consider, for example, the notable work of Martin Orne. He describes the psychological experiment as a context in which subjects agree to

> tolerate a considerable degree of discomfort, boredom or actual pain, if required to do so by the experimenter. Just about any request which could conceivably be asked of the subject by a reputable investigator is legitimized by the quasi-magical phrase, 'This is an experiment'. (Orne, 1962: 777)

He overstated things a little here – not *all* of Milgram's participants agreed to deliver those electric shocks, after all – but the statement is generally accurate. For one of his demonstrations, Orne asked his subjects to add the adjacent two numbers on pages filled with random digits. Each completed sheet required 224 additions, and Orne gave each participant several *reams* of paper! He then took away the subjects' watches, and left the room, telling them: 'Continue to work; I will return eventually.' Most subjects carried on with this bizarre task for a long time (Orne himself gave up after more than five hours). He then made the task even more ridiculous by instructing the subjects to tear up every sheet, once they had made all the additions on it, into 'a minimum of thirty-two pieces' (p. 777). Again, extended if not cheerful willingness – was the result. Orne concluded by saying that

> thus far, we have been singularly unsuccessful in finding an experimental task which would be discontinued or, indeed, refused by subjects…not only do subjects continue to perform boring, unrewarding tasks, but they do so with few errors and little decrement in speed. (pp. 777–778)

Not only did Orne's work reveal how easy it is to initiate and maintain participation, even in the most unprepossessing circumstances, it also suggested that subjects try to deduce what he called the 'demand characteristics' of the experiment. They try, that is, to be a 'good' subject by discovering what investigators are looking for, and then trying to provide it through their task performance. Once again, Orne's work echoed Pierce's description of the subject, happy and willing to help 'in every possible way, by reporting to [the investigator] those very things which he is most eager to find' (1908: 267).

Thus, the first point here is simply that most participants will do what is asked of them and, in a specific example of producing the 'socially desirable' response, will perform in ways that they think are being called for. The dangers are obvious. In situations in which people are willing to 'go along' to such an extent, how can we have any confidence in what they do, or tell us, or write on a questionnaire? We can return once more to Pierce for the second, and related, point: 'the very questions of the experimenter either suggest the shade of reply expected or act as powerful suggestions which inhibit the power to recall many important states of consciousness which were actually experienced' (p. 267). Well, the phrasing here is a little infelicitous, and Pierce's reference to 'states of consciousness' is not how we would state things today, but the general observation is again an important one. If one presents a questionnaire (say) to someone, the very act of giving it and, of course, the particular items contained in it, imply something about the salience and importance of the subject-matter – certainly in the mind of the investigator and, as we have just seen, very probably in the mind of the participant, too. That may already set up an artificial focussing of attention. A further complication is that many social enquiries constrain the allowable responses: a very common arrangement, of course, is to solicit marks of relative agreement along a scale. In other words, participants are not given the opportunity to speak or write their answers in any extended way at all. Quite apart from the inevitable truncating and blunting of responses that this means, the more subtle difficulty arises when the investigator, tallying responses and often seduced by statistical possibilities, aggregates check-marks in some mathematical manner. However this is done, no weighting is generally possible.

Suppose, then, that participants are asked to respond to a number of items, on 7-point scales, on some theme or other. Suppose further that this theme is differentially important: for some subjects, it is highly relevant, while others have never even encountered it; see Goot (1993) here, on the variations in intensity or 'passion' that undergird attitudinal ratings. Suppose that, both across and within subjects, some *items* are of great interest, while others seem trivial. Suppose that some items are ones about which (some) participants are knowledgeable, while others probe into ignorance. And so on. Remember, too, that virtually all participants can be expected to answer virtually all answers. What of value can possibly emerge from such an exercise? And yet it is on the basis of 'average responses' in such studies that hypotheses are tested and conclusions are reached.

An illustrative study in this regard was undertaken in Hawai'i by Choy and Dodd (1976), and it gives rise to yet another possibility that we could add to those just listed. Suppose respondents are given some small pieces of information (recordings of speech samples, for example) and are then asked to evaluate the speakers along a number of dimensions. One might be forgiven for thinking that assessments based upon extremely brief and disembodied behavioural snapshots would be of marginal value, at very best. But now, to further stretch credibility, suppose that some of the requested assessments involve judgements of characteristics that no reasonable person could be expected to make in the circumstances. In fact, Choy and Dodd asked teachers to evaluate schoolchildren along a number of dimensions: these included verbal fluency, intelligence and likely academic success – but also future social status and marital happiness! The inanity and inappropriateness of the requested ratings are notable but, for our purposes, the teachers' willingness to fill out all the scales is of even greater interest.

At about the same time, an increasing awareness of these problems led to some efforts to defuse them a little. Williams (1974, 1976), for example, discussed what he termed the 'latitude of attitude acceptance'. Not an entirely new concept in the larger domain of social psychology, this was an acknowledgement that raters' judgements can hardly be adequately expressed with a single mark on some semantic-differential scale. Williams argued that determining raters' range of acceptance might be a useful addition to that single mark. Beyond making a choice in the usual way, judges could also indicate other generally acceptable rating possibilities; likewise, ratings that would definitely be rejected could also be revealed. An example might be:

This child sounds: passive + : + : + : : – : – : – active

The three 'plus' signs towards the 'passive' end of the scale here could indicate ratings generally acceptable to a judge: his or her 'latitude of acceptance'. If one of these was circled or otherwise highlighted (I have put it in **bold** here), that could be taken as the judge's single best estimate. A position left blank (as in the mid-position, above) could denote lack of decision or neutrality, with the three 'minus' signs to the right of the mid-point indicating possibilities definitely rejected.

Another possibility was presented by Edwards (1979) in an Irish study of lower- and middle-class children. After listening to recorded speech samples of boys and girls, teachers were asked to make semantic-differential evaluations along a number of dimensions (fluency, intelligence, enthusiasm, likely school achievement, perceived degree of educational 'disadvantage', and so on). Accompanying each rating scale was a *second* 7-point scale on which the judges were asked to indicate the degree of confidence they had in the 'substantive' rating they had just made. With this, the nub of the experiment, several important findings emerged (including some interesting gender-of-judge effects), the most salient of which for present purposes is that – while, predictably enough, all judges dutifully provided ratings along all dimensions – they were clearly less confident with some than with others. They were more certain about aspects of personality that might conceivably be acknowledged as somewhat relatable to the speech sample (e.g. fluency, reading ability, pronunciation), and much less comfortable when asked to assess such things as the happiness of the child and family socio-economic status. The implications here are obvious, and of particular moment considering that, in the vast majority of such evaluative exercises, investigators have nothing to go on beyond 'substantive' assessments, no way to differentially weight responses: no opportunity, in other words, to go beyond *belief* and determine at least a little of *attitude* (see the following section here).[6]

Beyond the problems of assessment and interpretation discussed above, there is an important final matter here, and it has to do with those people who refuse to provide their assistance in attitudinal exercises. There may be relatively few of these in the immediate and personal contexts within which most social-scientific experiments take place, but there are many who avoid participation in other settings. Sociological and political polling, for instance, must regularly deal with large numbers of non-responders.

Turgeon (2009) presents an interesting analysis from the perspective of public-opinion polling and its discontents. After touching upon the problems of sampling error, question order, the effects of wording, and low or inconsistent response rates, he turns to a central difficulty. Those informants who cannot or will not respond to questionnaire items, who produce what polling agencies refer to as 'non-opinion responses', are not randomly distributed across populations. Rather, they are more likely to be found among 'the poor, the young, the less educated, women and African Americans'. The connecting thread here is level of knowledge: 'the less knowledgeable give more non-opinion responses' (p. 354). As Turgeon then puts it, 'polls generally sing with a more "knowledgeable" accent than those they represent because of the greater tendency of the less knowledgeable to remain silent' (p. 353). Or, to put it another way, the views of those having greater knowledge receive greater weight once 'non-opinions' are filtered out of analysis. Some may not think this to be an entirely bad thing, but the fact remains that overall representativeness is reduced. Drawing upon work in Brazil and the United States, Turgeon demonstrates that simple measures exist to reduce these non-opinions, in effect to add more people's views to the mix. These measures range from simply asking informants to wait for a short time before recording their response, to providing relevant information before presenting questions: stimulating thought seems, indeed, to decrease non-opinions. Interestingly (but, on reflection, not surprisingly), this works among those who are less knowledgeable to begin with; among the more knowledgeable, however, the stimulation of 'extra thought' tends to make them 'become more uncertain or ambivalent' (p. 370).[7]

Another recent study reflects several of the important problems discussed above and, in some ways, illustrates the most basic of all difficulties. Not only does the general public often have but a 'dim awareness' of many social and political matters, some people are 'willing to provide substantive responses' to enquiries about *non-existent* topics, even when allowed the opportunity to make a 'no opinion' answer (Sturgis and Smith, 2009: 67). These 'non-attitudes' emerge, it is reported, because respondents wish to 'conform to the protocols...and to avoid appearing ignorant' (p. 68). They do not arise, as some have speculated, on the basis of some mental 'coin flip'. Rather, respondents try to ascertain what the issue *might* reasonably be about, and then construct what they consider to be an appropriate answer. About 15% of Sturgis and Smith's British respondents were willing to make 'substantive responses' to fictitious issues, roughly the same proportion found in earlier American work; it is worth noting, however, that the proportion has been shown to reach about one-third if respondents are not provided with any 'no opinion' option. One of the troubling practical implications here is that opinion surveys are liable to be 'contaminated' by responses made by those who have no knowledge of the topic. In an echo of Turgeon, the authors conclude by noting that further work needs to be done to investigate whether given groups or populations are more or less likely to willingly engage with fictitious issues or, in 'real-life' settings, with matters of which they are partly or wholly ignorant.

Attitude, behaviour and belief

Although 'attitude' has long been the cornerstone of traditional social psychology, it remains problematic in some settings.[8] Part of the reason is that, like many other psychological terms, it is also an extremely common concept in popular discourse. There are of course psychological neologisms, terms that have arisen for specific social-scientific purposes, but, in a great many instances, 'popular' words are adopted to become part of the more formal parlance. That is, the usual alternative to the production of neologisms – many of which seem ugly and unwieldy and therefore, we might suggest, to be avoided wherever possible – is to adopt existing terms. This is of course much more possible in the area of psychological enquiry than it would be in, say, the remoter echelons of astrophysics. But such adoption always involves adaptation or, at least, an attempt to closely specify what a given term is to signify in its formal dress. The person on the street may continue to use 'attitude' in an imprecise way, but it must be properly delimited for scholarly purposes. The difficulty is leakage. Researchers may construct tight definitional containers, but faithful adherence has proved difficult: the attractiveness of more fluid connotations tends always to seep in. Indeed, scholars may sometimes *want* to depart from their own containerisation, and use terms in their 'street' sense.

Social science has generally considered 'attitude' as a disposition to react favourably or unfavourably to a class of people, events, objects and so on. As noted above, the concept is defined to have three elements: thoughts or beliefs (the cognitive component), feelings (the 'affective' component) and predispositions to act in a certain way (the behavioural aspect). That is, one knows or believes something, has some emotional reaction to it and, therefore, may be assumed to act on this basis. Quite apart, however, from the leakage or spillage mentioned above, there at least two other important difficulties to be taken into account. The first, as we have seen, has to do with the very frequent inconsistency between assessed attitudes and actions presumably related to, or based upon, them. The second is that there often exists a disjunction between *attitude* and *belief.*

Confusion between belief and attitude shows up clearly on questionnaires and interviews designed to tap the latter. In scholarly usage, as just noted, *attitude* includes *belief* as one of its components. Thus, a parent's response to a questionnaire item like 'Is a knowledge of French important for your children?' – where the response is to be of the 'yes-or-no' variety or, more commonly, made along a continuum anchored at one end by 'strongly agree' and, at the other, by 'strongly disagree' (or something similar) – indicates a belief. To gauge *attitude* would require further probing into the respondent's *feeling* about this expressed belief, would require adding the affective component to the cognitive one. Without this further enquiry, we cannot really say we have come to grips with attitude. For example, the informant might believe that French is important for children's career success while, at the same time, wishing it were not so because of a strong antipathy towards the French language and culture. The upshot here is simply that many 'attitude' questionnaires are, in fact, assessments of self-reported belief.

It is a testament to the thoughtfulness of his early work that LaPiere (1934: 235) touched on the matter:

> An honest answer to the question 'Do you believe in God?' reveals all there is to be measured...but if we would know the emotional responsiveness of a person to the spoken or written word 'God' some other method of investigation must be used.

Elsewhere, he acknowledges the potential usefulness of questionnaires in assessing factual information: 'if we wish to know how many children a man has, his income, the size of his home, his age, and the condition of his parents, we can reasonably ask him' (p. 236). And most pointedly, LaPiere observes that we ought not to mislabel those 'verbal reactions' to 'symbolic situations' that are commonly requested on questionnaires. This is, in part, because they typically depart from the elicitation of purely factual information and, in part, because there usually exists that 'attitude'–behaviour discrepancy (we must now put 'attitude' in inverted commas in this usage) already discussed. Hence, to call such responses 'a reflection of a "social attitude" is to entirely disregard the definition commonly given for the phrase [sic] "attitude"' (p. 237).

Allport (1958 [1954]) also discussed the attitude–belief distinction, noting that 'prejudicial statements sometimes express the attitudinal factor, sometimes the belief factor', suggesting that a statement like 'Japanese-Americans are sly and tricky' reflects a belief, while 'I don't want Japanese-Americans in my town' is more fully fleshed and attitudinal (p. 13). He also points out that, in many cases, distinguishing between the two components of prejudice is unimportant. 'When we find one,' he writes, 'we usually find the other. Without some generalized beliefs concerning a group as a whole, a hostile attitude could not long be sustained' (p. 13). Allport refers to work showing that prejudicial attitudes towards certain groups are typically correlated with the belief that those groups possess many 'objectionable qualities'. But he also points out that distinctions are often necessary, and cites the impact of educational programmes that have apparently succeeded in altering some of the beliefs that accompany prejudicial attitudes without substantially affecting the attitudes themselves. He writes that our belief systems have a way of 'slithering around to justify the more permanent attitude. The process is one of *rationalization* – of the accommodation of beliefs to attitudes' (p. 14). This of course brings us to the matter of 'cognitive dissonance' and the adjustments we make to reconcile disparate ideas which, if left unreconciled, would create unpleasant states of arousal or tension. Allport was essentially writing about cognitive dissonance *avant la lettre* – Festinger's (1957) introduction of the term appeared three years later.

Notes

1. Of course, it is not to my purposes here to discuss the *development* of racist and prejudicial attitudes, but it is worth mentioning their early appearance and their pervasiveness. There is abundant evidence to show that, while children may not be born prejudiced, their communities very often thrust prejudice upon them; see Aboud (1988, 2003), Connolly (1998), Lewis (2005), Troyna and Hatcher (1992) – and, for very recent discussions, Elton-Chalcraft (2009) and Barrett (2009). As Nelson Mandela reminded us, 'people must learn to hate' (1995: 749).

   The process begins early – certainly before school age, as Brown (2001) demonstrates in her investigations of racism and discrimination. And it is not surprising that other attitudes are well ensconced before children begin to go to school. Studies in England, Ireland, the United States and Canada have shown that hidebound conceptions of gender traits and roles are well in place in pre-school youngsters (Best *et al.*, 1977; Edwards and Williams, 1980). Teachers (and others, of course) are typically dismayed to find that gross, stereotypic and inaccurate images of sex, gender and 'race' are firmly present before children ever leave the parental nest. This is not so much to blame parents, of course, as it is to illustrate the pervasiveness and the reach of social assessments.

2. LaPiere adds, rather uncharitably, that the black soldiers themselves 'reveled in it, exhibiting in many cases those excesses which seem to accompany every sudden removal of restriction. They became intolerably arrogant and remarkably successful in the competition for the good graces of the French, or so it seemed to the white troops' (1928: 102). LaPiere's own state of racial enlightenment is not entirely transparent, either in this study or in the later (1934) article, but it should be remembered that he was writing at a time when casual and dismissive references to Jews, 'niggers' and others were frequently made in the pages of the best and most educated authors. Those times are not our times, but we may not have moved on as much as public discourse might superficially suggest: see the discussion, a little here, on the 'bogus pipeline' work, and so on.

   Notwithstanding the continuing illustrations of prejudice, expressions of hateful attitudes towards black and Jewish people is less now than once it was; this is true in the public sphere and within educated discourse, of course, but also within the broader society. On the other hand, there are still some groups who, in many contexts, can be attacked with impunity. I am thinking particularly of the travelling people, the Roma, the 'gypsies' (see Coxhead, 2007, for the most recent discussion, but see also the useful treatments by Mayall, 1995; MacLaughlin, 1995). They have remained 'acceptable' targets of racism and prejudice, as recent incidents in Europe amply demonstrate (Anon., 2008).

3. The most comprehensive studies of the attitude–behaviour interaction are those of the late Martin Fishbein and Icek Ajzen (Ajzen and Fishbein, 1977, 1980; Fishbein and Ajzen, 1975, 2010); see also Jaccard (1981).

   Since, as Ladegaard (2000: 230) has pointed out, attitudes may have more predictive value when 'broad behavioural patterns' are under study, it is hardly surprising that they are important in disciplines other than social psychology, disciplines more concerned with large-group dynamics: sociology and political science are notable here.

   Readers may be forgiven for thinking that, in their academic demonstrations of attitude–behaviour inconsistency, social-science scholars have once more rediscovered a wheel well known to 'ordinary people' for a very long time indeed. Emerson once famously observed that 'the ancestor of every action is a thought...to think is to act' (2007 [1841]: 41), and this is undoubtedly true, so far as it goes. But whether the thoughts we express to others (or, sometimes, to ourselves as well) are in fact the thoughts giving rise to the actions...well, that is another matter.

4. LaPiere's note is again a prescient one. A great deal of contemporary work within the social sciences, after all, is both technically sophisticated and trivial. Statistical significance is meaningless without real social significance.

5. I am prescinding entirely here, of course, from the more general difficulties dogging all enquiries which, in one way or another, rely upon self-reported data. These include outright fraud or lying, as well as the dubious assumption that we always know ourselves better than others and, hence, *can* report accurately if we wish to. The issue of the 'socially desirable' response, touched upon in the text here, can be the essential underpinning of misleading answers, but a 'self-favouring' bias is not the only one possible; in some instances, 'impression management' may involve heightening social distance, or presenting oneself in an unfavourable or negative light.

   A common justification for the use of interview techniques, as opposed to (say) questionnaires, is that one has a much greater opportunity of 'pushing' people towards a fuller or more truthful response; a cornered respondent is not always, however, an accurate respondent.

   Also important are the many ways in which questions can be phrased: clarity is central, but even clear questions can be posed in particularly suggestive ways. (Of course, as implied in the text here, simply asking a question – *any* question, in *any* way – can mean a departure from any sort of 'value-free' enquiry.) 'Double-barrelled' questions are a frequent occurrence; answers to queries like 'Do you approve of the Prime Minister's foreign policy, and do you think he is well advised by his cabinet? Yes or no?' cannot be clearly interpreted. We may also wonder if respondents properly understand the questions put to them, and if the understandings, accurate or not, are the same across all respondents. What are the advantages and disadvantages of closed- versus open-ended questions? And so on.

Some scholars have actually recommended jettisoning attitude study altogether, and putting discourse analysis of one sort or another at the heart of social psychology (see Edwards, 2010a). This, however, would be to discard the young Adam with his father's ale.

A satisfying overview of all the important issues involved in the design and administration of questionnaire, survey and interview instruments is that of Oppenheim (1992).

6. A little later I made the more general point: 'consider, for example, a case in which speaker A sounds more intelligent to judges than does speaker B. Might it not be valuable to probe further, to attempt to find out something of the reasons for the choice, to try and add the affective element to the belief component already assessed?' (Edwards, 1982: 31).

7. Voting behaviour is a very large topic indeed, but there seems to be a rough consensus that (other things being equal, of course) the behaviour of non-voters does not diverge significantly from those who do vote. That is, there is no general reason to think that, had the non-voters actually voted, the results would have altered greatly. This is providing, of course, that the non-voters do not constitute a distinct group of some sort or another; if a particular constituency were to abstain or to boycott the procedure, that would be a different matter. As well, this general finding obviously does not contradict what Turgeon (2009) and others have reported about those giving 'non-opinions' to questionnaire items.

I am indebted to Yvon Grenier (2009, personal communication) for this information; see also Blais (2000) and Evans (2004).

8. Any comprehensive social-psychology textbook will outline the matter; see, for example, Myers *et al.* (2009).

3
Are Attitudes Important?

An introductory note

Given the discussion in the preceding chapter, and as a precursor to the specificities that will be found in the following one, *this* chapter considers whether or not attitudes are as important as some have made them out to be. None of the three chapters in this part of the book, however, provides any sort of comprehensive overview of attitude enquiries; I have already noted the large social-scientific literature bearing upon attitudes *per se* and, within that, there is also a sizeable body of work dealing with language perceptions and motivations. Some excellent recent surveys by Howard Giles and his colleagues can be recommended: see, for instance, Bradac *et al.* (2001), Garrett (2010), Garrett *et al.* (2003), Giles and Billings (2004), Giles *et al.* (2006) and, for a succinct discussion, Giles and Edwards (2010).

In their review, Giles and Billings (2004: 187) refer to the wealth of studies from a generation or more ago: 'over the past forty years, a substantial amount of research on attitudes to language variation has emerged around the world and across disciplines'. (I have, of course, just revisited work that is *another* forty years before the investigations referred to by Giles and Billings.) They go on to write about the 'seminal investigations' of the 1960s and 1970s, and spend some considerable time on them; as they point out, 'the earliest studies...are still heavily cited today' (p. 188). Work on language attitudes has of course moved on, but not always in a straight line from these earlier enquiries – and it is part of my job here and in Chapter 4 to remind readers of their impact.[1]

The importance – and the unimportance – of language attitudes

Just as the study of attitudes has long been an important feature in social psychology *per se*, so it has contributed more specifically to enquiries into the social life of language. In the preface to *Language Attitudes: Current Trends and Prospects*, Shuy and Fasold (1973: v) observed that the study of subjective reactions to language was a very recent development in America, and that it was a 'new and exciting area of language research'. It was recent elsewhere, too. The literature review provided in Giles and Powesland (1975) shows that, on both sides of the Atlantic, empirical work in the area got off to a rather tentative start in the late 1960s.

To begin with, we should remember that the more informal record clearly demonstrates that language attitudes have always existed, and have often been forcefully expressed. Both John Hart, in his *Orthographie* of 1569, and George Puttenham, in his *Arte of English Poesie* (1589), stated that the best English was spoken in the royal court at London, or, at least, within the area immediately surrounding it: what we would now call the home counties. Nor has the passage of time weakened such opinion within the academic cloisters. Robert Chapman, a classical scholar who oversaw the first appearance of the *Oxford English Dictionary* in 1928, observed that Standard English was 'one of the most subtle and beautiful of all expressions of the human spirit' (1932: 562). Two years later, the linguist Henry Wyld wrote of 'RS' (Received Standard English – now generally referred to as Received Pronunciation, or 'RP') that

> if it were possible to compare systematically every vowel sound in RS with the corresponding sound in a number of provincial and other dialects, assuming that the comparison could be made, as is only fair, between speakers who possessed equal qualities of voice, and the knowledge how to use it, I believe no unbiased listener would hesitate in preferring RS as the most pleasing and sonorous form, and the best suited to be the medium of poetry and oratory. (p. 607)

In this argument for the superior *aesthetic* quality of a standard dialect, Wyld makes several scholarly qualifications and, in so doing, anticipates the empirical comparisons of accents and dialects that would follow thirty years later.[2]

Language attitudes have not, of course, been restricted to varieties of one's own tongue. Indeed, some of the most pointed assessments are those made of other people's languages: hardly surprising, given the much broader social criticism that has always existed across national borders. The sixteenth-century Holy Roman Emperor, Charles V, is supposed to have rather neatly distributed his linguistic fluencies, speaking Spanish to God, Italian to women, French to men, and German to his horses. A little later (1614), Richard Carew wrote of the 'excellencie' of English – and of the pleasant but flaccid Italian, the delicate and feminine French, the majestic but fulsome Spanish, and the harsh masculinity of Dutch. In the eighteenth century, Voltaire partially echoed the Emperor's linguistic allocations. Visiting Berlin, he wrote that it was just like being at home: 'on ne parle que notre langue. L'allemand est pour les soldats et pour les chevaux'; see Waterman (1966: 138). In 1783, we find George Lemon echoing Carew:

> Others then may admire the flimsiness of the French, the neatness of the Italian, the gravity of the Spanish, nay even the native hoarseness and roughness of the Saxon, High Dutch, Belgic and Teutonic tongues; but the purity and dignity, and all the high graceful majesty, which appears at present in our *modern English tongue*, will certainly recommend it to our most diligent researches. (pp. 6–7)

There is also Rivarol's well-known assertion (1797) that French was synonymous with clarity, and that English, Greek and Latin were mediums of ambiguity.

Such sentiments continued to be expressed throughout the nineteenth century. In his famous *Minute on Education* (1835), Thomas Macaulay observed that 'the claims of our own language it is hardly necessary to recapitulate. It stands pre-eminent even among the languages of the West' (see Sharp, 1920: 110). Edwin Guest wrote (1838: 703) that English was becoming 'the great medium of civilisation', George Marsh (1860: 23) argued that 'beyond any tongue ever used by man, it is of right the cosmopolite speech', and Edward Higginson (1864: 207) believed that 'there is not, nor ever was, a language comparable to the English'.

There is surely no need for further citations here, although two other points can be made. First, while my examples have English or French at their centre, it should be remembered that most, if not all, languages have thrown their weight around at one time or another. These are not opinions restricted to the 'large' varieties, either: many 'smaller' languages, particularly those engaged in struggles against encroaching cultures, have proclaimed their superiority. The claims made have a particular poignancy in such circumstances. One occasionally reads, therefore, a defence of some threatened 'small' or minority variety which is based upon its elegance of phrasing, its regularities, its linguistic 'purity' and its marvellous literature. Why should this language be shouldered aside by the insensitive hordes beyond its borders? Enlightened opinion, after all, confirms that it is just as good a medium as the hulking neighbour next door. Alas, as Mae West once said, *à propos* of diamonds, goodness has nothing to do with it.

The second point is that, while developments in knowledge, tastes and standards have made such blunt linguistic pronouncements increasingly less likely to be heard or read, they have not disappeared. They may be encountered less frequently in scholarly corridors – not only, we hope, because of political correctness, but because of heightened awareness – but they are easy enough to discover in more popular quarters; see also the relevant discussion in Chapter 2. Indeed, the letters pages of newspapers everywhere provide regular examples.

A recent insightful illustration is provided by Russell Smith (2007), a Canadian journalist. He had earlier noted that American pronunciations, like 'nooz' for *news*, or 'zee' for *zed* are variants, and not necessarily inferior to British versions or, touching an interesting regional vein, to Canadian usage. His observations prompted a flurry of response from readers who generally made stout assertions that pronunciations like 'nooz' reveal laziness, or perhaps too much exposure to American television. One correspondent wrote that 'it is sad to see our language deteriorate to almost slang'. The 'logic' card was played, too: we spell *pews* like *news* and nobody, not even those Americans, pronounces the former as 'pooze', nor do they say 'pook' for *puke*. Smith concludes by noting that the woman who essentially equated American usage with slang and deterioration went on to cite Churchill's famous wartime speeches as 'well spoken':

> I am guessing [Smith wrote] she means not only elegantly written but spoken in a British [sic] accent. The implication, I think, is that this accent saved us from Nazism and that this accent is therefore the language of valour and virtue, and one we should all emulate. This is what I mean about the conflation of usage and morality.

Moving from the historical, the anecdotal and the popular to those more rigorous investigations heralded by Shuy and Fasold, we can note the 1972 appearance of a book by Gardner and Lambert that concentrated particularly upon the influence and the importance of attitudes in the learning of second languages, a focus that has remained central within social psychology. Among other things, their book included an appendix reproducing a number of the important studies that had been conducted to that point. The first of these to appear was that of Gardner and Lambert (1959), which really initiated the modern interest and concern with language attitudes and motivation, and which introduced the distinction between 'instrumental' and 'integrative' impulses in language learning. In the 1972 volume, the authors summarise their research programme, which started with

> a simple question we asked ourselves about twelve years ago...How is it that some people can learn a second or foreign language so easily and so well while others, given what seem to be the same opportunities to learn, find it almost impossible? (p. 132)

Their conclusion, which has generated a great deal of subsequent work over the years, was that, beyond innate intellectual ability or language 'aptitude', learners' motivations were important. And these motivations rested upon attitudes. More specifically:

> we saw many forms the student's orientation could take, two of which we looked at in some detail: an 'instrumental' outlook, reflecting the practical value and advantages of learning a new language, and an 'integrative' outlook, reflecting a sincere and personal interest in the people and culture represented by the other group. It was our hunch that an integrative orientation would sustain better the long-term motivation needed for the very demanding task of second-language learning. (p. 132)

The perceived importance of attitude and motivation in language-learning exercises, and the enduring difficulties in encouraging and maintaining interest in classroom settings, have led to a specialist literature on language attitudes (or beliefs, of course: see Chapter 2). I am not closely concerned at this point with the technicalities of this literature; good overviews can be found in Dörnyei and Schmidt (2001), Dörnyei (2005) and, especially, Dörnyei and Ushioda (2009). The last comprises an excellent treatment, in eighteen chapters, by all the important current researchers in the field. Beyond the introductory and concluding sections, the two editors also provide substantive chapters themselves; additionally, there are noteworthy contributions by MacIntyre, Clément, Kormos, Segalowitz, Noels and many others. For recent treatments that embed discussions of attitude and motivation in the broader language literature, see Bhatia and Ritchie (2006), Ellis (2008: an encyclopaedic work of more than 1,100 pages) and Gass and Selinker (2008); the last can be particularly recommended as a comprehensive introductory text. Throughout the literature, the generality is that favourable attitudes contribute to the ease and depth of second-language acquisition. This has become a widely accepted point: 'motivation appears to be the second strongest predictor of success, trailing only aptitude' (Gass and Selinker, 2008: 426). While there is much room for detailed consideration of the varied forms that motivation may take, the general point seems so obvious that it would hardly merit detailed attention. Some years ago, however, Macnamara (1973) appeared to take a contrary view, asserting that attitudes were of *little* importance in language learning. His argument remains a succinct and noteworthy one; it is instructive even where it errs.

Macnamara first noted that necessity may overpower attitudes: a child who moves from Birmingham to Berlin will learn German. This point, which applies also to adults, is clearly correct and most people can corroborate it from personal or indirect experience. At about the same time as Macnamara was writing, an illustrative confirmation was found in the report of a large-scale language-attitude survey in his own *pays natal*. The use of Irish was found to be more associated with ability than with attitudes (Committee on Irish Language Attitudes Research, 1975). This unsurprising relationship does not mean that attitudes are unimportant but it does remind us that 'in certain contexts, attitudes are more likely to assume importance only after some minimal competence has been established' (Edwards, 1977a: 57). There is thus some reason to think that, in real-life contexts, attitudes may indeed be secondary in importance to ability.

Macnamara's second point also has to do with language learning in the real world. He refers to the adoption of English by the Irish population, a language shift not accompanied by favourable attitudes. Indeed, most historical changes in language use owe much more to socio-economic and political exigencies than they do to attitudes. However, Macnamara does acknowledge that attitudes of a sort – *instrumental* attitudes – may play a part in such broadly based shifts. For example, while a mid-nineteenth-century Irishman might have loathed English and what it represented, he may yet have come to grudgingly realise the usefulness of the language for himself and, more importantly, for his children. There would have been, therefore, no *integrative* motivation, no desire to learn English in order to facilitate cultural mobility, but a possibly reluctant instrumental one.

Interestingly enough, Macnamara rejects the possibility of any really significant instrumental motivation in such cases – on a technicality, as it were; he claims that Gardner, Lambert and others had reserved this term to describe present learning for future purposes. However, whatever the views have been of what constitutes instrumental motivation, it is clearly incorrect to deny the term's aptness for the experience of the child transported to Germany, or of the Irishman's shift to English. Just because the Irishman hated the English occupation did not mean that he could not appreciate the value of the language of his ascendancy masters. Just because the child cannot appreciate the future usefulness of German does not mean that he or she is unaware at some level of its present utility, and this is obviously an instrumental aspect.

All of this led me to suggest a distinction between *positive* and *favourable* attitude (Edwards, 1983). The two terms need not, after all, be synonymous: a positive position is one of certainty or assurance, but it need not be pleasant. 'I positively loathe it' is not an oxymoronic statement. To stay with the Irish example, we could say that the attitude of the mass of the nineteenth-century population towards the English language was positive and instrumental, but not favourable (and certainly not integrative).

The third strand to Macnamara's argument brings us to the classroom. He contends that traditional language learning at school has been an unreal and artificial affair, an undertaking in which communication is subordinate to an appreciation of language as an academic subject. It is this lack of communicative purpose, and not children's attitudes, that he feels underlies their poor language competence. Although I would agree that a great failing in language classrooms has been the absence of any realistic usage, I do not think that this means that attitudes are of small importance. It is rather a matter of attitudes taking their proper position, which in many cases is secondary to language ability. In instances of societal language shift (from Irish to English, say) as well as in cases of individual necessity, the point is not that attitudes are unimportant but that they are instrumental, if unfavourable. The argument that the classroom is an 'artificial' context may reflect a condemnation of traditional approaches, but it does not of itself indicate that attitudes are trivial. In fact, attitudes are clearly of *considerable* importance (in language learning, and in other subject areas) precisely *because* of 'artificiality'. If a context is *not* perceived as pertinent to real life, or does *not* arise from necessity, then attitudes may make a real difference.

If we return again to the Irish situation we can see, as well, that the notion of artificiality can extend beyond the classroom. With the establishment of the Irish state in 1922, and the subsequent revival emphasis upon schools as agents of Irish-language restoration, there arose a disjunction between official aims regarding Irish and actual, societal linguistic behaviour. An ever-decreasing level of native competence has been accompanied by an increasing minimal competence in basic skills, produced entirely through education. It can therefore be argued that schools, and the attitudes towards Irish which they have encouraged, have been of the greatest importance in the maintenance of Irish (such as it is: see Edwards, in preparation-a; see also the general discussion in Chapter 10 here).

The importance of language attitudes revisited

While we may take Macnamara's argument, and the wider historical examples that support it, as a salutary reminder of how important it is to place our investigations properly within their context, continuing interest in language attitudes is not at all misguided. The whole sweep of historical and contemporary life reminds us that the views we hold of ourselves and others – the bases, that is to say, of social life and human interactions of all kinds – draw from a deep and rich pool of perceptions. Among these are subjective reactions to language. It follows that attempts to influence perceptions, to change beliefs and to alter attitudes are equally central to human life. What could be more natural and reasonable, then, than efforts to encourage favourable and pro-social stances, and to try and soften or eradicate others? Writ large, isn't this the essential underpinning of education itself? Attempts to measure, analyse and ultimately influence language attitudes, with a view to improving acquisition, are then merely a sub-area (and a wholly worthwhile one) within a much larger enterprise. Insights into any aspect of language-in-society must take into account considerations of attitude and belief, of preference and prejudice, of approval and dismissal, of nuance and stereotype – in a word, of social perceptions in all their complexity. Our interests here, to repeat, do not lie with language *per se*, but rather with the ways in which language and other facets of social life can be studied – in their many ramifications, across their many intertwinings, and from many different starting-points – for the illumination they shed upon the human condition. Indeed, it would not be inaccurate to say that these complex interactions *are* the human condition.

The importance of *perception*, the most pervasive and the most compelling theme in psychology, is paramount here. We obviously do not react to the world on the basis of sensory input alone but, rather, in terms of what we perceive that input to mean. This is the foundation of all our social constructions, of all our individual and group relationships, and it is a foundation that reflects, in an ongoing fashion, our accumulated social knowledge. Perception, in this sense, is the filter through which sensory data are strained, and the establishment and maintenance of this filter are culturally specific and, within social groupings, individualised to a greater or lesser extent. For example, because every individual has accumulated a unique set of experiences, each set of perceptual spectacles is itself special to some extent. At the same time, there are many social perceptions that group members hold in common: at one level, we can think of these as *stereotypes*, at another as *culture* itself. At a group level, the most important feature here has to do with the acceptance of shared understanding. This is, in a great many instances, the only sort of understanding to which we have access, and we sometimes fall prey to the idea that *our* understanding is, in fact, the only sort possible. Nonetheless, we are aware (occasionally, at least) of the relative nature of social knowledge when we realise that others do not sort out their world in quite the same way.

Because language is central to human social life, and because perceptions are the basis upon which that life operates, it is hardly surprising that the study of perceptions (most notably under the rubric of *attitude*, of course) has long had a central position in the sociology and social psychology of language. Nor is it surprising that the results of investigations here have shed some light on the generalities just mentioned. It is easy, for example, to demonstrate that great variation exists in terms of people's reactions to (or evaluations of) different languages, accents and dialects (see Edwards, 1985, 1995). The question is what to make of this variation.

One possibility is that language attitudes reflect intrinsic differences across and within language varieties themselves. That is, variety 'A' might be evaluated more favourably than 'B' because it is a linguistically superior form. Although this is a view that has had considerable historical support, and while it remains common at a popular level in virtually all linguistically stratified societies, linguists have convincingly shown that languages and language varieties cannot be designated in terms of innate superiority or inferiority. Popular prejudice, then, profoundly misunderstands the nature of human language itself. Perhaps, however, different varieties vary in their aesthetic qualities and could then be ranked, in those terms, as better or worse than one another. More favourable attitudes might attach to those varieties that *sound* more appealing (more mellifluous, more musical) and, indeed, if inherent aesthetic qualities could be demonstrated, such evaluations would reflect reality. Again, however, empirical demonstrations have shown that aesthetic linguistic qualities are *not* inherent and invariable features. Our judgements of them rest, rather, upon our attitudes towards their speakers; more pointedly, favourable perceptions go hand in hand with assessments of the status of speakers.

If we are able to eliminate any 'logical', substantive or aesthetic grounds upon which to rank language varieties, we are essentially left with only one explanation for the hierarchy of perceptions that can so easily be elicited. Such a hierarchy, and such variation as is typically found in speech-evaluation studies, reflect social perceptions of the speakers of given varieties and have nothing to say about any intrinsic qualities of the varieties themselves. In short, listening to a given variety acts as a trigger or a stimulus that evokes attitudes (or prejudices, or stereotypes) about the relevant speech community. It is on this basis that language evaluations are made; fuller details here can be found in Edwards (1989, 2009) and in the next chapter.

Perceptions of speech and language occur in non-random ways. They are particular sorts of windows through which we can observe social life, and the things we see through them generally confirm what we observe from other perspectives. This is hardly surprising and, indeed, it would be strange if it were otherwise – always providing, of course, that we take into account misperceptions or inaccurately reported opinions. These can arise unintentionally or, more interestingly, from a desire to 'self-present' in some particular fashion. Most common here are attempts to adopt what is thought to be the politically correct or the socially acceptable posture, and social psychologists have written quite extensively about patterns of 'social desirability' that may, in fact, not reflect true feelings. I am unlikely, for instance, to contradict the person who is interviewing me for a job, even though I may strongly disagree with what he or she says.[3]

Interpretations are always difficult when people make favourable responses, report positive attitudes, agree with what others have said, and so on. These *may*, of course, accurately reflect personal opinions, but all sorts of social regulations may mean that they won't. On the other hand, unfavourable or negative opinions – particularly those expressed in ways that seem to violate or, at least, ignore such regulations – are much more likely to capture real feelings. Job applicants who are invited to explain just why they want the position are likely to say positive and favourable things, even though their real attitudes, intentions and aspirations may be quite otherwise. Consequently, we cannot be sure of the accuracy of their words. If, however, an applicant so invited said something like, 'I haven't got any other options at the moment, and working for your firm will keep me going while I look around for a *real* job' – well, we might question his or her interview technique, but we would be unlikely to disbelieve the candidate.

An extensive literature (again, see also the following chapter) reveals that evaluations of language, dialect and accent variation across speakers typically fall into two or three broad categories: some assessments (of characteristics like intelligence and industry) reflect speaker *competence,* some (helpfulness, reliability) reflect *personal integrity,* and some (friendliness, sense of humour) underlie *social attractiveness.* More recent work has suggested, in fact, that two particularly salient evaluational categories account for most of the variance: *social status* (which is more or less equivalent to competence) and *solidarity* (roughly combining integrity and attractiveness). Using these broad dimensions, and the more specific evaluational scales of which they are composed, researchers have been able to show that the speech of different regional, class and ethnic groups elicits different and, for the most part, quite unsurprising attitudinal evaluations (unsurprising, that is, given the non-random nature of language attitudes just mentioned). Lower-class, minority, and 'provincial' speech styles often have positive connotations in terms of integrity and attractiveness, for example, but their speakers are typically assessed as being less competent, less intelligent, and less ambitious than are those who enjoy some regional, social, or ethnic-majority status.

These findings are interesting for several reasons, but the single most important factor is their stereotypical nature. People are evaluated in terms of characteristics that, in a broad-brush sort of way, reflect perceptions of the group to which they are seen to belong. The implication is obvious: *individuals* – with all their personal strengths and weaknesses – are commonly viewed in stereotypical *group* terms. Studies have suggested that at school, in the workplace, in personal interactions of all kinds, in fact, negative stereotypes may hinder desirable developments. (It is also worth remembering that stereotyping can operate in the opposite direction, too: those with the socially 'right' attributes may have their progress unfairly expedited.)

In assembling evidence of linguistic stereotyping, and in language-attitude studies generally, social psychologists have typically presented recorded voices to judges for evaluation. Broadly speaking, this has been done either directly, by finding appropriate representatives of each of the speech varieties to be investigated, or indirectly. The classic indirect approach has been the 'matched-guise' technique, first introduced by Lambert *et al.* (1960; see Edwards, 2009), in which the same person assumes two or more speech varieties. The obvious advantage here is that any purely idiosyncratic features (which might, for example, occur with the first, direct method) are held constant across speech samples; the assumption, then is that judges' reactions must be to the variety itself and not to any such distracting or confounding features. Overall, social-psychological insights and methodologies have produced a sizeable body of evidence bearing on social perceptions, stereotypes and language attitudes. We can now predict with some confidence what sorts of reactions (in North America, say, or in Britain) will be elicited when people hear varieties of Black English, Newfoundland English, Cockney, 'Received Pronunciation', Boston English and many others. We can also make predictions about those varieties produced by non-native speakers of English that show the influence of the first language. We understand, at a general level, how these reactions come about, via the linguistic 'triggering' already noted, and how they reflect a set of attitudes (or beliefs) that listeners have of speakers.[4]

Further details needed

Investigators have not generally gone very much beyond fairly gross explanations in their attempts to relate speech evaluations to particular speech attributes. For example, although hundreds of experiments have revealed negative reactions towards Black English, we have very little information about possibly triggering characteristics, attributes that might include pronunciation patterns, particular grammatical constructions, dialect-specific lexical items (or, of course, any combination of these and other features).

Some moves have been made in this direction, however. For example, in 1982, Giles and Ryan called for fuller linguistic and acoustic descriptions of stimulus voices. I made a complementary observation in the same year, suggesting more probing of the *reasons* behind judges' evaluative decisions; see also below. Ladegaard (1998a) provided the main phonological and prosodic characteristics of seven different Danish language 'guises'; see also Ladegaard (2000). This opened the way for more fine-grained analyses and, in a third study, Ladegaard (2001) was able to link the varying linguistic features (phonological, prosodic and lexical) present in five speech samples with listeners' characterisations and assessments. In general, though, social scientists have done little in the way of isolating 'linguistic and acoustic' variables and relating them to evaluative judgements. It is to linguistic research that we must turn if we are interested in descriptions of features that characterise and differentiate language varieties. Indeed, in recent years, a considerable amount of work has been done here, work that focuses on those very social-class and ethnic varieties of particular social-psychological concern. Thus, linguists have investigated variations in pronunciation (some say *lock* and *loch* more or less identically; some pronounce the postvocalic /r/ -in words like *cart* and *mar*), in grammar (in American Black English, the present-tense copula verb may be deleted altogether – *they are going* becomes *they going* – where Standard English allows only contraction), and in vocabulary (some English speakers *brew* their tea, some *mash* it, some let it *steep*, some let it *set*, and so on); see Edwards (1999).

Nonetheless, while linguists have typically been the ones to describe such variation, they have either been relatively uninterested in its relation to differences in social evaluations or have simply assumed that the more obvious and salient linguistic markers provide the stimuli for differentiated ratings. Like psychologists, then, linguists have generally stuck to their specific lasts. (Of course, there are some notable exceptions: Labov and Trudgill come quickly to mind.) We would certainly benefit from efforts to bridge the work of psychology and linguistics in this regard; the effect would be to refine and particularise our knowledge of how *specific* aspects of speech elicit *specific* types of evaluative reactions. And such bridging is, in fact, beginning (see Milroy and Preston, 1999; Giles and Billings, 2004; and, for an extension of the argument to embrace sociology *per se*, see Mallinson, 2009).

Accommodation

The investigation of linguistic accommodation has been most thoroughly explored by Giles and his colleagues. It is not the only perspective but it is a comprehensive one and it takes into account the reactions of listeners as well as those of speakers, it acknowledges the importance of subjective perceptions of speech as well as objective markers, and it has demonstrated a potential to treat wide ranges of speech behaviour. Furthermore, the model has given special attention to interpersonal encounters as reflections of intergroup ones: that is, I may react to you more as a representative of my group than as an individual.

The essence of the theory of speech accommodation derives from social psychological studies of similarity-attraction and social exchange. The general finding was that we like others who are like ourselves. In outlining his 'attraction paradigm', Byrne (1971) set in motion a great deal of activity – after all, there are many ways to be similar: a current representative example of work in the area is that by Morry (2007). This rather underwhelming insight was supplemented by findings that reduction of existing dissimilarities will lead to more favourable evaluation.[5] Since the desire for social approval is 'assumed to be at the heart of accommodation', as Giles and Powesland (1975: 159) put it in an early overview, we see that the model involves reducing linguistic differences so as to enhance ourselves in the eyes of others. 'Accommodation through speech can be regarded as an attempt on the part of the speaker to modify or disguise his persona in order to make it more acceptable to the person addressed' (p. 158). Accommodative actions may include alterations in dialect and accent (see also Chapter 4), but also in speech rate, message content, implied attitude and so on.

A short digression here may be useful, one that illuminates some of the presumed wellsprings of accommodation theory while, at the same time, leading us towards still deeper waters. Since accommodation means change, and since change costs something, the model has also drawn upon the social-exchange literature. The classic work here is that of Homans (1961; but see also Blau, 1986; Cook, 1987; and a useful critique by Miller, 2005). Although not stressed in most of the accommodation literature, there are obvious similarities between social-exchange theory and Michael Banton's 'rational-choice' formulations. Banton had already published several important works on racial issues, when, in a short university working paper, he drew directly upon Homans's work, presenting rational choice not only as a powerful underpinning of intergroup dynamics but, in fact, as a theory to explain ethnic and racial relations (Banton, 1977). This was made clearer six years later, with the publication of a book in which Banton argued that competition was 'the critical process shaping patterns of racial and ethnic relations' (1983: 12; see also Barot, 2006). Central to both social-exchange and rational-choice theories are, of course, the 'economic' ideas of negotiation, of careful calculation, of cost-benefit analyses. At root, these are very simple and behaviouristic, characteristics that provide at once the appeal and the potential shortcomings of these formulations. It is clear enough, I think, that exchange of one sort or another can indeed be seen as one of the central pillars of individual interaction and, therefore, that it has necessarily developed on broader social levels, too. The danger, of course, is to limit the conception of exchange, such that theoretical formulations become stripped-down, reductive and, above all, unable or unwilling to grapple with subjective factors that enter into those cost-benefit calculations.

An example here is found in Banton's (2004) application of rational-choice theory to nationalism. Discussing recent Québec history, he notes that the difference between those many francophones who would like to see important changes in current federal-provincial arrangements, and the more pointedly nationalist members of the sovereigntist *Parti Québécois*, is that the former are not prepared to pay as high a price for desired changes. Invoking the concept of 'nationalism', Banton suggests, adds nothing to our understanding of each constituency: 'the actions of both the party members and the electors can be explained by the prices they put upon

their preferences' (p. 808) – that is to say, by the different cost-benefit calculus applied by each. Now, I certainly agree that 'economic' factors are
very important in social and political movements (much more so, in fact,
than many romantic apologists would have us believe). It is also true, as
Banton suggests, that 'nationalism' is often invoked in question-begging
ways. However, as I wrote in a criticism of his argument, without due regard
to nationalist history, impulses and emotions, 'we are left with no good
sense of how those very preferences arose to be priced' (Edwards, 2004:
838; see also O'Leary, 2001, for further critical comments on the thinness
of rational-choice and other instrumentalist theories of nationalism).

A fuller critique was provided by Stone (2004), and I reproduce some
of it here, since it applies to all exercises – including many within social
science – that hope to create something straight out of Kant's crooked
timber of humanity. The chief danger, in other words, is a social
procrusteanism.

> Rational choice is like Oscar Wilde's definition of a cynic, 'someone
> who knows the price of everything and the value of nothing'. In the
> real world, people are motivated as much by values as they are by
> prices, and attempting to reduce values to prices may superficially
> appear to describe behaviour, but fails to provide any serious expla-
> nation for motivation... [C]ircumcising the analysis with Occam's
> razor may well give the appearance of a more elegant solution... but
> it leaves us with an argument devoid of much theoretical or practical
> interest. (Stone, 2004: 841–842)

Revenons à nos moutons. The most basic premises of accommodation theory are that people wish to make changes that will instigate
or strengthen the approving perceptions of others, but also that such
changes will only be put in train where favourable cost-benefit ratios
can be achieved. In elaborations of the model, Giles and his colleagues
have made several other central points. First, speakers may not necessarily be aware of their accommodative actions: while some strategies are
clearly overt, others are not. Similarly, listeners may or may not detect
these actions. Like flattery, accommodation works best when undetec-
ted; indeed, just as detected flattery rebounds to the detriment of the
flatterer, so it is reasonable to think that awareness of another's accommodations may lessen their impact. An interesting subcategory here is
the situation in which accommodation is perceived as condescension,
something that actually reinforces status differentials rather than reducing them. Unlike with flattery, however, awareness of accommodative

actions need not always undo their effectiveness: we may feel that our own sense of superiority, or importance, or influence is quite justly being recognised by some minion's linguistic deferences.

Another important point is that accommodation (if it can still be called that in this circumstance) can imply divergence as well as convergence. Some speakers may want to *increase* the perceived distance between themselves and others, wishing to dissociate themselves from other people and other opinions. Divergence is often found when individuals act on the basis of their group membership (ethnic, class, and so on), where they wish to emphasise this identity and where, most specifically, this identity is not that of their interlocutor(s). Some further details can be found in Edwards (1995), where I also make a further salient point about speech accommodation: its operation and its reception demonstrate that, just as perceptions of context can influence the way in which we select from our linguistic repertoire, so too can language choice influence the psychological setting; for an early exploration of this, one that considerably predates the accommodation literature, see Herman (1961).

Notes

1. In a book that is in some ways complementary to this one (Edwards, 2010a), I expand a little on the way in which 'traditional' attitude studies, despite some contemporary disdain, remain important within the social psychology and sociology of language.
2. For useful overviews and many more historical citations dealing with attitudes towards varieties of English, see Mugglestone (1995), Fisher (1996) and Crowley (2003).

   Particularly germane to Wyld's qualification, of course, is the 'matched-guise' technique, introduced by Lambert *et al.* (1960).
3. One of the 'classic' treatments here is the work of Crowne and Marlowe (1964) on the 'approval motive', but this is of course only aspect of the much broader matter of 'self-presentation': see the discussion in Chapter 7.
4. The power of stereotypes is reinforced when we consider the operation of what has been termed (not very accurately, however) 'reverse linguistic stereotyping'. Here, speakers' language does not trigger stereotyped reactions from listeners. Instead, prior information about speakers' status – as non-native or non-standard-dialect speakers, for example – acts to 'cue distorted perceptions of . . . language style or proficiency' (Kang and Rubin, 2009: 442).
5. These are the sorts of observations – often called 'theories' – that can give social psychology a bad name or, at least, a reputation for laboured study of the blindingly obvious. In this case, after all, there are many proverbs in many languages that suggest that birds of a feather flock together. In fairness, there are lots of *other* proverbs that maintain that opposites attract . . .

4
Language Attitudes: Contexts and Features

Standard, non-standard and regional standard dialects

A standard dialect is one spoken by educated members of society, is that form used in writing and in the media, and is supported and encouraged (traditionally, at least) at school. Its particular form is often due to historical chance; for example, if York rather than London had become the centre of the royal court, no doubt Standard English today would be quite different. Standards are the dialects of those who dominate. As a dialect there is nothing intrinsic, either linguistically or aesthetically, which gives a standard special status. As a form reflecting power and dominance, however, it is in some sense *primus inter pares*.

Many studies in many contexts have shown that differential evaluations of speech and speakers occur along the *standard-non-standard* dimension; see also Chapter 3. Typically, standard accent or dialect speakers are rated more favourably along *competence* lines (on traits such as intelligence, industriousness and ambition) and receive the highest status or prestige judgements. On the other hand, lower-class speakers and others with non-standard styles are downgraded in terms of competence but receive higher ratings in *social attractiveness* (friendliness, warmth, sense of humour) and *integrity* (helpfulness, reliability, and so on). Standard varieties, then, are high in prestige and perceived competence but do not evoke the same level of interpersonal warmth and trustworthiness as do non-standard forms. Furthermore, these results seem to generalise across listener-status lines; that is, both standard-speaking and non-standard-speaking raters produce similar patterns of evaluation.

Early studies by Giles (1970, 1971) illustrate well the distinctions between standard and non-standard forms. He found that reactions to 'Received Pronunciation' (RP: the prestigious and non-regional standard) were favourable in terms of competence, but that regional dialects elicited higher integrity and attractiveness ratings. While there are some anomalies, the evidence over the past four decades continues to suggest that standard–nonstandard distinctions are quite robust. While the friendliness and warmth associated with non-standard styles are certainly positive features, and while they may contribute importantly to a sense of group bonding and solidarity, it may be suggested that friendliness and reliability are of lesser moment in many contexts (education, for example) than is a more basic competence. It might be simply argued, then, that a high-status standard style is generally more beneficial than a non-standard one of lower prestige.

However, all of this presumes that clear and consistent distinctions can be drawn between standard and non-standard forms. It is true, of course, that not all languages have standard forms and – as we shall see – there are settings in which the concept of a standard is accepted but where the standard itself varies, often along regional lines (Drake, 1977). The most unequivocal findings along the standard-nonstandard dimension, in terms of differential evaluations, derive from British studies; here, the existence of a widely accepted, widespread and non-regional speech form (RP) perhaps makes a standard-nonstandard distinction more clear-cut.

In other contexts, however, things are not so clear, as some early studies suggested. For example, an Australian study by Berechree and Ball (1979) found that the so-called 'Cultivated Australian' evoked high competence judgements, higher indeed than those accorded to two other varieties ('Broad' and 'General'), but was *also* associated with greater personal attractiveness. If we accept that the 'Cultivated' Australian form is analogous to British RP (see Eltis, 1980), these results are intriguing. Another possibly anomalous finding is that of Carranza and Ryan (1975), who reported, in a study of reactions to Spanish and English speakers by Mexican- and Anglo-American students, that English was perceived more favourably than Spanish on integrity and attractiveness traits, as well as on those reflecting status. Spanish speakers were seen more favourably in solidarity terms than in status ones but, when compared with the English speakers, fared worse across the dimensions. We can note, then, that there may be conditions in which high-prestige styles also connote social attractiveness, and it would be useful to investigate the relevant criteria for this. It may also be that, in some circumstances, the relatively clear nonstandard-standard distinctions found in certain contexts do not apply or do not adequately represent local dynamics.

Apart from the possibility that the power of the standard may in some cases extend beyond competence to attractiveness and integrity as well, there is also the possibility that when a standard is unclear, variable, or simply not present in a given study another variety may be evaluated as a standard, along the lines noted above. Two Irish studies were illustrative here. Edwards (1977b) provided groups of student raters with five Irish accent guises, representing speakers from Galway, Cork, Cavan, Dublin and Donegal. The last of these received the most favourable competence judgements while the Dublin variety, least favourable on this dimension, evoked the highest social attractiveness evaluations. It was argued that the Donegal guise operated in this context as a standard, while the others were non-standard regional variants (the Cork, Cavan, and Galway varieties occupied intermediate positions between the other two). Now, while this result may be seen to reflect long-standing historical views associated with Northern Irish drive, ambition and industriousness, the experimental stimulus voices did not include the Irish non-regional variety, perhaps the best analogue for British RP.[1]

This raises questions about previous experiments in Britain and elsewhere which have included a clearly accepted national standard variety. How might results have changed had such a form been omitted from those presented to judge-listeners? We might, for example, expect to see some evaluative ranking of other varieties; Giles (1970) found evidence, for example, for an accent continuum, in which RP was most favourably perceived in terms of rated competence, but where distinctions appeared between regional accents (like Welsh and Somerset) and specifically urban forms (like Cockney and Birmingham varieties). There is, in fact, a well-established gradation along which non-standard urban varieties of English tend to be evaluated less favourably than those from rural settings (see Edwards, 1989). Hiraga's (2005) updating of Giles's early work confirms this, in an interesting study that involved both English and American voice samples. Received Pronunciation and 'Network American' (i.e. the speech of educated media commentators) were thus evaluated, along with urban (Birmingham and New York) and rural samples (West Yorkshire and Alabama). The overall findings put RP and Network American at the top, followed by the two rural samples, with the two urban varieties at the bottom. When status and solidarity scales were considered separately, RP and Network American were again in the one-two position on status dimensions. In terms of solidarity, however, the latter retained its rung, while RP slipped to fourth; see also the discussion of American English, below. And a very recent, if rather idiosyncratic, study by Smith and Workman (2008) also showed that Yorkshire (rural) accents were judged more favourably than those of Birmingham.

The second Irish study is that of Milroy and McClenaghan (1977). Employing Belfast undergraduates as evaluators, the authors presented four voices, two of which were 'Ulster' (probably very similar to the Donegal guise used in Edwards, 1977b) and the British RP. Here, the latter attracted the most favourable competence ratings. While in this study the Ulster voice was obviously a local variety, and in the Edwards study it was not (my investigation was conducted in Dublin), the presence of an RP stimulus voice in a Northern Irish context seems clearly to have altered the pattern of evaluations received. In any event, the fact of a variety being local (which need not, of course, be a factor at all when RP is involved) has hitherto not been thought of as being as important as its position on the standard-nonstandard continuum. It seems possible, however, that interesting interactions may result when 'local' and 'standard' are not mutually exclusive categories.

Given that the clearest previous work on standard-nonstandard distinctions has been done in contexts where a case can be made for a strong and widespread standard form, given that not all languages have standard forms and – more to the point here – given that some have several regional standards, the central question of interest arises here. How will regional standards be evaluated? On the one hand, their use by the educated, middle class of an area would suggest high perceived competence evaluations but, on the other, their very local, regional character might lead us to expect high ratings in social attractiveness and integrity as well (a fuller theoretical account may be found in Edwards, 1989).

These considerations prompted a study in a mainland Nova Scotian context, one in which the notion of *one* over-arching standard is hard to support (Edwards and Jacobsen, 1987). As in the United States, the Canadian linguistic scene is one in which the concept of regional standards may be more applicable. While it is true that, in both countries, there are educated and uneducated speech styles, and while in the broadcast and print media some attempt is made at standardisation, the fact remains that 'acceptable' speech has a greater variability than is the case in, say, Britain. In this study, a local variety with broad regional acceptance was contrasted with three other styles (from Cape Breton, Massachusetts and Newfoundland). The general hypothesis was that mainland Nova Scotian English (Cape Breton is an island part of Nova Scotia) would act as a regional standard and, compared to other varieties (ones more locally restricted *within* the region), would thus evoke more favourable judgements of competence *and* social attractiveness and integrity.

Analysing judges' evaluations along a number of dimensions, we found that the mainland Nova Scotian speakers were more favourably perceived than were the others in terms of competence, there were no differences between ratings given to Massachusetts and Cape Breton speakers, and the Newfoundland speakers received significantly poorer evaluations than the rest. This finding by itself would suggest that, in this context at least, the mainland speakers possess the greatest prestige and may be thought of as 'standard-bearers'. However, we took the lack of significant differences, across all four speech styles, on the scales reflecting integrity and attractiveness, to mean that those speakers also had regional standing. They evoked the higher competence evaluations associated with standards and, because of their local or regional nature, did not lose ground, as it were, to the others along the lines of integrity and attractiveness – traits typically seen to relate to in-group solidarity.

This raises, of course, the question of the very definition of a standard. Certainly, the study indicates potential difficulties if the definition is to depend upon ratings obtained along given dimensions in experimental situations. However, this is not the usual direction. Usually, a standard is initially *assumed* on the basis of a group's social status, degree of education, economic power, and so on – then, on the basis of experimental work, it is found to have certain associations (and lack others). But, the present findings do at least indicate (together, perhaps, with some of the Australian data) that a variety which is nearer to standard than others, and/or which has regional standard status, can evoke the usual high competence judgements *without* being downgraded in terms of attractiveness and integrity. And this in turn suggests that, in some cases, such a variety may possess greater all-round favourable connotations than does the typical standard form. While it is sensible, on the basis of earlier literature, to suggest that regional standards may thus elicit *both* favourable status *and* solidarity evaluations, the Edwards and Jacobsen study seemed to be the earliest demonstration of this. More attention to standards and regional standards is clearly called for, since these findings are strong and clear, but also limited in scope.

In general, the results of the Edwards and Jacobsen (1987) study support the idea that, in contexts possessing regional standards, these varieties may have a greater all-round favourability than what the standard varieties typically possess in settings where more clear-cut distinctions can be made between a single standard and other, non-standard forms.[2] The explanation for this presumably relates to the fact that regional standards are at once regional *and* standard, and so may be expected to elicit both status *and* solidarity reactions.

The dynamics of powerful standards

An interesting possibility, for example, is that regional standards may sometimes be countrywide; this might go some way towards explaining Berechree and Ball's (1979) findings. That is, their 'Cultivated Australian', while still being viewed as a national standard, may also elicit solidarity responses from Australian listeners who have some remaining attachment for an external variety of English: the obvious candidate here would be British RP. This sort of colonial reflex found some support in work done by Ball (1983) in Australia, Huygens and Vaughan (1983) in New Zealand, and Chia and Brown (2002) in Singapore, in which RP-accented English received high status evaluations. It is touched upon in recent work by Giles *et al.* (2006), who note that the status of RP transcends national boundaries, within and beyond the anglophone world (see also Giles and Billings, 2004; Bishop *et al.*, 2005; Garrett *et al.*, 2003). One might imagine, however, that the increasing global presence and status of American English could affect the world prestige of RP, and this is indeed reflected in empirical work. Bayard *et al.* (2001: 44), for instance, suggest that 'overall, the American accent seems well on the way to equalling or even replacing RP as the prestige – or at least preferred – variety, not only in New Zealand but in Australia and some non-English-speaking nations as well'. Mugglestone (1995) adds that, even within Britain, the status of RP is not what it once was, even suggesting that it can be 'the loss rather than the acquisition of RP which creates the more positive image' (p. 276). It is also noteworthy (perhaps) that RP-speaking characters are now often the villains in films, but, as Jenkins (2007) points out, many regional varieties continue to have negative connotations in the media. The famous phonetician, Alfred Gimson, suggested that the negatively stigmatised variant here is what he called 'Refined RP' – that is, a particularly marked form, one that strikes many as affected; it is this form that emerges from the mouths of Disney villains, or, alternatively, from those who are 'figures of fun' (see Cruttenden, 2008).[3]

Old perceptions die hard, however, and the prestige of English accents generally, and RP more specifically, continues (see Jenkins, 2007; Ladegaard, 1998b, 2006). This is so even in America or, perhaps one should say, *particularly* in America. Jones (2001) devotes a monograph to anglophilia there, with a great deal of attention given to linguistic markers and the responses elicited by them: one chapter is entitled 'Gee, I Love Your Accent' (see also Stewart *et al.*, 1985).

When an American speaker says *kyōō´pon* instead of *kōō´pon*, we have an example of 'hypercorrection', arising from the notion that, if higher-status speakers say *styōōd´nt* rather than *stōōd´nt*, then an analogous pronunciation must surely be 'correct' for *coupon*. The further interest here is that the more prestigious American pronunciation of *student* is itself a conscious adoption of British usage, and recent work by Boberg (1999) reveals some pitfalls. The American 'nativisation' of foreign words spelled with <a> that have entered the lexicon (words like *macho* and *pasta*) has, Boberg suggests, a strong 'aesthetic' dimension. This favours a rendering of the sound as /a:/ (as in *father*) rather than as /æ/ (as in *fat*). And this 'aesthetic' sense derives from the idea that British usage – in which the /a:/ pronunication is considered more typical – is prestigious usage. Ironies arise, Boberg shows, when the American /a:/-based pronunciation of such foreign imports, based upon perceptions of British elegance and 'correctness', in fact *diverges* from the /æ/ pronunciation given to such borrowings in standard British English; see also Edwards (1999).

An interesting ramification of changing perceptions of the most desirable English, or of the English variety having the greatest status and prestige, or, simply of English versus American English, has to do with the variety chosen to be taught in schools around the world. Similarly, given that English is now universally acknowledged as the current global lingua franca, which English...? (See Jenkins 2007 for a good discussion; see also Crystal, 2003; Graddol and Meinhof, 1999; and the final chapters here.) In a brief but useful overview, Ferguson (2009: 117) begins by noting that 'the debate over the model of English most appropriate for teaching [around the world]...is a longstanding one' (see also Ferguson, 2006). There are many issues here, and they go well beyond the alleged decline of RP, and even beyond the rise and clout of American English. Some of the most highly politicised issues have to do with language 'ownership', the inequalities that may result when non-native speakers of a localised variety of English are compared unfavourably with native speakers, even though the former may be entirely fluent. Here, as Ferguson (2009: 119) notes, there may be quite reasonable efforts to 'reposition ELF [English as a Lingua Franca] speakers as competent speakers of their own variety as opposed to imperfect users of a British/American standard English'. Interesting questions also arise here about errors and variations. If the various 'new Englishes' differ substantially from older varieties, for instance, is this always to be taken as localised and unexceptionable innovation? Should different norms apply to written English? Many of these questions have pressing pedagogical implications, to be sure, but they are also highly politicised. Having opened his paper by remarking on the extent of English-as-lingua-franca debate, Ferguson concludes – rather neatly for our purposes here – by noting that

> the greatest obstacle probably is attitudes, and in particular the historically ingrained assumption that native-like proficiency and conformity to L1 standard norms is the most secure benchmark of achievement in second language learning. (p. 131)

Two concluding points should be made here. First (and generally), all enquiries in the sociology of language must be regularly repeated, since the intertwined nature of varieties, and the particular linguistic occupancy of the status categories themselves, are dynamic and not static. As the social world alters, so too do its linguistic markers. Second (and specifically), we can see that the investigation of *regional* standards can provide particular insights into status relationships, illuminating as it does perceptions within regions, within countries and – especially (but not only) in cases of historical colonisation – across international boundaries.

The Queen's English

The need for repetition of enquiry applies at all levels. The dynamic nature of RP that I touched upon above is treated by Fabricius (2006: 119–120), who points out that its speakers may be perceived as 'posh' or 'snobbish', their speech reflective of an 'élitist discoursal stance'. Young people in particular, it is suggested, are now likely to repudiate 'attitudes that sustained accent prejudice'. We can recall that Smith and Workman (2008) showed Yorkshire accents outstripping RP in terms of perceived intelligence. Relevant here, too, is Mugglestone's observation (above) and, more generally her (1995) chapter on 'the rise (and fall?) of Received Pronunciation'; see also Trudgill's (2002) discussion of the 'sociolinguistics of modern RP'.

Even the Queen's English, traditionally taken as the apex of RP, has altered over the last half-century, now showing some influences of 'Estuary English', a combination of London working-class speech and RP, first described by Rosewarne (1984, 1994). Analysing the Queen's vowel sounds over four decades of her annual Christmas messages, Harrington *et al.* (2000: 927) found significant changes, evidence of a 'drift in the Queen's accent towards one that is characteristic of speakers who are younger and/or lower in the social hierarchy'. Her accent has moved closer to what the authors style 'standard southern British', although it remains 'clearly set apart' from it. Besides raising the intriguing notion that the Queen no longer speaks the Queen's English the way she once did, the import of these studies is a bit broader. It is one thing to describe the rise and appeal of the new estuarine accent among younger speakers, but it is another to show its effects upon existing speakers, especially RP speakers. The fact that the speech of the Queen herself is influenced by change suggests that, for more 'ordinary' individuals, the alterations are likely to be greater. As Harrington *et al.* conclude (p. 927), 'the extent of such...influences is probably more marked for most adult speakers, who are not in the position of having to defend a particular form of English' – to which we might add that they also live in rather closer proximity to those influences than does Elizabeth R.[4]

The dynamics of dialect evaluation

One of the most poignant aspects in the social life of language is the long-standing tendency for speakers of non-standard dialects to accept and agree with unfavourable stereotypes of their speech styles. This internalisation, this feeling that one's own speech is not 'good', has historically been a very common phenomenon indeed, for reasons that are as clear as they are unfair. In some contexts (like the classroom) it is particularly disturbing and potentially destructive, the more so because it may be directly and indirectly reinforced by those in positions of authority (like teachers). Halliday (1968: 165) once observed that

> a speaker who is made ashamed of his own language habits suffers a basic injury as a human being; to make anyone, especially a child, feel so ashamed is as indefensible as to make him feel ashamed of the colour of his skin.

Some have debated the depth of the injury here; no enlightened opinion, however, doubts the unfairness of the process.

Lambert *et al.* (1960) referred to a linguistic 'minority-group reaction', in which the perceptions and stereotypes of the 'mainstream' are accepted by those outside it. French-speaking judge-listeners, for example, not only evaluated English 'guises' (see Chapter 3) more positively than they did French ones, they also gave less favourable responses to the *French* guises than did English-speaking evaluators. Other early language-evaluation studies demonstrated the breadth of the reaction. Tucker and Lambert (1969), Carranza and Ryan (1975), Ryan and Carranza (1975) and Ryan *et al.* (1977) – to cite only a few of the representative publications of the period – were able to illustrate the minority-group reaction among black, Hispanic, and several different regional white populations in America.

The reaction is, of course, a particular, linguistic manifestation of the much broader interplay between social dominance and subordination. And, in his classic studies in the American inner city, Labov (1976) confirmed another familiar pattern: those whose speech includes nonstandard or stigmatised forms are typically their own harshest critics. The reverse of this coin is that talking 'posh' is often seen as an affectation, and any attempts on the part of non-standard-dialect speakers to expand their repertoire are liable to be met with scorn. Bragg and Ellis (1976) reported the Cockney opinion that if a child were to speak 'posh', friends would label him (or her, of course) as 'a queer'.[5] They also quote one speaker saying to another, 'You won't end up on the Board of Directors with a voice like that'. Thirty years on, Marlow and Giles (2010), in a Hawaiian study embedded in the 'language-criticism' literature have just made the same point: the title of their article is 'We won't get ahead speaking like that!'. These are long-standing tendencies indeed.

Both social relationships and their linguistic markers are dynamic, of course. The black respondents to whom Labov spoke in the 1970s are not the same as those interviewed by Ogbu (1999) a generation later. The latter found, in fact, that linguistic attitudes appear to have become more complex, since his adolescent informants continue to believe that 'white talk' is 'proper', and that Black English is not (it is viewed as slang or, less pejoratively, as 'just plain talkin'). At the same time, there is a pride in the use and the 'solidarity functions' of their vernacular that was not felt or, at least, not expressed, in earlier investigations. Rather more pointedly, Fordham has reported (1999: 272) that Black English is now the 'norm against which all other speech practices are evaluated', at least by secondary-school students. Standard English is no longer privileged; indeed, 'it is "dissed" (disrespected) and is only "leased" by the students on a daily basis from nine to three'.

These perceptual changes notwithstanding, it is clear that Black English remains the 'low' variant in a diglossic situation. Although his respondents did not articulate the notion, Ogbu also found a sense of being caught: the Black English that represents home, familiarity and group identity is threatened by the mastery of 'proper' English, a mastery that is seen as necessary for school and work success. They believe, in other words, in a sort of 'subtractive bi-dialectalism'. The 'dialect dilemma', the belief that the necessary acquisition of standard English will tend to erode the vernacular, is sometimes reinforced by a feeling (both within and without academia) that this process is part of the assimilatory intent of 'mainstream' school and society.

This 'dialect dilemma' is the same phenomenon that Smitherman (2006: 129) discusses under the heading of 'linguistic push-pull', a linguistic contradiction whereby black speakers simultaneously embrace their vernacular and dislike it:

> On the one hand, Blacks have believed that the price of the ticket for Black education and survival and success in White America is eradication of Black Talk. On the other hand, Blacks also recognize that language is bound up with Black identity and culture.

This 'push-pull' situation obviously affects many non-standard-language speakers in many settings. The solution, a theoretically plausible bi-dialectalism by which you can eat your linguistic cake while still having it, is not always easy to maintain.

It has been argued that the perceived 'dilemma' does not, in fact, reflect actual practice. After all, a more or less stable bi-dialectalism is the norm in many contexts, and it is certainly part of the repertoire of large numbers of black Americans. Is there, then, any real dilemma here? It is clearly possible, just as 'subtractive bilingualism' is possible – where the acquisition of a new language gradually ousts an existing one – but, in both cases, any 'subtraction' that occurs is a symptom of larger social forces that make resistance unlikely to succeed. In the case of black American culture and its current pervasiveness, which extends well beyond the boundaries of the black community itself, I should think that a diglossic relationship between Black English and more standard American English is likely to endure for the foreseeable future. On the other hand, a perceived 'dilemma' is a psychologically real one, whatever the facts on the ground. Ogbu's informants clearly felt that, when a black person 'is talking proper, he or she is *puttin' on* [italics added] or pretending to be white or to talk like white people' (1999: 171–172). They told him that it is 'insane to pretend to be white', that speaking standard English is a pretense, a fake. They don't actually speak of betrayal of the group here but the implication is plain, and quite similar to the *vendido* possibility (see below; see also the following section, for further details on Black English in particular).

Overall, the most relevant literature here – largely from the 1960s and 1970s, when such work was at its apogee – is an extensive one, and it confirms what has been well understood at a popular level for a long time. The speech patterns of regional speakers, of ethnic minority-group members, of lower- or working-class populations (categories that frequently overlap, of course) elicit negative evaluations, most importantly in terms of perceived status, or prestige, or 'educatedness', and this stereotypic pattern seems to hold whether or not the listeners are standard-dialect speakers themselves. Some of the early studies, undertaken before the more recent emergence of black or Hispanic 'pride', do reveal hints of linguistic and psychological developments to come. Flores and Hopper (1975), for instance, found slight preferences on the part of Mexican-American judges for the speech styles of *compañeros* who referred to themselves as 'Chicano'. But it would be naïve to assume that negative language stereotypes are generally waning in a broad societal sense. This is borne out by the Marlow and Giles (2010) study cited above, and by other recent overviews and surveys, including those of Bradac *et al.* (2001), Garrett *et al.* (2003), Giles and Billings (2004), Giles *et al.* (2006), Giles and Edwards (2010) and Garrett (2010). All of these suggest, again, that the general pattern of results I have been discussing here is a robust one.

Pride in one's culture often involves a new or renewed affection for one's own dialect or language. Linguistic pride and self-confidence can be resurgent when groups previously oppressed, discriminated against and thought to be inferior, rediscover a broader social strength and assertion, and this can be as true for cultural sub-groups and dialects as it is for larger populations and languages. Though it may be lacking in general social prestige, *any* language or dialect may function as a powerful bonding agent, *any* variety can be the voice of group identity, a central element in the revitalised 'consciousness' of non-standard-dialect speakers.

But the solidarity function of language – the symbolic role of language, that is to say, in the articulation of group identity – is clearly not restricted to situations in which earlier self-denigration has now given way to admiration and allegiance. For we also observe a disinclination to alter speech styles on the parts of groups that seem not to have experienced any sudden upsurge in group pride, and who continue to adhere to the larger society's unfavourable stereotypes of their speech patterns: speakers of low-status dialects of urban British English are examples here. Can we put this down to a more generally liberal attitude towards speech variants *per se*? It is true that views are not as rigid as they once were. The linguistic variation to be found now in the mainstream media is an indication of this, and an even more interesting development is the aping of non-mainstream behaviour, attitudes and speech style by certain middle-class constituencies (notably young people: see also the discussion of 'covert prestige', below). But prejudicial views obviously persist, even if their force has lessened in some quarters. Consequently, the title of Ellen Ryan's often-cited 1979 article ('Why do Low-Prestige Varieties Persist?') continues to be an intriguing one – even more intriguing now than it once was, according to some commentators, because the models and the opportunities for linguistic alteration are greater now than before. Why would someone, anyone, continue to talk in such a way that others would regularly think less of them in important ways? All dialects are valid systems and none can be branded 'substandard': this is the scholarly, enlightened and, we believe, correct perspective on linguistic variation. Logically, then, it is perfectly clear that no one need be ashamed of his or her language, either at the individual level or as one of the cultural markers of the group. But we also know that the world beyond the study generally thinks otherwise; see also Chapter 5.

To alter a famous phrase: *proponent docti, disponit vulgus* – which is to say that scholars may propose, but society disposes.[6] Nevertheless, even if it be non-standard and non-prestigious, every language variety can be powerful and general. Group identity is a known quantity, and in that sense is safe. Attempts to alter one's speech style, to jettison a low-status variant, or even to add another dialectal string to the bow, on the other hand, are risky undertakings. Failure may lead to a sense of marginality, a sense of not being a full (and fully accepted) member of *any* social group. As noted earlier, the Mexican American who abandoned Spanish for the socioeconomic rewards of English risked being labelled a *vendido*, a 'sell-out', a linguistic quisling. The individual who wishes to add, and not to replace, may also fall between stools. The maintenance of Spanish (language and culture) may exist uneasily alongside the acquisition of English, particularly in a world in which bilingualism is often a way-station on the road to a new monolingualism, a world in which English increasingly threatens other variants (see Edwards, 1995, and the final chapters of this book). After all, as de Swaan (1998b: 120) has pointed out, if a language community has become bilingual 'and diglossia is well-nigh complete', the maintenance of the original variety may 'cost' more than it is 'worth', and outright shift towards a new monolingualism may ensue; see also the discussion in Chapter 11.

There is another very obvious factor that deters some non-standard-dialect speakers from attempting to 'improve' their speech styles. If we consider, for instance, that negative reactions to Black English typically reflect broader social or racial attitudes, then it follows that, for a black person or any other member of a 'visible minority' group, learning and using a standard dialect may not necessarily alter things very much. Indeed, there is some suggestion in the literature that black speakers who sound 'white' may elicit *more* negative attitudes. Some early studies by Giles and Bourhis (1975, 1976) demonstrated this among West Indians in Cardiff, and similar observations have been made in Canada and the United States (see Edwards, 1989).

We have already seen here that it is not invariably (or in all contexts, at least) the case that lower-class speakers consider their own language patterns to be inferior variants. Altered social circumstances, such as a reawakening of group 'pride' or 'consciousness', may obviously lead to altered self-perceptions, including linguistic ones. This process is underlined by the increasingly common tendency to exaggerate or heighten, whether consciously or not, speech styles that were previously disparaged both within and without the group. What was once an 'inferior' variety goes beyond mere equivalence with erstwhile 'better' forms, and comes to be seen as superior to them: more direct, more pithy, more animated. In this way, non-standard speech comes to possess a new status for its speakers. Furthermore, as a reflection and, at the same time, a reinforcement of such rejuvenated status, we find that non-standard language may come to possess attractions for some middle-class and more or less standard-dialect-speaking adolescents. As implied above, there is a 'street prestige' now associated with Black English and its speakers that extends throughout much of popular culture. The attractiveness of non-standard dialect is not restricted to adolescent and young-adult cultural consumers, however: there is also the socially broader phenomenon of *covert prestige*.

'Covert prestige' rests upon the related facts that the perceived directness and vibrancy of non-standard speech are understood as 'macho' qualities, and that masculinity itself is a favoured quantity. The continued existence of non-standard forms and the disinclination to abandon them will clearly be strengthened if their allure crosses group boundaries. Labov (1977, 2006) commented upon the phenomenon in New York, contrasting its effects with the 'hypercorrect' usage of non-standard speakers who may (he suggested) feel linguistically insecure about 'stigmatised' features of their dialect, and who may attempt higher-status speech forms, particularly in formal contexts. In fact, in settings of the greatest formality, Labov reported that his lower-class respondents' use of prestige forms actually surpassed that of upper-middle-class speakers. Furthermore, when asked about their *customary* linguistic practices, the former tended to exaggerate their use of higher-status forms. The point of interest here, of course, is not the lack of accuracy of such self-reports but, rather, the psychological underpinnings that give rise to them; see the discussion of Boberg's (1999) work, above. Of course, the downgrading of personal speech styles that is revealed by hypercorrection rarely leads to wholesale abandonment of maternal non-standard dialects, and it is here that the more latent prestige of the dialects can be seen as a sort of counter-balance. As implied above, in fact, this latent attractiveness does more than act as an anchor on the affections of non-standard-dialect speakers.

Work in Britain has supplemented and confirmed the American findings. In a summary, Trudgill (2000) notes that the masculinity of working-class speech may derive from the tough or rugged nature of working-class life. The generality rests upon evidence assembled much earlier; in 1972, for instance, Trudgill had asked respondents in Norwich to indicate the pronunciations they usually gave to words commonly having more than one pronunciation (e.g. the word *tune* may be pronounced either *tyōōn* or *tōōn*, with the former being the more 'prestigious' variant). While Labov had found a general tendency for respondents in New York to over-report the use of higher-status pronunciations, Trudgill's results indicated that *males,* both working-class and middle-class, often claimed to use *non-standard* forms even when they did not customarily do. (The trans-Atlantic variation, it has been argued, might be the result of a weaker assimilation of middle-class norms among members of the English working class, or to Trudgill's more subtle analyses of sex differences.) It seems clear that working-class, non-standard forms have an attraction that cuts across class boundaries, and it is this attraction which provides the covert prestige associated with such forms. Since it is based upon associations between non-standard speech and masculinity, covert prestige is essentially a male phenomenon. Thus, Labov (2006) notes that the positive masculine connotations of non-standard speech for men are not balanced by similar positive values for women. Again, the work of Trudgill (1972) in Norwich had borne this out. Unlike their male counterparts, the women in his studies there tended to claim more *standard* usage than they actually employed.

None of the foregoing means, of course, that significant changes in patterns of communication never occurs. Quite the contrary, in fact.

Language shift, after all, is a poignant reality for many whose 'small' varieties have become less powerful and less 'prestigious' than larger neighbours that have come to threaten them. Sometimes such contact leads to bilingual or multilingual accommodations, but it has historically proved difficult to maintain indefinitely a language when external pressures are increasingly potent. The pattern of immigrant languages in the 'receiving' countries of the new world is instructive here: it is often a trajectory from one monolingualism to another over the course of only three or four generations. Beyond that, there is a very large literature on 'endangered' languages generally, one that clearly shows that even languages having long-standing official status are not immune to global linguistic pressures; fuller details here may be found in Edwards, 1995, 2009, 2010b.

Within languages, accents and dialects that elicit unfavourable reactions because of their regional or class or ethnic association may also be 'lost'. Nonetheless, just as bilingualism can be a solution in situations of language contact, so many speakers of non-standard dialects become, to a greater or lesser degree, bi-dialectal. In some circumstances, in fact – particularly in settings where people have remained for a long time, either voluntarily or because mobility was not possible for them – bi-dialectalism can have a much longer existence than bilingualism (or, if not actual or formal bi-dialectalism, then certainly 'bi-stylism' or other selective dipping into one's linguistic reservoirs). Thus, while bilingualism is often a transitional stage on the way to language shift, bi-dialectalism can be a much more permanent phenomenon: two dialects, for instance (one reflecting group solidarity, let us say, and the other elicited by practical or instrumental needs brought about by desired group contact and social mobility) can be maintained at much less cost than can two languages. Dialects often imply mutual intelligibility, after all, and share many common features.[7] As well, while dialect speakers may customarily inhabit different subcultures, they are by definition all united under one language and cultural banner. Dialect variation can thus remain where language variation may not.

Just as resistance to language shift and bilingualism is often built upon perceptions of group identity and the importance of language as a marker of that identity, so within-language variation along the dimensions of dialect, accent, style, jargon, and so on – can also be explained as non-random and 'identity-driven' selection from those linguistic reservoirs just mentioned. I will probably speak in slightly different ways to my wife, my students, my children, the vicar, the policeman who stops my car, the doctor, my friends in the pub, the bank manager, and so on. (Indeed, we would find it immediately odd if there were no such variation across people and places – just as we would be taken aback if our doctor spoke to us the way our mechanic did, or vice versa.) In short, we select from a repertoire which, for most of us, is quite broad, according to our perceptions of situational constraints and demands.[8] This is all about identity and its presentation; relevant here is the social psychological work on linguistic accommodation that has already been discussed and, as part of the treatment of language and gender to come a bit later (in Chapter 7), I shall discuss some of the work of Erving Goffman and others on 'self-presentation' and 'performance'. The linkage with attitudes is clear: if language attitudes *per se* have given us some insight into the perception and presentation of identity, then accommodations made in social life will reveal those attitudes in action, as it were, while at the same time illuminating the very grounds on which attitudes are formed.[9]

Ebonics

Investigations of American Black English, most notably by Labov and his associates (see Labov, 1994) remain compelling and instructive. I am not going to repeat here the well-known work that firmly demonstrated Black English to be a valid dialect – dispelling completely, for the enlightened mind at least, any notions of incorrectness, of inadequacy, of some random approximation of 'proper' English – and, by extension, effectively reinforced the view that *all* dialects are fully fledged systems. While they obviously differ from one another, in grammar, vocabulary and pronunciation, all obey grammatical regulation. While giving the lie to older assertions that some varieties are *sub*standard, studies of Black English and other non-standard dialects have naturally emphasised points of variation across dialects, but it is useful to remember that dialects typically have more shared than unique features. Labov noted that most of the rules governing Black English, for instance, are the same as the regulations in other English dialects; he added that the 'machinery' of English is available to speakers of all dialects (see note 7). Needless to say, the observation applies to all dialects in all languages. It is also necessary to remember, however, that the results of scholarly enquiries do not eradicate ignorant and uninformed assessments of dialect inadequacy. Nor, because of the associations often made between 'poor' language and 'poor' cognition, do such enquiries root out continuing views that hold that speakers of certain dialects are both verbally and intellectually deficient. These observations do not, of course, mean that linguistic investigations should give up, or resign themselves to some internal scholarly dialogue: on the contrary, efforts to take their findings out of the laboratory and into the street should be redoubled.[10]

As it is, our current knowledge of the linguistic validity of dialects and, therefore, for the communicative competence of their speakers, remains unavailable to the general public and poorly understood among teachers. Niedzielski (2005: 259–260) discusses work demonstrating that, 'while African-Americans make up approximately 12% of the US population, they make up an astounding 41% of the students in American schools labeled "educably mentally retarded"'. Attributions here rest largely on language evaluations that persist in finding more incorrectness, more impurity and more speech pathology in Black English. Indeed, some of the most recent developments – specifically in the story of Black English, but obviously of much wider significance – reveal the continuingly potent intertwining of linguistic matters with social, political and even legal ones. The American *Brown v. Board of Education* decision of 1954 rejected educational segregation, even when masked under the specious 'separate but equal' provisions, and promised a future of real educational equality. Things have not turned out as hoped, however, because social obstacles to black progress have remained firmly in place. Among these are the 'tremendous linguistic divisions between those who trace their ancestry to African slaves and those who do not' (Baugh, 2006: 91).

A powerful demonstration of the fact that, in many instances, debates about language are in reality debates about other matters, is found in the 1996 resolution of the school board in Oakland (California) that declared Black English, under the title of *Ebonics*, to be the native *language* of its black students.[11] Because of the original and obviously contentious claim that Ebonics had a 'genesis' unrelated to English, an amended resolution was passed the following year: now, the variety was described as not *merely* an English dialect. At one level, then, the Oakland discussion revolved around relatively uninformed opinions about language–dialect distinctions. At a much more interesting level, it gave us an unusually informative chapter in the sociology of language.

Of course, no linguist would hold that Ebonics is a separate language (Baugh, 2002, 2004), but this hardly implies any diminished concern for the speakers of Ebonics-as-dialect. Many of those who argued for Ebonics-as-language, however, were motivated by their awareness of the common (but, of course, mistaken) belief that 'dialect' signifies an inferior, incomplete or inaccurate variety. Given their concerns for schoolchildren and, by extension, for all speakers of Black English, they hoped that an acceptance of the 'language' label would facilitate and focus desired actions. It is clear that, while some sincerely believed Ebonics to be a language, others did not: all the proponents of the equation, however, realised that, in the popular imagination, a language was rather more important than a dialect.

Wright (2005) assembled a considerable bibliography of references, both academic and popular, to the Oakland affair. We find, for example, that a number of prominent black scholars rejected the basic thesis while endorsing the underlying motivation. Henry Louis Gates found the original declaration 'stupid and ridiculous', but sincerely motivated by the educators' assessments of the grave problems of inner-city schools (Rich, 1997). Jesse Jackson initially decried the declaration: to say that black students spoke a language called Ebonics, rather than English, was an insult and a disgrace (Todd, 1997). Other prominent black Americans, from Maya Angelou to Bill Cosby, were also critical of the Oakland approach (Lippi-Green, 1997). And Brent Staples, a black *New York Times* journalist, wrote that Oakland fully deserved the scorn that greeted its mistaken assertion that 'broken, inner-city English [is] a distinct "genetically based" language system' (1997).

One could agree or disagree with the attitudes of black commentators who are not linguistic scholars, but they are neither foolish nor unfeeling. Black critics of Ebonics who believe it to be a deficient variety may be fairly criticised for not properly informing themselves of the relevant scholarship. They cannot be criticised, however, for their genuine concern for black children, nor, obviously, can they be accused of rejecting Black English on racially prejudiced principles. This *is* an accusation, however, that can be levelled at many of the 'popular' reactions to the Ebonics debate, reactions that are merely specific manifestations of long-held stereotypes, and hateful and prejudicial opinions.

Language difference as language deficit: the social power of attitudes

As we have seen, attitudes towards language variants have always been both widespread and strongly held; indeed, most socially stratified societies – which means virtually all societies, except for a very few (and increasingly rare) small 'tribal' groupings – have had firm ideas about 'correct' and 'incorrect' language, about 'substandard' dialects, about the insidious influences of 'slang', and so on. My earlier discussion of Russell Smith's examples is a case in point, where 'popular' views are concerned. In fact, however, these firm ideas have typically been most explicit in the classroom, since school has traditionally been a forceful supporter of 'proper' language (usually for the best of motives, it must be said). An important corollary has been the school's role – strongly articulated within its walls, and strongly if sometimes implicitly reinforced from without – in the eradication of 'substandard' varieties.

In accepting that some speech styles are simply wrong, schools have of course reflected extra-mural deficit views of disadvantage in general and of language in particular. These views, incidentally, have been remarkably similar across social groups, for it is a commonplace (and, after a moment's thought, the psychology here is not difficult to comprehend) that those with socially stigmatised speech styles often come to accept 'mainstream' perceptions of their low status and deficiency; see also the discussion, above, of the 'minority-group reaction'. The school's role in linguistic disadvantage has typically been a circularly reinforcing one: children arrive speaking a variety that is considered deficient; teachers, acting from those best of (but, sadly, ill-founded) motives, aim to replace this with a standard variety; they may also make attributions, based upon their perceptions of speech, about the intelligence, educability and likely scholastic progress of their pupils. The vicious circle implicit in Rist's famous 'self-fulfilling prophecy' (1970) is completed when children, treated differently because of presumed deficiencies, do in fact come to perform less well than others.

There is little doubt that, in many jurisdictions, schools are more tolerant of language variation today than they once were; again, this is related to the more liberal attitudes beyond the school gates. But 'tolerance' rarely rests upon whole-hearted acceptance. Contemporary assessments of 'social inclusion', of the evils of 'marginalisation' and 'stigmatisation', of the inequities marked by race and class – these, rather than more fundamental shifts in belief and understanding, may be the operative principles at work in many instances. The dubious insights of the late Basil Bernstein, with his notions of 'elaborated' and 'restricted' codes of language, and the more recent speculations of John Honey about the superiority of standard dialects continue, however, to exert a baleful influence upon educational thinking; fuller discussion of their specific arguments will be found in Edwards (1987, 2010a). It may well be that we have not, after all, moved beyond deficit views of certain speech patterns.[12]

One or two recent investigations will make the point. Edwards and McKinnon (1987) asked 96 primary and secondary teachers in rural Nova Scotia for their views of educational disadvantage in general, and language matters in particular. Ten schools were involved here; while they served communities that were predominantly white and English-speaking, they also had sizeable groups of French Acadian and black pupils. Most teachers held an implicit 'deficit' point of view; here are two representative comments (p. 337):

> disadvantage suggests an informational and experiential inferiority...an inability to make full use of novel information and, conversely, to call upon past experiences in novel situations;

> [disadvantaged children have] lack of experiences, poor language development...usually disorganized. They usually are not motivated by long-term rewards. Goals must be short-term. These students generally come from lower economic levels, but not always. A further characteristic of [disadvantaged) families I would say is disorganization and a low priority placed on learning.

Certainly, not all teachers phrased their feeling in such terms – which, indeed, show some familiarity with the literature or, at least, the jargon – but the general tenor of opinion is fairly reflected in these comments. There is some suggestion in these and other observations that teachers may have adapted new information to old attitudes; this is particularly evident in phrases like 'informational and experiential inferiority' which are redolent of the environmental-deficit literature.

Turning to language matters specifically, teachers pointed to poor grammar, vocabulary, articulation and reading as important aspects of disadvantage. Again, differences were generally seen as deficits. Here again are some representative comments will illustrate this (p. 339):

> [children often cannot] articulate their thoughts and feelings in such a way that they satisfy both themselves and their audience;

> the common element of experience among all disadvantaged children is infrequent interaction with adults in discovery activities where opinions and experiences can be shared;

> both receptive and expressive skills seem to have low levels of value and priority when it comes to developing accuracy and fluency.

These, once more, are beliefs that correspond strikingly with views expressed in the language-deficit literature. Children are seen to be unable to communicate adequately, they lack the experiences and interactions which are necessary for developing language skills and indeed, it is suggested that their 'receptive and expressive' talents are not greatly valued anyway. This last point is particularly reminiscent of the linguistically misguided sentiments of deficit theorists of the 1960s, those whose work prompted Labov's famous and important investigations. Several teachers commented extensively on the 'poor' English learned at home, and the consequent need to teach children 'correct' English. This task, some felt, was analogous to teaching a new language altogether. The various programmes and activities suggested as useful here were again echoes of the dreary recommendations of language-deficit theorists: language drills, speech therapy, and so on. The speech patterns of minority-group children were often singled out for attention. Many put black and Acadian children at the top of the lists of those having language difficulties. A fairly general view was expressed by one teacher as follows: 'Blacks have a slang language all their own. They will not use proper English when opportunity arises' (p. 339). In the secondary school having the most black pupils, 11 of the 22 teachers commented explicitly on the children's language problems.

Such findings are consistent with those reported elsewhere. In her discussion of the educational situation of Puerto Rican children in America, Walsh found teachers whose views seem to have 'effectively summarized all of the conclusions drawn from Bernstein's theories of restricted and elaborated codes' (Lippi-Green, 1997: 111):

> these poor kids come to school speaking a hodge podge. They are all mixed up and don't know any language well. As a result, they can't even think clearly. That's why they don't learn. It's our job to teach them language – to make up for their deficiency. And, since their parents don't really know any language either, why should we waste time on Spanish? It is 'good' English which has to be the focus. (Walsh, 1991: 107)

Could we ask for a clearer or more succinct statement of the 'deficit' position? The very persistence of such views, more than two decades after the demonstrations by Labov and his colleagues is noteworthy in itself, of course – noteworthy and (as Lippi-Green observes) indicative of 'how seductive such rhetoric can be' (p. 111). In any event, it is deeply disturbing to think that teachers still approach the children in their classrooms with this set of warped, and warping, assumptions; see, again, the plea made in note 10.

The disadvantaged children reported on above were Spanish-English bilinguals, and this is important for at least two reasons. First, as with Edwards and McKinnon's (1987) French-speaking youngsters, we are reminded that linguistic 'deficits' are commonly alleged to exist both within and across language boundaries. The inner-city black children whose speech was the primary focus of both deficit and difference theorists were monolingual English speakers, so their 'problem' was at the level of dialect. In other contexts, however – with indigenous or immigrant ethnic-minority children – the problem is at the level of language itself: pupils arrive in the classroom without a knowledge of English (for instance). There are of course some interesting wheels-within-wheels here. For instance, many non-English-speaking minority-group children will be disadvantaged in ways other than linguistic or cultural. Because of this, it is very likely that the English they soon begin to acquire will not be some standard-like variety; on the contrary, it is generally a non-standard dialect. The potential for jumping from a language frying-pan into a dialect fire is obvious.

Second, we note the impression that bilingual children can make on the linguistically naïve teacher: they (and their parents, too) are 'mixed up' and do not know either language very well. Such a misguided perception is perhaps more predictable when teachers who know only one language themselves and who live in an essentially monolingual environment are considering the competences of children who are at once materially disadvantaged and bilingual. But it is not limited to them.

Overall, the argument that I made in the second edition of a book about language and disadvantage (1989; see also Edwards, 2006) – and complementary suggestions made by Crowley in the second edition of *his* book on standard language (2003) – seem justified. Various types of 'deficit' models continue to have adherents, both within and without the educational world. There are 'important continuities with the thinking of the past, including the repetition of many of the same points of confusion and difficulty' (Crowley, 2003: 231). In similar fashion, Wolfram (1998: 105) recently acknowledged that 'entrenched myths about language inadequacy are like a jack-in-the-box that keeps springing back up'; he goes on to say that

> the exposure of one line of reasoning as objectively unjustified and illogical doesn't mean that linguistic equality will be attained. If the bottom-line belief is that one cultural group – and by extension its language – is inferior to another, then another line of reasoning will simply replace the old one.

Perhaps there is something inherent in the nature of socially stratified societies that will always find a way to translate cultural difference into deficiency. But even if this rather gloomy assessment is correct, even if we can only hope to scotch and not kill the snake, we should make whatever assaults we can on inaccurate and prejudiced interpretations; see, yet again, note 10.

Prejudicial and ill-conceived attitudes continue to turn language and dialectal differences into deficits. Whatever the scholarly evidence may suggest, questions of the 'goodness' of language are typically political ones, resting upon social bedrock that is both wide and deep. Society disposes. The scholarly evidence – as adduced by Labov, for instance, in his celebrated studies of urban American Black English – may have led some to imagine that the era of inaccurate 'deficit' thinking was nearing its end, but this conceit was a naïve one indeed.

Notes

1. The non-regional and prestigious southern Irish accent is now almost entirely a reflection of social class. It may be said, however, to be somewhat derivative of earlier religiously marked styles: the so-called 'Ascendancy' accent, or the speech of the 'West British'.
2. Hiraga's (2005) finding that 'Network American' in the ears of English judge-listeners was ranked (with RP) at the top of the 'status' hierarchy, and (with RP dropping a couple of places) *also* at the top of the 'solidarity' continuum, is interesting here. Another interesting situation is that in which more than one 'standard' may exist in the same region, and at the same time. Kristiansen (2001) has thus argued for the coexistence of a standard 'media' Danish with a more long-standing 'educated' Danish. Ladegaard (2001) identified other Danish regional standards. Long and Yim (2000) report that, in both Korea and Japan, the line between standards and regional standards is often blurred.
3. Gimson's observation reminds us that RP is not, itself, a monolithic entity. In the third edition of his famous work on English pronunciation (1980), he suggested three subdivisions; Wells (1982) suggested four.
4. A sampling made in 2008 by SpinVox – a firm that develops and markets software that converts voice messages into text, and then forwards them to recipient's email inboxes – suggested that three-quarters of the population of Britain 'don't like the way they talk' and, if it were possible, they would like to speak 'the Queen's English'. The investigators further pointed out that this desire to speak RP would mean sharing 'the sound of their voice not only with the Queen but with celebrities like Liz Hurley and Hugh Grant' (see Jackman, 2008). All three are now presumably enclosed within that 'estuarine' variety which some consider a modern form of Cockney. Her majesty will soon be dropping her h's, I suppose. Her majesty need not, of course, pay the slightest attention, either to language usage in general or to her own speech in particular. She could cite an old regal precedent, in fact. At the Council of Constance, convened in 1414 to discuss heresy, schism and church reform, Emperor Sigismund's language was corrected by a minion. His lofty reply was that *'ego sum rex romanus, et supra grammaticam'*.

5. A related phenomenon extends things from dialects to languages. Orwell famously observed that 'nearly every Englishman of working-class origin considers it effeminate to pronounce foreign words correctly' (1970 [1941]: 74). The gender is important here, I think. Males of my post-war 'boomer' generation will no doubt remember their own secondary-school experiences in French and German classes as confirming Orwell's point. These attitudes persist, and may in part reflect a larger phenomenon. Kissau (2006), for instance, reports that Canadian high-school boys feel that the French classroom is a 'female domain', and not a place for males. One language teacher observed that 'there's still a lot of sexist thinking that a man doesn't learn languages. A man does math or engineering' (p. 415; see also Carr and Pauwels, 2006).

6. It was the fifteenth-century mystic, Thomas à Kempis, who observed that *homo proponit sed Deus disponit* – 'man proposes, but God disposes'. The phrase comes from the nineteenth chapter of the first book of *De Imitatione Christi*.

7. As Labov (1976: p. 64) once put it: 'the gears and axles of English grammatical machinery are available to speakers of all dialects'. His observation clearly applies to all dialects of all languages.

8. An informal but not inaccurate treatment of variations in style choice is found in Joos (1967). He provides a continuum of stylistic formality/informality, the five points on the scale being frozen, formal, consultative, casual and intimate; for a full discussion, see Edwards (1995).

9. At this point, readers may wish to return to the discussion of language accommodation in Chapter 3, and also to look ahead to the treatment of identity in Chapters 5, 6 and 7.

10. See also some of the introductory observations in Edwards (2010a), where I make a plea for the provision of fuller information about dialect variation and its meaning to teachers. This is not, of course, any sort of suggestion that teachers are somehow more ill intentioned than others, but rather that their knowledge, attitudes and practices are of particular importance in the lives of non-standard-speaking children.

11. The term *Ebonics* was coined by researchers taking part in a conference in St Louis; as Robert Williams (1975) points out, this neologism represents a combination of 'ebony' with 'phonics', and arose from the desire to define and describe black language from a black point of view.

12. Cheshire *et al.* (1989: 6) note that 'the legacy of Bernstein lives on', and their collection demonstrates the persistence of deficit views among teachers in many European countries. And a recent number of *Language and Education* includes a piece by Myhill and Dunkin (2005) in which reference is made to Bernstein's hypotheses. The reference is only a passing one, but it appears in a list of citations concerning classroom talk and there is no indication at all that some insights may be more equal than others. Wiggan (2007) also comments on Bernstein's analyses without making any critical observations; consequently, they are simply presented as part of a very long, but very shallow, overview of studies in the area.

Part 2
Identity Matters

5
Language, Group, Identity: General Considerations

An introductory note

We live in an age when matters of group identity seem particularly important. This is because recent times have seen many social and political transitions – and transition often implies the negotiation or re-negotiation of social identities. At a minimum, transitional times cast things in more obvious relief. They are almost always uncomfortable: certainly so, when destinations are unclear, and sometimes even when destinations seem desirable. And they can be much more than merely uncomfortable. Classic examples include the break-up of the Soviet Union and the subsequent problems among the former republics; new arrangements within eastern European countries, and between these countries and a western European federation that is itself experiencing many social, cultural and religious tensions; reworked perspectives on nationality and its attributes, following the events of 11 September 2001; the continuing agonies of Africa and the ripple effects of these well beyond its borders; the rise of economic powerhouses in India, Asia and South America; the rethinking of multicultural accommodations – in the traditional immigrant destinations in the new world (Canada, the United States, Australia), but also in Europe – brought about by fears of social disintegration, of balkanisation, of violent internal discord; the attention now given to, and often demanded by, the stateless populations of the world – the regional minorities of Europe, for example, but also aboriginal and indigenous peoples around the world; and so on. These and other social settings are in flux, and the complexities are increased when we realise that none exists independently of the others, particularly given more or less universal electronic penetration and interconnection. There have, of course, been many other historical periods when the dynamics of group 'belonging' have become particularly marked or salient, but there is a speed and immediacy today that is new.

Leaving aside some of the more violent settings, we can consider western Europe as an instructive case study. It is a continent that is increasingly unified: since the formal establishment of the European Union in 1993, that organisation has grown to include 27 countries, with several others waiting in the wings to join. Yet internal arrangements have hardly proceeded without a glitch, and one of the most insistent pressures has to do with the reconciliation of a successful federal Europe with a 'Europe of the regions', where local interests and requirements are satisfactorily attended to. Notwithstanding the formal (some would say theoretical) allowances made for regional diversity in the Maastricht foundation documents, it is entirely reasonable to ask what an ever more centralised and more bureaucratic Europe will mean for the cultures and languages that enjoy official support and, even more pointedly, for those fifty or so 'stateless' varieties whose voices are increasingly raised (and occasionally responded to beyond the pieties of lip-service).

In October 1993 – just before the Maastricht Treaty came into force, essentially creating the European Union – Václav Havel addressed the General Assembly of the Council of Europe, meeting in Vienna. His subject was European unity and identity, and he argued that it was an 'erroneous belief that the great European task before us is a purely technical, a purely administrative, or a purely systemic matter' (Havel, 1993). To any student of language and culture, the observation is a truism, and many would also agree, today, with what Havel went on to say almost twenty years ago: that the continent lacks an overarching ethos, a shared imagination, a generosity of spirit and that, in a word, a new and truly unified Europe cannot be built upon partisan lobbying interests.

At about the same time, the *Fundacío per a les Idees i les Arts* in Barcelona undertook a survey of the opinions of twenty European scholars and intellectuals (Acta, 1993). The respondents included writers, artists, philosophers and historians, and among the best known were Alain Touraine, Günter Grass, Robert (Robèrt) Lafont, Cornelius Castoriadis, Ralf Dahrendorf and Ernest Gellner. All were asked about European dynamics and their implications for identity. What form should European integration take? Will increasing unification be beneficial for the 'stateless' communities? Is there such a thing as a *European* culture and is there, or could there be, an emergent *European* identity, one that transcends national borders? Could such a continental sense of belonging coexist with regional identities? It is apparent that these questions remain as important now as they were in 1993.

Approaching twenty public intellectuals, united only by virtue of being 'members of the world of thought and culture' (p. 222), does not a scientific survey make. Nonetheless, since it is the diversity of opinion that is the most interesting aspect of the enterprise, considerations of sampling and procedure become rather less important. Most of the respondents agreed that there was a general European cultural heritage, and most valued linguistic and social diversity (at least at a theoretical level). Beyond that, however, the intellectual bases for continental federalism appeared far from rock-solid or broadly shared. The thorny questions of models of integration, of the resolution of regional, state and national loyalties, thus remain open. The most interesting remarks bearing specifically upon identity were those of Robèrt Lafont, the Occitan writer, activist and former president of the Institut d'Estudis Occitans; he suggested, among other things, that

identities which are not 'reinvested' in living realities, which can no longer generate political projects and have no strategy for change, are doomed. A defensive attitude is itself the death knoll [sic]. I am always bothered in discussions between 'minorities' by the non-historical discourse, the discourse on identity. I would prefer something much bolder. (p. 280)

These are notable sentiments from a scholar who was passionately concerned with the fate of all minority languages and not just his own, notable because Lafont argues here against the stasis that so many enthusiasts and revivalists seem implicitly to endorse. Hopes for the rejuvenation of flagging varieties are a central feature within the minority-language literature, and reinvigoration and revival are *active* steps, of course. They are often seen as necessary counters to the depredations of those larger linguistic neighbours who have denied the 'smaller' language and culture its rightful place in the world. And yet, the implication often seems to be that – once old wrongs have been righted, once threatened languages have been set on their feet again, once a more acceptable balance of forces has been achieved – the social landscape will somehow remain in its new-found harmony. This is a curiously *static* view, not only unlikely on its own merits, but particularly bizarre since it affects to ignore the dynamism of history and the very social tectonics that brought the 'small' language to its present pass. When Lafont refers to the lack of any 'strategy for change' and 'a defensive attitude', he touches upon matters that remain at the very heart of all discussions about minority languages and the identities of their speakers. It is not unreasonable, of course, to attempt a defence of a beleaguered variety, but both contemporary and historical examples show, over and over again, how short-sighted such defences are if they are unable or unwilling to confront a future which will undoubtedly be at least as dynamic as the past. I am tempted here to refer to the important, and often tragic, differences between immediate and forceful military action and appropriate 'exit strategies'. Once the battle has been won, and once the soldiers have been withdrawn, how will the subsequent peace then unfold?

The matters that I have just discussed in the European context are, of course, equally important elsewhere, and readers can easily summon up other settings in which altered conditions of linguistic and cultural contact have thrust 'identity politics' on to the stage. The particular tensions and pressures will vary, of course (matters of language, religion, politics, economics, class, race and geography are among the most frequently recurring markers) but struggles on behalf of 'groupness', belonging and identity are always at the heart of things. A classic expression here, in terms of culture and language, is Saussure's (1980 [1916]) distinction between 'provincialism' and 'intercourse'. On the one hand, he argued, *l'esprit de clocher* keeps a linguistic community close, connected and more easily faithful to old traditions and practices; however, such parochialism *rend les hommes sédentaires*, and can become cloying and undesirable. So, on the other hand, we see communities pulled towards the larger world, attracted by mediums of 'wider communication' and unwilling to remain forever in the comfortable but static shadow of the village steeple. This was the principle of *intercourse* (Saussure used the English term, and his editors decided to retain *cette pittoresque expression*). We have, then, a centripetal-centrifugal opposition, one that Saussure felt was applicable to all human dynamics, not just linguistic ones. Many others, too, have attempted to capture this opposition. One of the earliest efforts was the classic distinction that Tönnies (1887) made between *Gemeinschaft* and *Gesellschaft*, but to mention such dichotomies as 'roots and options', 'state and community' and 'tribalism and globalism' is to cite only a few from a long list.

Not all of the attempts to capture and then to describe the tensions and pressures that are of such particular moment in minority-language settings are exactly equivalent in either their force or their intent. Nevertheless, it is clear that the human conditions that inspire them are broadly similar, and of very long standing.

The centrality of the group

The single most obvious facet of the language-and-identity relationship is the human need for psychosocial 'anchors'. It is clear that a sense of identity is at the heart of the person, and the group, and the connective tissue that links them. It is also clear that identities very rarely exist singly or in isolation from one another: on the contrary, we all possess a number of identities or, if you prefer, sub-components of some overall umbrella identity. Not all aspects are equally salient at all times, of course. Rather, different features will assume greater or lesser centrality according to circumstance and context. Since the general thrust of this book treats issues at the societal level, group markers and attributes of identity are more central than individual ones. As I have just implied, however, it is salutary to keep in mind the connections between individuals and assemblages here, if for no other reason than that 'group' encounters and tensions typically involve varying degrees of individual impetus. It is rare indeed to find people interacting with one another on group matters at such a 'representative' level that we can safely ignore individual motivations altogether. Thus, I want to preface my later remarks here by pointing out that personal and group identities are intertwined, and are joined in reciprocal fashion. One way to further describe the relationship is to recall the argument that language-contact settings are unique in the weighting and distribution of elements that are, themselves, common across contexts; for fuller details, see Edwards (2010b).

Similarly, the components of individual identity are not unique but are drawn from some common social pool. There is uniqueness at the level of personality, to be sure, but, once again, we can understand that it is built upon the particular combinations and force of those broadly shared elements. On the other hand, the social 'pool' itself is an assembly of constituent personalities. Limitations of time and space prevent further discussion here – of, for instance, the very old notion that the assembly is more than the collection of individuals, that the societal whole is greater than the sum of the personal parts, that there is a sort of *Gestalt* that both summarises and goes beyond specific components. Speculation here has fuelled discussions from the Greek golden age, to the reactionary impulses of nineteenth-century commentators worried about revolutionary upheavals, to contemporary social-psychological investigations.[1]

If we attend mainly to matters of identity at the level of the group, we immediately realise how varied 'groupness' itself. It will be understood that my main concern here is with collectivities that, if not always entirely 'involuntary' groupings, nevertheless have a significance that is at once broad and historically deep. This implies more attention to ethnic, national, religious and gender affiliations – to name only the most obvious categories (hardly watertight social compartments, of course) – and less to the linguistic features of membership in voluntary organisations, in narrower congregations. Naturally, what may appear as immutable memberships to some may seem more 'constructed' or 'contingent' to others. It is a matter of some considerable interest in the current literature, for example, whether ethnic and national affiliations have some 'primordial' status as fundamental components of human social arrangements, or whether they are better thought of as dependent variables, subject to instrumental construction – and reconstruction. Is nationalism a modern phenomenon, a product of the modernity that disrupted older social arrangements and created the need for new allegiances? This was the view of the late Ernest Gellner (1964, 1983), in opposition to the earlier idea that ethnonational affiliations were a natural and, indeed, perennial fact of human life. Other contemporary scholars, however, have argued that these affiliations must rest upon 'pre-modern' collectivities of long historical standing. The titles of important books by Anthony Smith and John Armstrong – *The Ethnic Origins of Nations* (1986) and *Nations Before Nationalism* (1982), respectively – are suggestive of this latter argument; see also Leoussi and Grosby (2007). Leoussi (2001) provides excellent coverage of these and related issues in ethnic and national 'groupness'. I will return to the matter in the next chapter; see also the discussions in Edwards (2009, 2010b).

Group memberships that are more self-consciously or voluntarily acquired may also, of course, involve linguistic features of great depth and importance. That multiplicity of identities or sub-identities that I mentioned above will often bring the more voluntary (and sometimes, indeed, the more ephemeral) memberships into close connection with those that are more deeply engrained. This accounts to considerable degree for the breadth and the dynamics of the language repertoires to which most people have access. Multiple identities imply a range of speech styles and behaviour. It is not only bilinguals and multilinguals who have more than one variety at their disposal: variation also exists at the within-language levels of dialect, accent, style, register, jargon, and so on. Considered from this perspective, we can see that the pools of linguistic possibility available to all normal individuals – even if the type and extent of capacities are rarely examined, and simply taken for granted in automatic or unconscious reactions to the exigencies of particular social roles and situations – are deep ones and that, therefore, the nuances of identity structure and presentation are manifold. A final point here, and one that suggests even greater possible shadings of language and identity, arises from demonstrations that reveal how easily and quickly groups can be created, how boundary-markers can be at once trivial and potent, and how groups summoned from nothing can then be manipulated without difficulty. One or two 'classic' studies will illustrate the point.

Sherif (1956) and Sherif *et al.* (1961) reported on an experiment conducted during a three-week summer camp for eleven-year-old boys in Oklahoma. It represented the culmination of a series of studies which had begun in the late 1940s, and it was carefully planned in three phases. In the first week, the boys were divided into two groups, and were generally kept apart, although some 'chance' meetings were arranged. Internal cohesion, choice of leaders and friends, and various markers of solidarity (slogans, flags, and so on) developed rapidly, but the awareness of the other group also gave rise to a 'spontaneous clamour' for competition. The 'Rattlers' and the 'Eagles' soon met on the sports field and, from there, further rivalries developed apace. Strong in-group solidarity was accompanied by disdain for the 'other'. Hoping to restore harmony, the camp administrators then brought the two groups together for enjoyable social occasions, but without success:

> These situations only served as opportunities for the rival groups to berate and attack each other. In the dining-hall they shoved each other aside, and the group that lost the contest for the head of the line shouted 'Ladies first!' at the winner. They threw paper, food and vile names at each other at the tables. An Eagle bumped by a Rattler was admonished by his fellow Eagles to brush 'the dirt' off his clothes. (Sherif, 1956: 57–58)

Further interventions did, in fact, break down these experimentally created group boundaries, and the boys travelled home together peacefully enough.

The import of Sherif's work, of course, was to demonstrate the ease with which allegiances can be created, and how solidarity *within* groups typically coexists with competition *between* them. Indeed, within-group allegiances are notably strengthened through comparison, competition and, perhaps, conflict. The suggestion is that an important part of group identity rests upon a sense of what one is *not*, of the 'out-group', of the 'other'. Defining by exclusion, after all, is a common enough exercise. Sherif's work has, at the same time, been seen as an exercise in cooperation: the unpleasant rivalries set in train by the experimenters were also reduced by them. It is important to realise, however, that conflict resolution was achieved at considerable cost, inasmuch as it rested upon the break-up of the two groups: the 'Rattlers' and the 'Eagles' were in effect eliminated as separate entities by the end of the three weeks, and the boys went back to their homes in the undifferentiated way in which they had left them. Consequently, the study does not directly address situations in which conflict reduction is desired but where separate group identities are to be maintained – situations, that is, more likely to occur in real-life settings. Nonetheless, the fact remains that 'in just three weeks, the Rattlers and Eagles experienced the kinds of changes that often take generations to unfold: they formed close-knit groups, went to war, and made peace' (Brehm *et al.*, 1999: 144). This is the crux of the issue: if, in a contrived setting and within a very short time, groups can form, allegiances can solidify, and both cooperation and competition can be demonstrated, then it is easier to realise how longstanding historical forces create and sustain 'groupness' and all its ramifications in the larger world arena.

Related work soon followed, in which 'ordinary' people were induced to assume extraordinary roles. Thus, in his famous 'shock' studies, Stanley Milgram led his subjects to give what they believed were powerful and painful electric shocks to others, when those others made mistakes in a memory experiment (Milgram, 1963, 1974; see also Blass, 1992). The most dramatic aspect of this 'obedience to authority' was, of course, the suggestion that we are all capable of performing unpleasant actions (and worse) with very little provocation. Milgram and his collaborators were able to produce their results with minimal constraints, after all; they had no real way to enforce compliance with their instructions to the subjects; they carried no weapons other than a contrived scientific legitimacy. The comfortable 'us-and-them' divisions that so often sustain us when we hear or read of people doing bad things to other people seemed rather harder to hold on to after this work. The other well-known work in this connection is Philip Zimbardo's 'mock prison' investigation (Haney *et al.*, 1973; Zimbardo *et al.*, 1973). University students were randomly assigned the roles of prison guards and inmates and, in a jail built in the basement of the Stanford psychology department, they were set to act their parts. Over the course of (only) a week, the 'guards' exercised more and more power; the 'prisoners' became increasingly passive and demoralised. Once again, the 'us-and-them' distinctions that separate men from monsters were challenged; after all, the 'guards' were not psychopathic bullies, but emerged via a coin-toss from the same pool of volunteers that provided the prisoners.[2]

These powerful experiments revealed how very minor manipulations can have quite major effects and, in so doing, they became cornerstones for much broader and more pedestrian social-psychological studies of *minimal groups*. Some of the earliest work was conducted in the 1970s by Henri Tajfel and his students and colleagues at the University of Bristol. They showed again how easy it is to divide people into groups on the basis of unimportant criteria (for example, expressing a preference for one of two painters, neither of whom had been heard of before), following which rivalries and antipathies will predictably arise. Indeed, Tajfel pointed out that, in one experiment, the 'height of absurdity was reached...each subject was explicitly and visibly assigned to one group or the other on the basis of a random toss of a coin' (Brehm *et al.*, 1999: 146): shades of the role assignment in Zimbardo's work. This is probably the most 'minimal' criterion for group formation; yet, even in these circumstances, within-group solidarity and its consequences can be demonstrated among those who 'were not long-term rivals, did not have a history of antagonism, were not frustrated, did not compete for a limited resource, and were not even acquainted with each other' (Tajfel, 1978: 33–34).

The importance of names and narratives

The work just discussed shows, among other things, that simply putting different labels on different groups may be enough to generate solidarities and antipathies. After all, one cannot simultaneously be both an 'Eagle' and a 'Rattler'. There are other senses, too in which group names are important. The generality here is that names influence our perceptions of others, these perceptions then enter the psychosocial contexts in which we all find ourselves, and these contexts contribute to, and frame, both personal and group identities. Furthermore, the names by which we call *ourselves* – not assigned by outside agencies, now, but self-generated – can influence those same contexts. In fact, the socially circular reactions of which names are a part constitute a specific example of a more general phenomenon described in yet another 'classic' study: Herman's (1961) description of the looped relationship in which language choices influence our perceptions of contexts, and where contexts affect language usage.

While groups' names for themselves obviously arise in many different ways – variants of 'people of the river' or 'mountain-dwellers' are common, for instance – self-descriptions also often suggest that those outside the group are qualitatively different. There is a basic, if rather disturbing, message in Stewart's (1975: 68) observation that many group names simply mean 'we' or 'the people', and imply that members of other groups 'are not human in quite the same sense'. The Ainu, Bantu, Berber, Chuchi, Inuit, Salish and Washoe communities are examples here (see also Green, 1996; Wilson, 1998). In similar fashion, Pečujlić *et al.* (1982) and Poser (2006) discuss North and South American groups whose self-references typically involve ascriptions like 'the real people' who are speakers of 'the real language' and where the terms applied to those outside the group reveal a powerfully ethnocentric bias. A particularly striking example is found among the Asmat of Irian Jaya: while they are 'the human beings', they classify everyone else as *manowe*: the 'edible ones'. Such ethnic naming conventions are also found in religiously based groups. Thus, some interpretations within Islam divide the world into those within the sacred 'house' and those without; and, as Castoriadis (1997) reminds us, the Christian bible echoes with racism, with accounts that describe the 'other' as impure, unclean, idolatrous, evil and depraved.

Biblical examples are hardly the only illustrations of names for 'outgroups' that go some way beyond simply 'not the real people'. While the Welsh call themselves *Cymry* (meaning something like 'fellow countrymen'), the English name for them derives from the Anglo-Saxon *w(e)alh*, via the Germanic *Wälsche* ('stranger', 'foreigner', or even 'barbarian'). The Khoisan speakers of southern Africa call themselves *Khoekhoe* ('men of men'), but it was the Dutch who called them 'Hottentots' (stutterers). In seventeenth-century Muscovy, foreigners were called *nemtsy* ('mutes'), a Russian labelling now restricted to Germans: 'mute' is *nemoi* (немой), German is *nemets* (немец) and the German language is *nemetskii* (немецкий). And so on.[3]

Since they are an important feature of identity, at both individual and group levels, it follows that the misuse or the appropriation of names, and the narratives of which they are a part, can be both an insult and an attack on one of the most intimate facets of 'belonging'. Contemporary complaints of 'voice appropriation' arise from the resentment felt by many 'small' communities that the names by which they are most widely known are not of their own choosing and, relatedly, that their important myths and legends are related by and for outsiders. This cultural theft is generally seen as a continuation of colonialism. If we link the resentment here with the earlier note that, for better or worse, many groups have seen only themselves as 'the real people', we can understand that the wound becomes deeper still. To have to put up with unpleasant or unwanted naming and narrative practices from outside the group is one thing; to realise that these have been imposed by people who are, by community definition, not even 'real' is another, and more bitter, one. A further implication here has to do with an erosion of aspects of the age-old sense of group identity. If outsiders who have been traditionally considered as inferior, alien or, indeed, not fully human have come to achieve such obvious social dominance, what does this suggest to the 'insiders' about the validity of their traditional descriptions, about their self-esteem, about the tenuous nature of their cultural continuity?

Still, no matter how much one may sympathise with individuals and cultures who have been badly treated by more powerful societies, 'appropriation' is not always clear-cut. In works of fiction, for instance, 'appropriation' of one sort or another is paramount. More generally, a logical extension of the appropriation argument might lead to the conclusion that no one could ever write about anything beyond one's own immediate experience. Only 'insiders' could write about their lives and cultures. Consider, too, that an embargo along these lines, one that would prevent majority-group outsiders from writing about the lives of those in 'small' or culturally 'at-risk' groups, would logically also prevent minority-group members from commenting upon the 'mainstream'. Furthermore: are women never to write about men, blacks never about whites, Germans never about Spaniards? This is clearly nonsensical, an imposition that would have stifled an overwhelmingly huge proportion of the world's literature, and of the knowledge we have of one another as human beings. But at the same time, it is not difficult to understand the grievances that arise when the narrative boundaries that are crossed separate groups of significantly different socioeconomic clout. This is why the more thoughtful commentaries on 'voice appropriation' have not stated matters in some either-or fashion but, rather, have argued about the *degree* of cross-border commentary that might be reasonable, the circumstances and contexts in which it ought or ought not to occur, and so on (see Clunie, 2005; Ziff and Rao, 1997).

Language as instrument and symbol

Both the centrality of the group in human life and the importance of the names and narratives that we construct for ourselves suggest that, whether oral or written, language has much more than some prosaic communicative function. In fact, it has always been abundantly clear that, in discussions of the linkage between identity and language, one must keep in mind the distinction between that instrumental function and the social, political, psychological and sometimes purely symbolic aspects of language. The fact that this latter linguistic dimension is by definition less tangible than the former does not imply peripheral or ephemeral value; on the contrary, the intangibles of human life can prove very resilient indeed.

The twin aspects of language generally coexist in 'mainstream' or majority-group cultures: for members of such groups, the language in which they do their shopping, go to work and talk to their neighbours is also the ancestral variety, the medium of history, legends and poetry. The aspects are separable, however, and the linguistic coexistence experienced by majorities is often lost in minority groups. That is one of the central reasons for focusing upon such groups when discussing the maintenance and loss of communicative language. Linguistic matters will necessarily have a greater immediacy there than they do in those larger communities having the luxury – or is it, in fact, a misfortune, a blunting of a useful sensibility? – of not thinking about language very much at all. A related reason is that, where communicative language shift is occurring, or has occurred, the symbolic aspects of language often receive closer attention; indeed, those aspects are sometimes accorded a level of value that would have seemed very exaggerated in earlier days. A language that has lost most or all of its communicative functions can retain symbolic status for a long time.

Some have suggested that when language operates at only a symbolic level, it is no longer really language. It is certainly true that 'symbolism' coexisting with communication is not the same as symbolism divorced from communication: Irish for most Irish people, Polish for most fourth-generation Polish-Americans, and so on. Still, it should be remembered that language, unlike other purely emblematic markers, is a system that is at least theoretically capable of regaining an instrumental and communicative status. My general point is simply that, even if they are often joined, the two functions of language *are* separable, and that ignorance of the distinction between them can lead to lack of clarity and misdirection of action (among linguistic nationalists, for example). And there is a further important proviso here. Although the functions are separable, and although the symbolic aspects can long outlast communicative-language shift, these aspects are first given life by a vernacular, not the other way around. The implication is that the loss or abandonment of a language in its ordinary communicative role must eventually lead to the dilution or, indeed, the disappearance of its symbolic or 'associational' role.

Whether or not the two facets of language remain joined, it is its symbolic and emotional weight that is the most important component of individual and group identity. A threat to the instrumental standing of a language is of course real, and may well be resisted, but people tend to go the barricades only when deeper matters are in play. To put it another way: if language were only a tool, if it existed only for mundane purposes, it is unlikely that we would see the highly charged reactions that follow upon linguistic and cultural contact and that animate so much of the research and writing in the social psychology, the sociology and the politics of language. Three examples will amply illustrate the point.

Animating much of the contemporary relationship between Québec and the rest of Canada – one that often brings to mind the words of

Lord Durham, who reported in 1839 that he had found 'two nations warring in the bosom of a single state' (Craig, 1963: 23) – are Québec fears that their francophone 'voice' is in danger, that a once special or 'charter' status is under attack, that a co-founder of the Canadian federation is being relegated to a lesser position. The desire to exist as a nation within Canada, and not merely as a province among other provinces has always been strong. In some manifestations, of course, the desire has been stronger still: a zeal for sovereignty or independence. Now, in some nationalist movements, matters of linguistic and cultural protection are proxies for underlying economic or political grievances. Among modern Québec *indépendantistes*, however, it is not socioeconomic deprivation or lack of adequate political representation that most accurately fuels the dynamic. It is, rather, a more 'classic' (one is tempted to say 'purer') sense of nationalism, in which the coincidence of nation with state is the paramount concern, and in which the French language and culture are not negotiable commodities.

In latter years, this has become more and more allied with the perception that a sovereign Québec could, in fact, prosper; and this, in turn, accounts in part for the continuation of the sovereigntist agenda. It was not always so: earlier yearnings were dampened by thoughts of an unpleasant economic future and, for all but the most unbending nationalists, the risks were simply thought to be too great. There is now, however, a revitalised sense of being *maîtres chez eux*, and – with a huge and rich geography, 7.7 million people, and a GDP of about $300 billion – many economists point out that an independent Québec could be better off than a great many existing countries. ('Could' is perhaps the operative word here, since economic predictions obviously rest upon many variables whose values cannot now be accurately assessed. It is also the case that the rosiest forecasts are those of pro-sovereignty economists, and that others paint a rather darker picture.) Nonetheless, the important point here is simply this: nationalistic aspirations without economic plausibility can lead to frustration; nationalism allied to economic viability can be a recipe for change.

Another example of the power of language-as symbol is found in the Balkans. In the former Yugoslavia, there was a language called Serbo-Croatian, a common variety among not just Serbs and Croats, but also Bosnians and Montenegrins; see Greenberg (2004) and Busch and Kelly-Holmes (2004). To be sure, it was not identical in all its regional and dialectal variants and, as might be expected in that troubled part of Europe, many historical, orthographical and grammatical points were contentious ones. Nonetheless, an agreement reached in Vienna in 1850 may be said to have formalised Serbo-Croatian as an accepted medium, and a later imprimatur was bestowed on the language in the famous (or infamous) Novi Sad agreement of 1954. Novi Sad is an important Serbian city, and given this location, the organisational background of the meeting, and the status of the participants, it was argued in some quarters that the agreement was in fact intended to advance the Serbian cause. A 1967 Croatian statement, for example, rejected the alleged 'forced unification' and the 'Serbianisation' of the Croatian language – a telling declaration, even though it was condemned by the Communist authorities of the time. As for the Serbs, they were the single most powerful group in the country and 'could thus affect broadmindedness and tolerance in linguistic matters' (Bugarski, 2001: 64). After all

> in language as in other things, as is well known, the larger nation as a rule insists less on its distinctiveness than the smaller one living next to it... [which] lays greater store by its separate linguistic and other identity, in constant fear of occupation or assimilation. (p. 64)

A slightly uneasy peace, then, prevailed until the break-up of Yugoslavia: Serbo-Croatian, with two standard pronunciations and two alphabets (Latin and Cyrillic), was the dominant medium, and considerable room was also made for the languages of other national groups (Bugarski, 2001; Edwards, 1985).

Now, however, Serbo-Croatian no longer has an official existence, having been replaced by Bosnian, Serbian and Croatian, and the hopes for linguistic unity that underpinned the Viennese agreement of 1850 were officially abandoned in 1990. The fractured components are, as Bugarski (p. 83) reminds us, 'the children of linguistic nationalism and, as such, impregnated with symbolic values'. And what has actually, linguistically occurred? In Serbia, Bugarski argues, 'the language itself has not visibly changed' (p. 84). In Bosnia, some moves have been made to emphasise 'Arabic-Turkish features in pronunciation, spelling, and especially vocabulary and phraseology' (p. 84), but the deeper levels of grammatical and lexical structure have been little affected. In Croatia, however, symbolic declarations have been accompanied by 'a campaign to actually make the language as different from Serbian (or Serbo-Croatian) as possible, and as quickly as possible' (p. 84). Further developments since he made these comments have only reinforced Bugarski's contention that the real dynamics here are political rather than linguistic. His bitter concluding comments on the forces of ethnic nationalism are worth reproducing here:

> Underlying these trends was the anti-historical, anti-civilizational notion, dear to the nationalist's heart, that members of one nation cannot live together with members of other nations unless they can dominate or assimilate them. Since the Yugoslav nations had in fact steadily intermingled for decades or even centuries, such a thesis could only be proved by...ethnic cleansing of territories, after which the argument about the impossibility of living together appeared as a self-fulfilling prophecy. (Bugarski, 2001: 85)

Without drawing any conclusions, here, about the relative merits and disadvantages of nationalist movements, one point is surely abundantly clear: the place of language in group identity is essentially a political matter, and it is as a symbol of belonging, rather than in its instrumental role, that it provides the greatest scope for boundary construction. The fact that active moves are also made to drive instrumental wedges, to try and make two languages where one once existed – these are best seen as servants to the larger symbolic cause rather than technical interventions meant to improve communication by smoothing out dialectal obstructions to grammatical standardisation, or regularising pronunciation, or introducing spelling reform. As Greenberg (2004: 14) has pointed out, questions of mutual intelligibility had 'no bearing on the debate regarding the status of Serbo-Croatian as a single language, or as three or four languages'. So, while it is deeply disappointing, it is hardly surprising to read that 'language planners are charged with the task of setting up new barriers to communication, rather than to the facilitation of mutual intelligibility' (p. 13).

A third illustration here rests simply upon an old equation: *traduttori-traditori*. Translators' linguistic competence provides entry to (at least) two language communities and, while their work is obviously useful, and often necessary, it may also lead to suspicion and apprehension. As George Steiner has pointed out (1992: 244), 'there is in every act of translation – and specially where it succeeds – a touch of treason. Hoarded dreams, patents of life are being taken across the frontier'. This reflects another venerable idea, that concealment is as much a feature of language as is communication. Privacy, the construction of fictionalised myths, legends and stories, and outright dissimulation are at once important and threatened by translation and translators; the matter of 'voice appropriation' is also germane here, of course. We see once again how the importance of language as a group marker may overshadow its purely instrumental function. If we were not afraid that those 'hoarded dreams' and those 'patents of life' were being taken across group lines, we would hardly equate translation with treason. And what are 'patents of life', if not the components of identity that are unique – or are felt to be unique, at any rate – to ourselves and our group?

The varied linguistic bearers of identity

There is a large literature, both scholarly and otherwise, dealing with the relative 'goodness' of different languages and dialects, with arguments about 'primitive' versus 'advanced' languages, with questions of linguistic 'decay' or 'impurity', and so on. Such matters have greater immediacy, of course, where communicative aspects of language are concerned. Perhaps, though, it would be possible for an 'impure' or 'unsophisticated' or 'primitive' variety to act as a symbolic boundary-stone of groupness, after all. Well, possible, perhaps – but not very likely. What self-respecting group would want to admit that its language is of an inferior cast? What external enemy would refrain from the argument that an inferior language must necessarily attach to an inferior community? It is necessary, then, to say something here about the perceived quality of linguistic expressions of group identity.

History is laden, of course, with evaluative comments about languages, and I reproduced a few of them in Chapter 3; see also Edwards (1995). While some of the more egregious comparisons have faded away, one can still find references to the allegedly greater concision of English (as opposed to French) or the greater aesthetic appeal of Italian (as opposed to German). Few scholars, perhaps, hold such attitudes these days, but they remain widespread outside the academic cloisters, in the popular media and on the street.

The question has sometimes been more thoughtfully considered where the languages involved are not closely related. Someone who would see little point in comparing members of the same language family (French and Italian, say) might perhaps feel on safer ground in suggesting better-and-worse distinctions between the mother tongues of communities widely separated in terms of 'development' or 'sophistication' (like French and Yup'ik, perhaps). Could there be some correlation, in fact, between levels of social and linguistic development? The idea has appealed to many in the past, and it retains considerable contemporary support. Even *within* those same scholarly cloisters I have heard discussions of the relative impoverishment of some 'third-world' varieties, and the richness of languages of the industrialised west. Within anglophone circles, for instance, it is common to hear variants on the argument that – blessed by history with a particularly large vocabulary – English contains more possibilities for nuanced expression and precision of definition than do other languages; see also Chapter 9.

In fact, however, linguists, anthropologists and other scholars are now more or less unanimous in their contention that languages are always sufficient for the needs of their speakers, that no language can be 'logically' described as better or worse than another. Given that language is an arbitrary system in which communication rests upon community agreement, it follows that the only 'logic' of language is to be found in its grammar (which is a logic of convention). What is grammatical in French (the use of two elements to express verbal negation, for example: 'Je suis heureux' and 'Je ne suis pas heureux') is not in English (where only one is required: 'I am happy' and 'I am not happy'). Who would wish to argue that this reflects upon the relative quality of the two systems? And, if we compare the language of a technologically advanced society with that of a more 'undeveloped' one, we find the same different-but-not-deficient relationship. Lenneberg (1967: 364) wrote that the notion of 'primitive' varieties was now 'thoroughly discredited by virtually all students of language', and in their influential survey, Gleitman and Gleitman (1970) bluntly observed that there are no 'primitive' languages. In fact, the famous linguist, Edward Sapir, had argued much earlier that 'the lowliest South African Bushman speaks in the forms of a rich symbolic system that is in essence perfectly comparable to the speech of the cultivated Frenchman' (1921: 22) and that, 'when it comes to linguistic form, Plato walks with the Macedonian swineherd, Confucius with the head-hunting savage of Assam' (p. 219).

Well, the phrasing here is no longer, perhaps, *comme il faut* – and there's more head-hunting now in corporate jungles than in those of Assam – but Sapir's words continue to be endorsed by virtually all linguists. This endorsement is based upon a great deal of research, over a great many years, with a great many languages.

Languages are best understood as different systems reflecting different varieties of the human condition. Although they may be unequal in complexity at given points, this does not imply that some have greater overall expressive power. To put it another way, we could say that not all varieties have the same capabilities: different social, geographical and other circumstances determine what elements will be needed and, therefore, developed. All language varieties are, however, potentially functionally equivalent. They differ in lexical, grammatical, phonological and other ways, but questions of overall linguistic 'goodness' are simply wrong-headed.

As with languages, so with dialects: they cannot be seen, linguistically, in terms of better or worse. However, while there may be (relatively) few people who would now argue that French is better than English, ideas that Oxford English is better than Cockney, or that Parisian French is better than *joual*, remain a more widespread prejudice. The very word 'dialect' has long been popularly considered to denote a deviation from some prestigious or more 'correct' form and, in fact, dictionary definitions have supported this view. Even the *Oxford English Dictionary* has noted that a dialect is 'one of the subordinate forms or varieties of a language arising from local peculiarities'. In a sense this is correct, but it is incorrect to assume (as the definition would imply to many) that 'subordinate' status has any inherent *linguistic* basis (social judgements are quite another matter, of course). Neither should it be thought, as some have traditionally done, that 'better' varieties are inherently more *aesthetically* pleasing than others. These and other 'myths' are briefly treated in the collection edited by Bauer and Trudgill (1998).

The general point here is simply that *all* languages and dialects are valid and adequate systems for the communicative needs of their speakers. If needs change, if environments alter, if contacts with other groups introduce new lifestyles, then varieties are more or less infinitely adaptable. I do not present any evidence to support the point but, as readers may imagine, there is a great deal of it: scholarly assessments of the 'goodness' of all varieties are based upon data gathered from all corners of the world (see Edwards, 1995, 2009). I am only concerned here to establish that, since all varieties are valid *communicative* systems, there is no reason to doubt their *symbolic* identity-bearing capabilities.

There is a final point of importance here. Every society in which internal linguistic differences are found reveals linguistic prejudices. It is one thing to demonstrate that no dialect, for example, can be seen as superior to another on linguistic or aesthetic grounds, but it would be quite another to expect such a demonstration to have much impact on the street. As we saw in the previous chapter, the power of social convention, attitude and prejudice regularly translates difference into deficiency. Dialect varieties that are simply variants of one another in scholarly eyes – whose description as 'nonstandard' is a non-pejorative acknowledgement of the historical forces that have elevated one section of society and, therefore, its ways of speaking – are popularly viewed as 'substandard', a word that does not exist in the linguist's lexicon. The social power of perception creates its own reality, and varieties broadly viewed as inferior *are*, for all practical intents and purposes, inferior. It is entirely understandable, then, that throughout history people have moved away from stigmatised maternal varieties, or tried to. In other circumstances, it is also understandable that a reinvigorated group self-esteem may be able to recast non-prestigious varieties into forms to be proud of, linguistic flags of a renewed group solidarity. Group members may even exaggerate previously scorned features in this process, and their dialect may become attractive to majority 'out-group' members.

All of this is clearly relevant for considerations of identity, and the generality is this: regardless of the evaluations made by speakers of their own dialect, that variety can always act as a carrier and a portrait of solidarity and belonging. It may be thought of as debased, or incorrect, or slovenly, or vulgar, but it still links people to their group; recall here Ryan's (1979) famous paper, already remarked upon. While it is true that in some cases the presence of other group markers, more indelible than language, suggests that attempted dialect mobility might be fruitless, or worse, it is also simply the case that even the most socially ill-favoured varieties perform symbolic identity duties for their speakers.

Notes

1. I prescind here from the interesting discussion about the extent to which, in some *Gestalt* fashion, groups may be more than the sum of their individual parts, or that the coming together of individuals initiates new phenomena at the collective level. The discussion, of course, is an extremely long-standing one. People have always been interested in the idea of the 'group mind' and, when they have considered it in any sort of detail, they have typically worried about it! From the discussions of the 'mob' by Livy and Tacitus (see the modern editions edited by de Sélincourt [1971] and Lloyd-Jones [1964], respectively), to Machiavelli's observations about social manipulation (see Max Lerner's [1950] edition), to the nineteenth-century speculations of Gustave LeBon (1895) about the behaviour of crowds, to conceptions of the 'diffusion of responsibility' that the anonymity of crowds permits, to the modern social-psychological work of Reicher and his colleagues (Reicher, 2004) – there is at least a two-thousand-year record of concern.
2. I have reduced the discussion of Milgram's and Zimbardo's work to the barest bones. There are many interesting nuances that qualify the blunter and more well-known generalities here, although the broad points I highlight here are not inaccurate. Zimbardo's (2007) recent overview of his own experiments, of Milgram's studies, of some contemporary reworkings of his famous prison exercise, and of real-life manifestations of evil done by seemingly good people – from Eichmann to Abu Ghraib – is particularly recommended.
3. Saussure (1980 [1916]: 262) made the same point many years ago, observing that
    > chaque peuple croit à la supériorité de son idiome. Un homme qui parle une autre langue est volontiers considéré comme incapable de parler; ainsi le mot grec *bárbaros* paraît avoir signifié ‹bègue›…en russe, les Allemands son appelés *Nêmtsy*, c'est-à-dire ‹les muets›.

6
Language, Group, Identity: Secular and Spiritual Allegiances

An introductory note

The previous chapter introduced some of the most basic elements that link languages, groups and identities. This chapter now turns to a consideration of three of the most basic identity-bearing collectivities – and, as well, to some contemporary ecological arguments which, it is claimed, will put the dynamics of language contact on a new and improved footing. To begin with, however, I present a cursory overview of an interesting framework for understanding the nature, the dimensions and the strength of linguistic bonds within groups.

Ethnolinguistic vitality and its implications for group contact

In an earlier chapter, I briefly discussed the accommodative practices that can regulate our linguistic interactions. In some of these interactions, it is clear that our group memberships form an important backdrop, as it were, to the dynamics of accommodation. To put it another way: while we obviously relate to others, in our daily interactions, as *individuals*, we sometimes present and 'carry' ourselves as group representatives. In many instances, then, our language behaviour may suggest an underlying interplay of both individual and collective traits or dispositions. Arguments over the policies of different states or regions are illustrative here and so, at a less important level, are those between supporters of different sports teams, clubs, societies, and so on.

In the development of their accommodation paradigm, Giles and his colleagues were led to consider the assessment of those collective traits, an exercise put under the rubric of *ethnolinguistic vitality*. In an early

formulation, Giles *et al.* (1977) outlined three factors central to our perceptions of group vitality (or, of course, the lack of it): demographic
variables, status and institutional support. Thus, population numbers
and concentrations, levels of socioeconomic well-being, and the position of the group's language and culture in important social settings
(education, government, religion, etc.) will all affect a group's overall
standing. Subsequent connections linking the accommodation perspective with other work that has focussed upon divergence between
groups, and upon the actions required to achieve a desirable sense of
in-group identity and of group distinctiveness (see, for example, Tajfel,
1978, 1982; Turner and Giles, 1981), have come to suggest the value of
a unified approach to the understanding of language-and-group relations, as the recent overviews by Abrams and Hogg (1990) and Hogg
and Abrams (1988) have demonstrated.

A further development soon arose from the realisation that, while
objective markers of a group's 'vitality' are clearly important, so too
are more subjective perceptions. Thus, Bourhis *et al.* (1981) produced
a 'subjective vitality questionnaire', an acknowledgement that group
members may minimise or exaggerate group vitality in given circumstances (or, we might add, are unaware of some factors and inaccurately
understand others). In essence, this development was meant to flesh
out objective data with important if less tangible psychological perceptions. The items on the survey instrument largely reflect the three vitality dimensions noted above; see also Bourhis *et al.* (2007).

It is clear that perceptions of group vitality may have a powerful
bearing upon some of the linguistic consequences of group contact,
including language shift, maintenance and revival, as well as the
broader cultural issues of pluralism and assimilation that often underpin them. A recent collection (Bourhis, 2008a) has investigated these
matters as they pertain to the anglophone minority in Québec; see
also Bourhis (2008b). In general, it seems clear enough that low vitality may hasten language shift and assimilation, and that high vitality
may stiffen cultural and linguistic resolve in the face of powerful external pressures. A generation ago, however, Johnson *et al.* (1983) also
suggested that low vitality could actually *spur* maintenance efforts:
this sort of Dunkirk, backs-to-the-wall scenario is certainly plausible. Indeed, many maintenance and revival efforts only emerge when
the linguistic and cultural situation is considered parlous, when the
pressures of large neighbours have finally been recognised by many
people in many contexts, when the decline in 'vitality' has become
particularly marked.[1]

Ethnicity, nationalism and the protection of languages

At a group level, the intertwining of language and identity is nowhere as emotionally charged as it is with ethnic and national allegiances. Both the historical record and more contemporary ledgers show, again and again, how central a 'marker' language often is in such allegiances; indeed, some have argued that the 'original' group language is the single most important pillar of ethnonational identity. It is certainly the case that linguistic nationalists and 'activists' have always aimed to enshrine language at the centre of their concerns. In the eighteenth century, Herder asked if a nation has 'anything more precious than the language of its fathers'; Humboldt wrote in 1797 that 'absolutely nothing is so important for a nation's culture as its language'. In the nineteenth century, Thomas Davis suggested to Irishmen that 'a people without a language of its own is only half a nation'. In the twentieth century, Eamon de Valera assured his republican constituency that 'Ireland with its language and without freedom is preferable to Ireland with freedom and without its language' (see Edwards, 1995, for the sources for all of these citations). Heady stuff, to be sure.

Such linguistic sentiments arose, of course, in the romantic era that followed upon the French revolution. Nationalism became god, and language was often its messenger: something to galvanise the oppressed, to rally supporters, to alarm the rulers. Thus, Herder outlined a philosophy of linguistic nationalism, in which ancestral language and national continuity are intertwined. As he wrote in a 1772 prize essay about the origin of language (*Ursprung der Sprache*), all nations cherish – and are right to cherish – their particular language, their 'collective treasure'. A little later, in one of his several philosophical incarnations, Johann Gottlieb Fichte translated many of Herder's ideas into broader sociopolitical positions. In his *Addresses to the German Nation* (1808), he praised the German language and deprecated others, as part of an ingenious extrapolation from Herder's contention that loss of language entailed loss of identity. Among the Europeans, only the Germans had remained in their original location, retaining and developing their original language (unsullied by Latin, that is to say). And, if the language was better than other varieties, it followed that the German *nation* was superior.

While it would be an oversimplification to assume that the linguistic nationalism of the time was purely a German production, there was a powerful and systematic German influence here, one that was enthusiastically received in other quarters. Indeed, the sentiments of the German linguistic nationalists have remained important ever since, particularly in those contexts where 'small' languages and cultures have struggled against larger neighbours. Wherever and whenever linguistic issues of this sort arise, and whatever is claimed about the 'superiority' or 'purity' of one ancestral language or another (incorrectly, of course), the essence of the matter is group identity and the role of the language is in its symbolic, rather than its instrumental garb.

Once this is understood, it becomes easy to understand the activities of language institutions, councils and academies. While they are ostensibly working to 'improve' the language, to resist foreign borrowings, or to rationalise spelling or orthography, their real task is group boundary maintenance. Once a relationship has been established between a particular language and a particular group affiliation, the 'protection' of the language often becomes paramount. This typically takes the form of purist and prescriptivist impulses and actions, all essentially in the service of *identity* protection.

The clearest examples of language protection are found in the existence and the works of academies. The most well-known of these – and the one whose intentions and activities can be said to have set the standard for its many, many successors around the world – is the *Académie française*, founded in 1635. Its forty 'immortals' were given 'absolute power...over literature and language' (Hall, 1974: 180). In modern times, the *Académie française* has become best known for its attempts to keep French free of foreign borrowings and to create where necessary French terms for the products and processes of science and technology. It has thus acquired a modernising function to supplement the original 'purifying' objective. The special aim of keeping English influence at bay began in the nineteenth century and has strengthened since then. Purification plus gate-keeping: these are obvious undertakings on behalf of the maintenance of group boundaries and identity. The French academicians may have been designated as immortal, but this has not brought about divine success; earlier grammatical and lexicographical productions were typically not very well done, and later attempts to intervene in the dynamics of language use have also foundered.

Almost every European country has, or had, a language academy. They are also widespread throughout Central and South America (typically modelled on the *Real Academia Española*), in many Arabic-speaking countries, throughout Africa and many parts of Asia. Conspicuous by their absence from this assembly are American and British academies. Both Britain and the United States required some accepted authority, of course, and in each we find lexicographers replacing academic councils: one-man academies, in effect. Samuel Johnson published his famous dictionary in 1755; and, in the United States, Noah Webster followed suit in 1827. Webster shared many of Johnson's lexicographic principles but, unlike his English counterpart, he had a more overtly political interest, wanting to contribute his mite to the linguistic independence of the United States. In particular, he hoped that a separation of the English and 'American' languages would come to mirror the political separation. Webster's view was one that we have seen before: 'a national language is a bond of national union', it 'belongs' to the people, and its maintenance is their responsibility (Quirk, 1982: 65).

The prescriptive successes of formal institutions may not be very marked, but this hardly detracts from their importance as manifestations of will and intent, nor does it vitiate their symbolic role. The establishment of language academies and councils, and their continued existence despite a poor track record, tell us much about the importance of language as a marker of national identity. Thomas (1991: 111) noted that 'it has become fashionable to lampoon language academies for their stuffiness, their smugness and their otherworldliness', but he was quite aware of their powerful symbolism.[2]

Of course, organisations charged with linguistic prescriptivism often arose to deal with very real problems of the regularisation necessitated by technical advances, increasing literacy, and more formalised conceptions of national 'groupness'. These issues did not simply arise in the minds of some nationalist élite aiming to forge or strengthen group solidarity. Consider Caxton, having to make a selection from varying English dialects because of the imperatives of printing; consider Samuel Johnson, who was at once contemptuous of any attempt at linguistic 'embalming' and hopeful that his dictionary might somehow 'fix' an English that he saw as degenerating. In his own writings, we find that Dr Johnson represents very well the general English ambivalence: on the one hand, the idea of some élite body imposing their will on the language was distasteful; on the other, the need for some guidelines was perfectly obvious, in an era when spelling and usage were fluid, and when language was seen as a potential servant in the cause of identity.

The tension between a prescriptivism arising from narrow and often unfair conceptions of social inclusion and exclusion, and desires and needs for at least *some* standardisation is surely important in any consideration of the work of 'language planners'. Decisions have to be made when national languages 'emerge', when some print standardisation becomes necessary, when endangered languages are at issue, when choices have to be made among dialects, and so on. All such decisions involve social and political matters that go beyond purely linguistic concerns. The literature of 'language planning', then, is replete with studies of the selection and codification of languages, as well as their implementation, maintenance and elaboration in changing social circumstances. Language-planning exercises are, however, never merely technical or instrumental operations; rather, they are driven by quite particular social and political desires and requirements. Language planning certainly calls for considerable linguistic skill but, if any degree of 'real-life' success is envisaged, those who engage in it are better considered as the servants of much larger political agendas than as independent creators. On the one hand, planners are like management scientists, called in as required to collect, organise and analyse information; their conclusions and their recommendations will be attended to only to the extent that they bolster existing or desired political stances. On the other hand, the literature is full of what are rather disembodied language-planning theses. Here, the independence and the creativity of the scholarly researchers and writers are not in doubt, but their efforts typically remain within the academic cloisters, precisely because they have neither the imprimatur nor the attention of those who wield real power and influence.

Putting these sorts of social-contextual requirements aside, and considering only developments within an existing medium, the broad scholarly stance has been a non-interventionist one. We have already seen something of the long tradition of concern with language attitudes, and this has been supplemented more recently by a revived interest in 'folk linguistics' and 'perceptual dialectology'. Nonetheless, this attention has coincided with arguments against prescriptivism, on the grounds that is is neither desirable nor feasible to attempt to intervene in the social life of language.[3] A deliberate renunciation of prescriptivism, of course, is more like atheism than agnosticism: a conscious non-belief is, itself, a belief and, as Hohenhaus (2005) has recently observed, a refusal to intervene is a sort of 'reverse purism' (see also Crystal, 2006c). In any event, it is arguable that, in their rush away from prescriptivism, linguists may have abdicated a useful role as arbiters, and may have left much of the field open to those less well-informed. Bolinger (1980) was one of the few contemporary linguists willing to participate dispassionately in debates about this aspect of the 'public life' of language: he rightly criticised the obvious crank elements, but he also understood the desire for standards, the frustration with perceived 'decay' and 'incorrectness', the onslaught of weasel words and jargon. In my view, there remains a need for much more illumination of that persistent no-man's-land between academic linguistics and public language.

Language ecology

A great deal of the contemporary discussion about language-and-group linkages – particularly in those highly charged contexts in which large languages are dominant and small ones are endangered – appears under the heading of 'ecology'. While fuller treatments may be found elsewhere (e.g. Edwards, 2002, 2008; Mufwene, 2008), the current prominence of the ecological turn warrants some consideration here. It is an important and deeply flawed perspective.

Earlier and more comprehensive uses of 'ecology' have always emphasised some Darwinian sense of the 'web of life' within which we observe both beneficial and inimical interrelationships among plants, animals and their surroundings: 'the totality of relations of organisms with the external world', as Ernst Haeckel famously put it (Hayward, 1995: 26). When he popularised the term 'ecology of language', Einar Haugen (1972) was also concerned to highlight the linkages among languages and their environment, and, as Mackey (1980: 35) observed a few years later, linguistic environments (like all others) can be 'friendly, hostile or indifferent'. In a very recent ecological study of Ukraine, Goodman (2009: 19) writes that 'the language environment in the republics of the former Soviet Union could be fairly described as predatory'. Indeed it could. Mention of such unpleasantness is rare, however, in an ecology of language that is typically stripped of its necessary breadth and therefore reduced in scope. As Mühlhäusler (2000: 308) has noted,

> functioning ecologies are nowadays characterized by predominantly mutually beneficial links and only to a small degree by competitive relationships...metaphors of struggle of life and survival of the fittest should be replaced by the appreciation of natural kinds and their ability to coexist and cooperate.

No predation here. Rather, with this unrealistic, inappropriate and unwarranted limitation, we are shown a pacific world in which there is room for all languages, where the goodness of diversity is a given, where 'the wolf also shall dwell with the lamb'. In Mühlhäusler's kinder and gentler picture, the key word is 'should' and the key question is, therefore, whether the desire is also the reality. We might remember Woody Allen's reworking of that passage from Isaiah: 'the lion and the calf shall lie down together, but the calf won't get much sleep'.

Calvet (1999) is one of the few contemporary writers who have dealt with language ecology at some length, *without* restricting the discussion to its 'pacific' aspects. He is quite clear, for instance, in his monograph:

Je ne prends pas ici le terme *écologie* en son sens courant qui en est la traduction politique (défense de l'environnement) mais en son sens initial, 'science de l'habitat'…la présence du terme *écologie* dans le titre de ce livre ne [signifie] pas qu'il [est] consacré à défendre le droit des langues ou le droit à la langue, la survie des langues menacées de disparition, etc. …l'écologie linguistique [n'est] pas dans mon esprit synonyme de protection des langues en péril.[4] (pp. 17, 34, 289)

Of course, when we treat linguistic diversity here, we are not dealing with the obvious and non-problematic variation that separates speakers in Turkey, say, from those in the Bolivian Andes. We are discussing the diversity that is threatened by language contact, particularly that between 'bigger' and 'smaller' varieties. We are discussing, in effect, cultures and group identities considered to be at risk. I believe that most enlightened opinion would hold that such diversity is, *mutatis mutandis*, a 'Good Thing' (as Sellar and Yeatman might have put it). Any educated and informed perspective would surely vote for colour over monotony, for variety over sameness, for a multiplicity of expressions. But this is not the point.

To put linguistic diversity and its preservation at the heart of the 'new' ecology is to inappropriately restrict an undertaking whose name implies and promises contextual breadth. Nonetheless, the 'new' ecology takes linguistic diversity as an unalloyed good, to be defended wherever it seems to falter. This perspective is implicit in recent language-rights manifestos, covenants and declarations. Beyond the legalistic approach of formal proclamations, however, there are several bases upon which a defence of diversity has typically been seen to rest in the 'new ecology': moral, scientific, economic and aesthetic. Apart from assumptions of inherent language rights (to which I shall turn shortly), the *morality* of diversity suggests that language attrition – often seen to occur as a result of unfair or oppressive social contact – means loss of accumulated experience and knowledge. It is also sometimes argued that multilingual societies reach higher levels of achievement, and that linguistic 'encounters' aid *scientific* advance; this in turn suggests that language diversity is *economically* beneficial and that emphasis placed upon lesser-used varieties will prove more worthwhile than simply broadening the base of those who learn 'big' varieties. Finally and simply, an *aesthetic* appreciation values all diversity, and regrets all loss.

The moral argument is by far the most interesting one and, in fact, the others can be dealt with quite briefly. Scientific arguments that repertoire expansion involves enhanced intellectual capacity, for instance are not proven; and, as for diversity *per se* aiding discovery, it could just as easily be said that language differences typically constitute a barrier to international exchange.[5] Economic rationales for diversity are even harder to sustain. This is clearly the case at 'macro' levels, but social costs and social responses are, after all, built upon individual coral. As for the aesthetic argument, the perspective that holds diversity valuable beyond any crass instrumentality – well, this is clearly not something that can be argued on any factual basis. *De gustibus*, and so on.

The more interesting (and, were it to be accepted, the more immediately compelling) moral 'case' is at least debatable. We must of course agree with Dixon's (1997: 144) argument that 'once a language dies, a part of human culture is lost forever', providing, of course, that we accept that the language itself is the part that is lost. But such arguments typically imply more than that, of course. Skutnabb-Kangas (2000: 259) has written that, while 'traditional' knowledge might 'linger' after language shift, 'the richness and diversity of that knowledge cannot survive even one generation of language loss'. Phillipson (1992: 166) has even asserted that the spread of English entails the 'imposition of new mental structures'. Putting aside the last strange and strongly Whorfian point altogether, we might ask if the insights of the Greeks and the Romans have, in fact, disappeared completely. Well, since theirs was a literate world, one that left records of itself, some might perhaps think that fairer examples of language-loss-as-knowledge-loss should refer only to 'small' languages with oral traditions. There is of course no evidence for this nor, strictly logically, *could* there be any such evidence. But if, for the sake of argument, we were to accept that, when such varieties are lost, they *do* in fact take particular and irreplaceable cultural insights with them, then this would surely constitute a strong rationale for the promotion of literacy among currently threatened languages. Readers should keep this in mind when we come shortly to consider literacy attitudes among the 'new' ecologists.

To this point, however, my argument is twofold: first, there is a disingenuous and inappropriately limiting equation of ecology with diversity; second, the only logically defensible arguments for diversity itself are moral and aesthetic ones. I don't find these to be negligible matters, of course, but it is important to realise that the central base on which diversity rests is not generally presented clearly. This is because appeals to the rather more tangible footings of science and economics – appeals that are easily challenged, both within the academic cloisters and in the wider world of ordinary human interaction – are allowed or, indeed, encouraged to cloud the picture. The essential defence of the linguistic diversity that is thrown into relief into contact situations must ultimately rest on perceptions of morality and aesthetic preference. These are the animating articles of faith that bolster all 'new' ecological expression.

Underpinning the implication that cultural and linguistic attrition is stupid, oppressive and essentially immoral are matters of linguistic human rights. Such rights constitute the central emphasis of an ecological thrust committed to diversity and, as such, figure prominently in the pronouncements of organisations formed expressly for the protection of endangered languages. Thus, the Terralingua society has asserted (1999) that 'deciding which language to use, and for what purposes, is a basic human right'. Existing language associations have also argued for rights: the Teachers of English to Speakers of Other Languages organisation (TESOL) passed a resolution in 2000 asserting that 'all groups of peoples have the right to maintain their native language…a right to retain and use [it]'. The other side of the coin, they argue, is that 'the governments and the people of all countries have a special obligation to affirm, respect and support the retention, enhancement and use of indigenous and immigrant heritage languages'. It is perhaps unnecessary to remark here that, while it is possible to legislate rights of language expression, it is rather more difficult to legislate rights to be *understood*.

As usual, Mufwene (2008) makes some insightful remarks here. He notes, for instance, that the advocates of language rights 'keep preaching to the victims without sensitizing the victimizers' (p. 247). The larger difficulty, however, is that they have not provided (nor, indeed, is it easy to see how they *could* rationally provide) any answers to what Mufwene calls 'the implicit question' of how the alternative and large-scale social, economic and political arrangements required in order to give real substance to their claims and exhortations might be brought about.[6]

Putting aside the obvious fact that many official and quasi-official pronouncements, charters and resolutions are vague, or useless, or cynical, there are deeper problems with language rights. Since discussions surrounding them are motivated by languages and cultures seen to be at risk, they are almost always meant to have an effect at the group level. This may sit uneasily with liberal-democratic principles that have historically enshrined rights in individuals, not collectivities. Questions surrounding language rights have become an important subset within broader discussions of feasible and desired social accommodation in societies that are at once democratic and heterogeneous. It is impossible to delve further into the matter here, but it should be noted that, while the treatments presented by notable scholars (Rawls, Dworkin, Taylor and Kymlicka among them) vary considerably in attitude and emphasis, they all demonstrate the inadequacy of isolated claims of language rights. Simple assertions that groups have language rights are not likely to advance matters very much.

There are some further, and more specific, issues of concern within the 'new' ecology of language. There is, for example, the proclaimed linkage with biology, with organic life. There is an obvious metaphorical connection, of course and, in his earlier work in the area, Haugen touched upon it. It was, he thought, a useful and possibly heuristic analogy but it ought not to be 'pushed too far' (1972: 58). More recently, while acknowledging that language is in truth 'no more an ecology than a mental organ or a calculus', Mühlhäusler argued that the biological metaphor helps 'in advancing a knowledge of human language'. As will become clearer below, I think that this is a mistaken view. Mühlhäusler was more accurate than he no doubt meant to imply when he suggested that metaphors are 'searchlights that selectively illuminate the terrain and leave others in the dark' (see Fill and Mühlhäusler, 2001: 3). Just so.

Biological metaphors for language have long been appealing. Franz Bopp, the famous nineteenth-century linguist, wrote that 'languages are to be considered organic natural bodies' (Edwards, 1995: 8), and it is easy to appreciate that a linkage between nature and culture, between what is provided and what is constructed, could be a valuable arguing point in a world increasingly aware of environmental issues. The advantages of adding anxieties about language decline to concerns with global warming, pollution and loss of natural habitats seem obvious. But metaphorical comparisons are just that, which is why it is a little alarming to find some scholars suggesting highly over-simplified connections between linguistic and biological diversity. Maffi (2000a: 175) has written that, since areas in the world rich in one are also extensive in the other, the two diversities are 'mutually supportive, perhaps even coevolved'. More pointedly still, Maffi (2000b: 17) suggests that 'the persistence of vigorous, thriving linguistic diversity around the world may afford us our best chance of countering biodiversity loss and keeping the planet alive and healthy'.[7]

Dubious argument apart, there is in any event a practical problem that any purported linkages between animals and languages cannot overcome: it is much more difficult to maintain the latter than it is to preserve the former. Despite all the obvious difficulties in mustering support and resources for saving rare species, we nevertheless have a potential level of control here that is impossible with human societies and their languages, unless we were willing to act in the dictatorial ways that are open to us with plants and animals. As de Swaan (1998b: 119) has suggested, language survival requires the concerted effort of a large number of people committed to 'maintain their speech and maybe their ways of life against the inroads of a changing social environment – a rather formidable task'; see also de Swaan's (2004) very pointed remarks about endangerment, ecology and 'linguistic sentimentalism', remarks on which I shall comment in a later chapter.

It is another commonly held assumption of the 'new' ecology that human interference necessitates management and planning. Mühlhäusler (2000: 310) tells us that, while 'healthy ecologies' are 'self-organising' and 'self-perpetuating', 'human actions [can] upset the original balance' Well, in what sphere of life have human actions *not* altered things? Indeed, what social spheres could there possibly be *without* such actions? This seems like lamenting the fact that we have two ears. We also note here the curiously static quality of much ecological thinking. The implication often seems to be that – once some balance is achieved, some wrong righted, some redress made – the new arrangements will, because of their improved moral basis, be 'self-perpetuating'. But history is the graveyard of cultures, and it is naïvely selective to pay attention to some and not to others. How many, I wonder, regret the passing of the British Raj? How many would argue that, because it once existed, it had a right to carry on existing? Of course, one could simply say that a 'bad' society like that forfeits any right to longevity: but how, then, do we reasonably argue such moral assessments, and just how are they to be brought to bear upon historical realities?

Yet another feature of the 'new' ecology is a distrust of literacy and education, an apparently odd position to take, given what I have discussed above. One might imagine that, eager to do everything possible to prevent the loss of 'traditional' or 'authentic' knowledge, the 'new' ecology would champion literacy for those communities where it is absent or restricted. In fact, the argument is that education often undercuts the preservation of linguistic diversity, that it works against 'linguistic vitality'. Literacy is often seen as a sort of bully, in the same way that large languages are the villains, and small ones the victims. Written varieties can push oral ones aside, writing is seen as sophisticated and, indeed, more likely to bear the truth, and so on. Literacy is also sometimes seen as a sort of Trojan horse, with speakers of at-risk varieties lulled into a false sense of security once writing arrives. Now, it is certainly reasonable to point out the cruel fallacy that literacy inevitably leads to social or political improvement, or to refer to the single-mindedness of literacy campaigns. It is also true that writing does not automatically augment veracity (do you believe everything you read in the papers?). It would surely be a dangerous instance of cultural isolationism, however, to try and purchase language maintenance at the expense of literacy.

The broader point here is the related suggestion that formal education is not always the ally of enduring diversity and bilingualism: it often has intrusive qualities, it elevates literacy over orality, it imposes foreign and external values and practices upon small cultures. Again, then, there is the idea of cultural bullying. It is not difficult to sympathise with laments about intrusive 'foreign' education paradigms but – given that all education worthy of the name is multicultural in nature – the argument is essentially self-defeating. Formal education necessarily involves broadening the horizons, going beyond what is purely local and 'traditional'. In an unequal world whose disparities create risks for languages, education will perforce become yet another evidence of those disparities. Those concerned with gaining a place in the media for minority languages have learned that they are double-edged swords. While it is clear that access to them is important, they also facilitate the transmission of those larger influences upon decline. There are similar 'risks' associated with the medium of education.

Within contemporary ecological currents we find a certain linguistic romanticism, often best understood as a more specialised manifestation of the more general ethnonationalist affections associated with jeopardised cultures. We find, for example, that some species of political villains are identified more readily and more frequently than others: unrestrained free-market capitalism, unfettered industrialisation, galloping globalisation. And, just as eighteenth-century romanticism was a reaction to more enlightened thought, so it has again become possible to find disparagement of secular culture and dismay with its 'privileging' of scientific knowledge over 'folk wisdom'. The special regard for 'small' cultures and local knowledges takes two forms: first, the simple, straightforward and, indeed, perfectly reasonable desire for the survival of such cultures and systems; second, the argument that they are in some ways superior to larger or broader societies and values. This view is generally expressed in some muted fashion, but occasionally the mask slips:

> without romanticizing or idealizing the indigenous cultures, it is clear that they are superior to the mass culture because their members retain the capability of living in at least relative harmony with the natural environment. (Salminen, 1998: 62)

Despite the half-hearted disclaimer, this is romanticism *tout court*. Or consider this dedicatory line in a recent anthology: 'to the world's indigenous and traditional peoples, who hold the key to the inextricable link between [sic] language, knowledge and the environment' (Maffi, 2001).

The unrealistic and potentially harmful romanticism that lies behind arguments for 'small' languages and cultures has been analysed by Geeraerts (2003). He discusses the assumptions made about the equivalence of all cultures, about the goodness of diversity, and about global English as international oppressor. In this last connection, Polzenhagen and Dirven (2004) have reminded us that the sanction of Standard English within anglophone societies has attracted accusations of dialect oppression and social exclusion. Yet, just as one could argue that Standard English actually levels a very bumpy playing field, so the use of English-as-lingua-franca in non-native contexts may permit a desirable unity of action (in movements for national liberation, for instance). Thus, Canagarajah (1999a: 207; see also 1999b) has argued that linguistic-imperialism models – like Phillipson's (1992) – may neglect its contribution to 'modifying, mixing, appropriating, and even resisting discourses'; see also the final chapters here.

To summarise: the 'new' ecology of language is not so much a refinement of scientific methodology in the face of new understandings and new challenges as it is a sociopolitical ideology. The critical remarks that I have made here are not directed at ecology *per se*, of course, for who could gainsay its essential elements? But I think that the underlying ideology of this new incarnation is insufficiently examined. It incorporates various assumptions as if they were unremarkable, and beyond enlightened debate. While some of its assertions may be appropriate in some cases, there can be little doubt that a wholesale acceptance of them would be both unwise and counterproductive.

Language, religion and identity

If language is one of the most obvious and most important markers of identity, religion is clearly another (Safran, 2008). There is of course a very large social-scientific literature on religion, and there is a reasonably extensive one devoted to the structures and functions of 'religious language'. There is remarkably little, however, on the interactions between language and religion, and on their often conjoined contribution to group boundary marking, even though history repeatedly shows the interesting intertwinings here (see Spolsky, 2003). Schiffman's (1996) chapter on the interrelated topics of language, religion, myth and purism is a notable exception, as are one or two contributions to the recent collection edited by Omoniyi and Fishman (2006), as well as

Safran's piece, just cited. This is not to say that religious and linguistic markers always march together – indeed, some of the most compelling manifestations show them in actual or potential opposition – but it is clear that both typically have roles to play in perceptions and postures of identity.

There are at least three important points of connection between language and religion, and two are immediately obvious: the language *of* religion, and the existence of language and religion as complementary markers of groupness. The third has to do with the work of missionaries. In all categories, however – and not just the second one – the threads linking language and religion stretch to include matters of identity.

Ancestral voices

As an extension of sorts to the section on 'names and narratives' in Chapter 5, we could begin here by noting that Steiner's (1992: 300) useful reference to the power and importance of linguistic 'enclosure and willed opaqueness' is seen most clearly in religious texts: works, that is, that are hallowed in and of themselves. While the Buddhist Sutras, the Hindu Vedas, the Christian Bible, the Holy Qu'ran, the Hadith, the Torah and the Talmud (and many other such collections) are codifications of consecrated systems, they are also intrinsically holy. The very words in which they are written have a divine quality. The idea of the holiness of 'the word' is an extremely old one. At some time during the twenty-fifth Egyptian dynasty (that is, between about 750 and 650 BC), an already existing theological discussion was inscribed on a stone, now in the British Museum. In this famous 'Memphite Theology', we read that the god Ptah, having first *thought* the world, created it by saying the name of all its elements. Names and things thus coincided, the former perfectly capturing the essence of the latter. This is exactly the case, too, in the Christian tradition. *Genesis* II:19 tells us that God formed all the birds and beasts, 'and brought them unto Adam to see what he would call them: and whatsoever Adam called every living creature, that was the name thereof'. And in the eighth book of his *Paradise Lost*, Milton records for us Adam's recounting of events:

> As thus [God] spake, each Bird and Beast behold
> Approaching two and two, These cowring low
> With blandishment, each Bird stoop'd on his wing.
> I nam'd them, as they pass'd, and understood
> Their nature, with such knowledge God endu'd
> My sudden apprehension...

With this exact equation between name and 'nature', where is the further connection that brings identity into the picture? It happens that, from the earliest times, the question of this Adamic language, this divinely perfect medium, was a question of the first importance, for, as Rubin (1998: 308) pointed out, those who spoke that language – or, at least, those who felt that they might claim them as ancestors – would obviously possess a very special identity indeed, one based upon an intimate relationship with divinity itself. The 'winner' here could, furthermore, assert a 'linguistic and cultural superiority over all other languages and cultures'.

Opera dei sunt verba eius: the works of God are his words. In the Christian tradition, as in the Egyptian, the mystical association of the 'word' (*logos*, the Greek λόγος, with its many related meanings of word, thought, pervading principle, and so on) with divinity has always been central. We read this at the opening of St John's gospel in the most forthright way: the 'Word' was there from the beginning, was not only 'with God' but, in fact, *was* God, and would later be 'made flesh' so that it might dwell among us. Thus, the 'Word', the scriptures, became incarnate in Christ. A recent summary was provided in April 2005, when Joseph Ratzinger (later to be Pope Benedict) said that 'from the beginning, Christianity has understood itself as the religion of the Logos'. Since further associations of the *logos* include logic and rationality, all orthodox Christians are able to maintain that, not only does their identity rest upon the most impeccable spiritual credentials, it also affords them an ideal grasp of *quaecumque sunt vera* ('whatsoever things are true'), as St Paul observed to the Philippians. Thus, Cardinal Ratzinger was able to further claim that Christianity was 'the religion according to reason' (see Ratzinger, 2005a,b). Not only, then, does Christianity arrogate to itself the possession of the true vessel of both spirituality and rationality; it makes the stronger claim that, under its banner, spirituality and rationality are one and the same, that there is an *identity* here, uniquely captured in the *logos*.

Tampering with the 'Word' is obviously an extremely serious matter. There are clear illustrations in Judaism and Christianity, for example, that translation is blasphemy. He who has 'been in Christ' must not (or, perhaps, cannot) repeat the *arcana verba* in mortal words (*Second Corinthians* XII: 4). And Jewish writings from the first century record the belief that the translation of the holy law into Greek led to three days of darkness (Steiner, 1992: 252). There are groups who believe that the name of God is never to be uttered, others who reserve this honour for the priestly caste alone, and still others who argue that *no* language at all is adequate for religious purposes; Sawyer (2001: 263) reminds us here of the 'Quaker predilection for silent worship'. (Refer, again, to the 'names and narratives' discussion in the previous chapter.) Levy (1993), Marsh (1998) and Cabantous (1998) all provide good overviews of blasphemy, of the act of speaking evil of that which is sacred.

Besides this sort of connection between language and religion, we also note that the spread of faiths has very often been accompanied by that of languages (see Mühleisen, 2007). Thus, the spectacular expansion of Islam in the seventh and eighth centuries, and the establishment of an empire stretching from Asia to the Atlantic, meant that Arabic became a world language. When the Emperor Constantine was converted in the fourth century, Latin became the lingua franca of Christianity and the old principle of *cuius regio, eius religio* – the religion of the ruler is the religion of his domains – was strongly reinforced. The principle was reaffirmed in the Holy Roman Empire of the sixteenth century, in the interests of international harmony.

Modern times: Israel and Ireland

The simultaneous contribution of both religious and linguistic markers to the identity of given groups has remained important. The Irish and Hebrew 'cases' are illustrative here, although hardly in identical ways. If we consider the latter first, we are confronted with a context in which the linguistic aspects are often seen to comprise the archetypal success story among revival efforts. Indeed, Nahir (1977) has counted all attempts at language rejuvenation as failures, with the sole exception of Hebrew. What accounts for its success in Israel?

With the coming together of a linguistically heterogeneous population, a real communicative need existed in Israel, one that is typically absent or attenuated in many other settings. And waiting in the wings, as it were, was an old language that had a powerful religious claim on that diverse population. This combination of circumstances suggests the uniqueness of the Israeli case while, at the same time, demonstrating that the rejuvenation of Hebrew is not quite the miracle it has occasionally been made out to be, particularly there are reasons to think that, while the language had indeed generally receded to purely liturgical status, it had also maintained a secular and diglossic existence in some European quarters; see the documentation provided by Fellman a generation ago (1973a,b). The alleged upshot here is that, when Ben-Yehuda first argued for official-status Hebrew in Palestine, in the last quarter of the nineteenth century, he set in motion a 'revival' that 'could – and did – proceed apace *without any overriding or insurmountable difficulties*' (Fellman, 1976: 17; original italics). To be sure, not all commentators fully agree with Fellman, but it is undoubtedly true that the

Hebrew success story rests more upon social and political bases than upon purely linguistic ones.

The Irish 'case' also illuminates the relationships among language, religion and identity. One of the central threads here is the use, or the attempted use, of a powerful religious element to bolster the fortunes of a 'small' and flagging linguistic one. With religion a central and continuing pillar in Irish culture, it was felt sensible to exploit its strength as a prop for the endangered language, to suggest that Catholicism was uniquely expressible through Irish. Irish, then, was celebrated as 'the casket which encloses the highest and purest religion that any country could boast of since the time of the twelve apostles' (Fullerton, 1916: 6). It was 'the instrument and expression of a purely Catholic culture' (O'Donoghue, 1947: 24).

At the same time, the language could assist the religious orthodoxy in countering foreign (i.e. English) secular culture (Clery, 1927). The lines were neatly drawn between 'Irish ideals and British sordid soullessness' (Butler, 1901: 2), and there were a great many expressions of this in the popular literature. Forde (1901) pointed out, for example, that the modern materialism that had turned the English away from God necessarily meant that anglicisation was evil; in any event, English was a Protestant medium and therefore unsuitable for Ireland *tout court*. There is a type of religious Whorfianism in all this, but the arguments of the time, however bizarre, do reflect a powerful possibility. If, after all, it had proved possible to convince the Irish people – a population almost entirely Catholic – that there was a necessary and indissoluble link between their strongly held faith and the Irish language, the fortunes of the latter might have shown a dramatic improvement.[8]

There is another interesting scenario, however, one that may be thought to correspond more closely to the development of the linguistic facts on the Irish ground. It is simply that, far from reinvigorating the fortunes of Irish, a strong Catholicism might actually have expedited its decline. If Irish identity was broadly felt to be secure, even though expressed through the foreign *Béarla*, because of a powerful religious allegiance that provided an obvious distinction between the *Gael* and the *Sasanach* – well, perhaps the language need not be maintained after all, perhaps the always-tenuous revival effort could be allowed to gently fade away.

Before these relatively modern developments in the fortunes of Irish, however, there was an earlier illustration of the language-religion-identity nexus, one quite different in nature. The Tudors and the sixteenth- and seventeenth-century penal laws for the suppression of Catholicism hoped to promote English by discouraging Irish. Since the dying years of the reign of Elizabeth I, however, formal attempts were made to *use* Irish as an instrument of Protestant proselytism. The Queen's establishment (in 1591) of Trinity College Dublin as an attractive outpost of the Reformation, together with her provision of type and press for an Irish Bible, marked a change of direction (though not, of course, of intent). The general hope was, in fact, twofold: to expedite the decline of popery and to hasten the demise of Irish via the apparently paradoxical means of supporting it. The ultimate aim was the transformation of a troublesome Catholic and Celtic Ireland into a Protestant and anglophone province of the United Kingdom.

The thrust waxed and waned, but picked up greater impetus with the evangelical activities of the nineteenth century. Dewar (1812: 143) noted that Irish could be invaluable in converting the peasantry from the 'errors of popery'; as well, supporting the language would surely hasten its decline, since suitably instructed people would more quickly come to see the advantages of English. Education *per se* was not of prime importance; Anderson (1818: 59) bluntly observed that the intent in 'teaching the reading of Irish, etc. is not to make those who are to be the subjects of that instruction a learned, or what may be called a reading people'. The more or less exclusive aim was simply to 'bring them acquainted with...[Protestantism]'. A little later in the century, we find the more nuanced view of Monck Mason (1846: 9). The 'primary object' of his Protestant mission to the native Irish was not, he said, particularly focused upon 'proselytism from any particular sect'. Since 'the sure result of the study of divine truth would be the abandonment of human error', one could be sure that the desired religious outcome would come about quite naturally.

Spreading the word

The activities of missionaries provide one of the most intriguing points of connection between language and religion. Much useful linguistic work has been accomplished by apostles over the centuries and, as Müller (1862: 135) observed in the middle of the nineteenth century, 'missionaries and travellers felt it their duty to collect lists of words, and draw up grammars'. More recently, Grenoble and Whaley (2006: 196–197) reinforced the sentiment, arguing that missionaries can play 'an important role in language documentation and other forms of language preservation'. Of course, this can be rather difficult to reconcile with the much more central religious impulse which, in essence, aims at broad cultural change. As with the activities of many churches in their indigenous social contexts – with those of the Catholic hierarchy in an

Ireland ruled by England, for instance – it is clear that religious workers in farther-flung vineyards must ultimately put saving souls above saving languages; see note 8. Varied stances and circumstances have meant that, while missionaries have sometimes attempted to replace local languages with their own, they have also employed parochial varieties in their work, encouraged the development of literacy, translated scriptural material into native vernaculars, and so on. In all cases, however, we can be sure that mundane languages are means to spiritual ends.[9]

The zeal with which missionaries typically approach their work has created great difficulties for those whose cultures are invaded, and who are told – whether subtly or bluntly – that their traditional practices are sinful. Dilemmas and conflicts increase when, as has often been the case, outsiders of different religious stripes stake out the same territory. Evangelical fervour has always been heightened by doctrinal rivalries in the great competition for souls, and an equation can be drawn between degrees of apostolic activity and indigenous cultural discontinuity. Samuels (2006) describes the work of some *two dozen* different Christian denominations among the Arizona Apache. Stoll (1990) recounts how, in 1984, the Catholic *nuncio* in Mexico called for all Latin American governments to curtail the operations of Protestant organisations. Apart from the pot-and-kettle flavour here, the anecdote suggests something of the depth of the antagonisms that have been felt from the highest ecclesiastical levels to the most local of missionary activities.

The body whose activities most exercised the Mexican apostolic delegate was the Summer Institute of Linguistics (SIL). Thousands of its members have worked in virtually every part of the globe, and they have generated a great many linguistic publications. The most well-known of these is their *Ethnologue*, a comprehensive and frequently updated catalogue of all the world's languages. The SIL was established in the 1930s, as the more secular face of an organisation called the Wycliffe Bible Translators, and in contemporary self-descriptions it likes to downplay its underlying religious remit, emphasising instead its concern for 'small' languages and cultures. Thus, a pamphlet cited by Mühlhäusler (1996: 166) trumpets its commitment to 'linguistic research, language development, literacy, and other projects of practical, social and spiritual value'. In the following year, an SIL member wrote that the institute's language activities were aimed at fulfilling the 'deepest needs' of ethnic communities (Kindell, 1997: 279). In the Mühlhäusler citation, only the word 'spiritual' suggests anything other than normal academic procedure, and Kindell's reference is indirect, to say the least. Such disingenuous descriptions, with their sins of omission, are typical of evangelical organisations.

Historically speaking, missionaries essentially have had their own way for a long time, with few at home doubting either their beneficent intentions or the value of their proselytising efforts. But when scholars also moved into the field, when anthropologists and linguists began to formally interest themselves in native languages and cultures, clashes of interest immediately surfaced. In an increasingly secularised world, the religious workers were generally the ones forced to find defensive positions. I would argue that this is eminently reasonable because – whatever one may feel about the trajectories of secularism – the work of religious zealots has always exploited, manipulated and attempted to reconfigure the central structures of local 'groupness' for purposes quite alien to people who are usually both susceptible and vulnerable. This would be regrettable even if one accepted the truth which presumably animates and sustains the missionaries themselves. (Among other considerations, it is clear that an acceptance of any one group's doctrine must necessarily mean that the activities of the rest are built upon spiritual sand and that, therefore, none of their interference in regional languages and cultures can be justified.) If, on the other hand, one is less certain about religious verities *tout court*, one would be forced to see the efforts of *all* the apostles as a particularly unhappy chapter in the story of language and identity.

Notes

1. From the early 1980s, it has been suggested that stronger motivations for learning an 'out-group' language may emerge, particularly for 'integrative' reasons, where group vitality is relatively weak; see the discussion, above. On the other hand, even 'instrumental' motivations for second-language learning may be weakened if group vitality is strong; see Giles and Johnson (1981), Giles and Byrne (1982), Beebe and Giles (1984). More recent accounts of language learning include those already mentioned, including Dörnyei and Ushioda (2009) and Bhatia and Ritchie (2006).
    These observations may be taken to heart when we turn, a little later on, to consider matters more closely related to language learning.
2. In many ways, the scholars working within the confines of academies, language councils and the like are simply more formal and more sophisticated versions of those perennial letter-to-the-editor writers, those more 'ordinary' citizens who, throughout the centuries, have penned feverish responses to linguistic borrowings, barbarisms and bastardisations.
3. Some contemporary 'activists', of course, see intervention as both desirable and feasible. It is, indeed, a moral imperative for some of them. Others see it

as desirable, but grudgingly admit that it is rarely feasible. There may, for the sake of completeness here, be another group who – considering draconian language policies of the past, perhaps –would argue that some interventions are feasible without being desirable.

4. At the end of his book (1999: 248), Calvet acknowledges the plight of endangered languages, and he is clearly not indifferent to it. 'La responsabilité du linguiste', he writes, is an ethical one. He shies away from direct intervention, however, suggesting instead that scholarly 'pratique descriptive et analytique constitue aussi une intervention dans les niches écolinguistiques, et qu'elle peut les modifier notablement'.

5. The old fears that individual linguistic diversity – bilingualism or multilingualism, that is – might retard or impede cognitive functioning are groundless: there is no such price to be paid for diversity. Equally, however, there is no compelling evidence that repertoire expansion heightens intellectual capacity. At a scholarly level, the research studies purporting to show such an association are always bedevilled by the lack of full experimental control. More popularly, we realise that most of the many millions around the world who speak two, three or more languages are not noticeably more intelligent than their monolingual counterparts. I am not denying for a moment that increased linguistic fluencies are by and large a good and desirable thing – but I *am* suggesting that there are no reasonable grounds for believing that becoming multilingual makes you smarter. See Edwards (1995) for further discussion here.

6. Mufwene (2008: 247 also ventures to ask if 'linguists are helping the [sic] humanity or helping linguistics?'

7. There is a simple error of logic and correlation at work here. Suppose I discover, for instance, that those adolescents who excel at secondary school spent much more time with their crayons and colouring books when they were five years old than did their duller class-mates. Am I then to imagine that intensive colouring programmes for small children will bring about heightened academic success?

The correlational errors into which some commentators have fallen are highlighted in recent and more sophisticated biological enquiries. Fincher and Thornhill (2008: 1290) note that biological diversity and, more specifically, 'human-disease species richness' increase as latitude decreases. In those more equatorial areas of 'high pathogen severity', the authors continue, it would make sense for human groupings to avoid contact with others, to lessen their risk of exposure to diseases for which they have developed no immunity. Cultural and linguistic isolation may then lead to the continuity of diversity.

Fincher and Thornhill acknowledge other hypotheses meant to account for greater numbers of languages in lower latitudes, including Nettle's (1999) argument that areas of the world having long or multiple growing seasons encourage human self-reliance and lessen the need for cultural and linguistic interactions with others: again, the persistence of diversity may then be expected. However, drawing particularly upon work by Cashdan (2001) and Sutherland (2003), as well as their own more detailed analyses, the authors reject this and other hypotheses. Their conclusion is that 'human language richness across countries positively correlates with parasite richness...as infectious disease levels increase so too does biodiversity' (p. 1293).

They are quite aware, of course, of the large and compelling literature on the benefits of 'outbreeding' and the costs associated with 'inbreeding', but they suggest that in some contexts – in those areas particularly high in that 'human-disease species richness' – the former reproductive strategy may become less attractive. Or, as they carefully put it, 'although close inbreeding is maladaptive under high parasite severity levels, distant outbreeding is too' (p. 1295).

Whether or not Fincher and Thornhill's arguments can be maintained, it is worth noting here that all the biologically based hypotheses that they examine (including their own) are as one in their implicit rejection of any simplistic 'co-evolution' of languages, plants and animals. The idea (as expressed by Maffi, 2000b, for example) that protecting linguistic diversity may help in sustaining global flora and fauna – or, indeed, vice versa – is, to put it charitably, a little naïve; see also Maffi (2005), however, for a somewhat more informed discussion.

8. At the same time, the Catholic hierarchy remained acutely aware of the temporal linguistic winds, and never forgot that saving souls rather than languages was their most basic duty.

9. In similar fashion, of course, missionaries have sometimes tolerated local religious practices, aiming at a gradual evolution to preferred beliefs – perhaps, as Christianity and other religions have done more extensively, adopting and adapting pagan rites and celebrations – while at other times have made rather blunter attempts at eradication and replacement.

7
Language, Group, Identity: Gender

Gender and identity: An introductory note

The two main points of intersection among language, gender and identity involve use and portrayal. Under the first heading we find differences – imagined, real or exaggerated – in the language and speech of men and women. Under the second are variations in descriptions of men and women. Both of them reflect and reinforce the cultural connotations of male and female identity: the specifics obviously vary with time and context, but they all rest upon stereotypes. I begin here with two illustrations of the power of social stereotypes, one bearing upon usage and the other upon description. I have chosen these examples because, in each case, the research reported is (at least in part) my own; more importantly, each demonstrates just how *early* social conventions seem to take effect.[1]

Even though physiological differences bearing upon speech production are not very marked in prepubertal children, reports in the literature have confirmed what every one has always known: by listening to speech samples, we can accurately guess the gender of young children. Children's early adherence to social conventions about male and female speech – well before the onset of actual physical differentiation in vocal quality – is clearly the factor that underpins this. In an Irish study, I investigated this phenomenon, adding social-class differences and perceptions of the masculinity or femininity of voices to the experimental mixture (Edwards, 1979). Adult judges listened to voice samples elicited from working-class and middle-class ten-year-olds, and were simply asked to identify the gender of each speaker. A second group of raters was asked to evaluate all the voices on four dimensions related to masculinity/femininity.

Among both girls and boys, the voices of working-class children were perceived as rougher and more masculine than those of their middle-class counterparts. Although the earlier accuracy in gender-identification was confirmed here (at about the 85% level, in fact), the errors made were not randomly distributed. First, female judges were more accurate than the male assessors in identifying children's gender; this accords with observations, both within and without the literature, of greater female sensitivity in interpersonal relationships in general, and in verbal interactions in particular. Second, a significant interaction was found, in terms of errors made, between social class and gender. Among the working-class children, few boys were mistaken as girls, but errors made about girls were considerably greater; for the middle-class children, the pattern was reversed, and more errors were made with the boys than with the girls.

It would seem that the greater general masculinity of working-class speech caused girls to be misidentified as boys by the (middle-class) judges. Middle-class speech, relatively more feminine, allowed the operation of what one might term the 'boys sound like girls' principle, a reflection of the fact that, at puberty, it is boys' speech that changes most markedly in assuming adult characteristics. In summary, then, the argument runs as follows: different social conventions operate for working-class and middle-class speech, young children are aware of these, and this awareness is exemplified by adherence to the appropriate norms; differential accuracy in gender identification can be understood as resting upon this chain of social processes.[2]

Turning to the influence of convention and stereotype upon description, a series of studies has revealed that characteristics traditionally associated more with males or with females are learned early. American, Canadian, Irish and English children – often by age three, clearly by age five, and markedly by age eight – demonstrated that they understood women to be more gentle, affectionate and emotional, while men were strong, aggressive and dominant (Best *et al.*, 1977; Edwards and Williams, 1980; Widen and Russell, 2002; Williams *et al.*, 1975, 1977). At a time, then, when such blanket perceptions are subject to increasing challenge, and when the discriminatory practices which they often underpin have become (at least publicly) unacceptable, these findings suggest that older views persist. When the results of some of these studies were presented to teachers of the children who participated in them, the general reaction was one of dismay; female teachers in particular were annoyed to think that, by the time children first entered the classroom, they had already absorbed blunt and often prejudicial attitudes.

Erving Goffman and gender display

Introductory remarks

When we turn to consider some of the social features that underpin these sorts of findings – wishing to probe a little further, in other words, into the stereotypic substratum – we can do no better than to return to Goffman's (1979) famous investigation of 'gender advertisements', in which he used hundreds of pictures to illustrate several aspects of 'gender display'. I say 'return' but, in fact, for more than a few social scientists, the proper word would be 'turn', especially if we are (as we ought to be) more concerned with the text than with the interesting and often provocative images upon which Goffman's commentary is based. As Smith (2006: 127) has observed, this 'instant classic of visual sociology' stimulated many later studies, but perhaps it is not unfair to suggest that the novelty of collecting and analysing pictures was the chief heuristic feature here. This, even though much of what Goffman wrote in the book anticipated the work of later feminist scholars, most notably Butler's treatment of gender-as-performance (1990); see Cameron (1995), Smith (2006) and, more generally, Gill (2007, 2008, 2009).

Butler's idea that gender is a performance with no natural or biological basis is founded in Goffman's work, notably his treatment of the 'presentation of self' (1959), which undergirds and generally foreshadows his study of 'gender advertisements' that I shall turn to shortly. Goffman defined performance as 'all the activity of an individual which occurs during a period marked by his [sic] continuous presence before a particular set of observers which has some influence on the observers' (1959: 32). Important here is the 'front', which regularly defines the context in which the performance takes place: rank, clothing, gender, age, race, size, expressions and gestures can all contribute to the 'front'. When we take on an established social role, we typically find that a 'front' for it already exists.

Of course, Goffman acknowledged that many, perhaps most, of these roles are gendered. Indeed, more than any other social categorisation, gender provides a basis of

> what our ultimate nature ought to be and how and where this nature ought to be exhibited...gender expressions are by way of being a mere show; but a considerable amount of the substance of society is enrolled in the staging of it. (Goffman, 1979: 8)

Behind masculinity and femininity, then, is social conditioning, and Butler expands the thesis into a more feminist and constructionist argument. Her basic contention is that gender has little to do with bio-logical sex; it is, rather, a construction that passes itself off as reality through a series of performances.[3]

As I have implied, Goffman's work remains important. Eckert and McConnell-Ginet (2003: 28) refer, for example, to his 'still compelling discussion'. The first section in the first chapter of Romaine's (1999) book on language and gender is called 'Doing and Displaying Gender', the earliest of the four works that she cites on the subject (on p. 29) is Goffman's, and she returns to it several times throughout the book – also referring to other work, to be sure, but never implying that his seminal insights have been eclipsed. In part, this is because of the acuity of his observations, but the continuing significance also rests upon the remarkable constancy of the most basic gender stereotypes. Thus, Kang (1997), Hovland *et al.* (2005) and Lindner (2004) have all found remarkably similar patterns to those earlier outlined by Goffman. I selected these three studies from a considerably larger pool for the following reasons: first, the work of Hovland *et al.* ranged well beyond the western, anglophone world; second, because the images collected and analysed in the other two articles were taken from magazines aimed specifically at women (*Vogue, McCall's* and *Mademoiselle*); third, because Lindner surveyed magazines across a fifty-year span (from the middle 1950s).[4] Yet, as I say, the portrayals of gesture and appearance, of status, glamour and beauty, were (as we shall see) essentially those found and illustrated by Goffman a generation earlier. The implications for the continuity of gendered descriptions and portrayals, and their linguistic components in particular, are obvious.

An interesting and relevant demonstration of the consistency of 'gender display' is found in the careful and convincing work of Hirdman (2000), who examined visual representations of men and women in the Swedish media over a sixty-year period (acknowledging Goffman throughout her study). In the journalism of 1925, men were dominant in both text and picture. Where images of the 'New Woman' – that is, the modern and more emancipated post-war woman – appeared, they emphasised beauty. Hirdman writes, simply, that 'women were visually represented as actresses' (p. 228). The earlier and slightly immoral connotations of 'rouge and powder' now faded as women became depicted as 'idols of consumption', as girlish creatures who were 'coquettish and narcissistically self-absorbed' (p. 229). Their narrow *amour propre* was, of course, held up as exemplary.

In her snap-shot survey of 1955, Hirdman finds more pictorial representations of men and women in groups, but the older senses of men as the serious decision-makers remain.[5] In illustrations of families, for instance, men are shown as essentially protective and, therefore, often a little on the periphery: domestic sentries, if you like. Women are at the heart of the family, of course, often bending down towards their children, touching them, and so on. Women's central obligations to home, hearth and children – one is reminded here of the (in)famous triple duty to *Kinder, Küche und Kirche* – are not unconnected, Hirdman suggests, to the view that, having helped outside the home during the war, women were now to be encouraged to return to their rightful, domestic sphere. Of course, none of this implies that earlier concerns with physical attractiveness were shunted aside; the central theme in women's magazines was still 'getting and keeping a man' (p. 231).

Another thirty years pass, and Hirdman finds that, in her 1987 sampling, many more pictures now appear in which men and women are shown in extra-domestic social roles. However, while pictures of politicians (for example) now appear more frequently in the newspapers, the women among them 'do not give the same impression of power as do the male leaders', they are not so likely to be found together in group pictures, and they are often shown gesticulating and smiling more often.

Overall, the most striking features here, of course, are not the temporal changes but, rather, the continuity of some basic threads. Hirdman herself summarises this – without using the word 'objectification' – by observing that women are much more likely to be portrayed as 'representatives *for* something outside themselves, and in contexts not directly related to the individual' (p. 235; original italics). They may be shown as 'silent bodies', or 'altruistic pleasers', or secondary players in the public arena, but, across all the time periods under review here, images of 'masculinity and public power' predominate (p. 236). Hirdman closes by noting that 'the establishment of masculinity as norm and the emphasis on the female as a form symbolising various values' is the continuing influence 'which has guided, and which still controls, the gender ideology of press images' (p. 236). It is thus unsurprising to find that, despite the view that the 'serious' press often takes of itself, stereotypic assumptions underpin its activities just as much as they do in the tabloid media.

Goffman re-examined

If we can agree on the continuing presence of remarkably similar gender stereotypes – nicely exemplified in the studies just touched upon, to be sure, but also abundantly clear to more casual observers – we should turn now to Goffman himself, his interesting observations, and his exemplification of some of the points I have highlighted from Hirdman's work.

Goffman (1979: 25) presents us with more than 500 photographic images of men, women and children, an admittedly 'un-randomly collected' assortment meant to show 'advertisers' views of how women can be profitably pictured'. But, of course, this is hardly the whole story. How does the 'gender-relevant behavior' depicted here relate to 'real life'; or, we might better ask, from what deeper social pools do the images emerge? In her brief introduction to Goffman's book, Gornick (1979: vii) cites his argument that both advertisers and societies have the same job: 'both must transform otherwise opaque goings-on into easily readable form'. What is this if not a comment on the stereotypic shorthand that is common – and, indeed, essential – to both? What, if not a justification for stressing the 'display', the 'performance' of gender? As Goffman puts it, rather nicely, himself:

> Natural expressions [of gendered behaviour] are commercials performed to sell a version of the world under conditions no less questionable and treacherous than the ones that advertisers face.

He remakes the point:

> Advertisers...draw upon the same corpus of displays, the same ritual idiom, that is the resource of all of us who participate in social situations, and to the same end: the rendering of glimpsed action readable.

And ends by noting that

> Advertisers conventionalize our conventions, stylize what is already a stylization, make frivolous use of what is already something considerably cut off from contextual controls. Their hype is hyper-ritualization. (p. 84)

An acceptance of this insight, especially by quantitatively minded social scientists, may mean that the non-randomness of Goffman's picture gallery becomes less important. It also suggests that when the writer and critic, Anne Hollander (1979), considers that Goffman has given us 'pictorial conventions' rather than 'real life', she rather misses the point. It *is* fair comment, however, to note that Goffman may have missed the intentionally ironic nature of some of his advertising images. And, as Anatole Broyard (1979) added, some modern advertising is 'not only read as parody, but intended as parody as well. Much of the humour of advertising depends on this double meaning, which is a play on the oversimplification being depicted.'⁶

Returning to a point that I touched upon earlier: while the very idea of presenting hundreds of pictorial advertisements may have been what captured those sociological imaginations that followed Goffman, it is the strength of his textual observations that are most important. He organises these under half a dozen headings (see also Gornick, 1979; Smith, 2006).

First, men are almost always shown as physically taller and more imposing than women, except in those rare instances where they are depicted as socially or occupationally inferior. This might be seen as a more or less accurate rendition, were it not for the fact that physical size is so often accompanied by greater 'social weight'. In advertisements, as in social life, 'what biology and social selection facilitate, picture posing rigorously completes' (Goffman, 1979: 28).

Second, while women are often shown as doing things with their hands, they rarely grasp, manipulate or shape; rather, they display various types of light, delicate, 'feminine' touch or caress. Woman's touch is ritualistic and stylised – nothing as crass and 'utilitarian' as the more forceful male variety. The butterfly touch can be a sexual signal, of course, and Goffman also mentions the frequently depicted female 'self-touching' as 'conveying a sense of one's body being a delicate and precious thing' (p. 31).

Third, men typically occupy any 'executive roles' shown. They are the instructors, women their acolytes. The distinction here is often shown within an 'occupational frame', but it is equally noticeable elsewhere. Goffman presents a number of pictures of the more active and tutorial male stance, and the most general observation is simply that men provide help and women receive it. There is an interesting sub-category here, one in which men are shown 'in the domains of the traditional authority and competence of females: the kitchen, the nursery, and the living-room when it is being cleaned'. In some representations, men may be shown simply looking on, thus 'avoiding either subordination or contamination with a "female" task'. In others, a man may be made to appear 'ludicrous or childlike' in some unrealistic or caricatured fashion; this means that 'the competency image of real males could be preserved' (p. 36). And, in a particularly felicitous turn of phrase, Goffman suggests a third possibility:

A subtler technique is to allow the male to pursue the alien activity under the direct appraising scrutiny of she who can do the deed properly, as though the doing were itself by way of being a lark or a dare, a smile on the face of the doer or the watcher attesting to the essentially unserious essayed character of the undertaking.

And, he adds, 'when females are pictured engaged in a traditional male activity, a male may (as it were) parenthesize the activity, looking on appraisingly, condescendingly, or with wonder' (p. 37).[7]

Goffman singles out illustrations of the family as a fourth category here, of special interest because men, women and children may be simultaneously present in their various postures. He had already touched upon the depiction of children under his status or function rubric, where he wrote that the 'cuteness' of their representations often rests upon the fact that they are shown being serious about things that, to adults, are not serious at all. He had also made the briefest of references to some earlier work on gender stereotypes in children's picture books, and this is not unconnected to an observation he makes here, in the 'family' section, where he notes the greater activity of boys and the greater passivity of girls. (Readers will recall here the four-country research, cited above, on the early absorption of such broad gender stereotypes.) Goffman's images imply, he says, that while boys 'have to push their way into manhood, and problematic effort is involved... girls merely have to unfold' (p. 38). Another part of the family portrait, this one reminiscent of Hirdman's account, is that

> often the father (or, in his absence, a son) stands a little outside the physical circle of the other members of the family, as if to express a relationship whose protectiveness is linked with, perhaps even requires, distance. (p. 39)

The fifth of Goffman's descriptive compartments, and the one most abundantly illustrated, has to do with the 'ritualization of subordination' of women. They may not always be pictured lying on beds or sitting on the floor at a man's feet (common though these postures are), but 'men tend to be located higher than women... [even when] a certain amount of contortion may be required' (p. 43). Women's status vis-à-vis men is often revealed in posture and stance, in the lowering of head or eyes, in what Goffman refers to as the 'bashful knee bend' (p. 45), in 'body cant' and 'head cant':

> Although a distinction can be made between body cant and head cant the consequences seem to be much the same. The level of the head is lowered relative to that of others, including, indirectly, the

viewer of the picture. The resulting configurations can be read as an acceptance of subordination, an expression of ingratiation, submissiveness and appeasement. (p. 46)

Demureness, coyness and modesty are other adjectives that come to mind, too, and Goffman might plausibly have seen these as the 'softer' faces of subordination, although I don't think he uses the terms in his book. As part of his discussion of women's smiling ('more the offering of an inferior than a superior'), however, Goffman does refer to arch and impish images (he uses the word 'puckish'; p. 48). This acts as a lead-in to a discussion of the many childish and playful postures in which women are shown.

Taken together, representations of shyness, of coyness, of childishness, suggest a lack of seriousness; this leads to one of Goffman's most interesting *aperçus*:

> The special unseriousness involved in childlike guises and clowning suggests a readiness to be present in a social situation garbed and styled in a manner to which one isn't deeply or irrevocably committed... as though life were a series of costume balls... the costume-like character of female garb in advertisements locates women as less seriously present in social situations than men. (p. 51)

Goffman writes that, while men are also sometimes portrayed in 'different' clothing, the range is typically much more restricted ('formal, business and informal gear') and, on the rarer occasions when they are shown in a guise beyond this continuum, there is 'little sense that one's whole appearance is a lark' (p. 51). In terms of the broader thesis here – that a common emphasis upon gender *display* is what unites advertisement and reality, what makes the study of the former useful for understanding the latter – it is also important to realise that the much wider range of elements contributing to their physical appearance in advertisements is related to the greater time, in reality, that women spend in 'shopping for clothes and preparing for appearances', to the fact that 'women set considerable store on the appreciative or depreciative response they produce' (p. 51). (*Why* women's behaviour takes these forms is, of course, the nub of the larger issue.)

Still under the heading of ritualised subordination, Goffman also discusses the various physical 'holding' positions that join men and women. Men, he writes, may 'employ an extended arm, in effect marking the boundary of his social property', or may use a 'shoulder hold'.

In both cases, but especially in the latter, the physical asymmetry with which Goffman opened his discussion is reinforced, because both of these proprietary gestures come more easily to those who are taller. With what he calls 'the arm lock', Goffman illustrates another mark that 'a woman is under the protective custody of the accompanying man'; as the woman is holding on to her man's arm, she 'shows herself to be receiving support... [while] both the man's hands are free for whatever instrumental tasks may arise' (p. 55).

Sixth and finally here, women are frequently shown engaging in 'licensed withdrawal' – a drifting away, with 'faces lost and dreamy' (Gornick, 1979: viii), that is permissible because of the presence of a capable and protective male. Gaze aversion, Goffman notes, can thus signify both submission and trust, often shown in conjunction with the lowering of the head or eyes. Women have the luxury of 'mentally drifting from the physical scene around them' because of the 'aliveness' and the 'readiness' of the man with them. (Goffman adds here that 'the male may well wear a wary, monitoring look'; p. 65.) In another 'lost' variant, women are often shown as unprepared and helpless – hands over the mouth, eyes wide with horror – in the face of misfortune, or when reacting to something with fear or remorse. Alternatively, hand-over-mouth can be an accompaniment of shyness, of coyness or, indeed, of laughter.

This last, 'licensed withdrawal', category summarises most of the other characteristics outlined in Goffman's picture gallery; or, at least, it is the psychological outcome to which many of them point. Women are not as strong or as serious as men, their activities are less important (even their interactions with children can only occur within a protective cocoon that they themselves cannot construct), they are subordinate in all important ways and, of course, they are consumed with and by the attractive but essentially trivial world of fashion. It might perhaps be suggested that, under all these circumstances, some degree of 'withdrawal' – of psychologically 'going away', as Goffman puts it – could represent a strategic retreat, an acknowledgement of the inevitable, a resigned acceptance of an existence which, after all, can be quite safe and comfortable. But remember that the withdrawal is 'licensed' by someone else... and licenses can be withdrawn. In an earlier discussion, commenting upon men's and women's speech, I wrote that if women are occasionally depicted as being on some social pedestal – 'higher' than men in some ways, perhaps because they are politer, or kinder, or more nurturing – it is as well to remember that they have been *placed* there – 'and pedestals offer little room for movement' (Edwards, 1995: 201).[8]

I justify this little section – with its extensive direct quotations from Goffman himself – on the grounds that the material presented remains of the greatest relevance. Should any reader disagree with the main thrust of these paragraphs, I would only ask him or her to go through a selection of contemporary magazines and newspapers, have a look at contemporary cinema and, perhaps most strikingly, consider the content and the style of modern music videos.[9] The findings can then be set against Goffman's interpretations of a generation ago. One outcome I predict is that such an exercise will suggest that, however much more enlightened viewpoints have become in the academy, things have not changed very much on the street. And even in the academy and other supposedly enlightened social corners, an arguable thesis is that a great deal of psychological 'compartmentalisation' occurs. After all, many of those who move in such precincts watch 'reality' television now and again, and read the tabloids or some formulaic book: Mills and Boon or Harlequin bodice-rippers, or perhaps some Dan Brown or Jeffrey Archer. Perhaps these forays into 'low culture' are more common among the keepers of the flame than we imagine; perhaps, therefore, the post-adolescent tastes of those university women I refer to in note 9 simply reflect the same sort of excursion (ratcheted up a bit, of course).[10] Still, I *do* remain concerned about my self-described feminist students who apparently enjoy even the most sexist of 'music videos', those raucous displays whose underlying theme is surely manipulation and misogyny. I find unconvincing the argument that the women who take part in those displays are revelling in the power of their sexuality, that it is *they* who are the conscious puppet-masters of the piece, and so on. Two things, at least, are clear, however: we need much more disinterested investigation, from a variety of disciplinary perspectives; and we could do much worse than to use Goffman's insights as a starting point.

Back to language

Having paid some attention to the variety and the pervasiveness of gender stereotypes writ large, we can focus upon more specifically linguistic matters with some greater confidence. The most immediately obvious topic has to do with gendered speech differences. While there are both historical and contemporary examples of gender-*exclusive* usage (of terms used *only* by women, or *only* by men), gender-*preferential* variations are much more common. It is a common and, in most instances, accurate argument that women's speech tends to be more conservative, more 'standard' and more 'polite' than that of men. In a much-quoted study, and one that continues my emphasis upon the early awareness and reproduction of social conventions, Fischer (1958) found that, among a sample of twenty-four young children in New England – twelve boys and twelve girls, equally distributed in two groups (ages 3 to 6, and 7 to 10) – the little girls were much more likely than the boys to use *-ing* rather than *–in'* for the ending of the present participle. The implication is that the social conventions bearing upon females elicit more 'correct' usage; and there are, of course, many common threads linking 'correctness' to 'politeness' to 'standard-ness'. We have already noted that, in broader application, those conventions involve status differentials, relative degrees of social power and subordination – but also a certain 'protected' status within which female delicacy, playfulness and, of course, sexuality are highlighted. It is not difficult to see the connections between those wider features discussed by Goffman and more specifically linguistic directions. In their femininity, however constrained and constructed it may be, women will naturally be expected to pay closer attention to what is 'proper' in language and, conversely, to eschew profanity, obscenity, slang and other such unattractive practices. My point here, of course, is not that politeness or the avoidance of profanity are bad things, but rather to suggest that we can read something interesting into social influences that have traditionally constrained one gender more than the other.

A subordinate social role may be taken to imply less linguistic expansiveness and more markers of insecurity and uncertainty. These are exactly the characteristics that were illustrated by Robin Lakoff in her much-cited work on women's language (see Lakoff, 2004, for the most recent overviews here; see also Talbot, 2003). Lakoff highlighted such generalities as the frequent use of polite and euphemistic terms, the avoidance of swearing, and the 'softening' of direct requests. She also discussed some specific features that have continued to attract research attention: they include lexical 'hedges' or 'fillers' (*you know, sort of, you see*); tag-questions (*she's very nice, isn't she*); emotional, expressive but often 'empty' adjectives (*divine, charming*); intensifiers (*I like him* <u>so</u> *much*); emphatic stress (*it was a* <u>brilliant</u> *performance*); diminutive forms. Many of these usages have been taken as reflections of subaltern and deferential status, of a stance that is not too assertive, contradictory or definite; in the picture given to us here, verbal intensifiers and emphases are so over the top that they constitute no serious declaration of strong opinion. Still, Lakoff and others have noted that, collectively, they also contribute to collaborative rather than competitive interactions. And this, after all, is one of the broadest and most general of female conventions, evoking and reinforcing as it does images of helping, of caring, of nurturing.

Despite conceptual and methodological difficulties, Lakoff's illustrations have an enduring relevance, and her taxonomic efforts have been widely recognised and applauded (see Crawford, 1995; Colley, 2005). The most interesting features are those involving either emphasis or understatement, because each of these can suggest nervousness, insecurity, a desire to mollify, and an avoidance of unpleasantness. And, reflections of nurturing and caring aside, it would be easy to see virtually all the features as supporting cross-gender comparisons that are generally unfavourable to women. This perspective is only reinforced when we add in evidence arising from male–female conversations: men dominate these conversations by steering the topic, by interrupting more, and by employing more forceful intonations; women, once again, are more recipients than initiators, provide more conversational feedback, make more encouraging and facilitating remarks, and so on.

This, at least, has been the received wisdom. After all, the linguistic (and paralinguistic) variation discussed here nicely complements the broader treatment with which I began this section. In language as elsewhere, women are submissive, manipulable, eager to please, and less serious. Their areas of expertise – 'women's work' in the home, with the children – may be acknowledged as important, but they are also of clearly restricted scope; and, when expertise is taken outside the home (in nursing, in professional child-care, and so on), that restricted scope still applies. Any work that women traditionally do, in fact, is likely to be considered of lesser status; it is certainly less rewarded in terms of the usual coins of society. If we return to language usage, especially in the context of the traditional 'home-maker', could there be any possible doubt about the relative importance of an extensive and fine-grained colour vocabulary, or an expanded capacity to endlessly discuss and dissect 'relationships', when compared to the discourse of engineers, surgeons, philosophers and other traditionally male groupings? Even at a time when more and more women are moving into professional areas that were once almost exclusively male preserves, the persistence of these perceptions and the tenacity of long-standing convention and stereotype are both unsurprising and depressing.

This is because, while one would have to be very naïve indeed to imagine that scholarly insights rapidly percolate through society at large, there is more and more evidence that challenges the received wisdom of the high street. The speech characteristics traditionally associated with women are not, after all, exclusively theirs. Male and female uses of the same features do not always signify the same thing. We are told, for example, that, while women's questions may be meant to maintain or facilitate conversation or, indeed, to invite an extended discussion, men's questions are simple requests for information (see Coates, 2004). This leads to many misunderstandings.

Cameron (1995, 2006, 2007) has reminded us of the large overlap in the way men and women speak, and she is particularly critical of some of the 'popular' literature that has reinforced our sense of gender miscommunication. Commenting on the well-known work of Tannen (1986 and 1990, for instance), Cameron notes that language interactions often have more to do with power than with gender. When the man says to his wife, 'is there any ketchup?', the message is really 'bring it to me'. If the daughter asks the same question, it is much more likely that the mother will respond by telling her that it is in the cupboard. This reminder brings us squarely back, of course, to the powerful underpinnings illustrated by Goffman. Cameron (1995) goes on to note that many 'popular' treatments are in fact self-help books aimed at women: they deal only with adaptation and tolerance, not coming to grips with the reasons for either behaviour or stereotype – and thus make no contribution to any possible change; see also Holborow's (1999) perspective on language, gender and power from a Marxist perspective.[11]

There are other important demonstrations of difficulties with that 'received wisdom'. Cameron (2006, 2007) shows that women can be as conversationally aggressive as men in terms of turn-taking and interruption. There is also abundant evidence that men talk more than women (Holmes, 1998; Leaper and Ayres, 2007), although context and topic are important factors. And, to consider the other end of the conversational continuum, we find that silence or restraint is another example of a characteristic that is not only differentially observed but, more importantly, is differentially interpreted. Silence may proverbially be the best ornament of a woman, and an approved marker of inferior status but, in a man, silence may be associated with wisdom, authority and potency (Kiesling, 2007; see also Mills, 2006). Tag-questions do not always imply female uncertainty, non-assertiveness, or conversational facilitation; they can also be confrontational ('You see what I'm telling you here, don't you?'), in which case readers would be right to believe that men are the more frequent users. In an insightful analysis, Holmes found that about 60% of women's tag-question use was facilitative, about a third of it expressed uncertainty, and only about 6% had a 'softening'. Men's use was clearly less facilitative (about 25%) – but about *twice as likely* to be used to 'soften' an utterance, or to express uncertainty. These findings seem to turn stereotypes on their heads. Can men really be more conversationally diffident than women and, if so, why are they not as 'facilitative'? A possible explanation here is that men are more linguistically aggressive than are women, and hence feel a more frequent need to moderate their expressions; similarly, they may forge ahead with ill-informed points of view, only to have to back-pedal somewhat later (see Edwards, 1979, 1989, for a discussion of variations in 'confidence' and subsequent 'softening'; see also Chapter 2) . None of this need touch upon the 'facilitation' function that, indeed, seems to be taken more seriously by women.

Other analyses suggest that greater female politeness, increased use of standard variants and so on, may all imply more about genuine facilitative and supportive desires than they do about insecurity and lack of confidence. In fact, many of the 'classic' features identified by Lakoff, and intensively investigated afterwards under headings having to do with gender differences, do not discriminate particularly well between men and women. It is noteworthy that some of the commentaries in the revised edition of Lakoff's classic work (2004) – that is to say, more recent assessments in the area – are now suggesting that it was always more about ideology and power than about this or that specific linguistic feature. Joseph's (2006) recent treatment of 'gendered language' within a broader discussion of power and politics is an insightful summary, particularly his remarks on the modern applications of discourse analysis.[12]

A broader point is that men and women sometimes use language for different social purposes. After all, if we accept that variations in socialisation practices constitute the major influence on gender traits, it is only logical to acknowledge that linguistic characteristics must be part of the package. Alleged differences in men's and women's 'gossip' are instructive here. The latter is traditionally seen to focus on personal relationships, experiences and problems, in a generally supportive atmosphere in which 'networking' is key. The former is more concerned with factual information, often in a competitive or combative format; of course, the tradition for men avoids the word 'gossip' altogether. Eckert and McConnell-Ginet (2003) provide an excellent discussion of the vagaries and vicissitudes of 'networking' and its organisation, in which it appears that much of women's activity is, in fact, driven by practical necessity, and much of men's gossip is intensely personal. Folk-wisdom is turned on its head. If one were to put together a corpus of women's exchanges about child-rearing, and compare it to a similar assemblage of men's talk about work or sports – just to remain in traditional arenas here – the inconsequentiality of the latter would likely be in stark contrast to the practicality and applied value of the former. Leet-Pellegrini (1980) succinctly remarked that men typically ask themselves if they have won in conversational exchanges, while women ponder whether or not they have been sufficiently helpful.

A nuanced perspective would surely hold that, in all considerations of 'gendered language' or of cross-gender communication, both *dominance* and *difference* are to be kept in mind. As Pennycook (2001: 153) notes in a brief but insightful treatment, emphasising power alone runs the risk of simply dichotomising what is, in reality, a rather more complicated picture, of presenting something that is 'too clumsy and limited to understand a broader set of social relations'. The other emphasis – upon differences in communication – is built upon the existence of different patterns of socialisation: here we may view women's language (for instance) as 'separate but different' from that of men (perhaps 'different-but-equal' would have been a more apt phrase here). In practice, and through some of the more 'popular' works in the area (those by Tannen, for example: 1986, 1990, 1994), this emphasis has often shaded over into a 'celebration' of women's talk. Pennycook's gloss is that 'the dominance position has needed greater complexity, while the difference position has needed more politics' (p. 153). This is neatly put – and accurate, as far as it goes. But the difficulty here is implied in Pennycook's own sentence: the 'dominance' position needs further work, but the 'difference' one actually needs to be folded *into* that dominance position. To put it more simply: as with all examples of social variation, linguistic or otherwise, the force of convention regularly translates those differences into deficiencies. Power, once again, translates different-but-equal positions into different-and-distinctly unequal ones.

While there are obvious and, indeed, compelling reasons that discussions of gender, language and identity focus principally upon women (as, in fact, I have done here), the best recent treatments have attended to *both* women and men (e.g. Cameron, 2007; Coates, 2004; Holmes, 1995; Holmes and Meyerhoff, 2003; Johnson and Meinhof, 1997). These all make the point, for example, that assessments of women's politeness, or swearing, or use of tag-questions, are often built upon unexamined assumptions about the men's speech from which women's is seen to depart. Despite considerable recent advances in both information and sensitivity, we must continue to be alert to the danger of seeing the speech of one gender (need I say which?) as the norm from which that of the other differs or deviates. Why say women are more polite than men, or swear less, or are more conversationally facilitative, or hedge their linguistic bets? Why not ask, rather, why men are ruder, more confrontational and more unreasonably assertive? An answer was provided a generation ago by Frank and Anshen (1983: 46):

> If it were shown that men speak more surely than women, hesitating less, this would certainly be greeted as another sign of masculine superiority. The halting speech of women would be seen as evidence of their tentative, feminine nature. Yet, when Jespersen found just the opposite phenomenon, that men hesitate more than women when speaking, he naturally attributed this fact to a greater desire for accuracy and clarity among male speakers, which leads them to search for just the right word.

This is the same Jespersen who, standing at the head of a long line of later authors, both male and female, felt obliged to include in his *Language* (1922) a chapter on women but none on men.

I cannot leave this section, of course, without at least a brief reference to what is perhaps the most 'visible' topic under this rubric: sexist language. A relatively mild, but still controversial and often annoying, aspect is the use of what is termed the *generic masculine*: the use of the masculine form of a word to refer to both men and women. Here are some examples[13]:

> ...in this stage of catatonia, the patient appears extremely preoccupied. He is uncommunicative, even mute, and appears generally uninterested in all that surrounds him;...eye fixation...is largely dependent upon the infant's ability to coordinate his eye movements.

> ...as the child lives in his environment, so he will daily encounter many frustrating occurrences.

> ...for the therapist to respect the patient, his behaviour, and his attitudes.

Contemporary responses to this matter (in English) have included simply replacing 'he' and 'him' with 'she' and 'her', substituting 'he or she' (or, perhaps, 's/he') or 'his or her' for the masculine usages, or introducing 'gender-neutral' neologisms (*e* and *tey*, for instance). None of these has achieved particularly wide currency: replacement simply changes the direction of the sexism, substitution is unwieldy, and neologisms are, at least for the moment, seen more as curiosities than as solutions. The most frequent adaptation is simply to cast singular into plural: in the first of the four examples above, then, 'patient' and 'he' would simply become 'patients' and 'they'.

More pointed definitions of sexist language, however, stress 'discriminatory language practices...[and] trivialising or demeaning references to women', particularly worrisome inasmuch as these are understood to 'reflect and contribute to the reproduction of broader social inequalities' (Swann *et al.*, 2004: 277). Mills (2008) provides particularly good recent treatment of language and sexism. She makes the point that, while direct or overt sexism in language may be on the decline – it is the form 'most contested by feminists and which has, as a result, become stigmatised by most language users...[it] still exists but it is seen by many as anachronistic' (p. 12) – more indirect forms have developed. Here, she suggests an indirect sexism that uses irony and humour in an attempt to forestall criticism. Her point, however, is that 'does not change the nature of the sexism itself, but rather simply changes the way it can be responded to' (p. 134); see also Lazar (2005), Benwell (2006) and Benwell and Stokoe (2006). Things that are indirect are often more insidious and harder to combat, particularly when any criticism can easily be deflected by reference to inappropriate severity or lack of humour:

> Saying serious things in jest both creates camaraderie and allows the speaker to avoid responsibility for anything controversial...it's just a joke, after all – can't you take a joke? (Lakoff, 1990: 270)

As Lakoff goes on to add, accusations of humourlessness are among the most biting of all.

'Overt' sexist language may indeed have become 'stigmatised' and 'anachronistic' in some segments of society – although even in educated circles, it is hardly rare in (for instance) all-male conversations – but it probably remains more prevalent in society at large than Mills seems to recognise. But this amendment, if correct, only heightens the force of her concluding comments that, in this matter as in others, active moves to counter linguistic discrimination and abuse are always to be lauded. It may well be that attempts to eradicate any currently unpleasant or hurtful usage will simply lead to the rise of new forms, but this in itself is no particular recommendation for inaction. One does what one can, when one can. More importantly, since linguistic usage can be understood as a representation of much larger issues of equality and participation, any success, however minor, may contribute its mite to the broader discourse (see also Holmes, 2001; Hellinger and Pauwels, 2007).[14]

Notes

1. Ehrlich's (2010) substantial encyclopaedia entry on language and gender provides a good introduction to the area. Talbot (2003) presents a brief but satisfying overview of the main issues under the rubric of gender stereotypes.
2. Readers may recall here the classic study of Condry and Condry (1976), in which men and women were asked to describe a film of an infant confronting various stimulus objects. Half of the viewers were told that the baby was a boy, the others that it was a girl. Different types and levels of emotions were reported, the variations resting upon the gender of the viewer-judges and, more importantly, on the gender attributed to the baby. For example, when the child was labelled a boy, judges were more likely to see its reaction to a jack-in-the-box as being more angry and less fearful.
3. These paragraphs linking Goffman with Butler draw more or less directly upon the work of Emily Edwards (2007).
4. Some of Goffman's 500-plus images were taken from non-English-language sources. One cannot say exactly how many, since most of the pictures were without any words at all, either in the photograph itself or as a caption. Of those *with* some words, however, there were three German, two Italian and five French images. There were, as well, five pictures in which women appeared completely naked, and I assume that these were not found in American or British magazines of the period; indeed, in two instances, accompanying words revealed Italian and German origins.
5. In this and other work (including Goffman's), it is always worth considering who is likely to have made all these images; as Edwards (2007) puts it, the lens itself is gendered.
6. Among several others, I spent about a week in Goffman's company – in 1979, just as *Gender Advertisements* was making its appearance. Even on this brief acquaintance, I feel certain in stating that irony was not Goffman's strongest suit.
7. The work of Mulvey (1975, 2009) on the dominance of the 'male gaze' is relevant here – but it is important to bear in mind the author's heavy reliance upon such scientific principles as patriarchy and phallocentrism.
8. I am prescinding here from the interesting literature that purports to show that women are more acquiescent than I have suggested here in occupying the various roles and taking on the various postures that Goffman and others have illustrated. Equally, I leave for another discussion the question of *intra*-sex desires and pressures.

   By an odd coincidence, I am just now re-reading Mario Puzo's *The Godfather*. In Chapter 20, Don Corleone observes that 'women and children can afford to be careless, men cannot'. It is unlikely that he was thinking of Goffman's 'licensed withdrawal', however.
9. Again, further discussion of these modern representations is called for, and I would particularly emphasise increased attention to music videos. While many of these portray women in flagrantly stereotypic style, in veritable

orgies of sexuality and objectification, it is interesting (to say the very least) that they are eagerly watched by women as well as men, and that their positive reactions must somehow rest upon something rather more selectively powerful than simply a willing suspension of disbelief.

The subject has come up for discussion many times in my university language seminar and I have, of course, been particularly interested to compare notes with my young, well-educated and socially aware female students, most of whom are self-described feminists. Interested, but also disappointed, because almost all of these women said that they watched and enjoyed the videos, even those whose pictures and lyrics were the most blatantly sexist. We have reached various conclusions at this senior undergraduate level, but the area cries out for sustained scholarly attention. There has already been some, of course. Mills (2008), for example, cites remarks bearing exactly upon the ambivalence that I report here.

10. Studies of 'popular fiction' suggest that the female readership is rather wider in social-class terms than might be imagined; see Radway (1984) and McCracken (1998). Citing a contributor to W. H. Smith's *Trade Circular*, McAleer (1992: 110) noted that 'every kind of woman reads romantic novels'. These authors confirm what Queenie Leavis had written much earlier, in her famous survey of reading habits: 'there is no reason for supposing that novelettes are bought exclusively by the uneducated and the poor' (1932: 277; see also Hoggart, 1993).

11. Books about miscommunication between men and women are not the only type of self-help manuals with a particular audience in mind. Almost all 'popular' books about 'relationships' are aimed at women. A new book dedicated to 'getting along with your in-laws' (Apter, 2009) is merely the latest in a very long line. It may be – as a perceptive reviewer pointed out recently – a 'cogent' treatment but 'realistically, it assumes its readership will be pretty much confined to women' (Martin, 2009: 27). In all such manuals, men are apparently to be 'handled' or, indeed, 'cajoled'.

12. In a recent book (Edwards, 2010a), I criticised 'discourse analysis and its discontents' – and I wish that I had made mention there of Joseph's brief but accurate analysis of 'critical discourse analysis' (CDA). Like me, he believes that there is considerable potential in this perspective, particularly for a better understanding of political rhetoric. Also like me, however, he takes CDA to task for its adoption of quite particular ideological stances. He comments, for instance, that typical CDA consideration of official statements dealing with immigration, civil rights and 'the Other' is slanted, inasmuch as texts are not selected at random for analysis. Rather, the examples chosen for interpretation are generally those 'produced by members of conservative or far-right parties' (Joseph, 2006: 130).

As Joseph says, those within the current CDA camp are probably not troubled by such selectivity, since their basic remit is to expose the excesses of 'hegemonic' power as it exercised by the political (and other) establishments. I am reminded here of the similar lack of balance that exists within contemporary treatments of language ecology (see Chapter 6) and some of the more pointed views about the spread of English (see Chapter 8). I am sure that Joseph would agree with my claim that, while there is nothing essentially wrong with any avenue of enquiry assuming any political posture that it chooses, there *is* something disingenuous about attempting to imply a broader and more inclusive scope.

Joseph suggests that the methodologies of CDA *per se* are potentially useful for a range of linguistic enquiries and – since 'CDA wears its political commitments on its sleeve' (p. 130) – its present tendencies could quite easily be detached, and its fuller value thus enhanced. Here, Joseph shows himself to be more generously disposed than me. I think that the 'leftist' tendencies inherent in CDA are *not* made sufficiently transparent, with the result that readers may be led to imagine that the linguistic unravellings set before them pertain to a much wider slice of the broad social narrative.

This aside, it is clear that Joseph's essential interpretations are accurate and incisive:

> CDA thus shares a fundamental weakness with [the] hegemony-based analysis of the spread of English...Any intellectual framework that requires a particular political commitment, and cannot open itself to application by people holding a variety of political views, has no place in the secular academic context. It is an ideology masquerading as a scholarly method. (p. 130)

13. These examples are all from undergraduate essays that I wrote in psychology classes in the late 1960s. I need hardly add that this usage of the 'generic masculine' occasioned absolutely no comment at that time. It simply was the norm.

14. Readers interested in a brief discussion of feminism, gender and language within a larger study of 'political correctness' may find Hughes's new book (2010) of some interest. He suggests that 'the fundamental issue is whether linguistic changes affect underlying attitudes or are merely cosmetic' (p. 289), and he tends towards the latter possibility. For an altogether lighter touch, see Kingsley Amis's entry for 'feminism in language' in his guide to modern usage (1997: 67–68).

Part 3

Language Contact and Its Consequences

8
Language and Imperialism

An introductory note

Writing about the breadth of devotion to Gaelic – largely passive, but no doubt genuine enough – Shaw (1977) used this phrase as his title: *'bithidh iad a'moladh na Gàidhlig, ach 'sann anns a'Bheurla'*. This means 'they praise Gaelic all right, but in English'. A generation later, Phillipson (2001) gave a 'conference paper bashing global English, in English' (Li, 2003: 49). According to Li (2003), Phillipson told his conference audience that he was reluctant to call himself a native speaker of English. This strange contortion was apparently meant as a vote in sympathy with learners of the language around the world, learners who have accepted the 'mythology' of the superior linguistic attributes of mother-tongue speakers.

How languages spread

Some initial remarks about the reasons for language spread are in order. Since they are not at all hard to grasp, my brief notes here will detour around a large literature, important elements of which include the following works. Good overviews, first of all, can be found in McArthur, Crystal and Bailey, all of whom are contributors to the collection edited by Mugglestone (2006); see also Tonkin and Reagan's (2003) anthology, Ferguson (2006), Wright (2004) and Wardhaugh (1987). Cooper's (1982) collection remains useful, especially the chapters by Lieberson, Ferguson, Paper, and Cooper himself. For discussions of some specific consequences of contacts between English and other languages – obviously the most important contemporary context involving linguistic spread (and retreat) – see Mair (2003a), Fishman *et al.* (1996),

Anderman and Rogers (2005), Cenoz and Jessner (2000), Harder (2009), Pennycook (1994, 1998), Mazzaferro (2002), Maurais and Morris (2003), Duszak and Okulska (2004), Ricento (2000) and Phillipson (2003b; for insightful comments on Phillipson's thesis, see Davies, 2006; Ammon, 2003). One thing is quite clear, or should be. The spread and scope of English, like those of all previous lingua francas, have virtually nothing to do with any qualities of the language *qua* language. After acknowledging that English has 'certain strengths', Smith (2005) goes on to list its weaknesses: it is difficult to pronounce, it is notoriously irregular in its orthography and grammar, it is both complex and ambiguous, and so on. Since 'the ideal lingua franca should be easy to learn' (p. 58), these difficulties hardly recommend English as the best candidate, and Smith argues that something like Esperanto would be a better universal second language. Since, however, that development is quite unlikely, he suggests that we might at least push for linguistic reforms within English. My point here, of course, is that none of the 'weaknesses' or irregularities of English has the slightest bearing upon its utility and its appeal. Its 'certain strengths' rest upon factors quite apart from its linguistic niceties.

On the particular, and particularly poignant, history of contact between French and English, Calvet's (1987) remarks are instructive. He suggests that contemporary efforts to sustain French in the face of global English pressures have neglected a fundamental fact: cultural arguments cannot prevail when the spread of language is driven by 'un moteur économique'. On the one side, America, science, technology – but also rock music and Coca-Cola. On the other, trench warfare ('guerre des tranchées') fought for the language of a 'communauté culturelle'. 'Ce contraste [Calvet writes] porte la marque de deux analyses du monde, de deux idéologies. Peut-être nous dit-il aussi l'issue finale du conflit' (p. 270). The reason why Calvet's remarks are so interesting is not that they summarise the spread of English and the retreat of French; after all, many others have done the same. It is, rather, because they imply a continuing disdain for anglophone 'ideology'. In the superficial world we are now forced to inhabit, it may have won the day, but only as the vehicle of that crass world and not as a deeper cultural torch-bearer. An interesting, but not wholly surprising reaction from a francophone quarter.

The single most important point here is that language spread has typically been a relatively unconsidered accompaniment of other social processes. Concerted attempts to impose one's language upon subordinate or conquered populations are historically rare, certainly up until the eighteenth-century enlightenment. The Greeks and Romans, for instance, coupled a disdain for subaltern groups with the certainty that obvious and unofficial pressures would ensure movement away from local varieties and towards their own powerful languages. During at least part of their history, indeed, the Romans felt the acquisition of Latin to be 'a privilege to be sought, like citizenship' (Lewis, 1976: 180). Neither the Ottoman nor the Austro-Hungarian rulers cared a great deal about the many languages spoken under their banners. Under the *ancien régime* in pre-revolutionary France there was considerable tolerance as well; political harmony and regular payment of taxes were far more important than any concern with the languages of the peasants. Generally, as Clark observed, 'when a country was governed by a limited ruling class, it did not matter much what language the masses spoke, as long as they kept their place' (Spencer, 1985: 389; see also Sahlins, 1989; Safran, 2008).

Common, then, from remote to fairly recent times was a benign linguistic neglect on the part of rulers, coupled with a belief that their own language was, in any event, superior and would naturally be adopted by anyone of sense. Indeed, as Haugen (1985) remarked, a *laissez-faire* policy was often sufficient insurance for the continuation of language shift. There were exceptions to this but, given linguistically diverse empires, peace and fiscal reliability were the major links between rulers and ruled. This was the situation that changed once a romanticised link between language and nation became strongly forged. Particularly in the century following the French Revolution, language became a rallying-point, something to galvanise the downtrodden, to rally supporters, and to alarm the rulers.

Beyond latter-day links with nationalism and identity – and, of course, not disappearing even when these links were at their most dynamic – language spread has always been closely allied to trade, to military conquest and expansion, and to hopes for religious conversion and proselytism. Some cultures have had more explicit policies here than have others: compare, for instance, the *mission civilisatrice* of the French with the more pragmatic attitude of the English. Still, all imperial powers have, directly or indirectly, made their languages attractive and sometimes necessary to subaltern or colonised groups. Linguistic roads, as well as the *viae publicae*, have always led to Rome. Because of power, and because of opportunities available to those who learn their languages, expansionist regimes often become associated, over time, with a cultural prestige which coexists with the simple trappings of dominance and which often long outlives them. This is a factor in the continued adherence to European languages which exists in former colonial areas (though it is not the only factor nor, perhaps, the most central one).

The reasons for language spread in the first instance need not be those which maintain and further it. English, for example, spread initially through trade and military action, subsequently buttressed by imperialist political unification. Once Britain's dominance declined, however, the language that it had established overseas, most notably in America, took on new and greater global significance, again animated largely by commerce and technological exigencies. Second, the degree to which a language community is open to the use of 'its' variety by others is often important. Consider, again, the differences between the English and the French. The latter have traditionally been much more possessive of their language and, while working hard to bring it to those unfortunate enough not to already speak it, have also been zealous in protecting its 'purity', both within and without *la francophonie*. English, on the other hand, has not been treated in the same guarded way. We see books on the 'New Englishes' and journals like *World Englishes*, but there are no such volumes for French. English is thus becoming truly international in a way that French is not, at least in terms of the acceptance of local varieties, and a language once tainted by imperialism is rapidly becoming 'ours' in many parts of the world; see the useful treatments by McArthur (1998, 2001), Mesthrie and Bhatt (2008) and Melchers and Shaw (2003), all of whose titles reflect a plurality of 'Englishes'; see also Ferguson (2006), Pennycook (1994, 1998).

The growing (and increasingly accepted) 'localisation' of English may, as Sonntag (2003) has noted, actually be reinforced by the spread of English outward from the first two of Kachru's 'circles'. Local adaptations of English around the world may have begun as straightforward results of language contact, accent transfer and so on, but it is not at all unreasonable to think that, faced with the ever-increasing clout of the global language, more self-conscious motivations may have come to contribute to the localisation thrust. Or, as Sonntag has put it in the current jargon of 'hegemony' and 'subalternity': 'globalization pushes forward global English hegemony, but in so doing it creates its own antithesis...politicizes the language issue and..."potentializes" a reaction' (p. 123). See also Ives (2009a).

Another important, and related, point in the linguistic expansion of competing varieties has to do with the position taken by 'third parties'. English and French, once again, provide good examples. Even as the former was growing in international clout (through trade and empire), the latter remained the language of diplomacy, widely endorsed around the world for important conferences, negotiations and treaties. Particularly after the second world war, however, the shifting sands of global policies and alliances – and, of course, the powerful presence of the United States – increasingly favoured English. Today, English is not only the dominant diplomatic vehicle, it also holds sway in the worlds of science and technology, finance, popular culture, and so on. It has consolidated an unprecedented across-the-board superiority.

The contemporary reach of English

Some years ago, Kachru (1985, 1986, 1988) presented his now well-known model of the 'three circles of English'. In the 'inner circle' (Britain, the United States, Canada, Australia and other 'traditional bases' of the language, described by Kachru as the 'norm-providing' areas) we find the 'first-language' varieties. The 'outer circle' includes all those countries, particularly former English colonies, where the language has come to occupy powerful and accepted 'second-language' roles. The varieties of English here are seen as 'norm-developing' ones; this, as we shall see, constitutes an important facet in the story of the spread of the language. There is also an 'expanding circle' of regions (China and Japan figure prominently here) in which the status of English is more 'foreign' than it is in ex-colonial contexts but where, nevertheless, its international utility is widely recognised.[1] This recognition is reflected in the increasing teaching of 'English as a foreign language'. Kachru suggested, by analogy with the other two 'circles', that this third area was a 'norm-dependent' one. This seems reasonable at the moment, but it is of course quite possible to imagine that, over time, we may come to see some 'norm development', too. In many ways, it is the growth of both the status and the use of English in the outermost of the circles that is especially noteworthy and indicative (see Fennell, 2001). Finally, it should be noted that, roughly useful as it may be, Kachru's tripartite division is rather crude and, indeed, since he first wrote on the theme, matters have become much more complicated and intertwined. Citing several authors, Clyne and Sharifian (2008: 5) point out that 'world Englishes have not remained comfortably within their traditional circles'; see also Bruthiaux (2003).

In 1995, I estimated the number of English speakers in all three 'circles' – that is to say, mother-tongue speakers and all others considered together – to be about 1,400 million. This figure, admittedly an upper estimate, placed English ahead of Chinese (with about 1,000 million speakers), and well ahead of Hindi, in third place with 700 million speakers. My estimate was seen in some quarters to be too high, but later analyses have borne it out. Crystal (2003, 2006a: 425) puts the figure at about 1,500 million, which 'suggests that approximately one in four of the world's population are now capable of communicating to a useful level in English'.[2] Actual numbers aside, there can surely be little disagreement with Crystal's (2003: 189) simple observation that 'there has never been a language so widely spread or spoken by so many people as English', nor with Spolsky's (2004) related comment that English is not only stronger than any other contemporary language, but also stronger than any other 'historical' language. International lingua francas have come and gone throughout history, but never 'ones that had shared ownership to the extent of English' (Sussex, 1999: 123). McArthur (2001) provides a number of citations – dated between 1982 and 2000, and emerging from within and without academia – attesting to the global lingua franca status of English. Algeo (2006: 211) has put it this way:

> Three truths are obvious. First, English is now the world's de facto interlanguage. Second, English is consequently influencing more languages than has ever happened before in human history. Third, some people do not like either or both of the preceding truths.

In order to reinforce the point from a number of different disciplinary, ideological and 'national' perspectives, I present various statements taken from a discussion about languages in Europe, a discussion among five very prominent intellectuals that was initiated by Abram de Swaan (holder at the time of the *Chaire européenne* at the Collège de France (Bourdieu *et al.*, 2001). De Swaan himself argues for the adoption of a European 'langue véhiculaire', and 'il va de soi que cette langue est l'anglais' (p. 54). He also maintains, however, that English must be 'appropriated', that it should no longer be in the sole possession of its original speakers. Arguing against some of the pretensions of his colleagues, he writes that 'il faut éviter les énoncés pieux ou illusoires', and reiterates his proposition that English be accepted as the vehicle of 'communication paneuropéenne' (p. 63).[3] Claude Hagège, linguist and polyglot professor at the Collège de France, argues that aiming to appropriate English from the British and the Americans, 'pour devenir nous-mêmes de parfaits anglophones' is 'totalement utopique et injuste, voire extrêmement dangereux' (p. 55). He makes a point that emerges frequently from within *la francophonie*: English is to be resisted, and the French 'coalition' of some fifty countries is the obvious leader. This familiar thesis is extended when Hagège suggests that French action in this regard is not to be seen as for the defence 'du seul français' but, rather, as the spearhead of an attempt to help *all* languages currently menaced by global English. Needless to say, it is a bit rich for the French to attempt this sleight of hand, to try and place themselves within the ranks of the 'small others' threatened by English, when it is perfectly clear that their interests remain quite self-centred (and why not, indeed?) and that their concern for members of the 'coalition' is hardly altruistic. As de Swaan notes, French has already 'dévoré six langues régionales' (p. 63).

Marc Fumaroli is the holder of the sixth *fauteuil* in the *Académie française* and here he expresses his great hope for a continuing multiplicity of languages, reiterates the familiar (and, of course, entirely correct) argument that language is more than a mere instrument of communication, but concludes that 'nous avons perdu la bataille de la communication... l'anglais est devenu la *lingua franca*' (p. 44). (Since, a little later in the discussion, he takes the part of Hagège, it appears that he very much regrets having to admit this.) Pierre Bourdieu, fully aware that the controversial forces of global English were once carried by French, agrees: no longer 'la langue de l'Angleterre mais de l'empire économique et culturel américain... l'anglais est devenu la langue dominante' (p. 45). There is no simple throwing in of the towel, however, for Bourdieu writes also of 'une hégémonie linguistique' to be resisted, not so much for the language itself but for the cultural influences that it tends to convey. He asks if it might prove possible 'd'accepter l'usage de l'anglais sans s'exposer à être anglicisé dans ses structures mentales' (p. 48).

Immanuel Wallerstein is best known for his pioneering studies of the 'world system' and, in his contribution to de Swaan's symposium, suggests that, while English will continue to be dominant in the twenty-first century, it will not be *as* dominant as it is at the moment – not, he adds, 'en raison de son déclin, mais parce que les autres langues reprendront leur place' or, at least will agitate for a return (p. 50). A little later, he restates things more bluntly: 'Je prévois ainsi un déclin relatif de l'anglais. La domination actuelle de l'anglais est une situation transitoire de distribution du pouvoir dans le monde et ne doit pas être envisagée comme étant de toute éternité' (p. 51).

Wallerstein also makes the point that, left to their own devices, people will make pragmatic choices: 'quand il y a une nécessité d'apprendre des langues, les gens les apprennent... s'il y a une atmosphère politique en Europe favorisant l'apprentissage de langues multiples, les gens le feront' (pp. 61–62). De Swaan agrees: 'Au fond, savoir quelles langues parleront les citoyens de l'Europe n'est pas tout à fait une question pour les institutions européennes. Cela relève de leur décision et il n'y a pas besoin d'un énoncé politique' (p. 64).

The imperial thesis

To some commentators, the breadth and depth of the spread of English has suggested something rather more pointed than the 'relatively unconsidered accompaniment of other social processes'. Spolsky (2004) thus refers to a virtual conspiracy theory, making specific reference to the work of Phillipson (1992). Of course, Spolsky does not deny the widespread scope of English, but he describes Phillipson's feeling that this linguistic dominance must represent 'the working out of some conscious policy on the part of governments, civil servants, English-teaching professionals and their elite collaborators and successors in the peripheral [sic] countries' (p. 79). Spolsky spends considerable time in rebutting this case, essentially on the twin grounds that the 'linguicism' (of which linguistic imperialism is taken as the central component) suggested by Phillipson implies efficiencies of language management and planning that are simply not plausible, and that, in any event, the 'accompaniment' scenario is more than sufficient to account for the facts on the ground; see also Spolsky (1996) for a more context-specific version of the argument.

Pennycook (2001) suggests that, for Phillipson, neither 'intentions' nor 'effects' are at the heart of the case; rather, the spread of English is seen as a broader and more structural matter. We are not obliged to think of groups of powerful managers coming together to plot desired courses. We are to think, instead, of the 'hegemonic' ways in which dominant values and standards are promulgated. And what is hegemony? It is an all-pervasive 'body of practices and expectations...a set of meanings and values...dominant ideas that we take for granted' (Phillipson, 1992: 72). There are at least two difficulties here, however. First, Phillipson spends considerable time discussing various institutions and enterprises that are underwritten by officialdom; this does rather suggest some intentionality. Second, without formal intention, the idea of 'linguistic imperialism' rather collapses. It is no doubt true, as he observes, that 'imperialism does not depend for its functioning on wicked people' (p. 72), but it certainly does rest upon a great deal of formal and highly purposeful activity. (Unless, of course, Phillipson agrees with Seeley [1883: 10], who wrote that the British seemed to have assembled their empire 'in a fit of absence of mind'.[4])

So it seems that, after all, the core of the dispute *is* the degree of conscious intention that animates the spread of English. In a rebuttal to Spolsky, Phillipson (2007) assembles a number of quotations from British and American politicians, all to the effect that a desirable global domination is inextricably linked to the ever-increasing spread of English. He cites, for instance, the view of the then managing director of Kissinger Associates, who wrote that it is in the American interest 'to ensure that if the world is moving toward a common language, it be English' (Rothkopf, 1997: 45). It is both clear and entirely unsurprising from a historical point of view that apologists for important political regimes would make such comments. It is even reasonable to assume that they will do whatever they can to encourage certain linguistic outcomes. Davies (1996) agrees with the suggestion that Phillipson makes on the first page of his 1992 book that English has been 'actively promoted' as an instrument of the foreign policy of Britain, the United States and other anglophone countries. There is certainly evidence for this – in the workings of the British Council, for instance, a quasi-governmental organisation established in 1934 to promote British interests through educational, cultural and linguistic initiatives; see also Phillipson (1994). But I think that Davies, a fierce critic of the 'linguistic imperialism' thesis, is actually a little too generous to Phillipson's observation: it is literally accurate, but it over-emphasises the centrality of the linguistic policy thrust to foreign-policy enterprises. Ammon (1996: 263) suggests that, since the spread of English has occurred because of a variety of social, political and economic factors, it 'does not really need additional support through language-spread policy' – which means that, where one actually observes such policy, it can reasonably be termed linguistic imperialism.

Ammon's is a useful observation, to be sure. One could hardly argue for the complete non-existence of specific policies with specific intentions, and one could certainly put such policies under the rubric of imperialism. However, as Spolsky (1998: 77) notes, 'language diffusion efforts of English-speaking countries have tended to be attempts to exploit worldwide desires to learn the language. There has been little need to fan the interest.' In any event, the existence and the force of such policies is as nothing compared to the powerful and multifaceted thrusts that 'push' English around the world and, at the same time, 'pull' it into ever-larger areas. Without the latter, the former would be silly, the work merely of language enthusiasts of one stripe or another. A focus upon such work, a focus upon admitted examples of linguistic imperialism – whose contribution to the bigger picture is relatively minor and, in any event, parasitic on the factors of *real* importance – represents a massive misdirection of effort. In some cases, this misdirection can be attributed to ignorance or naïveté; in others, perhaps, there are rather more wilful ideological issues in play.

Phillipson's 'case' has also been seen by many commentators (not least by those for whom English is not the mother tongue) to downplay the 'agency' of those on the receiving end, to imply that their linguistic choices are naïve and uninformed, to suggest that they are gullible and easily manipulated. This is the substance of a brief comment by Esseili (2008), and it is representative of the views of many in Kachru's 'third circle'; see also Clayton (1999). Brutt-Griffler (2002) provides a more sustained critique. Her essential point is that 'speech communities are not the passive recipients of language policy that they are often implicitly assumed to be' (p. 63). The treatment of (English) linguistic imperialism, then, often

> conceives Western agency alone...the 'colonized peoples' barely appear at all, except insofar as they are oppressed by the irresistible forces of imperialism. Even after they free themselves (or are freed?), they remain subject to ideological control through 'hegemony', a nebulous force by which the former 'masters' continue to impose their will on their former 'subjects'.[5] (pp. 63–64; see also Davies, 1996)

It is also interesting to add here that the ideological tendencies inherent in discussions of linguistic imperialism are not left-leaning enough in even stricter circles. Thus, in her marxist approach to language and politics, Holborow (1999) takes the thesis and its chief architect to task. While she thinks that Phillipson may be on the right track, his simple centre-versus-periphery model is insufficient, and his 'theoretical framework' is thus 'inadequate to explain how national states are themselves enmeshed in global capitalism' (p. 76). Besides, 'linguistic imperialism' is a misleading term, implying that 'language is somehow a decisive tool in the world order' (p. 79). There are deeper forces at work here, of which language is merely a signifier. Perhaps her most stringent criticism – not surprising, emanating as it does from a marxist perspective – is that, in arguing for less 'centre' dominance, the linguistic-imperialism thesis 'leads in nationalist directions' (p. 79). While they have been of historical usefulness in struggles against empire, these directions are essentially underpinned by narrow sentimentalities (Edwards, 1995) and their continued existence can only retard the completion of the socialist struggle.[6]

Crystal has written (2003: x) that the force of English is now so great that 'there is nothing likely to stop its continued spread as a global lingua franca, at least in the foreseeable future'. Issuing from the mouths of native English speakers, such opinions have been criticised as 'triumphalist' (Reagan, 2005). Indeed, in a review of the first edition of Crystal's book, Phillipson (2000: 96) writes that his 'story of globalising English is fundamentally Eurocentric and triumphalist, despite his protestations to the contrary'. There have certainly been many crass expressions along these lines, although Crystal himself is clearly not guilty of anything so unscholarly. Infelicitous phrasing apart, however, it is hard to deny the underlying facts of the matter. A Guyanese lawyer, educator and Commonwealth Secretary-General (from 1975 to 1990), Sir Sridath Ramphal noted in 1996 that English had become the world language:

> It is not the language of imperialism; it is the language we have seen that has evolved out of a history of which we need not always be proud, but whose legacies we must use to good effect...there is no retreat from an English-speaking world. (Crystal, 2003: 26)

'Sonny' Ramphal's pragmatism is widely shared throughout Kachru's 'expanding circle' of English. Are we to see this, too, as 'triumphalism' – or is it something else?[7]

The collection on 'post-imperial' English edited by Fishman *et al.* (1996) brought together contributors writing about contacts between English and indigenous languages in many contexts: in Cuba, Mexico, the Philippines, Puerto Rico, Canada, Kenya, Uganda, South Africa, Sudan, Nigeria, Tanzania, Cameroon, Singapore, Saudi Arabia, Sri Lanka, Malaysia, Israel, India and Papua New Guinea, to be precise. Clearly no fan of 'big' languages, Fishman (1996) summarised these efforts in terms of fears about imperialism, alienation from local cultures and languages, even 'linguacide': 'Almost all of the reports independently prepared by our authors simply do not confirm such fears. Instead, they imply the establishment of a functional division of labor between English and the local vernacular(s)' (p. 637). He goes on to write that the current position and clout of English around the world is not so much a 'reflection of externally imposed hegemony...as it is part of the everyday discourse of various now substantially autonomous societies, all of whom are essentially following their own "commonsense needs and desires"' (p. 639). Fishman is quite clear on this point. It is not a matter – hardly to be suspected in his case, in any event – of 'blaming the victim' or 'identifying with the aggressor'. Rather, it has to do with acknowledging the widespread utility of English and the active agency of those many people for whom it is now 'part and parcel of indigenous daily life'. Along with the force of global English, there is also a 'similarly powerful trend...in the direction of asserting, recognizing and protecting more local languages, traditions and identities...than ever before in world history' (p. 639).

Fishman doesn't explicitly state that this second phenomenon is actually reinforced by the first, but it is a reasonable argument, and has been made by others: a utilitarian acceptance of English that is, at the same time, coupled with an awareness of its prodigious penetrative power, can obviously spur activity on behalf of local varieties. Fishman does observe that both directions are being followed simultaneously in the contexts represented in his edited collection, and, in a rather nice summary, he writes that 'to call the former trend "the imperialism of English" is as antiquated and as erroneous as to call the latter trend "the chauvinism of the losers"' (1996: 639). As might be expected, Phillipson (2000) – generally found to be pulling in the same direction as Fishman – has raised some objection to the latter's remarks. Relevant here is Wright's (2004: 168) observation that the force of Gramscian 'hegemony' is a sufficient explanation for the growth of English 'as the prime medium in all transnational political domains without coercion. The acceptance of English in its lingua franca role is consensual. There is little actual direction or compulsion, except for the dominant groups' refusal to communicate in any other medium.' (Of course, without that last condition, the hegemonic force of the dominant would be somewhat less than it is.)

Continuing with questions of the 'agency' of those who are, in some eyes, on the receiving end of linguistic imperialism, we can find evidence of struggles which – putting aside the conclusions reached – demonstrate that a simple acceptance of external pressures is an unlikely phenomenon. Ngũgĩ wa Thiong'o (1981: 59) was scathing in his condemnation of some African government offices in which 'the ability to speak the Queen's English...is the sole criterion for employment and promotion'. As for writers like himself, he is clear that only African languages should be used. He is not only making a nationalist and 'anti-imperialist' assertion here, for he goes on suggest very practical advantages:

> I have no doubt that writing in an African language is as commercially viable as writing in any language. Market pressures might even have the added advantage of forcing those who express themselves in African languages to strive for local relevance...because no peasant or worker is going to buy novels, plays or books of poetry that are totally irrelevant to his situation. (Ngũgĩ wa Thiong'o, 1985: 153)

As for himself, Ngũgĩ wa Thiong'o (1986, 1993) describes in several powerful essays his decision to write in Gĩkũyũ rather than English, a decision that underpins his many impassioned pleas for the linguistic and cultural 'decolonising' of the African mind. For him, 'African literature can only be written in African languages' (1986: 27; incidentally, he rejects the argument that European varieties have *become* African ones, although, as Mair [2003b] notes, he accepts pidgins and creoles). Ngũgĩ wa Thiong'o is of course particularly concerned with 'decolonisation' in literary and dramatic contexts, but he touches upon political ones as well. He mentions Léopold Senghor, who admitted that French had been forced upon him but who yet remained 'lyrical in his subservience' to the language (p. 19), as well as Hastings Banda, who created an élite English-language academy in Malawi, expressly designed to encourage able students to be sent to 'universities like Harvard, Chicago, Oxford, Cambridge and Edinburgh' (p. 19); all the teachers were recruited from Britain.

An equally prominent African writer, Chinua Achebe, took an opposite tack, although not without misgivings:

> Is it right that a man should abandon his mother tongue for someone else's? It looks like a dreadful betrayal and produces a guilty feeling. But for me there is no other choice. I have been given the language and I intend to use it.[8] (Achebe, 1975)

Achebe goes on to suggest that parallel literatures in 'local' languages and in 'big' ones might be a solution here; another might be the emergence of 'new Englishes', those localised variants that are, indeed, becoming more and more common around the world.

Mair (2003b: xvii) argues that each of these two 'strategies' can be understood as valid postcolonial postures. He suggests that, by rejecting the colonial language altogether as a literary vehicle, Ngũgĩ wa Thiong'o is making 'the superficially safe bet' against external cultural influence. Perhaps, however, he underestimates the possibility that 'the very same oppressive discursive practices might quickly reconstitute themselves in an indigenous language' if social power structures are unchanged. And besides, Mair adds, English has 'shown itself able to accommodate African experience' (p. xviii). Achebe's adoption of English, on the other hand, 'looks like the riskier course' to Mair: take the language, use it, and 'write back' with it. In any event, we see once again that a focus upon language alone is likely to miss bigger and more important factors of economic, social and cultural power. Indeed, stressing linguistic forms of 'imperialism', and resistance to them, may be akin to shooting the messenger.[9]

It is worth pointing out here, by the way, that the English-speaking countries are hardly alone in setting up institutions to promote themselves: consider the *Alliance française*, established in 1883 as the bluntly named *Association nationale pour la propagation de la langue française dans les colonies et à l'étranger*; or the *Instituto Camões*, founded in 1992 but based upon much earlier initiatives; or the *Società Dante Alighieri* (1889); or the more recent (1951) *Goethe-Institut*. This is only a sample of the sorts of councils and institutes that many countries have set up to promote their languages, cultures and commercial interests. Ammon (1996) observes that *all* countries try to spread their languages. If they could emulate the success and the scope of English, they would certainly do so. Indeed, two of his edited collections (Ammon, 1994; Ammon and Kleinedam, 1992) outline the efforts of France, Germany, Spain, Portugal, Brazil, Japan, Russia, Italy and other countries (including some that were recently colonies) in this regard.

Above all, we should remember that no institutional efforts – even if we were to concede that they were both active and central components of official policy – would achieve much success unless they were moving in the same direction as much broader currents. In fact, those broader linguistic currents don't really require such formal institutional services at all. Compare, for example, the poor results achieved by the *Academie française* on behalf of the defence of the French language in the face of a global English penetration that seems to have made great progress with virtually no formal assistance: it certainly lacks the centuries-old influence of a well-endowed academy which has, in addition, spawned any number of more specialised bodies and, since 1970, has had its basic remit strongly reinforced by the *Organisation internationale de la francophonie*, a very well-funded 'Commonwealth' of dozens of member-countries collectively concerned to promote French language and culture.

It is neither reasonable nor necessary to conclude that attention to language in any sort of free-standing way has ever figured largely on the bureaucratic agenda; see also Saraceni's apt comment (2008) and Pennycook's (1994, 2001) more broadly considered treatment. It is questionable whether or not it is important to try and combat the spread of English, but it is quite unreasonable to expect that any substantial gains can be made if the language is made the central target of action. This is exactly the error that language revivalists repeatedly fall into. Language comes as part of a larger cultural package and, unless one were willing to take radical steps to open and then repack that parcel – a revolutionary step that, even were it thought feasible, most activists shy away from – then meaningful change is unlikely, to say the least.[10]

The expansion of English

Whatever the interpretation or ideological stance, it is clear that the spread and scope of English is immense. In Chapter 9, I shall point out that this has not always been the case and, indeed, its dominance once seemed an extremely improbable development. To conclude here, however – and to foreshadow that fuller discussion – we might recall that English was for a long time a localised variety of little cross-cultural use or prestige; it occupied a subordinate position not unlike that of many varieties that must exist, today, in its considerable shadow. Barber (1993: 234) points out that Shakespeare was writing for a community 'of only a few millions, whose language was not much valued elsewhere in Europe and was unknown to the rest of the world'; see also Fennell (2001). Richard Mulcaster, a grammarian and lexicographer, was a contemporary of Shakespeare and a believer in the potential of English vis-à-vis Latin, at least within England. 'I honour the Latin,' he wrote, 'but I worship the English'. Still, he was obliged to acknowledge that 'our English tung...is of small reatch, it stretcheth no further than this Iland of ours, naie not there ouer all (1582: 256).[11] As Levin (1986: 24) pointed out, 'for centuries there were far more Englishmen learning French than Frenchmen learning English'. And, as Bailey (1991) and Wright (2004) have more generally observed, this means that, for a very long time, the English were by necessity assiduous language learners; see also Chapter 10.

Things change, however. As part of his late sixteenth-century praise of English, Mulcaster suggested that it was the equal of any language in 'pith and plainness'. At exactly the same time, Richard Stanyhurst – historian, lawyer and priest – referred to 'so copious and fluent a language, as oure English tongue is' (1582: 5). A decade on, his great friend, the poet Philip Sidney, wrote of English: 'But for the uttering sweetly and properly the conceits of the mind, which is the end of speech, that hath it equally with any tongue in the world' (1973 [1595]: 140).[12] It is clear enough that perceptions of the value and utility of English went hand-in-hand with expanding fortunes in many other fields of endeavour. This, after all, was the age of Drake and Raleigh, of the establishment of the Newfoundland colony, the first building block of empire. But, more immediately relevant perhaps, it was also the age of Shakespeare, that most eminent of all wordsmiths, and of the King James Bible – surely the most noble literary work ever produced by a committee (the 'high-water mark of English literary prose', as Jeffrey [(1993: 441] put it).

By the eighteenth century, commentators of the stature of Lord Chesterfield and David Hume were writing of the important status of

English and its undoubted spread and expansion (Bailey, 1985, 1991; Crystal, 2003). After reproducing the thoughts of an anonymous mid-eighteenth-century commentator – that 'the affectation of Englishmen who prefer any language to their own' is rapidly disappearing, and that 'in many places abroad…it is become the fashion to study the English Tongue' – Bailey (2006: 346) goes on to note that:

> It would not be long before the old idea that English people were adept at foreign languages had been stood on its head. The new idea, emergent in the middle of the eighteenth century, was that English was destined to be a 'world language' and that those who did not gain it as a birthright would learn it as a necessity.

By mid-nineteenth century, Bailey writes, this 'new idea' became part of the anglophone orthodoxy (with, of course, its unfortunate corollary of 'a stubborn resistance to multilingualism'). The nineteenth century was a time of growing pride in the language, and heightened anticipation of an ever-greater global role.[13] Many relevant citations can be found in Crowley (1989) and Edwards (1995), but a section from Thomas Macaulay's famous 1835 'minute on education' can be taken as representative: 'The claims of our own language it is hardly necessary to recapitulate. It stands pre-eminent even among the languages of the West' (Sharp, 1920: 110).[14] While claims do not always reflect reality, particularly those emanating from within the anglophone community itself, supporting observations from those outside that community can easily be found. Addressing the Royal Academy in Berlin in 1851, Jacob Grimm said that English was now a 'language of the world…destined to reign in future with still more extensive sway over all parts of the world' (Bailey, 2006: 353). Buttressing his case that, by 1900, English was already dominant in world politics and economy, Crystal (2003: 85) cites a comment made by Bismarck who, in 1898, said that 'the fact that the North Americans speak English' was the 'decisive factor in modern history'.

Melchers and Shaw (2003), Spolsky (2004), Mair (2006) and others have suggested that the global expansion of English really escalated after the Second World War. As Mair notes, however, the first great war also provided a turning-point of sorts: in a reversal of long-standing diplomatic practice, the Treaty of Versailles was drafted in English and then translated into French. He also points out that, in terms of scholarly publications in the sciences, medicine and mathematics, English began to draw away from the others during the interwar years, and by the mid-1930s a gap opened between it and French, German and

Russian that has continued to increase. Bollag (2000) has cited the opinion of Eugene Garfield, the founder of the Institute for Scientific Information, which spawned *Current Contents* and the *Science Citation Index*: of the 925,000 scientific articles published in 1997, 95% were in English. But only half of this 95% came from authors in anglophone countries. By the end of the twentieth century, English-language publications accounted for almost 91% of the total; at the same time, publications in the humanities were about 83% English-language.[15]

A possible exception to these trends is found in the place of English in the electronic world. The popular perception is that, as the *New York Times* reported in 1996, the language of the internet is English, and it is true that the first 'major study of language distribution on the Internet' suggested an overwhelming (about 82%) presence of English (Crystal, 2000b; 2000c: 229). Commenting on the situation five years later, Lambert-Drache (2001) was particularly upset that French usage in cyberspace accounted for only 3.5% of the total: English led with 47.6%, followed by Japanese, Chinese, German and Spanish. And why? Her answer was that 'la représentation relativement faible du français reflète la lenteur des pays francophones à entrer dans la société de l'information' (p. 30). She has of course put *la charrue avant les boeufs* here: it is the relative *faiblesse* of French that has led to its diminished place in the electronic ether.

As the web grows, however, more and more languages are represented, and Crystal's own estimate is that something like a quarter of the world's languages now 'have some sort of Internet presence' (2006c: 233). It is particularly notable, although hardly surprising, that many 'small' or endangered languages are found in the ether. It is, of course, important to ask (as Crystal does) just how much *use* is made of sites in languages other than English. Still, his prediction is that 'the character of the Web is going to be increasingly multilingual' (p. 236). His discussion of a new technology that is still in its infancy is admirable, particularly in its frank acknowledgment of rapid developments into as yet uncharted waters (see also Antieau, 2009).

Notes

1. Some recent figures from Japan (National Center for University Entrance Examinations, 2008) are particularly striking. At the secondary-school level, where foreign-language learning generally begins, English is the choice of more than 99% of the pupils. In the foreign-language category of the 2008 national entrance examinations for university admission, English was taken by 497,101 candidates, about 99.9% of the total (497, 971). The

remaining 870 applicants opted for Chinese (460), Korean (142), French (152) and German (116).

2. Crystal's proportion is based on 1999 estimates. Current world population is about 6,800 million but, since English competence may be keeping rough pace, there is no particular reason to think that the one-in-four suggestion requires any great adjustment. For another set of figures, see Ostler (2005), who acknowledges the possibilities and suggests the reasons for large variations in estimates. Graddol (2006) has remarked that, within another five years or so, some two billion people will be learning English: this, in addition to those already possessing some competence.

3. De Swaan's contribution to our discussion will be taken up more fully in Chapter 11.

4. Porter (2004: 169) notes that Seeley's point was 'uncannily' anticipated in an anonymous contribution to the *Westminster Review* (1870); the writer was in fact John Robinson, who became the first Prime Minister of Natal, in 1893.

   A more complete version of Seeley's famous observation is this: 'we seem, as it were, to have conquered and peopled half the world in a fit of absence of mind' (1883: 10). And a still fuller contextualisation (in the preceding sentence) describes the empire as 'this mighty phenomenon of the diffusion of our race and the expansion of our state'. Seeley's comment was a product of sarcasm and disappointment, part of his criticism of the neglect or marginalisation of imperial history in books and classrooms (Porter, 2004).

   If I may be permitted a digression from a digression: Seeley writes, on the first page of his book that, while the fortunes of England continue to grow and develop, other peoples have seen their former greatness disappear. For countries like Holland and Sweden, then, history might 'pardonably' be seen 'as in a manner wound up' (p. 5). Shades of Francis Fukuyama (1992)....

5. As Hall (2003) points out, in a detailed review of Brutt-Griffler's book, both Pennycook (1994) and Canagarajah (1999b) have provided nuanced treatments of the 'linguistic imperialism' thesis, more convincing than what he styles the 'rather caricatural aspect of a larger story' (p. 446) represented by Phillipson's (1992) argument. Hall suggests that, on occasion at least, Brutt-Griffler 'slips into a simple reversal of Phillipson's image' (p. 446). It may indeed be the case that she has sometimes been blunter than necessary, although she would no doubt argue that strong expressions are needed to combat a widely cited, but inaccurate, thesis. Phillipson's (2003a) reaction to Brutt-Griffler's work is worth reading, if only for his opening statement: 'my wife and fellow critical scholar, Tove Skutnabb-Kangas, warned me, when I wrote *Linguistic Imperialism* (1992), that I would need to develop a thick skin. Joshua Fishman wisely advised me that it is preferable to be demonised rather than ignored' (p. 324).

6. There is a lengthy, and extremely satisfying review of Holborow's book by Joseph (2001). It is worth citing at some length here:

   > Chapter Three takes on the 'linguistic imperialism' thesis of Phillipson (1992), targeting all its blatant flaws on mostly the same grounds non-Marxist critics have raised against it (see Davies, 1996). Phillipson fancies himself the opponent of an international 'hegemonic' structure, and one meets less independent-thinking Marxists than Holborow who assume it is their duty to stand in solidarity against this supposed conspiracy by

the 'centre' to wipe out other cultures and languages...But Holborow is having none of it, because 'Phillipson's centre–periphery, north–south categorization...locks him into an anti-imperialist strategy of nationalism and the promotion of national languages' (p. 77) and nationalism is of course the traditional obstacle to social class solidarity. (p. 285) Well, Joseph is certainly no fan of Phillipson – but he has his doubts about Holborow, too. 'The intellectual perversity of Holborow's Marxism lies in its deep materialist scepticism toward all categories and constructs except one, social class, for which it demands a credulity of religious proportions' (p. 286).

There is a briefer but no less interesting review of Holborow's book that is worth mentioning here. Scollon (2001: 323) remarks that 'Fairclough and Tannen, Bernstein and Saussure, Crystal and Kress, the Milroys and Foucault, Kachru and the British Council, Hume and Pennycook, Conrad and Fishman, Pinker and Chomsky, Cheshire and Trudgill, Holmes and Schiffrin, Lakoff and Labov, and a rather lengthy roster of others' are all united by the scorn in which their works are held by Holborow. None of them has paid sufficient attention, it seems, to Voloshinov, to Vygotsky or, most importantly, to Marx'n'Engels (as Joseph styles the socialist double-act: p. 284).

Holborow's powerful demolition job reminds me of a remark made by Alan Ryan (1993), in his review of a book about the inadequacies of contemporary American culture (Hughes, 1993). He wrote that 'Hughes's notion of defending a middle-of-the-road view is to settle a squadron of heavy tanks firmly across the central reservation and order rapid fire on both carriageways'.

7. The maligned British Council actually underwrote a study (Graddol, 1997) that its author described as 'neither triumphalist nor alarmist' (p. 3), and in which the future of English is seen as a little less all-enveloping than some others have forecast. Graddol suggests that the current 'near-monopoly' of English will give way to an 'oligopoly' involving other 'big' languages: Chinese, Hindi, Spanish and Arabic. Phillipson (2000) actually praises both Graddol and the British Council for the 'open, critical spirit' of the work, although he also writes that it 'reflects an unresolved tension between the urge to be scientifically sound and to produce a blueprint for an organization whose purpose it is to maximize the use of English' (p. 103).

8. This passage is also reproduced by Ngũgĩ wa Thiong'o (1986: 27), who obviously finds Achebe's conclusion a morally untenable one. See the useful discussion of these two writers by Mair (2003b).

9. Whatever one's ideological 'take' on the struggles of Achebe, Ngũgĩ wa Thiong'o and the many others like them, it is clear that they *are* struggles – and that, even if one rejects, as I obviously do, the crass linguistic-imperialism thesis, 'global English' remains an external force of great concern to many people. Roughly speaking, the degree and level of its influence exist in an inverse relationship with the strength of the languages and cultures with which it comes into contact. But it would of course be wrong to discount that influence when 'bigger' competitors enter the lists. I have scholarly colleagues in Québec, for example, who must repeatedly choose between French and English publication of their work. Some opt for the former, on nationalist grounds; some choose English for pragmatic reasons having to do with the breadth of potential readership; and some, indeed, essay various

combinations. All, however, are faced with decisions that do not affect anglophones. See also the collection edited by Carli and Ammon (2007), particularly the chapter by Flowerdew; de Swaan (1998b); and the discussion in Chapter 11.

10. In a terminological wrangle, Phillipson (2007: 379) also takes Spolsky to task for suggesting that he (Phillipson) defines linguicism as 'the intentional destruction of a powerless language by a dominant one'. This is certainly what Spolsky wrote (2004: 79) and it may well be that Phillipson never produced exactly that phrase. But the definition that Phillipson *does* endorse is this: 'ideologies, structures and practices which are used to legitimate, effectuate and reproduce an unequal division of power and resources (both material and non-material) between groups which are defined on the basis of language (on the basis of their mother tongues)' (p. 379).

    If we cut through this swollen phrasing, it is surely not unfair to suggest that 'practices' intended to produce inequalities of power are not a million miles away from Spolsky's balder statement, especially if we (reasonably, surely) imagine that such 'practices' are seen as ongoing and, therefore, cumulative.

    The debate about 'linguistic imperialism' has proved to be a highly contentious and long-running one, but I cannot detain readers with it any longer here – beyond pointing to Davies's (1996) review essay, Phillipson's (1997) rejoinder, Davies's final note of reply (1997), and the interchange of views found with Phillipson (2008).

11. Mencken (1999 [1935]: 86) cited Mulcaster, as well as the late sixteenth-century status of English, which, he suggested, 'stood fifth among the European languages, with French, German, Italian and Spanish ahead of it'.

12. Brennan (2003) provides some further illustrative citations here; see also Crowley (1989, 1991).

13. And not just in language, of course. The mid- to late-Victorian period was a time of unparallelled colonial expansion, based upon aspirations and policies that went virtually unquestioned in the corridors of English power and influence. It is then, after all, that Cecil Rhodes allegedly claimed that to be an Englishman was to have won first prize in the lottery of life. There's 'triumphalism' for you, there's the arrogant face of imperialism.

14. Rahman (1996) contextualises Macaulay's observations within the larger nineteenth-century debate about the best way – the best *linguistic* way – to maintain and expand British colonial power in India. The 'Orientalists' who believed in the value of indigenous languages were of course opposed to Macaulay's 'Anglicist' views. There were divergent opinions, too, among Indians themselves.

15. In presenting these data, Mair (2006) draws upon the more detailed work of Tsunoda (1983), Ammon (1998) and Mühleisen (2003); see also Ammon (1996), and the extremely useful collections edited by Ammon (2001) and Carli and Ammon (2007).

9
No Good Past Dover

An introductory note

Meeting a few years ago in Phoenix, a conference of the Association of Departments of Foreign Languages (part of the Modern Language Association) had as its theme the future of language teaching and learning. The participants were all department heads or administrators and, instead of papers on substantive scholarly topics, almost all the presentations were practical pieces, 'how-to' sessions and the like. Two main threads ran through the meetings. First of all, there was much lamentation over the sorry state of the language-teaching discipline, apparently trapped in a circle where declining enrolments mean fewer resources, where weakened resources mean decreased academic clout and respect. Second, it was easy to see the relative superiority of those involved in teaching Spanish language and culture. The Hispanicists were clearly the nuclear physicists of the discipline: they knew it and so did all their lesser brethren.

This chapter has grown out of remarks I made at that Phoenix conference, and, while their central context is thus American, the issues are of wider concern. At more or less the same time in Britain, for instance, the Minister of Education was announcing an 'awards programme' meant to encourage language teaching and learning, designed to heighten the motivation of language learners. It is of course interesting to consider why such programmes suggest themselves at all, and why they arise when they do. Further, the Minister's politically correct remarks on language learning in a diverse world imply something of the power behind an opposite thrust – the recognition of diversity as simply more fuel for the English juggernaut:

> The Government wholeheartedly supports the Europe-wide drive to stimulate language learning. It is increasingly important in a world

of international trade, commerce, advanced communication and tourism, where people and nations are interdependent. (Blackstone, 2000: 429)

The tensions that exist in a world increasingly dominated by English, but also a world of continuing linguistic and cultural diversity – these are the important matters which, perhaps unwittingly, the Minister touched upon in her rather formulaic remarks.

English in the world

These are difficult times for some languages – the small ones, the stateless ones, those of 'lesser-used' or minority status, and so on. A recent conference exchange is illustrative here:

> 'What do you think of Gaelic now – be honest!'
> 'Well, it's a language that may still do you some good in the Highlands and Islands, maybe still in parts of Cape Breton, but outside those little areas, it isn't going to take you very far...'
> 'Isn't it used in any other settings, then?'
> 'No, it's simple, really – no one to speak it with. Who did you have in mind?'
> 'Maybe Scots abroad...?'
> 'Listen, outside Scotland, Gaelic speakers hardly use the language at all, even amongst themselves.'
> 'OK, but what d'you think of the language itself – is it a good sort of language, or what?'
> 'Actually, I'm not too keen on it, as a language *per se*. It has become pretty bastardised, you know, bit of a mixture really – different dialects, English borrowings...'

This conversation surely has a familiar ring to it: a 'small' language struggling against larger forces, a variety increasingly confined geographically and socially, a medium whose intrinsic status (however illogically, from a linguist's point of view) is often felt to be degraded and impure. And, if it proves difficult to maintain such a language in something like its native state, what attraction does it possess for language learners elsewhere? Why would anyone study it at school or university? There is an elementary catch-22 here: how can you induce the learning of a language when its community of use is negligible, but how will the latter ever grow unless more join it? Who will, in due course, become the teachers of the language? The dreary downward drift seems fated to continue: a native community which is small, and a 'secondary' community which may become the preserve of a tiny band of consciously committed enthusiasts.

In fact, I have been deceitful here. The exchange about Scots Gaelic never took place. It is, however, modelled on this earlier passage:

'What thinke you of this English tongue, tel me, I pray you?'
'It is a language that wyl do you good in England, but passe Douer, it is woorth nothing.'
'It is not vsed then in other countreyes?'
'No sir, with whom wyl you that they speake?'
'With English marchants.'
'English marchantes, when they are out of England, it liketh them not, and they doo not speake it.'
'But yet what thinke you of the speech, is it gallant and gentle, or els contrary?'
'Certis if you wyl beleeue me, it doth not like me at al, because it is a language confused, bepeesed with many tongues: it taketh many words of the latine, & mo from the French, & mo from the Italian, and many mo from the Duitch...'. (Yates, 1934: 32)

This passage is taken from John Florio's *Firste Fruites*: published in 1578, it is a textbook and manual for the teaching of Italian to English gentlemen. The fruits 'yeelde familiar speech, merie Prouerbes, wittie Sentences, and golden sayings. Also a perfect Induction to the Italian, and English tongues.... The like heretofore, neuer by any man published' (as Florio modestly pointed out in his fuller title). Florio was an exceedingly interesting character, and he played several different roles, language teacher and translator among them. He provided, for instance, an engaging if rather loose translation of Montaigne's *Essays*, a translation read and used by Shakespeare. (His father, Michelangelo Florio, had translated the children's catechism of Cranmer. Published in 1553, this was the first Italian-language book printed in England.) In Florio's time (*c*.1553–1625), French, Italian and Spanish were the powerful 'international' varieties, widely studied in Tudor and Stuart England. Italian challenged the supremacy of French in both the cultural and the commercial worlds, and many prominent Elizabethans learned it. Indeed, the queen herself was a student, along with luminaries like Edmund Spenser and the Earl of Southampton, Henry Wriothesly – a literary patron to Florio and, more famously, to Shakespeare (Acheson, 1920; Yates, 1934).[1]

It is instructive to consider the position of English after the Norman conquest. Conquerors, after all, bring dominant languages with them, and prolonged occupation often involves linguistic assimilation. Of course, the much more pronounced social stratification of earlier centuries was actually a blessing in terms of the preservation of vernaculars. No one of any status – or who hoped to gain some – cared very much what the peasants spoke. Within the Norman hierarchy, then, French was both the invading language and the prestigious medium to be learned. As Robert of Gloucester wrote in his thirteenth-century history: 'Vor bote a man conne Frenss me telþ of him lute, Ac lowe men holdeþ to Engliss'. That is to say, 'unless a man knows French, people make little account of him' (Barber, 1993: 136). The second line tells us that 'low men keep to English'. While recent commentators (e.g. Nevalainen and Tieken-Boon van Ostade, 2006; Townend, 2006) suggest that, within a century or so of the conquest, bilingualism was quite common, it was of course the French–English bilingualism of the middle and upper classes. The lower orders spoke only English. Nonetheless, their language obviously persisted, its continuing presence resting upon three important factors: a long written and spoken history among a large number of people; the increasingly intimate relationships linking the English with the Normans; and the early thirteenth-century military reversals on the continent that isolated the 'Anglo-Normans' in their new island home.

When the Norman conquest carried through to Ireland, in the twelfth century, it took with it French, of course, but also English. It found there an Irish language that had been secure for centuries, which had provided all of Europe with the only vernacular seen as suitable for education and literature, and which possessed considerable assimilative power over newcomers. With the coming of the Normans, a process of change certainly began, but it was neither rapid nor extensive. Only in towns within the Pale (roughly, the east coast, including Dublin) did French and English establish themselves. The Pale itself tended to shrink as the Gaelicising of the new settlers continued; they became, as the old phrase put it, *Hiberniores ipsis Hibernis*: more Irish than the Irish themselves. Telling articles of legislation, the Statutes of Kilkenny, were passed in 1366, telling because the intent behind them was to try and keep English settlers from adopting Irish and Irish ways. The laws were not very effective. By 1600, English flourished only within a diminished Pale and in one or two rural enclaves.

Further developments would soon occur, of course, but one point is this: as late as the early seventeenth century, very few people would have predicted global status for English, or anything like it. As implied in the previous chapter, it was a rather 'small' language, with four or five million speakers, well back in the linguistic sweepstakes. A related point: the fortunes of language rise and fall, and the variety that nowadays wields international influence on a scale never before seen was once of very secondary importance and restricted utility. On the other hand, consider what has become of Norman French and Irish.

At the moment, it is perhaps particularly easy to forget historical patterns, dynamics and vicissitudes, not only because of the current dominance of English, but also because we live in an age when historical knowledge, and the contextualisation of current events to which its application must inevitably lead, are commodities of little priority. It is sometimes imagined, then, that the global power of English represents a new phenomenon. We are actually seeing, however, only the most recent manifestation of a very old one, although the strength and scope of English are arguably greater than those possessed by earlier 'world' languages: the difference is one of degree rather than of principle.[2] Of course, I don't mean to argue that all this somehow lessens the impact of English upon other varieties; I simply want to suggest that social and linguistic struggles to resist the encroachments of English are not battles against demons never seen before. I would also not wish to belittle the anxieties felt by those whose languages and cultures are under threat. But all these things have happened before, and will no doubt happen again: it is an old play we are looking at here, a play whose plot endures while the cast changes – some eternal *Mousetrap*.

A related point is that the rise and dominance of English around the world have uniquely profited from historical circumstance. Consider the fate of other great *lingua francas* – Greek and Latin, for example. They must have seemed imperishable, yet they faded away with the declining power of their speakers. Languages of 'wider communication', after all, have no special linguistic capabilities to recommend them; they are simply the varieties of those who have power and prestige. It seems necessary to repeat this truism quite frequently – and not merely for the benefit of those languishing in ignorance outside the academy. Eoyang (1999: 27) spoke for many within the cloister when he argued that its current linguistic dominance

lies very simply in the fact that English is more responsive than any other language to the growing knowledge base that is the hallmark of these postmodern times. It is this ability to be eclectically open to new thoughts, new ideas, new concepts that has predisposed English to be the major medium of modern communication.

Now, it is undoubtedly the case that, more than (some) other languages, English has been (or, at least, has become) an open and 'loose' medium, ready to take what was needed from other varieties, to be flexible in the face of modern necessity, and so on – and equally, we should note, relatively unconcerned with local dialectal variations and, indeed, with the spawning of regional 'Englishes'. These are tolerances more available to the strong than to the weak, and it is an egregious mistake to imagine that 'openness' accounts for dominance. The truth lies in the other direction, and is rather more brutal. (I remind the reader here of the little discussion, ending with a reference to Mae West, presented in Chapter 3.)

Historical precedent would have suggested that the decline of British power meant the decline of English. But, as we all know, power shifted to the other side of the western ocean, and so English received a renewed lease on life. Less often thought about, perhaps, is what that current broad and American-backed presence of English means for the continuity of the language. We hear more and more, for example, about eastern economies, about the greatly increased presence of China and India, about the countries of the 'Pacific Rim' whose collective power may prove the replacement to American dominance. Maybe so, maybe not. In any event, however, it is a good bet that the *lingua franca* will probably continue to be the English that has already penetrated these regions. We have, then, the historically odd situation that regional power and prestige may *not* imply the necessity for others to know that region's language(s). English receives further injections of life: first from America and then from a wider world in which it has become widely accepted (at least as an instrumental necessity). The late Robert Burchfield, editor of the *Oxford English Dictionary*, and consultant to the excellent television series, *The Story of English* (McCrum et al., 1986), argued that the vibrancy and spread of English – including the development of many regional Englishes, something which he likened, with some misgivings, to the gradual transformation of Latin into mutually unintelligible European languages (see McCrum, 1986) – were likely to mean continued life 'for many centuries to come' (1987: 173). Indeed, he once made the rather more pointed remark that English dominance seems assured well into the future, unless something truly cataclysmic (Burchfield mentioned a 'nuclear winter') were to occur. In that case, all other bets would be off, anyway. It is interesting that only such an extreme event would suggest itself, to such an important scholar, as appropriate in the discussion of possible limitations to the spread and importance of English.[3]

While the contemporary force of English arises from sources other than 'openness', the latter quality is not insignificant. The current strength of the language makes a relaxed stance easy: as noted, a secure and powerful medium need not worry very much about borrowings and hybrids, about localisations and colloquialisms, about purism and prescriptivism. But even if we go back to periods in which English was *not* dominant, back (say) to the sixteenth and seventeenth centuries, when 'standard' national languages were beginning to emerge in Europe, we find English linguistic reflexes to be unlike those elsewhere. The most notable example is the lack of a language academy – to help standardise, yes, but usually also to protect, to keep out foreign influence, to manage neologisms, and so on. A generation ago, Quirk (1982) pointed to an 'Anglo-Saxon' aversion to 'linguistic engineering', a disdain for language academies and their purposes; he felt that these goals were 'fundamentally alien' to English speakers' conceptions of language. This is putting things too strongly, but it is certainly noteworthy that the United Kingdom and the United States are virtually the only countries not to have (or have had) formal bodies charged with maintaining linguistic standards. Given the obvious need for standardisation (even in English), it is also interesting to realise that both countries essentially appointed one-man academies. The great lexicographers, Samuel Johnson and Noah Webster, produced dictionaries that became the arbiters of English standards and of 'correctness' on both sides of the Atlantic; see also Chapter 6.[4]

The single most interesting aspect of English 'openness' is the degree of its localisation around the world, together with the attitudes attaching to this localisation. Consider the recent history of English compared with French, in this regard. The latter has seen its influence shrink dramatically, and it is unsurprising that the current stance is often one of protection and defence. Although the basic tendency has been there since the revolution, part of this involves a renewed vigour in what might be called linguistic centralism. French is certainly interested in expansion, in bringing Rivarol's language of clarity to more people, but this is to be accomplished in a guarded and centralist way. English, on the other hand, is much more *de*centralised, less guarded and more expansive. Local varieties achieve considerable status, with Indian English providing the single best example of a developing and accepted indigenised model. Some have predicted an increasing divergence, reminiscent of the birth of the romance languages; of course, there are strong counter-tendencies to this. In any event, a language once tainted by imperialism is rapidly becoming one of 'our' languages in many parts of the world. It is suggestive that we see books devoted to the 'new Englishes', that there are journals called *World Englishes* and *English World-Wide*, and that these have essentially no equivalents in French scholarly circles; see also Chapter 8.

The current world status of English is not an unprecedented phenomenon, nor is it likely to be the last word in global linguistic dominance. On the other hand, political, historical, commercial and technological features have combined to produce a world language that is stronger and more ubiquitous than any of its predecessors. World languages are no respecters of borders, and the case of Irish has already been cited here (in Chapter 6): it is the only Celtic language to have its own country, but that has not made it the most powerful in its family, nor has it managed to bar foreign linguistic influence at the customs-post. Irish is, of course, a minority language, and its subordinate role predates considerably the establishment of the Republic. English, however, also poses threats to more substantial rivals. In 1999, the *Nederlandse Taalunie* sponsored a meeting in Brussels devoted to the status and use of 'national' European languages. The real thrust of the conference was the place of smaller varieties (Dutch, Finnish, Swedish and others) in a Europe increasingly dominated by French, German and, above all, English. About seventy participants from all over the continent (and beyond) provided more evidence than any rational observer could possibly need that being a 'state' variety rather than a 'stateless' one hardly guarantees immunity from external influence.

Lending and borrowing

It is obvious that even 'big' languages now worry about English. On the one hand, its increasing use tends to crowd out other varieties in all sorts of contact situations. On the other, examples need hardly be given of English usages now commonly found *within* other varieties, the very 'borrowings' that continue to exercise national language academies and councils. It is worth noting that these usages do not simply fill *new* needs, or avoid translations for words in common international exchange; they can also push aside already-existing equivalents. It is one thing, then, to refer to *das Web-Design* or *der Cursor,* and perhaps another to employ *der Trend,* or *der Team* or *der Cash-Flow.* Such borrowings reflect the extra-communicative and symbolic appeal of English; or, more specifically, its ability – abetted by its hosts – to burrow its way into other varieties; or, more specifically still, its potency in advertising.

English itself, of course, has hardly been immune to the appeal of other languages, a matter famously commented on by George Orwell.

Since English has the biggest vocabulary of all, he asked why it borrows unnecessary words and expressions: 'where is the sense, for instance, of saying *cul de sac* when you mean blind alley?' (1970 [1944]: 157). He listed other French usages (*chemise, rendezvous*), and writes of the 'needless borrowings' from Latin, and (indicative of the time, of course) of the 'infestation' of German words (*Lebensraum* and *Weltanschauung*, but also *Wehrmacht* and *Panzerdivisionen*). He also criticised the tendency to 'take over American slang phrases without understanding their meaning' (p. 157). And Orwell was not very fond of what he calls 'standard English', either, by which he meant the 'dreary dialect' of officialdom whose worst characteristic is 'its reliance on ready-made phrases – *in due course...explore every avenue...take up the cudgels*' (1970 [1947]: 43). Finally here, he asks why it is 'that most of us never use a word of English origin if we can find a manufactured Greek one?' (1970 [1944]: 157). Why *antirrhinum* rather than *snapdragon*; why *calendula* instead of *marigold*?

Orwell acknowledged that, sometimes, a foreign borrowing is useful – but imports should then be anglicised: 'if we really need the word "café"...it should either be spelled "caffay" or pronounced "cayfe". "Garage" should be pronounced "garridge"' (1970 [1944: 157). In fact, some people *do* say 'garridge' (I do, myself) and one can also hear 'cayfe' (or 'caffey') in more than one anglophone context (admittedly, usually in a humorous or intentionally 'non-standard' way).

As usual, Orwell overstated his case a bit but, also as usual, his remarks are always interesting and illustrative. His attitude towards the work of William Barnes, by the way, is not recorded. The latter, an eighteenth-century teacher and linguist, also railed against foreign borrowings, which make 'our language less perspicuous and simple' (1830: 501; see also 1869). Like Orwell, Barnes also believed that the use of foreign borrowings discriminated against those who know no other languages than English. He suggested alternatives, terms that draw upon Germanic roots: thus, *birdlore* instead of *ornithology*, *speech-craft* rather than *grammar*, *inbringing* instead of *importation*. In providing further detail about Barnes and others who have been similarly motivated (including Orwell), Bailey (1991) reaches back as far as the sixteenth century, citing John Cheke and Thomas Wilson, both of whom were early 'Barnesians'. While bizarre and unnecessary neologisms (Barnes suggested *fore-begged thought-putting* for *hypothetical proposition*) have always attracted derision, Bailey observes that arguments for plain speaking, and against unnecessarily abstract or arcane usage, owe at least something to Barnes. In this regard, the antipathy of Nathaniel Fairfax (1674) to foreign borrowings is particularly noteworthy, as it was part of the emphasis that the 'new science' was placing upon plain and direct language. Bailey does not mention Fairfax, although he does touch upon the 'new science' when he cites the encouragement given by the Royal Society (founded in 1660) to clarity, bluntness and 'native easiness' in English usage.

Members of the Royal Society were almost immediately interested, therefore, in the formation of some institutional body charged with the 'ascertaining' and 'improvement' of English. A little later, Daniel Defoe (1697) proposed something along the lines of the *Académie française*, to

> encourage Polite Learning, to polish and refine the English Tongue, and advance the so much neglected Faculty of Correct Language, to establish Purity and Propriety of Stile, and to purge it from all the Irregular Additions that Ignorance and Affectation have introduc'd.

Jonathan Swift (1712) continued the effort with his famous proposal for countering the 'Infusion of Enthusiastick Jargon' and the 'licentiousness' that had come to corrupt English. He was also exercised by the chaos of spelling, the 'barbarous custom of abbreviating words' (like *rebuk'd* for *rebuked*, or *mob* for *mobile vulgus*), and the adoption of 'modish speech without regard to its propriety'. And, in his equally famous essay on 'polite conversation' (1738), Swift satirised the empty and cliché-ridden discourse of educated society, thus anticipating Orwell's criticisms of 'standard English' by more than two centuries (see also Partridge, 1963).

Thus, in the area of language adoptions, even a cursory historical awareness shows that English has been subject to the same pressures, which have then elicited the same reactions, as other varieties. At the moment, of course, it is more frequently the lender than the borrower. I have in front of me, for instance, three wrappers from Japanese sweets, picked up during a recent visit. Each has an abundance of Japanese-language product information, lists of ingredients, place of manufacture, notes of special offers, and so on; but each *also* displays English messages. We read, for example, that 'Meltykiss Chocolate' is a sweet that 'gently melts in your mouth like a snowflake available only in winter' (original absence of punctuation). Then there is 'Chelsea Yogurt Scotch', advertised on the packet as 'the taste of old Scotland...the candy with traditional Scottish flavour. Please enjoy its superior taste.' The third wrapper encloses 'Men's Pocky Chocolate', described as 'crispy pretzel dipped in dark chocolate for the type of person who enjoys the finer points of life'.

To focus on the oddity of usage here is to miss the point – which is that any such oddity is meaningless. Very few of the purchasers of these sweets will decipher these English words, and they will neither know nor care that yogurt or Chelsea and Scotland are not immediately related in the anglophone mind, nor that 'meltykiss' may have rather unintended connotations, nor that the idea of 'men's chocolate' – particularly if it is 'pocky' – would not be a strong selling point in London or New York. The powerful associations here lie not with the words but with the choice of language itself, and the more or less constant marketing surveys imposed upon the Japanese consumer, as well (of course) as actual buying patterns, reveal the positive consequences of this choice. This symbolic power is not restricted to the written word. Cheshire and Moser (1994: 451–452), for example, discuss Haarmann's (1989) finding that the use of English in Japanese television advertising involves 'no expectation that viewers will understand what they see *or hear*' (my italics). More generally, they point out – as I have done here – that English is working 'not as a system of signs, but as a sign itself'. Onysko (2004) discusses the motivations for anglicisms in German, most of which also stem more or less directly from their social and 'emotive' power. In some contexts, too, the use of English in advertising avoids having to make invidious choices among indigenous varieties; Murray (2003) discusses the Swiss case in this regard. (This last instance is a minor manifestation of the way in which 'big' languages acquire further muscle by acting – bizarre though this may seem to many – as a relatively *neutral* medium in linguistically heterogeneous settings, even those in which such varieties had earlier been colonial impositions.)

Languages fight back, of course. The *Verein Deutsche Sprache*, founded in 1997, regularly inveighs against 'Denglisch', and names particular corrupters or despoilers of the language. A *Sprachhunzer* is cited on a monthly basis, and a *Sprachpanscher* once a year; see also Brookman (2000). The *Academie française* and its Canadian counterpart, the *Office de la langue française*, also devote much time and energy to linguistic resistance efforts. In fact – and quite unsurprisingly, of course – many other official, semi-official and private organisations around the world engage in such activities.

In minority-language contexts where it might be thought that external pressures would create and reinforce internal solidarity, we often observe, instead, internal divisions and dissensions. Internal fissiparous tendencies are one symptom of the larger contact scenario itself and, in that sense, hardly unexpected; nonetheless, they have the effect of weakening resistance efforts, sometimes at the precise moments when they are most important. And, at the level of borrowings, at the disputed frontiers of 'Denglisch', or 'Franglais' or 'Spanglish' or 'Japlish' – thousands of examples of which are available at the touch of a Google key – we often find that external pressures often lead to internal division. While the term 'e-mail' is commonly used in French, the *Academie française* has endorsed *message electronique* (or *mel*, an abbreviated version), and Québec's *Office de la langue française* has plumped for *courriel*. It is perhaps not very surprising, either, that, within a wider language community, the more threatened sectors will tend to be the most linguistically watchful. A few years ago, Canada's sovereigntist *Parti Québécois* accused France of not being French enough, of not sufficiently guarding the linguistic barriers, when it was announced that Air France pilots would now speak English to air-traffic controllers in Paris. This is in line with international practice, in which English is the norm in aviation, but French has been allowed in Québec airspace for twenty years, and its place there became of considerable symbolic importance. French pilots who find themselves in difficulty may inform ground control that they are about to commence *le fuel dumping*, but their *Québécois* counterparts are more likely to refer to *délestage* (Séguin, 2000). (A note of interest here: despite the international endorsement of English as the language of the skies, it is certainly the case that some Air France pilots speak French to air-traffic controllers in France; similar 'local' usages occur quite widely elsewhere, too.)

The language of air-traffic control in Québec has been an important issue, more important than many language scholars realise, and more broadly relevant than it first might seem. Until 1974, English was the only language legally permitted in air-traffic control in Canada. At that time, attempts were made by francophone pilots and controllers to use French in Québec, attempts that were in fact supported by Ottawa. The largely anglophone air-traffic controllers' union protested and, in 1976, pilots went on strike in support of them. A predictable split of sympathies between the French- and English-Canadian publics ensued. By the end of the decade, however, and following the recommendations of an enquiry commission, bilingualism in aviation was given a green light by government.

Borins (1983) provides a thorough account. His third chapter presents the general arguments for and against bilingual air-traffic control, and the ninth and tenth discuss the findings and conclusions of the commission of enquiry. The commissioners found that 45 countries used English alone, while 83 others used more than one language in air-traffic control. They then examined the data relating to more than 17,000 aviation accidents that had occurred, world-wide, over a twenty-year period. They found that only one – 'a mid-air collision in 1960 over Rio de Janeiro between a United States aircraft being controlled in English and a Brazilian aircraft being controlled in Portuguese' – might perhaps have been prevented by a one-language policy (p. 185). Unsurprisingly, the commissioners wrote of their 'abiding conviction that there is nothing inherently dangerous in bilingual air traffic control' (p. 186).

So much for the 'proximate facts' of the case. The greater value of Borins's comprehensive treatment (at least for our purposes here) goes well beyond matters of safety in the skies. The air-traffic-language controversy was also sharply illustrative of French–English relations in Canada. In fact, all of the five major themes outlined at the beginning of Borins's book deal with these relations and the various 'players' involved in patterns of linguistic and cultural contact and conflict. The author's summary returns to the 'ultimate theme', first mentioned in the introduction – 'the viability of Canada as a nation' (p. 3) – by repeating that the central emphasis of the book has been 'conflict and compromise between English and French Canadians', an exploration of the coexistence of two language groups within one state (p. 243). This last is an echo of Lord Durham's famous observation about French–English relations in British North America. 'I expected to find,' he wrote in his 1839 report, 'a contest between a government and a people; I found two nations warring in the bosom of a single state' (Craig, 1963: 23); see also Chapter 5.

The implications of world English for language teaching and learning

In the next chapter, I shall present some facts and figures bearing importantly on the subject of this section. I anticipate some of them here only in a general sense, largely focussing upon the contemporary American scene.

As I implied in an earlier chapter (and as the material to follow will further attest), it is clear that foreign-language competence among anglophones has become more and more associated with formal educational instruction, and less driven by mundane necessity. Of course, this is a very general statement, and there are all sorts of exceptions to it. Nonetheless, the correlation between the social, political and economic dominance of the English-speaking world and the decline in its linguistic repertoire means that language learning becomes more a matter of the classroom than of the street. And this has clear implications for both students and teachers.

It is commonly accepted that favourable attitudes and positive motivations are central to successful second-language learning, and there is a very large literature on this subject (see earlier chapters here; see also Noels and Clément, 1998). The importance of favourable attitudes, however, would appear to vary inversely with real linguistic necessity. Historically, most changes in language-use patterns owe much more to socioeconomic and political pressures than they do to attitudes. Some have suggested, however, that one sort of motivation may play a part here. That mid-nineteenth-century Irishman whom I cited in Chapter 3, for instance, could well have loathed English and what it represented, while still realising the mundane necessity to change. This sort of *instrumental* motivation is, as I said, a grudging quantity, and quite unlike what has been termed an *integrative* one, an impulse based upon genuine interest in another group and its language, perhaps involving a desire to move towards that group in some sense. There might also be a useful distinction to be drawn here between *favourable* and *positive* attitudes (to cite the adjectives I used above). To return to the Irish example in Chapter 3, and to repeat myself here, one could say that the language attitudes towards English were typically instrumental (and positive, in the sense of commitment or emphasis) but not necessarily integrative or favourable. Of course, attempting to separate instrumentality from 'integrativeness' may prove, in practice, to be difficult and, as well, the relationship between the two no doubt alters over the course of language shift. But there *is* a distinction between, say, the English needed by Japanese engineers and that sought by Japanese professors of American literature; the difference is one of depth of fluency, to be sure, but it goes beyond that (see Edwards, 1985, 1995).

The language teaching of greatest interest often goes beyond language training; although it must build upon that, and although some students are primarily interested in acquiring what we could now call an instrumental fluency. It has been argued that, since attitudes (favourable ones, at least) are often of little consequence in real-life situations of language contact and shift, they are trivial elsewhere, too. My point (again, see the discussion in Chapter 3) is simply that attitudes may assume *greater* importance in many teaching settings. That is, if the context is *not* perceived to be very pertinent in any immediate or personal way, if the participant is *not* there out of real, mundane necessity, then attitudes may make a real difference. In this way, and leaving ability out of the equation, of course, language classes may become just like all others.

This does not always sit very well with language teachers, many of whom (most, perhaps) are concerned to tell the students how *different* their classes are from many of the others. Unlike history, or botany, or political science, the study of foreign languages is not usually presented as an end in itself, but rather as the acquisition of the key needed to enter another literature, another culture. The distinction is not, of course, absolute: on the one hand, it is possible to learn another language purely for its intrinsic interest; on the other, meaningful work in all disciplines requires the acquisition of specialised tools: some sort of apprenticeship is involved. But there is certainly a difference of degree, if nothing else, and this is clearly seen when the work of those in modern-language departments is compared to that of their colleagues elsewhere in the academy.

At other times, in other settings, instrumental motivations could be taken more for granted. As well, the inequalities in power and prestige that have usually given birth to these motivations have often reinforced broader and more 'integrative' tendencies. The commercial necessity which once led to the study of Italian existed most immediately because of the superior position of Italian business and finance, but there was an inexorably attractive dominance in other spheres, too. Mundane motivation may well have become, then, something less restricted. Beyond all this there was, until quite recently, a virtually unquestioned acceptance of the view that education involved languages. In fact, the matter of 'instrumentality' *tout court* hardly arose. An educated person knew some literature, some history, some geography – and acquired some level of foreign-language competence. Languages were simply part of the marrow of learning.

However, in societies that often seem to emphasise narrow and immediately applicable learning, in educational systems that are increasingly 'corporatised' and where research and teaching assessment exercises regularly test teachers for 'relevance', 'impact' and so on, in instantaneous electronic access points that lead students to confuse information with knowledge, and in a world made more and more safe for anglophones – in all these contexts, foreign-language learning and all its ramifications have lost the immediacy they once possessed. Not only does instrumental appeal lessen, but the more intangible and more profound attractions to which instrumentality can lead and with which it is entwined inevitably decline. These are the social constraints within which much contemporary teaching and learning occur, and they tend to dwarf more specific settings. A few years ago, Swaffar (1999: 10–11) made some suggestions 'to help foreign language departments assume command of their destinies' (a little grandiose, no?), and the usual suspects were pedantically rounded up: a redefinition of the discipline, 'as a distinct and sequenced inquiry into the constituents and applications of meaningful communication'; more emphasis upon communication and less upon narrow grammatical accuracy; the establishment of standards, models and common curricula (for 'consistent pedagogical rhetoric'). All very laudable, no doubt – but why do I think of Nero? It has always been difficult to sell languages in Kansas: wherever you go, for many hundreds of miles, English will take you to McDonalds, get you a burger, and bring you safely home again, and a thorough reworking of pedagogical rhetoric doesn't amount to sale prices.

Misconceptions continue to abound, it seems. I note that Straight (2009) has recently argued that, once American foreign-language departments sort themselves out, language learning will flourish: 'By changing our approach to cultures and languages, especially at the college level, the United States could lead the world in the delivery of truly multilingual higher education.' This is surely both inaccurate and immodest. On the other hand, Strong (2009: 623–624) has recently endorsed my 'Kansas' observation, although putting things rather more prosaically:

> The United States is big: generally, one does not in a day's travel encounter another country with another language. Additionally it has a hegemonic view of English. This is unavoidable: French is hegemonic in France, but four hours on the TGV puts you under another hegemon in Düsseldorf, a very different experience.

(We also note the jargon here, of course. If, like many others, Strong uses *hegemony* simply as a synonym for 'leadership' or 'dominance', then she [and they] would surely be advised to use one of those words; if she intends more Gramscian connotations, then the use is simply incorrect.)

Broadly speaking, there are two paths through these difficult woods, although occasionally they share the same ground. The first is for foreign-language teaching to satisfy itself with that shrinking pool of students intrinsically interested in languages and their cultures. These *are*, after all, the students who are generally nearest to teachers' hearts. The problem is that the 'natural' constituency here might prove too small to support a discipline at desired levels, and it is hard to nurture in any direct way. The other is to hope and work for a renewed instrumental interest, with whatever longer-term fallout that might lead to. To some extent, this is dependent upon a context which extends well beyond national borders, upon alterations in global linguistic circumstance which, while inevitable, are not always easy to predict. On the other hand, things might be done at home, particularly if home is a culturally diverse setting, in which the loss of a hundred native languages to English is seen as uneconomic, in which the rights of immigrants (especially, of course, those who are entitled to vote) attract social and political attention, and so on. If we think here of the American scene, for example, we inevitably think of Spanish.

The study of Spanish is self-evidently important. It is a language with a lengthy cultural and literary tradition, with many interesting branches from the original trunk and, at the same time, it remains a widely used variety around the world. With something like 380 million speakers, it runs fourth (behind Hindi, Chinese and English) in the usage sweepstakes. Academically, then, it is the ideal second language. In the United States, there are now significantly more people who speak Spanish as a first or second language (about 48 million) than there are African Americans (about 38 million); these figures translate to about 15.6% and 12.3% of the total population, respectively. In fact, the United States is the second largest Spanish-speaking country in the world (after Mexico, where about 98% of the 110-million population speak Spanish). Hispanic Americans are the fastest-growing minority, and their proportion of the total population is expected to double before mid-century. This would mean better than one in four Americans. In a fit of estimation, Carlos Fuentes (1999) suggested that three out of every five Americans will speak Spanish by 2050. Such future proportions are almost certainly inaccurate, particularly if we factor in what are likely to be gradually falling fertility rates.[5] Still, the Hispanic figures represent impressive growth. They assume greater importance, too, when we consider both numbers and concentrations; after all, millions of people living more or less together constitute a different sociological phenomenon than if they are widely scattered among others. At the same time, not all Hispanic people live in the southwest or the southeast. They are now the largest minority group in almost half the states of the union: not just in California, New Mexico, Texas and Florida, but also in Connecticut, Iowa, New Hampshire and Washington.

As it became immediately clear to me at that Phoenix meeting, and as the figures in the next chapter will demonstrate, Spanish is the linchpin of modern-language teaching in the United States. While the statistics for French and German indicate declining interest, and while those for some newly important languages (Chinese and Arabic, most notably) suggest only the beginnings of what may well prove to be future growth, Spanish figures are on the rise. Nonetheless, while Spanish university enrolments now account for well over half of all foreign-language entries, the actual numbers remain but a small percentage of overall college enrolments. Is the learning of Spanish in a healthy situation, then, or does it only seem so in comparison with weaker sisters? This may be an impossible question to answer. How many students *ought* to be studying Spanish – or archaeology, or computer-and-business combinations, or quantum mechanics, or sculpture? Still, one might expect that language study would be more immediately related to extra-educational factors (jobs, mobility, opportunity, and so on) and, if that is so, then one might wonder why the strength of the American Hispanic community does not bolster the educational effort more.

Despite America's multiethnic status in general, and its powerful Hispanic components more specifically, the country remains anglophone in all important domains and, indeed, the chief mainstay of English as a global language. Nonetheless, statistics show that foreign-language enrolments have remained quite stable over the last generation or so and, despite large (percentage) gains in students studying Arabic and Chinese, Spanish retains a dominant position; again, see the detailed figures in the next chapter. It is also true, as any casual observer can note, that all those in America with something to sell have been quite quick in preparing Spanish-language advertisements. As well, government documents, tax forms, and so on, are now readily available in Spanish, a development that would have been hard to predict until relatively recently. And finally, the large and important clusters of those Hispanics and 'Latinos' whose buying and voting power has not gone unnoticed represent a sea-change in American demography. It may well be that the central anglophone axes of the country are becoming less sturdy, and that we will see a larger and more enduring Spanish–English diglossia.

It is, however, still too early to tell. That famous melting-pot has historically been particularly effective at the level of language. While aspects of cultural continuity can be discerned in various groups, languages other than English typically last no longer than the second or third generation, and the 'normal' pattern has meant moving from one monolingualism to another. This has stayed true, even for the two 'special' cases, francophones in New England and hispanophones in the southwest – special inasmuch as they, unlike all other arrivals, remain close to their heartlands, the borders of which can often be easily and frequently crossed. The *timing* of language shift is naturally dependent upon such variables, but the overall shape of the curve has proved remarkably similar across groups.

All of this makes some of Fuentes's (1999) further remarks rather naïve, even though they are eminently understandable, reflective of the views of many and, indeed, attractive in their impulse. He asks why most Americans know only English, and he sees their monolingualism as a 'great paradox'. The United States is at once the supreme and the most isolated world power. Why, he continues, does it 'want to be a monolingual country?' All twenty-first-century Americans ought to know more than one language, to better understand the world and deal with problems. And so on, and so on. Obviously, monolingualism is not a paradox, and to say that Americans 'want' to be monolingual would seem to miss the point: it is simply that English serves across domains.

In more subtle ways, though, it could be argued that Americans do 'want' to be monolingual or, to put it more aptly, see no reason to expand their repertoires. They therefore resist the institutionalisation of other languages. In a climate like this, especially a long-standing one, such an outlook, arguably based upon perceived practicality, can expand on less immediate and more unpleasant levels. Not only do languages other than English appear unnecessary, their use can be seen as downright un-American, their speakers as unwilling to throw themselves wholeheartedly into that wonderful pot, their continuing linkage to other cultures a suspect commodity. It is surely not surprising that, given the right context (or should one say the 'wrong context'), these sorts of views would find formal expression, that organisations like *U.S. English* would flourish, that many states would enact English-only legislation, that bilingual education would be progressively de-emphasised and, in one or two notorious cases, scrapped entirely. Nor is it surprising that the central part of that context would be an increasingly worried sense that the non-anglophone 'others' are becoming too potent. English-only, therefore, typically means not-Spanish. And so another circle is completed. The very language community which, by its power and numbers, ought logically to blaze the way in foreign-language teaching and learning, is under attack by powerful opinions which represent either nostalgia-ridden yearnings for some selective status quo or, worse, reflect the most abhorrent social virus. The fact that many of its own members – however linguistically unenlightened scholarly outsiders may conceive them to be – are more or less willing 'shifters' is also a very important consideration, of course, and clearly not unrelated to the other tendencies and pressures indicated here.

A concluding note

This chapter has largely aimed at some elucidation of the social context relevant to languages and language learning. Large forces and weighty histories are at work here, and their presence should be acknowledged and thought about. As Mufwene (2008: 250) reminds us, 'language endangerment is certainly not a recent process, any more than globalization is'. For many, I know, English in lock-step with globalisation is a lowering villain depriving other mediums of their rightful inheritance.

I would simply reiterate that the factors at work here are neither unfamiliar nor unpredictable. We have seen transitional linguistic and social times before and transition is, almost by definition, a painful and wrenching experience for those whose lives are directly affected. Since this is true even in circumstances where transition is endorsed (whether grudgingly or wholeheartedly), how much truer must it be when individuals and groups feel transition as a manifestation of unwanted external pressure.

It is a truism to say that the teaching and learning of languages is influenced by the state of affairs outside the walls of the academy. It would be heartening – in a world in which, for all the power of English, bilingual or multilingual competences are still the norm – if the North American (or the British or, indeed any other 'large-language') academy were dealing with a constituency which acknowledged and accepted such repertoires. The products on offer would not then require such advertising; the demand would arise naturally and would not have first to be suggested to the consumers. But this is a setting in which some linguistic analogy of Gresham's Law seems to operate. As well, one recalls the (perhaps apocryphal) remark of that school superintendent in Arkansas who steadfastly refused to have foreign languages taught at secondary level: 'if English was good enough for Jesus,' he remarked, 'it's good enough for you' (Michaels, 1990: xvii).

We should recall, though, that linguistic and cultural diversity continues to be a visible and powerful quantity in many settings, America and Britain among them. We have also engaged, over the last few years, in an unprecedented debate about multiculturalism and pluralism, about identity and citizenship. The field here remains terribly disputed and highly politicised, but the debate is far from over and the valuable middle ground has yet to be properly mapped. Since an important part of this ground has always been linguistic, it is regrettable that the most powerful contributions (from political philosophy and related areas) have not always given this aspect its due. There seem to be changes for the better here, however, as some of the discussions and references in this book demonstrate.

Notes

1. Two recent discussions in which Florio figures prominently (Lawrence, 2006; Wyatt, 2005) suggest that the success of his manuals rested upon English interest in Italian reading proficiency rather than in facility with the spoken word. Desired access to Italian work in the arts, literature, history and philosophy was the spur here. This type of interest is itself of great significance, of course, and hardly negates the general point I am making about the

relative importance of Italian and English. It is also the case, however, that both Wyatt and Lawrence are more interested in the desires of the literati than in those of English travellers abroad, even though the Florio excerpt I present here reveals this to be too narrow a view. It would be more accurate to consider that the English gentleman-reader addressed by Florio was a man of culture *and* a traveller.

In a joint review of the Wyatt and Lawrence books, Healy (2007) notes that the production of Italian manuals by Florio and others could hardly be accounted for by the very small number of Italians living in post-Reformation England, and he thus supports the authors' overly narrow view. But this misses the point. The number of English people wishing to 'drinke at the wel-head' abroad (as Florio put it, in his *Second Frutes*) is more relevant than the number of Italians living in England.

While his rendering of Montaigne's *Essays* is Florio's main claim to fame now, his reputation with his contemporaries rested upon his linguistic efforts, as Yates (1934: 190) pointed out. She also reminds us that – even as his Italian handbooks were necessitated by the restricted usefulness of English – Florio was struck by 'the number, variety and picturesqueness of the English equivalents' he was able to summon for Italian words: 'And for English-gentlemen me thinks it must needs be a pleasure to them, to see so rich a toong out-vide by their mother-speech, as by the manie-folde Englishes of manie wordes in this is manifest.' Shades of further developments, perhaps, for that 'so rich a toong'.

Beyond his *Firste Fruites* (1578), Florio went on to produce a *Second Frutes* (1591), aimed at a slightly more upmarket audience, and imparted in a 'superior' tone more suited to the literati. His *Worlde of Wordes* followed in 1598, later expanded into *Queen Anna's New World of Words* (1611). The fuller titles of these interesting volumes are given in the References section here.

A final little note: while the advent of printing had initiated standardisation of spelling and grammar, the books of Florio's time were still relatively unconcerned with regularity. In the 'Epistle Dedicatory' to the *Second Frutes*, the catchword ('bounty') appears at the bottom of page A2; its repetition at the top of the next page, however, is given as 'bountie'! (Note also the variations within Florio's very titles.) (Readers who have seen old books will know that catchwords are commonly found in material produced before the arrival of modern printing methods; their presence was a reminder to both printers and binders of proper page ordering.)

2. Of course, one should take into account just what 'the world' has represented at various stages in history. If we consider, for instance, the extent of the known world in Roman times and if, in addition, we fold in conceptions of 'civilised' versus 'barbarian' regions, we might very well agree that Latin was a greater 'global' language than English is today.

3. Important scholars don't have infallible crystal balls, of course. At the conclusion of his book, Burchfield (1987: 173) suggested that, while American English had become numerically dominant, 'the Received Standard of British English remains the form admired and sought after by most foreigners'.

4. Further information about academies and dictionaries will be found in Edwards (1995); see also Edwards (in preparation-b).

202 Challenges in the Social Life of Language

5. The 'replacement' fertility rate for 'developed' societies is about 2.1, which is more or less the overall American rate at the moment. Among the American Hispanic population, however, the rate is 2.9. The difference has occasionally led to ugly comments from ugly quarters – just as the electronic ether is now full of bigoted warnings about Muslims 'breeding' their way to dominance in Europe – and we should always be on our guard against prejudiced arguments that touch upon such matters. In fairness, one must note that Muslim spokesmen themselves sometimes make (favourable) reference to fertility-rate differences.

Nonetheless, for a host of demographic and cultural reasons, the current Hispanic fertility rate *is* higher than the overall one. There is little reason to think, however, that the expected social dynamics will not bring about a gradual convergence. Beyond the United States, authoritative statistics suggest falling fertility rates among many of the groups in which the figures were traditionally high: this is true whether we consider members of those groups who have remained in their home countries, or whether we look at those who have emigrated elsewhere. Westoff and Frejka (2007) have demonstrated this, for instance, among Muslim populations in Europe.

Overall, it seems clear that – in the United States as in Europe – anxieties (whether prejudiced or simply 'popular') about minority groups somehow gaining the upper hand through sheer weight of numbers are not supported by demographic analyses.

10
Language Learning in Anglophone Settings

An introductory note

It is both a fact and a frequent lament that English speakers lag far behind others in foreign-language competence. The teaching and learning of foreign languages in North America and Britain have seemed more difficult and less attractive undertakings than they are in Europe. Do we observe here some genetic anglophone linguistic deficiency? Are the British and the Americans right when they say, 'I'm just no good at foreign languages'? Are they right to envy those clever Europeans, Africans and Asians who slide effortlessly from one mode to another? The answers here obviously involve environmental conditions, not genetic ones, but I present these rather silly notions because – to the extent to which they are believed, or half-believed, or inarticulately felt – they constitute a type of self-fulfilling prophecy which adds to the difficulty of language learning. I use the word 'adds' here because the real difficulties, the important contextual conditions, the soil in which such prophecies flourish, have to do with power and dominance. Anglophone linguistic laments perhaps involve some crocodile tears or, at least, can seem rather hollow: the regrets of those who lack competence, but who need not, after all, really bother to acquire it.

Given what I've said in the two previous chapters, one could reasonably assume that English speakers, when not globally dominant, were assiduous language learners. Indeed, as late as the dawn of the twentieth century, the idea that the British were somehow innately ill equipped to speak foreign languages would have seemed ludicrous, and a great many educated people (not just the royals, not just Victoria and Albert chatting away in German) were, in fact, bilingual or better. Less well-educated people, of course, formed another category. With the great nineteenth-century expansion of continental travel, many such individuals were able to go abroad for the first time. In one of his famous travel guides, John Murray discussed the misunderstood Englishman, whose 'morose sullenness' is generally due to the 'involuntary silence arising from his ignorance of foreign languages... which prevents his enjoying society' (see Sillitoe, 1995: 24.)

On the other hand, there are counter-indications, and one of these takes us back exactly to Florio's day. In *The Merchant of Venice* (I:ii), Portia complains to her maid, Nerissa, about one of her suitors: Falconbridge, she says, 'understands not me, nor I him; he hath neither Latin, French, nor Italian'. All her admirers, including a Scot, are criticised, 'but only the English one is slated for linguistic incompetence' (Oulton, 2000).

Well, we need not take Shakespeare, cleverly observant as he was, as an infallible guide to language abilities. More to the point, there is no real paradox to be explained away. Educated English speakers were, at once, more broadly capable in foreign languages than they are now, and increasingly less capable – because of the growing clout of their maternal variety – than their continental colleagues. Bailey (2006: 345) suggests that, up to the end of the seventeenth century, 'the prevailing opinion among the English was that they were especially skilful at learning new languages' (see also Bailey, 1991). He cites Richard Carew, the sixteenth-century poet, translator, antiquary and politician – and one of the earliest champions of regional varieties (especially Cornish: see Blank, 2006):

> turne an Englishman at any time of his age into what countrie soever allowing him due respite, and you shall see him profit so well that the imitation of his utterance, will in nothing differ from the patterne of that native language. (Bailey, 2006: 345–346)

The dawn of the eighteenth century, however, marked the beginning of an important change. As the international fortunes of English improved, so the learning of other languages began to decline. An anonymous author, writing in 1766, acknowledged that the 'affectation' of some Englishmen led them to 'prefer any language to their own' and to suggest that 'our tongue wants universality'. However, he continues, 'I have been assured, by several ingenious foreigners, that in many places abroad, Italy in particular, it is become the fashion to study the English Tongue' (Bailey, 2006: 346). So, by mid-century, the old idea that the English were good at foreign languages was being more and more replaced by the notion that their own would become a powerful medium, 'and that those who did not gain it as a birthright would learn it as a necessity' (p. 346). As Bailey goes on to note, while it would take another century for this new idea to become firmly entrenched, the seed of resistance to multilingualism had been well and truly planted; see also Chapter 8.

Popular assessments

In the first paragraph of the previous section, I touchd upon some common estimates of anglophone language-learning capacities. If we look a bit more closely, we will certainly find some strange and inaccurate judgements; reminding ourselves, however, that perceptions can often create social realltles, and putting aside the common academic rejection of 'amateur' assessment, we will also find some points worthy of attention. This is particularly the case if we leave aside comments of the letters-to-the-editor variety and, instead, turn to analyses made by those who, while not professional social scientists, nevertheless possess some substantial credentials.

First of all, we might consider those affectations, just noted, which combine disdain for one's own community with (as that anonymous eighteenth-century author put it) a preference for languages other than one's own. At a general level, such language preferences have always been widely remarked upon, particularly within the broader cultural context. In 1797, for instance, George Canning established the *Anti-Jacobin*, a newspaper whose general purpose, given the timing of its founding, is rather obvious. As a complement to swiping at the revolutionaries across the Channel, the paper 'valorized roast-beef-of-England traditionalism' (Edgecombe, 1998: 484). In the first issue, Canning wrote that the paper was 'partial to the Country in which we live, notwithstanding the daily panegyrics which we read and hear on the superior virtues and endowments of its rival and hostile neighbours' (Hinde, 1974: 60). His jingoism was exaggerated for political effect, and Canning certainly didn't claim that things English were perfect. He was, however, genuinely exasperated with the 'steady patriot of the world alone / The friend of every country – but his own' (p. 61). These famous lines are taken from Canning's *New Morality*, a long poem that appeared in the last (July 1798) issue of his short-lived newspaper.

About a century later, Benjamin Disraeli (1877) gave a speech at the Guildhall in London, reported in the next day's *Times*. In it, he mentioned those 'cosmopolitan critics, men who are the friends of every country save their own'. And one cannot omit mention here of

206 Challenges in the Social Life of Language

'As someday it may happen', the Lord High Executioner's song (better known as 'I've got a little list') from *The Mikado* (Gilbert and Sullivan, 1985). Noting the many victims who 'never would be missed', Ko-Ko sings of 'the idiot who praises, with enthusiastic tone / All centuries but this, and every country but his own'.

Considering these and many other similar accusations, past and present, – I think it is entirely possible to separate right-wing ravings from more temperate criticism of those persons for whom something else, or someone else, or somewhere else, is always better. Sometimes the stance is an affectation of sophisticated superiority, while at others it may be better understood as a guilt reflex. Either way – sneer or self-reproach – the posture is unattractive and often crippled. As an exercise, readers may wish to consider the extent to which such postures are detectable in the sociology-of-language of literature, particularly in that segment of it that currently goes under the rubric of 'language ecology' (see Chapter 6).

But if, on the one hand, we find many snobbish and posturing rejections of this sort, another side of the coin is much more likely to turn up, the one that reveals limitations to foreign-language acquisition. George Orwell, so good on the politics of language, clearly went off the rails a bit here. He suggested that 'the English are very poor linguists' because 'their own language is grammatically so simple'. And yet 'a completely illiterate Indian will pick up English far faster than a British soldier will pick up Hindustani' (1970 [1947]: 42). Furthermore, Orwell (p. 18) also writes that 'the peculiarities of the English language make it almost impossible for anyone who has left school at fourteen to learn a foreign language'. This is why, in the ranks of the Foreign Legion, British and American soldiers 'seldom rise out of the ranks, because they cannot learn French, whereas a German learns French in a few months' (p. 18). Orwell also suggested that, even when living abroad for long periods, the English refuse to learn foreign languages; and, of course, 'nearly every Englishman of working-class origin considers it effeminate to pronounce a foreign word correctly' (1970 [1941]: 85).

In all this, Orwell is really speaking only of working-class people. The 'upper classes learn foreign languages as a regular part of their education', a fact which only feeds lower-class hostility: 'travelling abroad, speaking foreign tongues, enjoying foreign food, are vaguely felt to be upper-class habits, a species of snobbery, so that xenophobia is reinforced by class jealousy' (1970 [1947]: 18). Orwell would have been amazed at the astronomical growth of working-class holiday opportunities abroad, and at the fact that curry is now the most popular English food, but he might not have thought it necessary to revise his remarks about language learning. Among other recent writers, Carr and Pauwels (2006) have suggested that discomfort in speaking foreign languages 'properly' remains an issue, particularly for males; see also Edwards (2010a). Nonetheless, it is clear that anglophone difficulties with language learning now have more to do with the ubiquitous nature of English, and rather less with either 'class jealousy' or xenophobia.

Writing at about the same time as Orwell, Henry Mencken (1999 [1935]: 88) suggested that 'to most educated foreigners [English] seems so simple that it strikes them as almost a kind of baby-talk' – a perception, he adds, that is soon amended 'when they proceed from trying to speak it to trying to read and write it'. Still, 'so long as they are content to tackle it *viva voce* they find it strangely loose and comfortable, and at the same time very precise'. Mencken was a clever and committed scholar, and his *American Language* (1919–1948) is still well worth reading (or at least dipping into), but these observations are passing strange.[1]

Mencken also suggests that, while English has flourished due to its global dispersion, its native speakers 'have been, on the whole, poor linguists, and so they have dragged their language with them, and forced it upon the human race' (p. 87). Where English has come into contact with rivals, he writes, it has 'sought every opportunity whether fair or unfair' to upset what were initially reluctant linguistic compromises. Needless to say, these statements hardly capture the essence of the matter (and one would like to know more about the distinction between fair and unfair treatment). Given that Mencken was no sort of anglophile – Nelson (1999: 669) notes the 'anti-British animus' that pervades his *American* Language, and Teachout (2003) provides many references to his Germanophilia, an affection that became something of an affliction during both world wars – it is both interesting and praiseworthy that he acknowledged that linguistic contact has generally led to a 'win' for English through 'the sheer weight of its merit'. A more pleasant observation, at least in anglophone ears, but, alas, no more accurate than the other sociolinguistic opinions cited here.

Preceding Mencken by just over a generation, Mark Twain (1882) wrote an amusing essay on American vis-à-vis English English. He notes that, as late as mid-century, Webster's dictionary gave the pronunciation of 'basket' as *bahsket* – interesting, when one considers that part of Webster's purpose was to encourage and strengthen American usage; in terms of vocabulary he actually supplied the desired alternatives (*color* for 'colour'; *center* for 'centre'; etc.). Twain was of course an excellent observer, but he was not infallible: his comparison of the English, 'I haven't got any money', with the American, 'I haven't any money', is exactly reversed. These minor points apart, Twain's essential thesis was the modern one that differences do not constitute deficiencies.

Language learning in anglophone settings: Statistics

The main thrust of this chapter is neither with historical nor 'popular' information, but with some rather harder data relevant to the current state of foreign-language learning. Most of the numbers here pertain to Britain and the United States, but I begin with some briefer notes about Australia and Canada.

Australia

Nettelbeck (2009) reports that the vast majority of students entering university study no languages at all; few of those do carry on with their language course. Asian languages have actually fallen in popularity, while European ones have strengthened somewhat: Spanish accounted for 80% of the growth here, but it was suggested that this reflected a serious problem of language decline at school. Thus, Anne Pauwels was recently cited (by Lane, 2009): 'The number of students completing a language other than English at school has gone down over the past twenty years, from approximately 48% to about 13%, as a result of removing a language requirement for entry to higher education'.

Canada

At the beginning of the century Spanish enrolment was 'booming' in many Canadian universities (Charbonneau, 2001; see also Hendry, 2000), while the study of other languages was either 'flat' (German, Italian) or in decline (Slavic languages). Charbonneau cites Statistics Canada figures showing that, between 1992 and 1998, the number of students 'majoring' in foreign languages (i.e. neither English nor French) went from 3,200 (in 1992), to 3,800 (1995) and back down to 3,100 (1998). Both English and French have suffered, too: 17,300 were studying the former in 1992, down to 13,600 in 1998; the comparable figures for French were 7,300 and 5,600. In western Canada, the eclipse of French has been particularly marked: university uptake figures in urban areas declined in the last five years of the twentieth century by 13%, and by 34% in rural settings.

In an interesting situation at the University of British Columbia, Japanese enrolments tripled between the mid-1990s and the end of the century, and the Japanese programme is now the largest in North America, 'with 1,500 students studying Japanese in one course or another' (Charbonneau, 2001: 17). However, most of these students are 'of Asian descent and most are taking the courses out of cultural interest' (p. 17). We will see that in other contexts, too, increases of this sort suggest rather less for *anglophone* language learning than a hasty consideration of the simple numbers might imply. A second cautionary note comes from the head of the Department of French and Spanish at Memorial University in Newfoundland: 'Across the country, enrolments in our [foreign languages] departments are pyramids with very, very broad bases and very narrow summits' (Charbonneau, 2001: 14). That is, more students begin programmes of foreign-language study than finish them. Indeed, statistics reveal that, for Spanish, French and other languages, most university students are interested only in entry-level courses, and few continue on to upper-level studies. This proves to be a second generalisable point, particularly marked in the American context; relatedly, we find that *postgraduate* language study has slumped significantly in many departments.

Kondro (2000) has argued for the relevance of cyberspace to declining interest in language learning, even though there is

> no shortage of other culprits. Globalization is a factor. Shortsighted administrators have played their part, as have lackadaisical students and an apparent diminution in Canadian pride in multiculturalism and bilingualism. [Nonetheless] the Internet appears to be the biggest single culprit in a disturbing trend now manifesting itself within the classrooms of the nation: the demise of foreign-language instruction and departments.

To bolster his case, he cites Linda Hutcheon, then president of the Modern Language Association (and a Toronto professor), who stated that the dominance of English makes people feel less inclined to learn foreign languages. Decline of interest at secondary-school level then leads inexorably fewer language students at universities: a 'domino effect', she suggests. Of course, this doesn't particularly strengthen his case at all, since the effects of English dominance are hardly dependent upon the internet; indeed, as we have seen (in Chapter 8), other languages have increasingly found their place in that medium.

Britain

At the beginning of the European Year of Languages, de Laine (2001) cited a Eurobarometer report suggesting that 70% of Europeans believed that everyone should be able to speak English. At the same time, King (2001: 28) noted that the central challenge for the UK during that year was that of promoting multilingualism in an English-speaking context, given the 'unmistakable desire of so many people to learn English'. His argument was threefold. First, more than half of European adults still don't have much English fluency. Second, he cited Graddol's (1998) point that the more English becomes the world language, the more the British will need skills in other varieties.[2] (At the same time, King writes, as more and more people around the world gain competence in English, there will no longer be a special advantage in being a native speaker, 'especially not a monolingual one' [p. 28].) Third, the British should develop their foreign-language skills because 'significant parts of the UK are operationally multilingual, whether measured in terms of the expanding numbers of Welsh speakers or the hundreds of mother tongues in London and other large conurbations' (p. 29). Including the Welsh here seems a bit odd, but the most important caveat is that, as elsewhere, those many London languages largely belong to immigrants, and not to the native anglophones whose fluencies one would like to see expand. Overall, however, King's points are well worth highlighting, because they are such familiar ones within those circles keen to encourage larger linguistic repertoires.

King (and CILT [Centre for Information on Language Teaching and Research], 2009) also provide some instructive figures about the state of secondary-level language teaching and learning in Britain. Table 1 provides some comparisons in terms of GCSE and A-level entries in modern languages.[3]

The CILT website also provides information on the proportion of 15-year-old students taking a modern language at GCSE-level (here I show numbers for England only): in 2000, 76% of all students took at least one language, a proportion that dropped to 44% in 2009. Those studying French and German have been getting fewer, but more are taking Spanish.

Table 1   Figures for secondary-level language learning

Year	Total*	(%age)**	French	German	Spanish
1995	(GCSE) 559,000	10.3	350,000	130,000	40,000
	(A-level) 49,000	6.7	27,000	11,000	5,000
2000	(GCSE) 573,000	10.1	341,000	134,000	50,000
	(A-level) 39,000	5.1	18,000	9,000	6,000
2009	(GCSE) 380,000	6.9	189,000	73,000	67,000
	(A-level) 37,000	4.3	14,000	5,800	7,300

Notes: Total*= *all* modern-language entries.
(%age)** = percentage of *all* subject entries represented by the language total.

In 2004, new government policy made language learning optional for GCSE-level children: the proportion taking *no* languages at that level jumped from 22% to 56% between 2001 and 2008; see also the figures in Table 1. There were, as may be expected, immediate demands for a review of this optional policy – some compensation for which, rather strangely perhaps, is meant to be found in the anticipated 'National Languages Strategy', which, from 2010, will entitle all primary-school children to learn a foreign language (Woods, 2005).

Leon (2002) had warned that this government policy of optional language learning would exacerbate the slide in the numbers taking language degrees, feeding a vicious circle of decline. Relatedly, Utley (2002) pointed out that university modern-language departments were concerned about their survival if such a policy was put in place, despite those efforts, just mentioned, to compensate with improved language provision at the primary level. She provided a statement from Hilary Footitt, a representative of the University Council of Modern Languages:

> the calendar proposed by the Green Paper would, in effect, mean a delay of some eight years between languages being dropped as compulsory at 14, and the first primary-taught young people getting to secondary school. That 'lost generation' would mean the death-knell for several language departments.

Fewer GCSE-level students studying languages means fewer at A-level and, therefore, fewer candidates for university degree courses. And indeed, at tertiary level, there has been a considerable decline in language enrolments. Of course, not all of the drop is a consequence of secondary-school policy, but the latter is clearly an extremely important factor. Statistics suggested a drop in entrants to modern-language degree courses from about 4,500 to 3,700 over the last four years of the 1990s (Anon., 2000). More recent findings stem from research conducted at the University of London and Stirling University: over the first decade of this century, the number of students accepted for degree courses in German has dropped from 2,300 to 600; in French, from 5,600 to 3,700. Numbers are slightly up for 'newly available' languages (notably Mandarin and Arabic) but, overall, the figures show a decline of about 25% (see *The Independent*, 2008). Michael Kelly, director of the British Subject Centre for Languages, Linguistics and Area Studies has recently reported that only about 2% of students choose to do modern-language degrees, and about the same percentage study languages as part of other programmes (Reisz, 2009; see also British Academy, 2009).

Overall, Kelly suggests that only 6% or 7% leave university with 'survival skills' in a foreign language, and only 5% can 'function effectively'.

When providing the percentages noted above, Kelly also noted that a number of students study languages through various extracurricular programmes, a reflection perhaps of the continuing desire of employers in the modern multinational economy to hire people with language skills. The London/Stirling University study mentioned above noted that

> for some companies, the specific languages were immaterial: they saw students with languages as much more flexible and adaptable, more likely to appreciate the need for intercultural communication skills, and more able to build relationships with counterparts or clients in other countries.

In fact, Leon (2002) went so far as to suggest that language provision at universities was 'buoyant' because many students who are not reading for language degrees nevertheless take language modules. Kelly (in Anon., 2000) – then head of French at the University of Southampton – also described a rise in the popularity of these language modules: 'French for lawyers, Spanish for chemists, German for engineers', he stated.[4]

There have been important knock-on effects at the teaching level. In 2000, German, Russian and Slavic departments were reported to be at special risk of closure (Anon., 2000). In 2002, Leon wrote that at least fifteen university modern-language departments were under threat, and that staffing complements had dropped dramatically in many instances. And seven years later, the British Academy (2009) reported the actual closure of perhaps one-third of university modern-language departments.

The United States

The most recent and comprehensive statistics about pre-university language learning in America are provided by Rhodes and Pufahl (2009). Their survey included about 3,500 primary and 1,500 secondary schools, both public and private. The response rate was about 76%, and they were able to make meaningful comparisons with earlier surveys (conducted in 1987 and 1997). Foreign-language provision were made at 22% of the primary schools in 1987, at 31% in 1997, and back to 25% in 2008. The pattern was similar, but at an overall higher level (72%, 75%, 58%) at middle schools, and higher again but more stable at high schools (95%, 90%., 91%). As primary-school offerings, both French and German programmes have decreased significantly, dropping from 27% to 11%, and 5% to 2%, respectively, over the last decade. Spanish, on the other hand, has strengthened (from 79% to 88%). At the secondary level (middle school and high school in combination), the relevant 1997–2008 figures show French provision down from 64% to 46%, German down from 24% to 14% – but Spanish stable, at 93%. Chinese and Arabic provisions are both slightly up over the time period, although the percentages of schools offering them remain very small. Some further details may be found in Klee (2002), Rodd (2002) and Jacobs (2002).[5]

Rhodes and Pufahl make the familiar (but, of course, entirely accurate) complaint about the shortage of highly qualified language teachers. They also make another point, one that is becoming familiar, when they write that about one-third of those public schools (both primary and secondary) that have language programmes report that their foreign-language instruction has been negatively affected by the 'No Child Left Behind'. Its intense focus on the tested subjects (mathematics and reading) has acted to the detriment of others (see Edwards, 2010a, for further details of President Bush's NCLB initiative).

Welles (2002) attempted to clarify what she claimed were misinterpretations about language-enrolment figures provided in earlier studies (see particularly Brod and Welles, 2000). She notes the common complaints (that have only intensified since the dramatic events of September 2001) about the great deficiencies in American language learning and teaching, but points out that the proportion of college students who study languages has remained stable (at about 8% of overall registrants) over the last quarter-century. Spanish now claims more than half (55%) of language enrolments, French and German about 24%, Italian and Japanese about 8% (see also Brod and Welles, 2000). Furthermore, since many primary- and secondary-level schools also offer languages, it seems clear that more than that university 8% have some foreign fluency. Welles provides some historical background, too, going back to the early twentieth century, and noting the spike in foreign-language enrolments (to almost 16% of the total) that followed the Russian launch of *Sputnik* in 1957: increased government spending on defence, science and education was fuelled by the fear of 'falling behind' the Soviet Union.

Welles also refers to a study of foreign-language enrolments (Goldberg and Welles, 2001) that reported on a survey of some 2,600 American university language departments (of whom about three-quarters responded). This survey showed, in fact, that many departments were experiencing either stable or increasing enrolments; an important proviso here, however, is that only the rate of growth or decline was reported, rather than actual numbers. Welles suggests, too, that many universities have 'eliminated all but the healthiest programs' (p. 254).

As in Canada (see above), there was an apparent slump in post-graduate foreign-language study during the 1990s. Welles (2004), however, shows that a 15% decline from 1995 to 1998 was substantially reversed by a 12% increase to 2002. 'Substantially' but not, of course, entirely – and this charting of percentage decreases or increases from year to year can mask significant alterations in actual numbers (as in the Goldberg and Welles report, noted above). Also as in Canada, the figures provided by Furman *et al.* (2007) show quite clearly the large disparities between entry-level and advanced foreign-language study at university. They summarise some of them as follows:

> For every eight enrollments in first- and second-year Arabic, there is only one enrollment in an advanced Arabic course; Chinese does somewhat better with a ratio of 9 to 2, whereas Spanish and Japanese, despite their proportional differences in size of total enrollments, both have one out of five enrollments in upper-level classes. (p. 4)

Welles (2004) presents an updating of the Brod and Welles (2000) figures; here, about 2,800 questionnaires were sent to two- and four-year colleges and universities and, incredibly, all but a dozen eventually replied. We also have a further set of comparative data (Furman *et al.*, 2007), which allows comparisons of foreign-language enrolments in 1998, 2002 and 2006. Table 2 provides some of the salient (rounded) figures, with the accompanying percentage increases. Not shown on the table are figures for Japanese and Chinese, each of which increased by about 20% between 1998 and 2002, followed by further increases of 27.5% for the former and 51% for the latter (2006 *numbers*: 67,000 for Japanese; 52,000 for Chinese). And Arabic? It rose from about 5,000 enrolments in 1998, to 11,000 in 2002, and 24,000 in 2006.

Table 2 Foreign-language enrolments at university

Language	1998	2002	2006
Spanish	657,000	746,000 (+13.7%)	823,000 (+10.3%)
French	199,000	202,000 (+1.5%)	206,000 (+2.2%)
German	89,000	91,000 (+2.3%)	94,000 (+3.5%)

Interestingly, the biggest increase by far (in percentage terms) was for American Sign Language: it went up by 432% between 1998 and 2002, and up again by 29.7% in 2006 (actual numbers: 79,000). Among the traditional 'big three' we find some significant alterations over the last four decades. In 1968, French, German and Spanish enrolments accounted for 34.4%, 19.2% and 32.4% of all foreign-language enrolments. By 2002, these had changed to 14.5% for French, 6.5% for German, and 53.4% for Spanish. In 2006, the percentages were 13.1% French, 5.9% German and 52.2% Spanish. Over the same period, Arabic enrolments increased eight-fold, from 0.1% of enrolments, to 0.8%, to 1.5% (Furman *et al.*, 2007).

We must bear in mind, of course, that *all* enrolments in higher education have increased: from about 14.5 million in 1998, to 15.6 million in 2002, to 17.7 million in 2006. Of these, enrolments in foreign-language programmes represented 7.9%, 8.1% and 8.6%, respectively. As already noted, these levels have remained the same since the early 1970s. Another very important point to bear in mind here: we know that the percentages of Spanish speakers in the United States increased by at least 50% over the last decade of the twentieth century, and the increases for other groups were even more dramatic: almost 100% for Chinese speakers, about 130% for Koreans, about 150% for Vietnamese. These reflect heightened immigration, of course, but their relevance here is suggested by Charbonneau's (2001: 17) point, noted above in the section on Canada: the majority of those students studying Japanese at the University of British Columbia are 'of Asian descent and most are taking the courses out of cultural interest'. The implication is that some of the increased uptake of Spanish in the United States may have little to say about improving *anglophone* competences.

We also have recent figures on trends among teachers of foreign languages. Drawing upon the National Study of Postsecondary Faculty – a representative sample of over 26,000 faculty members throughout the United States – the Ad Hoc Committee on Staffing of the Association of Departments of English (2009) reported that the number of teachers of foreign languages went from about 27,000 in 1993 to 35,000 in 2004, an increase of 32%. This compares to an overall increase of 17% in the ranks of university teachers overall, perhaps a promising difference. Less satisfactory, however is that the increase was greatest (almost 70%) among non-tenure-track teachers. In fact, in 2004, only 40% were full-time teachers on the tenure line: the others were either full-time but non-tenurable, or part-time. It must be said, however, that these figures – representative of important changes sweeping through post-secondary institutions in North America – are virtually identical to those obtaining among all teachers, across a score of disciplines.

Another recent report (Teagle Foundation Working Group, 2009) provides some further insight here. Statistics for 2004–2005 reveal that 17,433 bachelor's degrees (representing just over 1% of *all* such degrees) were awarded in foreign languages. Of those language degrees, about 48% were in Spanish language and literature, 14% in French and 6% in German. Only 208 degrees were awarded for the study of Chinese, and 21 for Arabic.

Overall, despite Welles's (2002) attempts at some reassurance, many continue to agree with the predominant theme of media commentary after the events of September 2001 – which harped, of course, on the lack of American linguistic expertise in dealings with an increasingly troublesome world. Welles cited a couple of representative instances herself. In the *New York Times* (2001), Dennis Baron had written that the study of foreign languages was declining in America, and so the country 'doesn't know what the world is saying'. In the *Washington Post* (2001), Paul Simon lighted upon that 'stable' 8% of foreign-language enrolments, arguing that it represented a deficiency. Within academia, too, alarm bells went off – and they continue to ring.

Within the modern-language area, for example, Blake and Kramsch (2007) introduced a forum on language policy in the United States by referring to a recent European Union survey. While about half of all Europeans reported some facility with a second language (one-third said that that language was English), the figure dropped to 30% in Britain, and only 9% in America. Allen (2007) and Al-Batal (2007) report considerable improvement in Arabic-language matters since September 2001: between 1998 and 2002, student enrolments in Arabic university courses increased by more than 90%, and they have been doubling annually since then. Arabic-language programmes at universities have also increased significantly. Further moves are discussed in a forum introduced by Byrnes (2009), as part of which Klee (2009: 618) cites a report by the Modern Language Association describing 'the current language crisis that has occurred as a result of 9/11' (Ad Hoc Committee on Foreign Languages, 2007).

English in Europe

With English fluency increasing around the world, with academic pressures to publish in English and, most pointedly, with English-medium education more and more widespread in non-anglophone countries, Kubota (2009: 614) points to the greater difficulties now for American exchange students to learn another language during their year abroad: this, on top of the fact that, in any event, 'one quarter of American students already choose English-speaking countries as their destination for study abroad' (see also Mok, 2007; de Wit, 2002). In this connection, Maiworm and Wächter (2002) surveyed higher-education institutions in 19 countries and found that, while only 1% of *entire* programmes were delivered through English, one in three universities had at least one English-language programme (*all* universities in Finland and Netherlands). (They also found, of course, a much larger number of individual *courses* taught in English.) The authors note that English-medium teaching is a relatively recent phenomenon, with most of it emerging in the late 1990s, and in the larger universities north of the Alps. Ammon and McConnell (2002) provided further relevant detail here. Beyond Finland and the Netherlands, English-medium provision (for complete programmes of study once again) was greatest in Belgium, the Czech Republic and Norway. In five countries – Spain, Italy, Switzerland, Croatia and Greece – the authors reported *no* such provision at all.

By 2004, almost one in five European universities were offering programmes in English. Since these are often crafted to attract non-native-English-speaking students from other countries, the universities are now competing with English, American, Canadian and other anglophone institutions for 'market share' of 'foreign' students. Also, in early 2004, German universities actually mounted a campaign to attract British students to their English-taught degree programmes (of which there were more than 300). Is this bad for the quality of English? Does it provide further evidence that the English 'weed' is choking European flowers, to cite Swain's (2004) title? Whatever the case, such trends clearly testify to the strength and appeal of English.

Within the European systems themselves, Eurostat figures from fifteen years ago were already showing that 90% of school-aged learners in the European Union were studying English (as opposed to 32% taking French, 18% German and 8% Spanish); see King (2001). And ten years earlier still, a survey of German, Belgian and Finnish university students had suggested that of the 69% who supported the idea of a single European language – not an uninteresting statistic in its own right – some 84% thought that that language should be English (Coleman, 2006).

Notes

1. Mencken was not a 'professional' linguist, but many academic reviewers praised his books and, indeed, he was often given work in philology and linguistics to review. Besides, many important efforts on both sides of the Atlantic have been made by gifted 'amateurs' (Nelson, 1999).

2. King's mention of Graddol suggests a 1998 book; in fact, the contribution is a chapter in a larger 'consultative report'. The accurate citation appears in my reference list here.

3. 'GCSE' stands for 'General Certificate of Secondary Education', a qualification awarded on the basis of examinations that mark, in England, Wales and Northern Ireland (the Scottish system is somewhat different), the end of compulsory secondary-level education. Students may then go on to take 'A-level' courses ('A' meaning 'Advanced') in preparation for a university career.

   Readers will find some minor discrepancies in the figures provided by King (2001) and the Centre for Information on Language Teaching and Research (2009).

4. Some readers will find this marketing-based instrumentality a little sad. Where is the cultural component that once informed language teaching? Malcolm Cook, Kelly's counterpart at the University of Exeter, thus found the modern scenario a bleak and depressing one, and the decline in literature as very serious. According to Kelly, however, modern students are not interested in reading *per se*, so why should we expect them to be interested in some 'fat nineteenth-century novel'? Universities are 'market-led, involved in designing attractive courses that lure students. If we do not do that, we are dead' (Anon., 2000).

5. The last of these three authors (Jacobs, 2002: 251) provides some interesting comments on the situation in the state of Hawai'i, where multiculturalism and multilingualism exist at a 'crossroads of the Pacific'. While the most commonly taught languages are Spanish, French, German, Japanese and Chinese 'unfortunately, despite the considerable numbers of people of Filipino, Samoan and Vietnamese ethnicity in Hawai'i, far too few aspire to higher education'.

   Indeed, Jacobs reports that secondary-school principals actually discourage language learning, and tend to push computer courses.

11
Language Contact: Present and Future

Predicting language dynamics: General notes

Coleman (2006: 11) has suggested that 'ultimately, the world will become diglossic, with one language for local communication, culture and expression of identity, and another – English – for wider and more formal communication, especially in writing'. It is clear that many feel this way, although not all of them are pleased by the prospect, of course, and some feel that it is an outcome to be resisted. Relatedly, Nettle and Romaine (2002: 191) have argued that such a bilingual or diglossic situation essentially transforms 'the majority of the world's languages [into] minority languages'. I don't think this is quite accurate or, if it is, it achieves accuracy only by sliding back and forth between different linguistic regions. Nonetheless, the increasing power and attraction of English certainly alters patterns of communication in important ways. It is undoubtedly accurate to add, as Nettle and Romaine do, that even those languages 'protected by national boundaries and institutions exist in a diglossic relationship with English'. It is also correct for the authors to write that 'this in itself is no cause for alarm' (p. 191). If the balance between a 'big' language like English and 'smaller' or more localised ones could remain more or less stable, more or less diglossic, then there would indeed be little cause for alarm. But what animates Nettle, Romaine and many other commentators is the possibility that such a balance is in fact *un*stable, and that in a marriage of unequal partners one will sooner or later fall to a distinctly subaltern status. In many ways, and for many people, this is the nub of the matter. There may be no easy or, indeed, desirable way of stuffing the big genie back into the bottle...but can we limit its powers once it's out?

While few prizes have been awarded for successfully predicting the future in any but the most trivial or obvious settings (see Maurais and Morris, 2003; Tsitsipis, 2005), we can agree that some opinions are more valuable than others: in the present case, then, we might imagine that the views of language experts will be particularly germane for linguistic futurology. It is worth pointing out, however, that experts often see the world through very particular, and sometimes myopic, spectacles. Within what is now a very large sociology-of-language literature, many books and articles are so much on language *alone* that the vision presented is of the tunnel variety; typically, in such treatments, the necessary contextualisation is lacking. The clearest examples of this, perhaps, come from the language-revival literature, in which desired outcomes are depicted as if they could be achieved in some stand-alone fashion, in which there is no recognition of the fact that linguistic shift and loss are *symptoms* of a larger dynamic. The logical but often insufficiently grasped implication is to attend to this broader dynamic: after all, you don't cure measles by covering up the spots. No one doubts that this is difficult. Although massive reweaving of the social fabric, or widespread social revolution, is always possible, it is relatively rare (and fraught with danger). A further complication is that broadly based alterations to the social fabric are rarely desired: what is usually wanted is some linguistic redress by which (for example) a given group retains its place within the modern mainstream, its mobility, and all desired current conditions – but is somehow enabled to revive its ancestral language. Related to this most basic point is the fact that many of those who write on topics like language contact, maintenance, shift and revival, or on themes like the spread of English around the globe, or on linguistic ecology, are themselves strongly or ideologically committed to particular lines of argument. The matter cannot be pursued here, but it is obvious that a combination of expertise with enthusiasm may pose some difficulties.[1]

Perhaps, then, it is not surprising that some of the best assessments of linguistic conditions (in a social sense, of course) have been produced by those whose original and more basic allegiance was sociology, or political science, or history, or anthropology. The need to graft an appreciation of language writ large onto a broader stem has often proved salutary. I don't mean to suggest, of course, that nothing valuable under the heading of 'the social life of language' has been produced by those whose complete academic *raison d'être* centres upon language. Nor could I deny that there are sociological, political and historical works which try to comment on language matters and fail abysmally. But the point is obvious here, I'm sure: it is essentially a plea for scholarly triangulation, and for fuller and more cross-disciplinary contextualisation.

To discuss 'language futures' means to consider the social factors that bear upon linguistic strengths and weaknesses, scope and influence. While 'small' or endangered languages naturally command our particular attention, their status is only defined in relation to others.[2] That is to say, in areas where inter-relationships are paramount, discussing *only* the small is just as blinkered as focussing solely on the powerful. Contact and its ramifications are the starting-point here – and generally the finishing one, too. In many instances of language contact between varieties that are unequal in important ways, some bilingual accommodation seems the obvious avenue: one language for home and hearth, another for the world beyond one's gate. Bilingualism, however, is often an unstable and impermanent way-station on the road to a new monolingualism. Formal language planning on behalf of beleaguered languages (to encourage a firmer diglossia, for example) can often do very little to stem the forces of urbanisation, modernisation and mobility, forces which typically put a language on the endangered list and lead to shift. In a word, decline in the existence and attractions of traditional lifestyles inexorably entails decline in languages associated with them. Short of unethical and draconian intervention, or of voluntary social segregation which has proved to be of extremely limited appeal, language shift often seems inevitable and bilingualism often unstable.

Despite the fact that people can breathlessly write about 'language loss' as if there were actually some period during which groups had no language at all, despite the fact that in many eyes *globalisation* has become the longest four-letter word, despite the imbalance of heat and light in discussions of the social life of language, we should try to remember that – both historically and linguistically – change rather than stasis is the norm. Environments alter, people move, needs and demands evolve, and such factors have a large influence upon language. When considering accusations that certain societies, or groups, or institutions can be singled out as villains in the story of some language or another, we ought to bear some generalities in mind. The desire, for instance, for mobility and modernisation is, with some few notable exceptions, a global phenomenon. Whether one looks at the capitalist world or the former communist one, at contemporary times or historical ones, at empires or small societies, at immigrant minorities or indigenous groups, one sees a similarity of pressures which take their toll, force change and throw populations into transitional states that have, naturally, unpleasant consequences (for some at least, in the short term at least, and so on). Original languages are frequent casualties here.

What to do with, and about, endangered languages has become a hot topic, the central element (as we have seen) within the 'new' ecology of language. A collection on the subject, by Robins and Uhlenbeck (1991), was not the first discussion of endangerment and death, but its organisational origins are important. The Comité International Permanent de Linguistes (of which both Robins and Uhlenbeck were officers) had argued, through its statutes, that more academic and official attention should be given to threatened varieties; as well, the collection comprised a special issue of *Diogenes*, a journal underwritten by UNESCO. Since the appearance of that collection, there has been a great deal of activity: particularly useful discussions include those of Grenoble and Whaley (1998), Nettle and Romaine (2002), Crystal (2000) and, most recently, Duchêne and Heller (2007) and Harbert *et al.* (2009). Fascination with the death or near-death of languages has also given rise to more 'popular' treatments, such as those of Dalby (2002) and Abley (2003).

I only touch upon the matter here because, for present purposes, we can understand much of the literature of endangerment as the reverse of the coin of 'global English'. It is worth pointing out, however, that the most pressing issues under this rubric involve the intertwining of the 'new' ecology of language, questions of language rights, and the appropriate roles for linguists and other concerned academics. My concern here is simply to make some suggestions about language futures in a world made increasingly safe for anglophones and – as will shortly be seen – to introduce two particularly level-headed assessments in the area.

Large and small languages

We can conveniently begin here with some attention to the fate of 'small' and 'stateless' languages, a fate that has certainly become more precarious in modern times. In a world in which the big lingua francas and the state-supported languages either ignored smaller and, it was presumed, unimportant mediums, or failed to penetrate their heartlands, the more localised forms continued on a minor but relatively stable basis. But that world has largely vanished. Now, the big languages (we could often say, I suppose, *the* big language) are everywhere; their penetrative power is ubiquitous. Their strength derives from the same sources as always, but their scope has increased dramatically because of technological innovation on a scale never before seen. Their progress is like some juggernaut which crushes all in its path. Thus do English and globalisation – sometimes, but not inevitably, a rough synonym for westernisation or Americanisation – march arm-in-arm around the world. But there is another factor in all this. Apart from the inexorable 'push' of a globalised economy, intent on selling the same shoes, soft drinks and sex, through English, to everyone from Boston to Bhutan, there is an almost equally powerful 'pull' factor.[3] Globalisation and its linguistic ramifications are welcomed by many who see in it upward mobility: physical, social, psychological. Spolsky (1998: 76–77) writes that 'the demand [for English] has continually exceeded the supply'. All of this is very serious for small languages without a state behind them, whose appeal to their once-and-future speakers increasingly rests upon abstract pillars of cultural continuity and tradition.

What of 'small' languages fortunate enough to have their own state? While the same pressures bear upon them as upon their stateless counterparts, it may be thought that they are significantly more well armed for resistance operations. Such varieties do indeed have better future prospects, but it would be a great mistake to assume that the acquisition of official status by a small language means that a corner has been decisively turned. Irish is the only Celtic language to have its own state, but that has not made it the most dominant in that family, nor has it managed to bar foreign linguistic influence at the customs-post. Other varieties (Dutch, Finnish, Swedish) are also finding that long-standing and official status is no guarantee of protection.

The evolving nature of the relationship between small languages and large ones is continuing grist for the scholarly mill, and there are some particularly instructive contexts to attend to here. Consider the European Union, for example, where we see a continent coming increasingly together while, at the same time, giving more regard to both 'stateless' languages and those varieties of limited scope. Can a future federal Europe coexist with a 'Europe of the Regions'? What is the status likely to be of languages like Danish and Finnish, to say nothing of Provençal, of Catalan, of Welsh? Of particular importance here, I think, is a deeper consideration of the technological 'shrinkage' of the world and its effects upon small varieties. On the one hand, for example, it can be argued that global technology assists the advance of English; on the other, that technology (together with European political restructuring) actually makes it easier for small cultures and their languages to have that desired place in the sun. See also my remarks, in Chapter 8, about the place of languages in cyberspace.

I have already hinted at another central issue: the emergence of a two-tiered structure within the ranks of the 'big' languages. We need to know much more about the likelihood of English becoming super-dominant, and the effects of this. This is not only important for the speakers of French, Russian, German, Chinese, Spanish and so on, because there are obvious knock-on effects which will touch the smaller varieties. A world – or even just a Europe – which evolves more and more to become 'English versus All The Others' will not be same as one in which the continuingly important presence of other large varieties interposes itself, as it were, between the super-language and the smaller ones. I have not, as yet, seen very much on this aspect of the topic.

Academic insights

In a world of language contact where several players hold the main part of the stage, and where a great many others nervously huddle in the wings, questions of intervention naturally arise (in some minds, at least). In fact, intervention in linguistic matters can be worse than doing nothing, if there has been inadequate preparation across a wide spectrum of social life. Prescinding from my comments (above) about scholar-advocates (see also note 1), I would argue that the particular and obvious contribution of academic linguists to this drama is to assist in data-gathering, and then (perhaps) in the translation of information into policy. Scholars are not usually prime movers here and as Elie Kedourie noted many years ago in a slightly different context, academic research 'does not add a jot or a tittle to the capacity for ruling [read also *policy-making*], and to pretend otherwise is to hide with equivocation what is a very clear matter' (1961: 125). While being appropriately modest, however, researchers can make real and important contributions.

First, and most generally, we should surely aim to cultivate a clearer and broader awareness of the *real* forces in the *real* world that bear upon language matters. It may be of interest to continue to point to the 'logic of languages' that all varieties possess, so as to reinforce the perceived validity of some given variety. Or, it may be useful to conduct studies showing the historical roots of that language, and to suggest that its continuity is bound up with that of its speakers' culture. It may be valuable to point to the imperialistic and basically unfair practices of those large linguistic neighbours who are stifling the re-emergence of the language, or who are preventing it from maintaining its own little place in the sun. These sorts of studies and concerns are, of course, eminently worthwhile from an academic and cultural point of view. If, however, we are concerned with *policy* and *planning* – and bearing in mind Kedourie's cautionary note – we should realise that none of this sort of work need have the slightest relevance to actual linguistic developments on the ground.

In line with previous comments in this book, and with a central theme in almost all of my work, I think it is important to remember that what is really under discussion is not so much language *per se* but, rather, questions of group *identity*. If language were purely an instrumental medium, then many elements of its social existence would resolve themselves and many of the most heated controversies and debates would vanish. Language planning, as a formal exercise, would become a very delimited undertaking. As we all know, however, language has deep psychological importance, and the deepest wellsprings are those of group identity. This is why the struggle between large and small varieties is so vehement, why we need always remind ourselves that our work takes us into heavily mined territories of emotion. Whatever future developments may unfold, this at least will be constant.

I began this chapter with a plea for more triangulation and interdisciplinarity, for keeping scholarly myopia at bay. In this regard, it is interesting to report that two of the most insightful forays into the thickets of language contact are those of Abram de Swaan and Philippe van Parijs. Neither is a language expert by background: the former is a political scientist, sociologist (and psychotherapist!), the bulk of whose work has dealt with transnational social and welfare policies; the latter is a philosopher and political economist whose research concerns have centred upon more equitable distributions, and re-distributions, of income. In a world in which one linguistic variety has become more dominant than any other ever has been, each of these scholars has approached the study of language with a cross-national perspective, concerned with macro-level analyses of the 'world language system'.

Language futures: The work of Abram de Swaan

Following some introductory remarks on the topic (1993a), de Swaan (1993b) provides a brief historical description of the various 'circles' occupied by European languages; he suggests – this is in 1993, remember – that 'the subject of language has been the great *non-dit* of European integration', that only English and French are widely used in political and bureaucratic discussions, and that there is, therefore, 'a tacit rivalry between the great language groups of Europe [essentially French, German and English] for predominance within the Community' (p. 244). De Swaan introduces a metric he calls the 'Q-value', the communicative potential possessed by given linguistic repertoires. Among other things, this heightens the appeal of acquiring second and subsequent languages that overlap with those of others. As de Swaan observes, 'speakers will prefer a repertoire that has languages in common with a greater number of *multilingual* speakers than another repertoire' (p. 246). Within a fairly dynamic linguistic context, the Q-value for English is 'consistently the highest: it has de facto become the connecting language of the European Community' (p. 250). De Swaan's conclusion is that the cross-national importance of English will only increase, while in more delimited contexts

> the national languages will prevail and English will not easily push the indigenous languages out of their domains. But this diglossia is an equilibrium, predicated on the robustness of the languages involved, and therefore dependent on continuing state support and protection of the national languages.[4] (p. 252)

In a later paper, de Swaan (1998a) reinforces his basic contention: within various circles of 'larger' and 'smaller' languages, English is 'at the galactic center', the one that allows the greatest breadth of contact among all the others. He notes that linguistic utility is, in important part, a function of its *prevalence* within a region and its *centrality*, and it is the product of these two factors, of course, that comprises the 'Q' value of a language, its essential *communicative value*. This can be expressed quantitatively. While German may be the most prevalent mother tongue in Europe, English overtakes it when second-language speakers are added to native ones; during the 1990s, de Swaan calculates, the Q-value of English in the EU was 0.50, that of German 0.12, and that of French 0.19. (I provide no justification for numerical derivation here; the only points of present interest are the relative positions.) De Swaan also approaches the question of relative 'value' through a discussion of languages as collective 'goods'; in fact, he suggests, they are 'hyper-collective' goods because their utility is widened as the number of their speakers increases. Their Q-value, that is to say, is a function of user numbers, and it is easy to see that as the circle of utility expands, so does the appeal of investment by new potential members of that language community.

(This, incidentally, is the central difficulty associated with the growth of 'constructed' or 'artificial' languages like Esperanto. Their existence and their appeal are logical, since they provide a relatively easy – that is, low-investment – communicative medium whose instrumentality does not oblige potential users to abandon their mother tongues or other existing elements of their linguistic repertoires. Still, *some* investment is required and, therefore, some return on that investment must be on the cards. Why, however, should one make even the minimal effort necessary to acquire Esperanto [for example] when the circle of users that will then be joined is so small? But how, proponents of constructed languages argue, will there ever *be* a significant circle unless new learners agree to sign a contract of agreement? The impasse is obvious.)

In a companion piece, de Swaan (1998b) returns to a subject I touched upon at a more subjective level in Chapter 8 (note 9): 'the dilemmas that confront authors...who must decide whether to address a relatively restricted audience in their native tongue or compete for a much larger public by either learning the more widespread language or relying on translations' (p. 109). He expands the argument by noting that the evident attractions of a language with a high Q-value may prove detrimental to the maintenance of diglossia (or polyglossia). Gradually, he suggests, varieties may be deserted and whole communities may 'tilt towards the new language like a ship making water and leaning over ever further until it capsizes'; then, shifting metaphors, he writes of 'a stampede out of the indigenous language and towards the imported tongue ensues' (p. 119).

Language shift may indeed ensue, and it is important to realise here (as we have already noted) that bilingualism and diglossia are no guarantees against it. After all, once most members of a language community have become bilingual, where original-language domains are increasingly eroded by the lapping linguistic waters of a more dominant variety, then 'the original language no longer adds much to the value of individual repertoires' and, consequently, may be abandoned (de Swaan, 1998b: 120). The context then may become one that is all too familiar to nationalists and revivalists of various stripes, whose appeals for language maintenance must increasingly be based upon cultural arguments. As I have suggested elsewhere, such appeals are neither ignoble nor trivial. Nonetheless, given the social and economic circumstances of most 'ordinary' people, part of the familiar picture I've just mentioned typically shows 'a small group of activists nervously glancing over their shoulders to see how much of the population they claim to represent is following them, and how closely behind them it is' (Edwards, 1995: 111).

As I foreshadowed in an earlier chapter, de Swaan (2004) has extended his arguments about the contemporary linguistic world to include some very pointed remarks about endangered languages and their place within the 'new' ecology. He begins by suggesting that much of the current literature on the topic is motivated by guilt. While most contemporary scholars 'speak and write flawlessly one or more major languages', many of them have 'a bad conscience' vis-à-vis 'smaller' languages and cultures' (p. 567).[5] Consequently, a 'new mission' has arisen: the protection of 'endangered speeches' (p. 568). De Swaan rejects the 'linguistic sentimentalism' that generally underpins efforts here, noting that, while the abandonment of a language is always a serious matter, it is one for speakers themselves to decide upon; he thus agrees with Ladefoged (1992) that it is not for scholars to pronounce on such matters, that combining research with advocacy is a risky undertaking. Faced with important problems, difficulties that almost always involve other variables besides language, communities are presented with

> a classical dilemma of collective action...that neither linguists nor sociologists or anyone else can resolve for them. It is not up to others to preach or admonish; the only helpful response is to clarify the dynamics of the dilemma.[6] (p. 577)

Current scholarly interest in 'language rights, against linguistic imperialism, against "linguicism and linguicide" has become unstuck from sociolinguistics. It favors imagery instead of theory' (p. 570), drawing especially upon the 'misleading metaphor' of plant and animal extinction. Linguistic sentimentalism, then, is 'an exaggerated appeal to familiar feelings with the aim of eliciting the traditional response of sympathy'. De Swaan singles out Skutnabb-Kangas and Phillipson as 'the village enthusiasts of linguistics'. It is a reflection of some sort of collective guilt ('who does not feel vaguely uneasy about the hegemony of the West?': p. 576), de Swaan implies, that their views 'though seldom taken seriously, are rarely openly refuted, either' (p. 570).

Implicit in this scholarly perspective is the view that diversity is ever and always an unalloyed good, and that all languages deserve their 'rights'. Quite apart from the practical obstacles that immediately present themselves to the open-minded, de Swaan observes that the greater the diversity, the better for English, whose hegemony is actually being 'hastened and consolidated by the promotion of a multiplicity of languages' (p. 573): he cites both current European policies and, more striking still, the results of post-apartheid South Africa's adoption of eleven languages as official. So there as elsewhere, de Swaan suggests, 'the more languages, the more English...[and] thus works the ruse of history: the opponents of English linguistic imperialism...have accomplished precisely the opposite of what they hoped to bring about' (p. 574).[7]

Moving towards his conclusion, de Swaan writes that 'like all forms of sentimentalism, linguistic sentimentalism is disingenuous at the core'. Among other things, this fuels European language policy which, in turn, contributes to 'a permanent circuit of conferences on the endangered and disadvantaged languages of Europe, which keeps the experts and the activists fully occupied' (pp. 575–576). His single most important point, however, is found in the concluding comments to his summary book on the subject:

> What matters more is to separate the hegemonic language from the hegemonic world views that it transmits. Almost every conceivable opinion, almost any human sentiment, is expressed in English; there is no language that more fully reflects the variety of human experience. The danger of global uniformity is not in the language. It is in the power relations that prevail in the global constellation, where English is the hypercentral language ... But, as the language of global communication, English also allows dissident voices to make themselves heard all over the world. If English is the language of the powers that be, it is also the language of empowerment. (2001: 192–193)

Is this triumphalism ... or the summary of scholarly analyses tempered by common sense and pragmatism? Readers may judge for themselves, of course, but my own opinion is, I think, clear.[8]

De Swaan (1998b: 119) pointed out that 'in principle, a language community should be ready to subsidize new speakers to join its ranks, since they increase the Q-value of its language'. Many agencies around the world do in fact underwrite language courses for immigrants, but de Swaan suggests that the British and the Americans (for example) might reasonably be expected to subsidise their languages for 'foreign' learners abroad, too. However, many of those learners will pay for their own books and tuition, 'since they want to improve the Q-value of their repertoire by adding a widespread language'. One implication, perhaps, is that the 'big' linguistic players can rather unfairly sit back and do nothing, content in the knowledge that their language communities will increase without any special cost to them; see the earlier remarks on Greek and Roman attitudes (in Chapter 8).

Language futures: The work of Philippe van Parijs

Matters of fairness and cost are what Philippe van Parijs has mainly interested himself in. He has stated bluntly that only English 'can hope to become the first (and predictably only) universal lingua franca' (2000a: 221). As a sort of counterweight, however, application of the 'territorial' principle – essentially, *cuius regio, eius lingua* – may be necessary for the protection of 'vulnerable' languages: 'When people intend settling in a particular territory, they should kindly but firmly be asked to have the humility to learn the local language' (p. 219). He notes elsewhere (2000b) that successful application of the territorial principle rests upon a high level of linguistic homogeneity in the region concerned. This is not, of course, always the case and, as well, van Parijs detours around tricky questions of 'nations' within 'states': Québec within Canada, for example. Two provisos (outlined in van Parijs, 2004a) – first, for a language to be 'given' a territory, there must exist a 'sufficiently vigorous movement' demanding it; second, the population of native speakers must not be the 'product of recent immigration' – are not entirely satisfactory here, as the author himself acknowledges. ('How many?' and 'how recent?' are only the two most immediate questions that spring to mind.)

More broadly speaking, things do not, and will not, exist in stasis. Van Parijs goes on to describe the mechanisms by which the scope and appeal of English are only likely to increase. And if this global 'linguistic flattening' were to continue, why should we worry unduly? On the one hand, the 'tremendous economic and cultural advantages of sharing the same language world-wide'; on the other, 'nothing more terrible than turning the whole planet into a large number of Republics of Ireland' (p. 225).

As readers may imagine, van Parijs immediately presents the arguments against this vision of future, on two grounds. First (and despite what we might think at the moment to have been a slight slip in inserting the word 'cultural' into the statement I have just quoted), linguistic diversity may be the only serious protection for cultural diversity – and the latter is arguably good for all of us. This is, however, a speculative argument. Another is rather stronger: those who do not speak the 'big' language incur costs for its acquisition, and this seems unfair. The injustice here may be 'limited to the transition period: the native English-speaking French in tomorrow's linguistically globalized world will not suffer from it...but the transition can be both long and tough enough to badly affect several generations' (p. 227).

What remedies suggest themselves here? Van Parijs notes, first of all, that various measures might be put in place to keep people at home, a home in which the territorial principle prevails, a home in which a 'local' language is broadly sufficient. These measures would include more tangible efforts (of transnational socioeconomic redistribution, for instance) and less tangible ones (the fostering of local allegiances, of pride in regional institutions). All such measures, however, can at best hope to alleviate some of the linguistic injustices in a world with 'big' and 'small' languages.

Van Parijs (2004a) stresses the need for English as a lingua franca as something that has arisen from 'no hidden conspiracy by the Brits, let alone the Americans, but [by] the spontaneous outcome of a huge set of decentralised decisions, mainly by non-anglophones, about which language to learn and which language to use' (p. 124). He acknowledges that incentives for learning 'foreign' varieties will decline as the spread of English increases but writes that this can be accepted 'without rancour or resentment' (p. 149) providing that 'fairness' prevails. And how is this to be understood?

Choice of a lingua franca 'unavoidably provides...undeserved advantages' to those whose mother tongue it is (p. 124). (Of course, this unfairness has always prevailed, wherever [for example] one dialect has been given some official imprimatur.) Van Parijs cites with approval Pool's (1991) observation that the only real way of overcoming unfairness is for the linguistically advantaged group to subsidise the acquisition of its language by others. The question, of course, is how and whether this can be meaningfully done. Van Parijs's curious suggestions for redress involves banning the dubbing of English-language programmes, as well as 'poaching' off the web; each of these represents a sort of compensatory 'free riding' that makes the acquisition of English somewhat less difficult – and expensive. These may seem a bit 'micro' in the overall scheme of things, but the (perhaps) more logical alternative of asking Britain and America to transfer funds to countries whose citizens have the unfair language-learning burden is rather unlikely to occur, particularly since those citizens 'spontaneously crave to learn English anyway' (p. 137). De Briey and van Parijs (2002) and van Parijs (2003) provide more of the economic details involved in the redress of linguistic disparity, as well as reinforcing the argument that at least part of the unfairness comes from the fact that the anglophone community grows and grows, as more non-anglophone speakers learn English. Not all commentators have agreed: Réaume (2009: 9), for instance, considers it unlikely that a benefit accrues to the anglophone community if 'someone in Tibet' with whom she will never speak learns English. One sees her point, but it would surely be more accurate to suggest that, in some instances, the benefits will take a little longer to be realised. (In the next section I turn more formally to criticisms of both van Parijs and de Swaan.)

Part of the alleged unfairness, van Parijs notes, is that with the spread of English comes the spread of a certain mind-set, of a particular system of ideas, leading perhaps to 'a worrying world-wide ideological domination by the United States' (p. 138). Furthermore, he admits that making it easier to learn English – via subtitles rather than dubbing, via web-poaching – might reinforce this tendency. But he immediately goes on to remind us that there is nothing in the language *qua* language that is philosophically offensive and that, in any event, the solution cannot be any sort of 'defensive retreat'; rather, it lies in more and more appropriation of English 'in order to spread through it whatever content we see fit' (p. 139). This is entirely in line, of course, with the localisation of various 'world Englishes'.

Criticisms of de Swaan and van Parijs

It is already apparent, I suppose, that I find myself in broad agreement with the theses advanced by de Swaan and van Parijs. The criticisms of their work that I present here – criticisms mounted by Grin, Phillipson, Réaume and Ives – are not at all sufficient, I find, to dispel this agreement. They are, however, extremely useful in focussing our attention on some of the most salient features of the work.

Van Parijs's work (in particular, 2004b) has evoked an interesting rejoinder from François Grin (2004). Grin is an admirer of van Parijs's efforts to deal with matters revolving around the choice and encouragement of a lingua francas, the unfairness that this can lead to, and the possibilities for reducing this unfairness. Nonetheless, he points out that the desirability of a single lingua franca is just an assertion (what of Switzerland, happy enough with three, and then four, official languages?). He also suggests that European competence in English may be somewhat less than van Parijs thinks and, in any event, 'l'auto-évaluation des compétences en langues étrangères est chose délicate' (p. 4). Despite compensatory efforts, Grin adds, non-anglophone countries continue to incur costs that do not have to be borne by the Americans and the British; and despite the best efforts of language learners, their competences will always be 'nettement inférieures à celles des locuteurs natifs' (p. 7).

And what of the 'effets symboliques qui accompagnent toute hégémonie linguistique' (p. 7), Grin asks? He notes that choosing Esperanto as the common link language would do away with all the injustice. As van Parijs has pointed out, Esperanto is not quite as 'neutral' as it is made out to be, but (Grin writes) it is certainly more 'neutral' than English (or, of course, than any other 'natural' language; see Edwards, 2010b). It should be mentioned that van Parijs has also taken the practical ground here by observing that, whatever the merits or demerits of a constructed language, its promotion would undermine all the efforts around the world that have already been made to acquire English.

Grin certainly endorses the idea of financial compensation for those who must learn English, an idea that is 'féconde et séduisante' idea (p. 10). However, can we really expect the large anglophone countries to make massive subventions? Unlikely, to say the very least. Gazzola and Grin (2007) provide further details here, and cite a number of important earlier works attempting to deal with questions of money and equity.

In a return engagement, van Parijs (2007: 72) bluntly observes: 'Let us not beat around the bush. In science and in all other domains which require communication across borders, we need a lingua franca. One lingua franca. As quickly as possible. And this lingua franca will be English.' He picks up Grin's point (which he had also touched on himself, of course), that the anglophone countries of the world are not going to provide financial subsidies for non-anglophone speakers to learn English; this would be a sort of 'tax that is most unlikely to ever come about' (p. 79). Why should they pay when millions of people around the world are learning English anyway, driven by individual and collective self-interest? How can we deal with this anglophone 'free riding'? Van Parijs suggests that some measure of European Union redistribution *might* be possible, but a more likely scenario involves that reciprocal 'free riding' already noted: 'compensatory poaching' of the web, for instance, means that all the information emerging from anglophone sources and presented in English is freely available to non-native speakers, too; on the other hand, information in other languages is largely unavailable to anglophones.

Réaume (2009) has criticised the 'simple rational-choice model' that van Parijs allegedly uses to in his discussion of the emergence and utility of English as lingua franca: 'Hard and soft imperialism practiced by English-speaking states plus anglophone intransigence, which is itself a side-effect of an imperial mentality, magnify and accelerate the rationality of the convergence on English' (p. 5). This seems reasonable, but Réaume's further observation that 'absent these sorts of forces, not only is it doubtful that English would become the lingua franca; it is questionable whether a single lingua franca would emerge at all' (p. 5) is rather less compelling. If the current state of affairs might not have come to pass without 'unjust power relations', she adds, 'it is less clear to me that the only task of a theory of linguistic justice is to determine how best to compensate [for it]' (p. 6). Again, the second half of her sentence might bear more weight if we could more easily accept the first.

234 Challenges in the Social Life of Language

At a more basic level, Réaume, like Grin, questions whether we do in fact *need* one overarching lingua franca. She notes that, given existing social and educational inequalities – rich children always do better than poor ones – acceptance of the point would only heighten an unseemly 'race to the top' (p. 12), a race to most closely emulate native-speaker competence, a race in which, at least for some considerable period of time, some will reap occupational and other opportunities denied to others.

It is perhaps worth inserting here the point that arguments for an open and egalitarian world, one in which a democratic expansion of lingua-franca knowledge is considered to be a good thing, may be somewhat compromised when we realise that not everyone is released from the starting-gate at the same time. (This is a difficulty found in many areas of social life, of course: one thinks immediately of educational programmes of a 'head-start' or 'affirmative-action' nature, programmes meant to try and level social playing-fields.) Henri-Dominique Lacordaire, the famous nineteenth-century Dominican activist, wrote that 'entre le fort et le faible, entre le riche et le pauvre, entre le maître et le serviteur, c'est la liberté qui opprime, et la loi qui affranchit' (1872: III: 494). A little later, Anatole France (1894: 118) made the same point from the other angle, writing about those same liberating regulations: 'la majestueuse égalité des lois, qui interdit au riche comme au pauvre de coucher sous les ponts, de mendier dans les rues, et de voler du pain'. Whether such points, in themselves, are sufficient grounds for rejecting the lingua-franca benefits endorsed by de Swaan and van Parijs is, of course, a different thing.

To return to Réaume. She correctly observes that 'a common language is not a sufficient condition for lively democratic engagement' (p. 8), adding that such engagement is rare even within speech communities. In the past – now seen by some as rather élitist – cross-community communication was infrequent enough that only a handful of professionals needed the multilingual competence to cope. Now, she says, we are told that everyone must be able to speak more or less directly to everyone else. 'But no human society has ever known such communicative richness...so it is difficult to see why the language barrier must be eliminated in order to better enable a level of communication that doesn't happen even when there is no language barrier' (p. 7). Apart from the fact that she seems to be replacing the idea of a lingua franca with some model of greatly increased multilingual facility here, Réaume leaves aside the simple fact that more and more 'ordinary' people *want* a lingua franca, or, more bluntly, want English. This is at the heart of the theses of de Swaan and van Parijs, and I have provided various illustrations in earlier chapters.

To reinforce the point, I can mention three more very recent publications: Sharifian (2009), Honna (2008) and Park (2009) – all simply selected from the book-review pages of a recent number of *World Englishes*.[9] The very titles are revealing: Park thus cites the 'local construction of a global language'; Honna writes of 'English as a multicultural language'; Sharifian refers to 'English as an international language'. In other words, all three books – referring to vast numbers of speakers – stress that English is no longer the 'property' of its first owners, suggesting (as we have seen elsewhere here) that notions of 'imperialism' now seems quaintly inaccurate. (None of the authors, it may also be noted, is a native English speaker.)

Park (2009) writes about South Korea, noting the 'near-obsessive quest' for English there; see also Jin-Kyu Park (2009). This has been criticised as a sort of feeding frenzy, a 'fever'; however, while these terms are intended pejoratively, they also highlight the strength of the across-the-board interest. English-language 'villages' – total immersion environments within the country – are also increasingly popular, particularly among those sections of the population who cannot afford *jogi yuhak* (overseas language education). Beginning with some remarks on Japan, Honna (2008) considers that English can no longer be thought of simply as a foreign language there; furthermore, 'English is not the language for us to use only with Americans [and] the British... [but also] with Chinese, Koreans, Bruneians, Thais, Malaysians, Singaporeans...Europeans, Africans, Arabs, South Americans' (p. 6). The third scholar, Sharifian (2009; see also Sharifian and Clyne, 2008), edits a collection that deals with settings in Europe, Asia, Africa and America. An important emphasis is the 'divide' that often continues to separate native from non-native speakers of English – both interesting and disturbing since, as the editor points out, most English conversations are now between members of the latter group. The overall concern, then, is to reduce this divide in the interests of fuller and fairer cross-cultural communication, but nowhere is it even hinted that there is any going back nor, more importantly, any strong *desire* to go back. Important matters have to do with improvement, not replacement.

To return to Réaume once again: she also observes that policies encouraging the breadth of use of a lingua franca give rise to two sorts of cost: there are the obvious costs incurred by those who must learn it, costs not borne by those fortunate enough to be native speakers; and there are also 'costs' in the sense that the growth of lingua-franca competence will negatively affect the viability of the 'smaller' languages. She also comments upon the fact that, until and unless non-native speakers 'catch up', anglophones will continue to have great advantages; since the time involved here is not negligible, 'the advantage of Anglophones will have a great deal of time to become very firmly entrenched' (p. 15). Over the long haul, however, there will be more and more 'defections', perhaps to the point where the 'smaller' language dies.

On the 'cost' of language learning, however, Réaume adds a bit later that 'it is odd to think of learning a second language as imposing a cost' since learning anything is generally reckoned a good thing. She then glides somewhat illogically to the point that, if learning is good *per se*, why don't speakers of the lingua franca want to engage in language learning? 'It is hard not to read disrespect for other language communities into this posture, especially given the history of quasi-imperialist [?] attitudes and practices' (p. 19). 'Disrespect' is hardly the *mot juste* here, of course: there are much more direct and obvious reasons why speakers of 'big' languages so often fail to learn 'small' ones. In a similar discussion in her earlier piece, Réaume (2003: 293) notes that, since personal bilingualism is not difficult to achieve ('as minority-language communities everywhere prove daily') its relative rarity among majority-language speakers must be due to 'the absence of support for second-language learning and, one suspects, an ideology of superiority'. Again, this hardly captures the essence of the matter. And a final odd note from Réaume: 'the only policy that will accord equal respect to language communities...is equal recognition of the use of each of their languages' (2009: 19) – odd, because we are not, in the main, talking about 'respect' for other groups, nor 'equal recognition' of other languages but other, rather more immediate considerations. Questions of maintenance and shift, or language use and disuse, may quite reasonably be discussed without the introduction of vague terms like 'respect' and 'equal recognition'. Such an introduction rather misses the point, in any case. For instance, I may fully recognise the use of other languages in other contexts, and I may (regardless of this, incidentally) also respect the inhabitants of those contexts, without this social-psychological posture having the slightest impact on either my own language use and learning, or on the linguistic exigencies facing members of those of other groups.

Van Parijs's suggestion that every 'small' language may reasonably have its own territory is also seen as less than ideal. Réaume's point here rests upon her linked assertions that convergence on a single lingua franca is not, in fact, inevitable or desirable, and that the use of such a variety is not inevitably beneficial. From this perspective, the territorial 'solution' still rather smacks of unfairness: one language group has only its own area, while another 'has both its own turf and the transnational arena as its linguistic playground' (p. 18; see also de Schutter and Ypi, 2009). Her own argument, of course, is for the maintenance of multi-lingualism, for the avoidance of language 'loss', for the continuation of speakers' 'ability to carry on as we can presume they would want to under normal circumstances' (p. 17). This could involve changing their language practices, of course, as need dictates, but changing it on their own terms. Apart from foreign borrowings and the development of neologisms, however, it is difficult to understand why a group would *ever* want to change their language 'on their own terms' (that is to say, in the absence of external social and linguistic pressures). The suggestion, then, that languages do die out, 'sometimes without even any unfair pressure on [their] speakers' (p. 19) seems baseless. Or, at least, it fails to recognise that – given our understanding of the validity of all varieties, and more general considerations of the basic respect due to all human beings – all pressure is essentially 'unfair'. But where does this bring us, if not back to the broadest of all historical generalisations about groups in contact, in which matters of 'fairness', especially where that quantity is seen primarily in terms of the maintenance of all groups, cultures and languages, have typically not played a central role. Réaume's closing note about 'the recognition of equal status of all viable language communities' (p. 19) is, therefore, either terribly innocent or woefully skeletal. After all, it is the palpable *inequality* of various important social commodities that goes to the very heart of the entire discussion.

Phillipson (2004) has mounted some criticism of de Swaan's argu-ments, noting first that the latter sees the global language system as essentially resting upon individual choice and self-interest. He is said to ignore 'the role of the state in providing an infrastructure in education that constrains choices' (p. 74), cultural imperialism and 'McDonaldization', and the 'clear evidence' of British organisational efforts 'strongly backing the maintenance of English' (p. 76). Phillipson refers to de Swaan's observation (one made by several others, too) that the promotion of many languages can actually improve the standing of one, where that one is stronger than the others. He cites the South African case, with its eleven official languages, as a policy derived from 'a wish to respect diversity' (p. 76) – a little naïve, surely – but can any-one doubt that English is stronger in South Africa than ever before? A small digression here may be illustrative.

McLean and McCormick (1996) have pointed out that the South African policy only *recognises* the eleven languages; it does not pre-scribe their use. One interpretation of the policy, as they note, is that it 'licenses the dropping of Afrikaans...leaving English as the only language of public discourse'. Mazrui (2004: 72) suggests that, in many eyes, 'Afrikaans was a language of racial claustrophobia' while 'English was a language of pan-African communication'. Thus, he continues, while English is theoretically reduced in status, 'in reality the new policy only demotes Afrikaans'. A second interpretation is that the use of *all* official languages is meant to move English 'from a dominant to an equal role' (McLean and McCormick, 1996: 303). The *de jure* status of English is clear enough but, the authors ask, does the new linguistic dispensation undermine the *de facto* position of privilege that it has held for two centuries? Their conclusion was as follows:

> The evidence from various domains...is that this policy thrust toward multilingualism is often intended and perceived as a symbolic statement, and that for instrumental purposes English remains the dominant language in South African public life. (p. 329)

Of course, McLean and McCormick were writing only a couple of years after the introduction of the new constitutional arrangements, and they acknowledged that the progress of further language developments was uncertain. If we move to the present, however, and if we consult the views of Mazrui (2004), Djité (2008) and Alexander (2009) – three of the best qualified commentators on the current South African language scene – we find reports of the undiminished importance of English (All three, incidentally, are critical of English hegemony, and argue for the increased use and scope of indigenous languages; this position is, of course, not my point in citing them here, although it does imply that their assessments of the place of English are very far from 'triumphalist' in tone.)

Phillipson's final criticism of de Swaan is that, as a native Dutch speaker 'who is impressively articulate in English' (p. 78), he has fallen prey to 'the final triumph of a system of domination, when the dominated start singing its virtues' (Ngũgĩ wa Thiong'o, 1986: 20). One would be interested to hear de Swaan's response to this.

Finally here, we can note the criticisms of both de Swaan and van Parijs made by Ives. He holds the rather blunt view that 'to give up one's language, by necessity or apparent choice, is to lose a culture and a sense of oneself and one's history' (2009b: 673–674). He may be an excellent Gramsci scholar (see below), but he is clearly not a close reader of the language-and-identity relationship; see Edwards, 2009).[10] Nor does he seem to have fully taken on board the social, political and historical intertwinings that determine the fate of languages:

> learning English may be technically a 'free choice' but it can in fact just further entrench cultural, psychological, economic and political imperialism...it is not the learning of English that is so problematic *per se*, but rather the very circumstances that lead people to make this so-called free choice and the psychological, social and cultural fragmentation that it fosters. (Ives, 2009b: 676)

De Swaan and van Parijs, Ives argues, 'do not grapple with the actual complexity of what language is and how it relates to democracy' (2004: 9). This seems curious at first blush, but Ives's real point soon becomes clearer. His central criticism of both authors is that they draw upon rational-choice theory and rely largely upon macro-level economic analyses: the implication here is of a certain 'coldness'. More specifically, and drawing upon the development of Italian in particular, Ives adds that historical European language policies have been underpinned by much more than a 'rational choice individualistic perspective' (2004: 9). He thus suggests that de Swaan and van Parijs naively see language only as a 'vehicle of communication' (p. 9), downplaying the important symbolic aspects of language (see also Ives, 2006). 'Symbolic' values were, he argues, central to the creation of standard national languages in Italy, France, Germany.

There are two points to make here, I think. The first involves a small repetition of something I wrote in Chapter 5 about the symbolic and communicative functions of language:

> Although the functions are separable, and although the symbolic aspects can long outlast communicative-language shift, these aspects are first given life by a vernacular, not the other way around. The implication is that the loss or abandonment of a language in its ordinary communicative role must eventually lead to the dilution or, indeed, the disappearance of its symbolic or 'associational' role.

The implication here is that it is a mistake to put the symbolic cart before the communicative horse, and the more pointed implication is that it is extremely unlikely that any meaningful national language policies – however important symbolic aspects may have been – have ever succeeded without paying central heed to the actual or potential scope of usage. The other point is broader still. De Swaan, van Parijs and all the others who have made significant contributions to the sociology-of-language choice, to matters of linguistic dominance and subordination, to questions of maintenance and shift, have all implicitly paid the closest attention to the non-instrumental aspects of language. This is for the simple reason that, were language to be only a communicative tool, then much of what is written and argued about would not be much of an issue at all. It is only when we add, directly or indirectly, the symbolic features of language that we enter the minefields of emotion, belonging and identity.

Ives weaves discussion of Gramsci through much of his thesis, because while the latter was interested in the idea of a common language, he never made the mistake – Ives tells us – of dividing the symbolic from the communicative, nor did he ever imagine that cultural and political power were absent from the picture. Ives (2009b: 669) points to Gramsci's particular concern that 'lack of access to dominant languages can exclude subaltern social groups from power, wealth and influence'. Furthermore, he quotes Gramsci to the effect that single-language advocates are motivated by a '*cosmopolitan*, not an international anxiety, that of the bourgeois who travels for business or pleasure, of nomads more than of stable productive citizens' (Gramsci, 1985: 27; further notes on the theme by Ives, 2009a). The implication here is that the acquisition of English does not always equip 'average people, not just élites, to actively participate in meaningful and effective dialogue' (Ives, 2009b: 671). The evidence presented elsewhere in this book suggests, however, that what may once have divided the cosmopolitan bourgeois from the 'average citizen' no longer applies. The latter now travel much more widely than they ever did and – much, much more importantly – one can now remain sedentary and the various media will bring the world into one's home, with the accompanying awareness of the value of English competence; see also Wright (2004) on Gramsci.

Ives (2009b) expands on Gramsci, noting that many who cite him are insufficiently familiar with his position on a common language as a link.[11] It is certainly true that Gramscian 'hegemony' – signifying, of course, not merely the dominance of an élite, but a dominance that has come to be accepted in one way or another by 'non-élite' groups, a dominance that is essentially the *manufacture of consent* (see Wiley, 2000) – has proved an appealing concept to left-of-centre theorists of imperialism. I say 'in one way or another' because, while no one doubts the *fact* of global English, many matters remain for discussion and debate: perceived *intention*, that balance between 'push' and 'pull' factors – have all those subaltern groups jumped, or were they pushed, or did jumping and pushing combine? – whether or not subordinate groups have essentially been co-opted, what Joseph (2004) discusses under the heading of 'attributions of blame and proposed solutions', and so on. 'Evidence,' as Joseph further points out, 'is not neatly separable from interpretation', and he aptly refers to 'undisprovable Gramsci-derived notions of hegemony' (p. 182). Just so.

Ives (2009b) discusses Gramsci's (obviously correct) idea that the emergence of any 'common language' is 'a political act' and that the language therefore cannot be 'neutral'. How this could become fuel for criticism of de Swaan and van Parijs is a little hard to fathom. The point, as well, is rather clearer for Gramsci's within-Italy context (or, if you like, with the mechanics of Hebrew in Israel) than it is for English around the globe. Ives goes on to imply that, just as a more democratically assembled Italian would have pleased Gramsci, so a less politically charged-from-the-centre English would be a more acceptable lingua franca, and he concludes by suggesting that a 'progressive' English hegemony would be one in which the language incorporates and does not replace 'various spontaneous grammars' (p. 677). He means local languages, dialects and idioms. This, of course, is precisely what happens in the formation of local 'Englishes'!

Notes

1. Fishman is a good example of the scholar-advocate. He writes of mother-tongue loss among groups who 'have not capitulated to the massive blandishments of western materialism, who experience life and nature in deeply poetic and collectively meaningful ways' (1982: 8), and he has devoted considerable attention to the question of 'reversing language shift', an undertaking that he styles a 'quest' of 'sanctity' (1990, 1991).
    See also the well-known piece in which Krauss (1992) called for more involved commitment on the part of linguists, noting with alarm the large number of the world's languages now at risk. We should go well beyond the usual academic role of description and documentation, he argued, to 'promote language development in the necessary domains...[and] learn...the techniques of organization, monitoring and lobbying, publicity, and activism' (p. 9). See also Ladefoged's rejoinder (1992), plumping for a more 'traditional' and 'disinterested' scholarly stance; and Dorian's (1993) response to both Krauss and Ladefoged.
2. It is a truism – but one that demands some repetition when so much research on minority languages focuses only on the speakers of those languages – that the attitudes of *majority*-language speakers are central. A recent specific example is given by Davis *et al.* (2010: 148), whose opening sentence is this: 'the future of the Welsh language is intimately connected with the attitudes,

culture, identities and language of those in Wales who do not speak Welsh'. Just so.

3. Coining a word that has since become well-used (over-used, in fact), Ritzer (1992) wrote about the 'McDonaldization' of the world, generally taken to mean a pernicious cultural imperialism. As Watson (1997, 2000) has pointed out, however, it is hard to imagine the success of such global market penetration (to use the terms of the enemy here) without acknowledging its appeal to large numbers of new consumers. Furthermore, as Li (2003) points out, in his useful discussion of the matter, there is evidence that McDonald's and other such firms have been quite innovative in using local suppliers, attending to local values and practices, and so on. Some readers may recall here the anti-McDonald's stance taken by the French political activist José Bové and his *Confédération paysanne* in 1999. The protest here, however, was not so much anti-American as against the restaurant's use of hormone-injected beef and its allegedly 'anti-organic-food' posture.

   I certainly don't want to endorse the spread of fast food – see the disturbing recent treatments of Schlosser (2001) and Spurlock (2004) – but only to reinforce the note in the text that, in most modern global phenomena, there are strong 'pull' factors as well as obvious 'push' ones. (Unless, of course, one is willing to accept, as some adherents of the linguistic-imperialism thesis seem to do, that those on the receiving end of things are powerless and without 'agency'.)

4. This is also the conclusion reached, by a different methodological pathway, by Laitin (1993: 238): 'the maintenance of multilingual repertoires rather than the replacement of competing languages in all domains by English will be the mark of the emerging world language system'. It turns out, of course, that the definition and the specificity of 'domains' is a key issue here, for it is certainly the case that, in many regional contexts, domains once 'reserved', as it were, for the more local variety are increasingly absorbed by powerful exoglossic elements.

   The articles by de Swaan (1993a, 1993b) and Laitin (1993) were published in a special issue of the *International Political Science Review* (14:3), devoted to 'The Emergent World Language System'. Three other valuable pieces (by Kreindler, Mazrui and Mazrui, and Dua) also appeared there, treating more specific contexts: Russia, East Africa and India. I list these in the references section here.

5. Guilt and conscience there well may be, but they do not lead to lifestyle alteration. Those who wax lyrical over 'small' or 'threatened' languages and cultures generally don't leave their rather more secure billets. A related comment was made by Quirk (1985: 6): 'disdain for élitism is a comfortable exercise for those who are themselves securely among the élite'. He was making an argument about the desire for 'standards' among 'ordinary folk', but the point could easily be extended to cover those 'ordinary' people who want access to powerful lingua francas.

6. Citing Kuter (1989; see also Edwards, 2009, especially Chapter 8) – de Swaan also notes at this point that: 'the preservation of a language community very often means the continued oppression of women, children, young people, the dispossessed, deviants and dissidents' (2004: 572).

A more mundane observation by Spolsky (1989: 451) reminds us that many 'ordinary' people have issues to deal with that are rather more immediate than language choice:

> A Navajo student of mine once put the problem quite starkly: if I have to choose, she said, between living in a hogan a mile from the nearest water where my son will grow up speaking Navajo, or moving to a house in the city with indoor plumbing where he will speak English with the neighbors, I'll pick English and a bathroom!

As de Swaan (p. 576) adds, choice of language is but one aspect of the social predicament often faced by those living in 'small linguistic communities'.

7. There are obvious similarities with the actions of another 'big' language: French. When the French government endorsed the European *Charter for Regional or Minority Languages*, it rejected the restriction to national minorities, preferring to 'recognise' minorities of all provenances. A big-hearted effort at inclusion, a desire to see rights extended to the furthest? Perhaps. Or perhaps, as cynics suggested, because the French strategy here was to widen the field so much that action for any would become impractical (see Edwards, 2003).

8. Mazrui (2003) provides a balanced and insightful review of de Swaan's book. One of his criticisms has to do with de Swaan's mathematical formulae; his 'Q-value' calculations and his 'economistic portrayals' of languages as 'collective goods' seem to Mazrui to be cold, biased towards the 'instrumental' aspects of language, and insensitive to intra-group perceptions (across class, gender and age lines, for instance). Cold – or, at least, cool – the workings of the Q formulae may be, but no one could possibly accuse de Swaan of excessive mathematising, either in his book or in the several articles that I have discussed here. The other two points are, I think, overemphasised: de Swaan is clearly most interested in macro-level and instrumental aspects of language, but he certainly does not neglect the 'symbolic' and other features that are stressed by language nationalists and their apologists.

9. I am of course indebted to the reviewers of these three books (Peter de Costa, James d'Angelo and Jamie Lee) for their summaries and interpretations.

10. There are, in fact, a number of curious observations scattered through the works of Ives that I refer to here: at one point, for instance, he suggests that 'one of the many benefits of linguistic diversity is precisely that it calls our attention to the constant need for translation' (2004: 10).

11. I have reported elsewhere (Edwards, 1995) that, at the time of the revolution, only a minority of people within *l'hexagone* actually spoke French. Ives (2009b) reminds us that, at the time of national unification (in 1861) in Italy, the number of Italian speakers was very much fewer: he cites de Mauro (1963), who suggests only about 3%, and Moss (2000), whose estimate is 12%. It is, in any event, easy to see why Gramsci paid some considerable attention to the nineteenth-century incarnation of the *questione della lingua*.

References

Abelson, Robert (1972) Are attitudes necessary? In Bert King and Elliott McGinnies (eds) *Attitudes, Conflict and Social Change*. New York: Academic Press.

Abley, Mark (2003) *Spoken Here: Travels among Threatened Languages*. Toronto: Random House.

Aboud, Frances (1988) *Children and Prejudice*. Oxford: Blackwell.

Aboud, Frances (2003) The formation of in-group favouritism and out-group prejudice in young children: Are they distinct attitudes? *Developmental Psychology* 39, 48–60.

Abrams, Dominic and Michael Hogg (eds) (1990) *Social Identity Theory*. London: Harvester Wheatsheaf.

Achebe, Chinua (1975) *Morning Yet on Creation Day*. New York: Doubleday.

Acheson, Arthur (1920) *Shakespeare's Lost Years in London, 1586–1592*. London: Bernard Quaritch.

Acta Foundation (Fundació per a les idees i les arts) (1993) *Europes: Els Intellectuals i la Qüestió Europea*. Barcelona: Acta.

Ad Hoc Committee on Foreign Languages (Modern Language Association) (2007) Foreign languages and higher education: New structures for a changed world. *Profession* (Annual of the Modern Language Association), 234–245.

Ad Hoc Committee on Staffing (Association of Departments of English) (2009) Education in the balance: A report on the academic workforce in English. *Profession* (Annual of the Modern Language Association), 180–245.

Ajzen, Icek and Martin Fishbein (1977) Attitude-behavior relations: A theoretical analysis and review of empirical research. *Psychological Bulletin* 84, 888–918.

Ajzen, Icek and Martin Fishbein (1980) *Understanding Attitudes and Predicting Social Behavior*. Englewood Cliffs, New Jersey: Prentice-Hall.

Al-Batal, Mahmoud (2007) Arabic and national language educational policy. *Modern Language Journal* 91, 268–271. [a contribution to a forum on 'National language educational policy': see Blake and Kramsch, 2007]

Alexander, Neville (2009) The impact of the hegemony of English on access to and quality of education, with special reference to South Africa. In Wayne Harbert, Sally McConnell-Ginet, Amanda Miller and John Whitman (eds) *Language and Poverty*. Bristol: Multilingual Matters.

Algeo, John (2006) Review of *In and Out of English* (Gunilla Anderman and Margaret Rogers). *Language Problems and Language Planning* 30, 211–213.

Allen, Roger (2007) Arabic – flavor of the moment: Whence, why, and how? *Modern Language Journal* 91, 258–261. [a contribution to a forum on 'National language educational policy': see Blake and Kramsch, 2007]

Allport, Gordon (1954) The historical background of modern social psychology. In Gardner Lindzey (ed.) *Handbook of Social Psychology, Volume 1: Theory and Method*. Cambridge, Massachusetts: Addison-Wesley.

Allport, Gordon (1958 [1954]) *The Nature of Prejudice*. New York: Doubleday Anchor. [first edition published by Addison-Wesley]

Amis, Kingsley (1997) *The King's English*. London: HarperCollins.

Ammon, Ulrich (ed.) (1994) *Language-Spread Policy, Volume 2: Languages of Former Colonial Powers and Former Colonies*. Berlin: Mouton de Gruyter. [= *International Journal of the Sociology of Language* 107]

Ammon, Ulrich (1996) The European Union (EU – formerly European Community): Status change of English during the last fifty years. In Joshua Fishman, Andrew Conrad and Alma Rubal-Lopez (eds) *Post-imperial English: Status Change in Former British and American Colonies, 1940-1990*. Berlin: Mouton de Gruyter.

Ammon, Ulrich (1998) *Ist Deutsch noch internationale Wissenschaftssprache? Englisch auch für die Lehre an den deutschsprachigen Hochschulen*. Berlin: Mouton de Gruyter.

Ammon, Ulrich (ed.) (2001) *The Dominance of English as a Language of Science: Effects on Other Languages and Language Communities*. Berlin: Mouton de Gruyter.

Ammon, Ulrich (2003) Review of *English-Only Europe?* (Robert Phillipson). *Language Problems and Language Planning* 27, 289–295.

Ammon, Ulrich and Hartmut Kleinedam (eds) (1992) *Language-Spread Policy, Volume 1: Languages of Former Colonial Powers*. Berlin: Mouton de Gruyter. [= *International Journal of the Sociology of Language* 95]

Ammon, Ulrich and Grant McConnell (2002) *English as an Academic Language in Europe: A Survey of its Use in Teaching*. Berlin: Peter Lang.

Anderman, Gunilla and Margaret Rogers (eds) (2005) *In and Out of English: For Better, for Worse?* Clevedon: Multilingual Matters.

Andersen, Roger (1988) *The Power and the Word*. London: Paladin.

Anderson, Christopher (1818) *A Brief Sketch of Various Attempts which have been made to Diffuse a Knowledge of the Holy Scripture through the Medium of the Irish Language*. Dublin: Graisberry & Campbell.

Anon. (2000) Innovative language teaching. *Times Higher Education Supplement*, 9 June.

Anon. (2008) Bottom of the heap: The dismal lives and unhappy prospects of Europe's biggest stateless minority. *The Economist*, 21 June, 35–38.

Antieau, Lamont (2009) Review of *Language and the Internet* [2nd edition] (David Crystal). *Critical Inquiry in Language Studies* 6, 350–353.

Apter, Terri (2009) *What Do You Want from Me? Learning to Get Along with In-laws*. New York: Norton.

Armstrong, John (1982) *Nations Before Nationalism*. Chapel Hill: University of North Carolina Press.

Bailey, Richard (1985) The idea of world English. *English Today* 1 (1:1), 3–6.

Bailey, Richard (1991) *Images of English: A Cultural History of the Language*. Ann Arbor: University of Michigan Press.

Bailey, Richard (2006) English among the languages. In Lynda Mugglestone (ed.) *The Oxford History of English*. Oxford: Oxford University Press.

Ball, Peter (1983) Stereotypes of Anglo-Saxon and non-Anglo-Saxon accents: Some explanatory Australian studies with the matched-guise technique. *Language Sciences* 5, 163–184.

Banton, Michael (1977) *Rational Choice: A Theory of Racial and Ethnic Relations*. Bristol: University of Bristol Research Unit on Ethnic Relations.

Banton, Michael (1983) *Racial and Ethnic Competition*. Cambridge: Cambridge University Press.

Banton, Michael (2004) Are ethnicity and nationalism twin concepts? *Journal of Ethnic and Migration Studies* 30, 807–814.

Barber, Charles (1993) *The English Language*. Cambridge: Cambridge University Press.

Barnes, William (1830) Corruptions of the English language. *Gentleman's Magazine*, June (100), 501–503. [Barnes writes here as 'Dilettante']

Barnes, William (1869) *Early England and the Saxon-English*. London: Smith.

Baron, Dennis (2001) America doesn't know what the world is saying. *New York Times*, 27 October.

Barot, Rohit (2006) Michael Banton's contribution to race and ethnic studies. *Ethnic and Racial Studies* 29, 785–796.

Barrett, Martyn (2009) The development of children's intergroup attitudes. In Michael Byram and Adelheid Hu (eds) *Interkulturelle Kompetenz und Fremdsprachliches Lernen: Modelle, Empirie, Evaluation*. Tübingen: Gunter Narr.

Bauer, Laurie and Peter Trudgill (eds) (1998) *Language Myths*. London: Penguin.

Baugh, John (2002) Linguistics, education, and the Ebonics firestorm. In James Alatis, Heidi Hamilton and Ai-Hui Tan (eds) *Linguistics, Language, and the Professions*. Washington: Georgetown University Press.

Baugh, John (2004) Ebonics and its controversy. In Edward Finegan and John Rickford (eds) *Language in the USA: Themes for the Twenty-first Century*. Cambridge: Cambridge University Press.

Baugh, John (2006) Linguistic considerations pertaining to *Brown v. Board*: Exposing racial fallacies in the new millennium. In Arnetha Ball (ed.) *With More Deliberate Speed: Achieving Equity and Excellence in Education*. Oxford: Blackwell. [= *Yearbook of the National Society for the Study of Education* 105(2)]

Bayard, Donn, Ann Weatherall, Cynthia Gallois and Jeffery Pittam (2001) Pax Americana? Accent attitudinal evaluations in New Zealand, Australia and America. *Journal of Sociolinguistics* 5, 22–49.

Beebe, Leslie and Howard Giles (1984) Speech accommodation theories: A discussion in terms of second-language acquisition. *International Journal of the Sociology of Language* 46, 5–32.

Benwell, Bethan (ed.) (2006) *Masculinity and Men's Lifestyle Magazines*. Oxford: Blackwell.

Benwell, Bethan and Elizabeth Stokoe (2006) *Discourse and Identity*. Edinburgh: Edinburgh University Press.

Berechree, Philip and Peter Ball (1979) A study of sex, accent-broadness and Australian sociolinguistic identity. Paper presented at the Second Australian Conference on Language and Speech, Melbourne.

Best, Deborah, John Williams, Jonathan Cloud, Stephen Davis, Linda Robertson, John Edwards, Howard Giles and Jacqueline Fowles (1977) Development of sex-trait stereotypes among young children in the United States, England, and Ireland. *Child Development* 48, 1375–1384.

Bhatia, Tej and William Ritchie (eds) (2004) *The Handbook of Bilingualism*. Oxford: Blackwell. [paperback edition, 2006]

Birks, John (ed.) (1962) *Rutherford at Manchester*. London: Heywood.

Bishop, Hywel, Nikolas Coupland and Peter Garrett (2005) Conceptual accent evaluation: Thirty years of accent prejudice in the UK. *Acta Linguistica Hafniensia* 37, 131–154.

Blackstone, Tessa (2000) England: National language thrust. *Modern Language Journal* 84, 429.

Blais, André (2000) *To Vote or not to Vote?* Pittsburgh: University of Pittsburgh Press.

Blake, Robert and Claire Kramsch (2007) National language educational policy: Guest editors' introduction. *Modern Language Journal* 91, 247–249.

Blank, Paula (2006) The Babel of Renaissance English. In Lynda Mugglestone (ed.) *The Oxford History of English*. Oxford: Oxford University Press.

Blass, Thomas (1992) The social psychology of Stanley Milgram. In Mark Zanna (ed.) *Advances in Experimental Social Psychology: Volume 25*. New York: Academic Press.

Blau, Peter (1986) *Exchange and Power in Social Life*. New Brunswick, New Jersey: Transaction.

Boberg, Charles (1999) The attitudinal component of variation in American English foreign <a> nativization. *Journal of Language and Social Psychology* 18, 49–61.

Bolinger, Dwight (1980) *Language – The Loaded Weapon*. London: Longman.

Bollag, Burton (2000) The new Latin: English dominates in academe. *Chronicle of Higher Education*, 8 September 47(2), 73–77.

Borins, Sandford (1983) *The Language of the Skies: The Bilingual Air Traffic Control Conflict in Canada*. Montreal: McGill-Queen's University Press.

Bourdieu, Pierre, Abram de Swaan, Claude Hagège, Marc Fumaroli and Immanual Wallerstein (2001) Quelles langues pour une Europe démocratique? *Raisons politiques* 2, 41–64.

Bourhis, Richard (ed.) (2008a) *The Vitality of the English-Speaking Communities of Quebec: From Community Decline to Revival*. Montreal: Centre d'études ethniques des universités montréalaises (Université de Montréal).

Bourhis, Richard (2008b) Notes on the demolinguistic vitality of the English-speaking communities of Quebec. *Canadian Issues – Thèmes canadiens* (Summer), 29–35.

Bourhis, Richard, Howard Giles and Doreen Rosenthal (1981). Notes on the construction of a 'subjective vitality questionnaire' for ethnolinguistic groups. *Journal of Multilingual and Multicultural Development* 2, 144–155.

Bourhis, Richard, Shaha El-Geledi and Itesh Sachdev (2007) Language, ethnicity and intergroup relations. In Ann Weatherall, Bernadette Watson and Cindy Gallois (eds) *Language, Discourse and Social Psychology*. London: Palgrave Macmillan.

Bradac, James, Aaron Cargile and Jennifer Hallett (2001) Language attitudes: Retrospect, conspect and prospect. In W. Peter Robinson and Howard Giles (eds) *The New Handbook of Language and Social Psychology*. Chichester: Wiley.

Bragg, Melvyn and Stanley Ellis (1976) *Word of Mouth*. London: BBC Television.

Brehm, Sharon, Saul Kassin and Steven Fein (1999) *Social Psychology*. Boston: Houghton Mifflin.

Brennan, Gillian (2003) *Patriotism, Power and Print: National Consciousness in Tudor England*. Pittsburgh: Duquesne University Press.

de Briey, Laurent and Philippe van Parijs (2002) La justice linguistique comme justice coopérative. *Revue de philosophie économique* 5, 5–37.

Bright, William (ed.) (1966) *Sociolinguistics*. The Hague: Mouton.

British Academy (2009) *Language Matters: A Position Paper*. London: British Academy.

Brod, Richard and Elizabeth Welles (2000) Foreign language enrollments in United States institutions of higher education, Fall 1998. *ADFL* [Association of Departments of Foreign Languages] *Bulletin* 31(2) , 22–29.

Brookman, Jennie (2000) Germans fight Anglo invasion. *Times Higher Education Supplement*, 22 September.

Brown, Babette (2001) *Combatting Discrimination*. Stoke-on-Trent: Trentham.

Broyard, Anatole (1979) Saved from seriousness. *New York Times*, 18 April.

Bruthiaux, Paul (2003) Squaring the circles: Issues in modeling English worldwide. *International Journal of Applied Linguistics* 13, 159–178.

Brutt-Griffler, Janina (2002) *World English: A Study in its Development*. Clevedon: Multilingual Matters.

Bugarski, Ranko (2001) Language, nationalism and war in Yugoslavia. *International Journal of the Sociology of Language* 151, 69–87.

Burchfield, Robert (1987) *The English Language*. Oxford: Oxford University Press.

Busch, Brigitta and Helen Kelly-Holmes (eds) (2004) *Language, Discourse and Borders in the Yugoslav Successor States*. Clevedon: Multilingual Matters.

Butler, Judith (1990) *Gender Trouble*. London: Routledge.

Butler, Mary (1901) *Irishwomen and the Home Language*. Dublin: Gaelic League.

Byrne, Donn (1971) *The Attraction Paradigm*. New York: Academic Press.

Byrnes, Heidi (2009) The role of foreign language departments in internationalizing the curriculum. *Modern Language Journal* 93, 607–609.

Cabantous, Alain (1998) *Histoire du blasphème en Occident*. Paris: Albin Michel.

Calvet, Louis-Jean (1987) *Guerre des langues et les politiques linguistiques*. Paris: Payot.

Calvet, Louis-Jean (1999) *Pour une écologie des langues du monde*. Paris: Plon.

Cameron, Deborah (1995) *Verbal Hygiene*. London: Routledge.

Cameron, Deborah (2006) *On Language and Sexual Politics*. London: Routledge.

Cameron, Deborah (2007) *The Myth of Mars and Venus: Do Men and Women Really Speak Different Languages?* Oxford: Oxford University Press.

Canagarajah, A. Suresh (1999a) On EFL teachers, awareness and agency. *ELT Journal* 53, 207–214.

Canagarajah, A. Suresh (1999b) *Resisting Linguistic Imperialism in English Language Teaching*. Oxford: Oxford University Press.

Carew, Richard (1614) The excellencie of the English tongue. In William Camden, *Remaines Concerning Britain...* London: Waterson. [Carew's work was written earlier, but was first printed in this, a 'reviewed, corrected and encreased' edition of Camden's work, originally published in 1605]

Carli, Augusto and Ulrich Ammon (eds) (2007) *Linguistic Inequality in Scientific Communication Today*. Amsterdam: Benjamins. [= AILA (Association Internationale de Linguistique Appliquée) *Review* 20]

Carr, Jo and Anne Pauwels (2006) *Boys and Foreign Language Learning: Real Boys Don't Do Languages*. Basingstoke: Palgrave Macmillan.

Carranza, Miguel and Ellen Bouchard Ryan, E. (1975) Evaluative reactions of bilingual Anglo and Mexican American adolescents toward speakers of English and Spanish. *International Journal of the Sociology of Language* 6, 83–104.

Cashdan, Elizabeth (2001) Ethnic diversity and its environmental determinants: Effects of climate, pathogens and habitat diversity. *American Anthropologist* 103, 968–991.

Castoriadis, Cornelius (1997) *World in Fragments*. Stanford: Stanford University Press.

Cenoz, Jasone and Ulrike Jessner (eds) (2000) *English in Europe: The Acquisition of a Third Language*. Clevedon: Multilingual Matters.

Centre for Information on Language Teaching and Research (CILT) (2009) Examination entry data for GCSE and A levels. www.cilt.org.uk.

Chapman, R. W. (Robert William) (1932) Oxford English. *Society for Pure English* 4(37).

Charbonneau, Léo (2001) Tongue-tied. *University Affairs*, March (42:3), 10–17.

Cheshire, Jenny, Viv Edwards, Henk Münstermann and Bert Weltens (1989) Dialect and education in Europe: A general perspective. In Jenny Cheshire, Viv Edwards, Henk Münstermann and Bert Weltens (eds) *Dialect and Education: Some European Perspectives*. Clevedon: Multilingual Matters.

Cheshire, Jenny and Lise-Marie Moser (1994) English as a cultural symbol: The case of advertisements in French-speaking Switzerland. *Journal of Multilingual and Multicultural Development* 15, 451–469.

Chia, Boh Peng and Adam Brown (2002) Singaporeans' reactions to Estuary English. *English Today* 18, 33–38.

Chomsky, Noam (1979) *Language and Responsibility*. Brighton: Harvester

Chomsky, Noam (2009) Back-cover encomium. In Jo Anne Kleifgen and George Bond (eds) *The Languages of Africa and the Diaspora: Educating for Language Awareness*. Bristol: Multilingual Matters.

Choy, Stephen and David Dodd (1976) Standard-English-speaking and non-standard Hawaiian English-speaking children: Comprehension of both dialects and teachers' evaluations. *Journal of Educational Psychology* 68, 184–193.

Clayton, Thomas (1999) Decentering language in world-system inquiry. *Language Problems and Language Planning* 23, 133–156.

Clery, N. (1927) Five miles from anywhere. *Catholic Bulletin* 17, 875–877.

Clunie, Barnaby (2005) A revolutionary failure resurrected: Dialogical appropriation in Rudy Wiebe's *The Scorched-Wood People*. *University of Toronto Quarterly* 74, 845–865.

Clyne, Michael and Farzad Sharifian (2008) English as an international language. In Farzad Sharifian and Michael Clyne (eds) *International Forum on English as an International Language*. Melbourne: Monash University Press. [= *Australian Review of Applied Linguistics* 31(3)]

Coates, Jennifer (2004) *Women, Men and Language*. London: Longman.

Cohen, Arthur (1964) *Attitude Change and Social Influence*. New York: Basic Books.

Cohen, Marcel (1956) *Pour une sociologie du langage*. Paris: Albin Michel.

Coleman, James (2006) English-medium teaching in European higher education. *Language Teaching* 39, 1–14.

Colley, Ann (2005) Review of *Language and Woman's Place: Text and Commentaries* [Robin Lakoff]. *Journal of Language and Social Psychology* 24, 421–428.

Committee on Irish Language Attitudes Research (1975) *Report, as submitted to the Minister for the Gaeltacht*. Dublin: Government Stationery Office.

Condry, John and Sandra Condry (1976) Sex differences: A study of the eye of the beholder. *Child Development* 47, 812–819.

Connolly, Paul (1998) *Racism, Gender Identities and Young Children*. London: Routledge.

Cook, Karen (ed.) (1987) *Social Exchange Theory.* London: Sage.

Cooper, Robert (ed.) (1982) *Language Spread: Studies in Diffusion and Social Change.* Bloomington: Indiana University Press.

Coxhead, John (2007) *The Last Bastion of Racism: Gypsies, Travellers and Policing.* Stoke-on-Trent: Trentham.

Craig, Gerald (1963) *Lord Durham's Report.* Toronto: McClelland & Stewart.

Crawford, Mary (1995) *Talking Difference: On Gender and Language.* London: Sage.

Crowley, Tony (1989) *The Politics of Discourse: The Standard Language Question in British Cultural Debates.* London: Macmillan.

Crowley, Tony (1991) *Proper English? Readings in Language, History and Cultural Identity.* London: Routledge.

Crowley, Tony (2003) *Standard English and the Politics of Language.* London: Palgrave Macmillan. [this is the second, revised edition of Crowley, 1989]

Crowne, Douglas and David Marlowe (1964) *The Approval Motive.* New York: Wiley.

Cruttenden, Alan (2008) *Gimson's Pronunciation of English.* London: Hodder.

Crystal, David (2000) *Language Death.* Cambridge: Cambridge University Press.

Crystal, David (2003) *English as a Global Language.* Cambridge: Cambridge University Press. [2nd edition]

Crystal, David (2006a) English worldwide. In Richard Hogg and David Denison (eds) *A History of the English Language.* Cambridge: Cambridge University Press.

Crystal, David (2006b) Into the twenty-first century. In Lynda Mugglestone (ed.) *The Oxford History of English.* Oxford: Oxford University Press.

Crystal, David (2006c) *Language and the Internet* (2nd edition). Cambridge: Cambridge University Press.

Dalby, Andrew (2002) *Language in Danger.* London: Penguin.

Davies, Alan (1996) Ironising the myth of linguicism. *Journal of Multilingual and Multicultural Development* 17, 485–496.

Davies, Alan (1997) Response to a reply. *Journal of Multilingual and Multicultural Development* 18, 248.

Davies, Alan (2006) Review of *English-Only Europe?* (Robert Phillipson). *Journal of Multilingual and Multicultural Development* 27, 521–523.

Davis, Howard, Graham Day and Angela Drakakis-Smith (2010) Attitudes to language and bilingualism among English in-migrants to North Wales. In Delyth Morris (ed.) *Welsh in the Twenty-first Century.* Cardiff: University of Wales Press.

Defoe, Daniel (1697) *An Essay upon Projects.* London: Cockerill.

Dewar, Daniel (1812) *Observations on the Character, Customs and Superstitions of the Irish: and on Some of the Causes which have Retarded the Moral and Political Improvement of Ireland.* London: Gale & Curtis.

Disraeli, Benjamin (1877) Lord Mayor's Day. *The Times,* 10 November.

Dixon, Robert (1997) *The Rise and Fall of Languages.* Cambridge: Cambridge University Press.

Djité, Paulin (2008) *The Sociolinguistics of Development in Africa.* Clevedon: Multilingual Matters.

Dorian, Nancy (1993) A response to Ladefoged's other view of endangered languages. *Language* 69, 575–579.

Dörnyei, Zoltán (2005) *The Psychology of the Language Learner.* Mahwah, New Jersey: Lawrence Erlbaum.

Dörnyei, Zoltán and Richard Schmidt (eds) (2001) *Motivation and Second Language Acquisition.* Honolulu: University of Hawaii Press.

Dörnyei, Zoltán and Ema Ushioda (eds) (2009) *Motivation, Language Identity and the L2 Self.* Bristol: Multilingual Matters.

Dua, Hans (1993) The national language and the ex-colonial language as rivals. *International Political Science Review* 14, 293–308.

Duchêne, Alexandre and Moncia Heller (eds) (2007) *Discourses of Endangerment.* London: Continuum.

Durham, John George Lambton (1839) *Report on the Affairs of British North America…Officially Communicated to both Houses of the Imperial Parliament, on the 11th of February, 1839.* Montreal: Morning Courier.

Duszak, Anna and Urszula Okulska (eds) (2004) *Speaking from the Margin: Global English from a European Perspective.* Bern: Peter Lang.

Drake, Glendon (1977) *The Role of Prescriptivism in American Linguistics, 1820–1970.* Amsterdam: John Benjamins.

Eckert, Penelope and Sally McConnell-Ginet (2003) *Language and Gender.* Cambridge: Cambridge University Press.

Edgecombe, Rodney (1998) *Little Dorrit* and Canning's 'New Morality'. *Modern Philology* 95, 484–489.

Edwards, A. D. (Anthony) (1976) *Language in Culture and Class.* London: Heinemann.

Edwards, Emily (2007) *Eating Disorders as Distraction from Problems of Self and Meaning for Women in Ireland.* PhD Thesis, Trinity College, Dublin.

Edwards, John (1977a) Review of *Report* (Committee on Irish Language Attitudes Research). *Language Problems and Language Planning* 1, 54–59.

Edwards, John. (1977b) Students' reactions to Irish regional accents. *Language and Speech* 20, 280–286.

Edwards, John (1979) Judgements and confidence in reactions to disadvantaged speech. In Howard Giles and Robert St Clair (eds) *Language and Social Psychology.* Oxford: Blackwell.

Edwards, John (1982) Language attitudes and their implications among English speakers. In Ellen Bouchard Ryan and Howard Giles (eds) *Attitudes Towards Language Variation: Social and Applied Contexts.* London: Edward Arnold.

Edwards, John (1983) Language attitudes in multilingual settings: A general assessment. *Journal of Multilingual and Multicultural Development* 4, 225–236.

Edwards, John (1985) *Language, Society and Identity.* Oxford: Blackwell

Edwards, John (1987) Elaborated and restricted codes. In Ulrich Ammon, Norbert Dittmar and Klaus Mattheier (eds) *Soziolinguistik: Ein Internationales Handbuch zur Wissenschaft von Sprache und Gesellschaft.* Berlin: Walter de Gruyter.

Edwards, John (1989) *Language and Disadvantage.* London: Edward Arnold.

Edwards, John (1995) *Multilingualism.* London: Penguin.

Edwards, John (1999) Refining our understanding of language attitudes. *Journal of Language and Social Psychology* 18, 101–110.

Edwards, John (2002) Old wine in new bottles: Critical remarks on language ecology. In Annette Boudreau, Lise Dubois, Jacques Maurais and Grant McConnell (eds) *L'écologie des langues: mélanges William Mackey.* Paris: l'Harmattan.

Edwards, John (2003) Contextualizing language rights. *Journal of Human Rights* 2, 551–571.

Edwards, John (2004) Rational nationalism? *Journal of Ethnic and Migration Studies* 30, 837–840.

Edwards, John (2006) Educational failure. In Keith Brown (ed.) *Encyclopedia of Language and Linguistics* (2nd edition). Oxford: Elsevier.

Edwards, John (2008) The ecology of language: Insight and illusion. In Angela Creese, Peter Martin and Nancy Hornberger (eds) *Encyclopedia of Language and Education: Ecology of Language*. New York: Springer. [Volume 9 of the 10-volume second edition of this encyclopedia]

Edwards, John (2009) *Language and Identity*. Cambridge: Cambridge University Press.

Edwards, John (2010a) *Language Diversity in the Classroom*. Bristol: Multilingual Matters.

Edwards, John (2010b) *Minority Languages and Group Identity*. Amsterdam: John Benjamins.

Edwards, John (in preparation-a) *Irish: The Triumph of Failure?*

Edwards, John (in preparation-b) Language management agencies. In Bernard Spolsky (ed.) *The Cambridge Handbook of Language Policy*. Cambridge: Cambridge University Press.

Edwards, John and Maryanne Jacobsen (1987) Standard and regional standard speech: Distinctions and similarities. *Language in Society* 16, 369–380.

Edwards, John and Margaret McKinnon (1987) The continuing appeal of disadvantage as deficit: A Canadian study in a rural context. *Canadian Journal of Education* 12, 330–349.

Edwards, John and John Williams (1980) Sex-trait stereotypes among young children and young adults: Canadian findings and cross-national comparisons. *Canadian Journal of Behavioural Science* 12, 210–220.

Ehrlich, Susan (2010) Language, gender and sexuality. In Kirsten Malmkjær (ed.) *The Routledge Linguistics Encyclopedia*. Oxford: Routledge. [3rd edition]

Ellis, Rod (2008) *The Study of Second Language Acquisition*. Oxford: Oxford University Press. [2nd edition]

Eltis, Ken (1980) Pupils' speech-style and teacher reaction: Implications from some Australian data. *English in Australia* 51: 27–35.

Elton-Chalcraft, Sally (2009) *'It's Not Just About Black and White, Miss': Children's Awareness of Race*. Stoke-on-Trent: Trentham.

Emerson, Ralph Waldo (2007 [1841]) *Spiritual Laws*. Rockville, Maryland: Arc Manor. [this is a 'separate' reprint of a piece first appearing in Emerson's *Essays: First Series*, published in Boston by Munroe]

Eoyang, Eugene (1999) The worldliness of the English language: A lingua franca past and future. *ADFL* [Association of Departments of Foreign Languages] *Bulletin* 31(1), 26–32.

Esseili, Fatima (2008) Comment 4. *World Englishes* 27, 274–275.

Evans, Jocelyn (2004) *Voters and Voting*. London: Sage.

Fabricius, Anne (2006) The 'vivid sociolinguistic profiling' of Received Pronunciation: Responses to gendered dialect-in-discourse. *Journal of Sociolinguistics* 10, 111–122.

Fairfax, Nathaniel (1674) *A Treatise of the Bulk and Selvedge of the World*. London: Boulter.

Fellman, Jack (1973a) *The Revival of a Classical Tongue: Eliezer Ben-Yehuda and the Modern Hebrew Language*. The Hague: Mouton.

Fellman, Jack (1973b) Concerning the 'revival' of the Hebrew language. *Anthropological Linguistics* 15, 250–257.

Fellman, Jack (1976) On the revival of the Hebrew language. *Language Sciences* 43(17).

Fennell, Barbara (2001) *A History of English*. Oxford: Blackwell.

Ferguson, Gibson (2006) *Language Planning and Education*. Edinburgh: Edinburgh University Press.

Ferguson, Gibson (2009) Issues in researching English as a lingua franca: A conceptual enquiry. *International Journal of Applied Linguistics* 19, 117–135.

Festinger, Leon (1957) *A Theory of Cognitive Dissonance*. Evanston, Illinois: Row, Peterson.

Fichte, Johann Gottlieb (1808) *Reden an die deutsche Nation*. Berlin: Realschulbuchhandlung.

Fill, Alwin and Peter Mühlhäusler (2001) Introduction. In Alwin Fill and Peter Mühlhäusler (eds) *The Ecolinguistics Reader*. London: Continuum.

Fincher, Corey and Randy Thornhill (2008) A parasite-driven wedge: Infectious diseases may explain language and other biodiversity. *Oikos* 117, 1289–1297.

Fischer, John (1958) Social influences on the choice of a linguistic variant. *Word* 14, 47–56.

Fishbein, Martin and Icek Ajzen (1975) *Belief, Attitude, Intention and Behavior*. Reading, Massachusetts: Addison-Wesley.

Fishbein, Martin and Icek Ajzen (2010) *Predicting and Changing Behavior*. New York: Psychology Press.

Fisher, John (1996) *The Emergence of Standard English*. Lexington: University Press of Kentucky.

Fishman, Joshua (1970a) *Sociolinguistics*. Rowley, Massachusetts: Newbury House.

Fishman, Joshua (1970b) Preface. In Joshua Fishman (ed.) *Advances in the Sociology of Language: Volume 1*. The Hague: Mouton.

Fishman, Joshua (1972) *The Sociology of Language*. Rowley, Massachusetts: Newbury House.

Fishman, Joshua (1982) Whorfianism of the third kind. *Language in Society* 11, 1–14.

Fishman, Joshua (1990) What is reversing language shift (RLS) and how can it succeed? *Journal of Multilingual and Multicultural Development* 11, 5–36.

Fishman, Joshua (1991) *Reversing Language Shift*. Clevedon: Multilingual Matters.

Fishman, Joshua (1996) Summary and interpretation: Post-imperial English 1940-1990. In Joshua Fishman, Andrew Conrad and Alma Rubal-Lopez (eds) *Post-imperial English: Status Change in Former British and American Colonies, 1940-1990*. Berlin: Mouton de Gruyter.

Fishman, Joshua, Andrew Conrad and Alma Rubal-Lopez (eds) (1996) *Post-imperial English: Status Change in Former British and American Colonies, 1940-1990*. Berlin: Mouton de Gruyter.

Flores, N. and Robert Hopper (1975) Mexican Americans' evaluations of spoken Spanish and English. *Speech Monographs* 42, 91–98.

Florio, John (1578) *Florio his First Fruites: which yeelde familiar Speech, merie Prouerbes, wittie Sentences, and golden sayings. Also a perfect Induction to the Italian, and English tongues, as in the Table appeareth. The like heretofore, neuer by any man published.* London: Woodcocke.

Florio, John (1591) *Florios Second Frutes, To be gathered of twelue Trees, of diuers but delightsome tastes to the tongues of Italians and Englishmen. To which is annexed his Gardine of Recreation yeelding six thousand Italian Prouerbes.* London: Woodcock.

Florio, John (1598) *A Worlde of Wordes, Or Most Copious, and exact Dictionarie in Italian and English, collected by Iohn Florio.* London: Blount.

Florio, John (1611) *Queen Anna's Nevv Vvorld of Words, Or Dictionarie of the Italian and English tongues, Collected, and newly much augmented by Iohn Florio, Reader of the Italian vnto the Soueraigne Maiestie of Anna, Crowned Queene of England, Scotland, France and Ireland, &c. And one of the Gentlemen of hir Royall Priuie Chamber. Whereunto are added certaine necessarie rules and short obseruations for the Italian tongue.* London: Blount & Barret.

Flowerdew, John (2007) The non-anglophone scholar on the periphery of scholarly publication. In Augusto Carli and Ulrich Ammon (eds) *Linguistic Inequality in Scientific Communication Today.* Amsterdam: Benjamins.

Forde, Patrick (1901) *The Irish Language Movement: Its Philosophy.* Dublin: Gaelic League.

Fordham, Signithia (1999) Dissin' 'the standard': Ebonics as guerrilla warfare at Capital High. *Anthropology & Education Quarterly* 30, 272–293.

France, Anatole (1894) *Le lys rouge.* Paris: Calmann-Lévy.

Frank, Francine and Frank Anshen (1983) *Language and the Sexes.* Albany: State University of New York Press.

Fuentes, Carlos (1999) A cure for monolingualism. *Times Higher Education Supplement,* 17 December.

Fukuyama, Francis (1992) *The End of History and the Last Man.* New York: Free Press.

Fullerton, Robert (1916) *The Prudence of St Patrick's Irish Policy.* Dublin: O'Brien & Ards.

Furman, Nelly, David Goldberg and Natalia Lusin (2007) Enrollments in languages other than English in United States institutions of higher education, Fall 2006. (www.mla.org/pdf/06enrollmentsurvey_final.pdf) (published online, November 2007)

Gardner, Robert and Wallace Lambert (1959) Motivational variables in second-language acquisition. *Canadian Journal of Psychology* 13, 266–272.

Gardner, Robert and Wallace Lambert (1972) *Attitudes and Motivation in Second-Language Learning.* Rowley, Massachusetts: Newbury House.

Garrett, Peter (2010) *Attitudes to Language.* Cambridge: Cambridge University Press.

Garrett, Peter, Nikolas Coupland and Angie Williams (2003) *Investigating Language Attitudes.* Cardiff: University of Wales Press.

Gass, Susan and Larry Selinker (2008) *Second Language Acquisition.* London: Routledge.

Gawronski, Bertram (2009) Ten frequently asked questions about implicit measures and their frequently supposed, but not entirely correct answers. *Canadian Psychology* 50, 141–150.

Gazzola, Michele and François Grin (2007) Assessing efficiency and fairness in multilingual communication. *AILA* [Association Internationale de Linguistique Appliquée] *Review* 20, 87–105.

Geeraerts, Dirk (2003) Cultural models of linguistic standardization. In René Dirven, Roslyn Frank and Martin Pütz (eds) *Cognitive Models in Language and Thought: Ideologies, Metaphors and Meanings*. Berlin: Mouton de Gruyter.

Gellner, Ernest (1964) *Thought and Change*. London: Weidenfeld & Nicolson.

Gellner, Ernest (1983) *Nations and Nationalism*. Oxford: Blackwell.

Gilbert, William Schwenk and Arthur Sullivan (1885) *An Entirely New and Original Japanese Opera, in Two Acts, entitled The Mikado, or, the Town of Titipu*. London: Chappell.

Giles, Howard (1970) Evaluative reactions to accents. *Educational Review* 22, 211–27.

Giles, Howard (1971) Patterns of evaluation in reactions to RP, South Welsh and Somerset accented speech. *British Journal of Social and Clinical Psychology* 10, 280–281.

Giles, Howard and Andrew Billings (2004) Assessing language attitudes: Speaker evaluation studies. In Alan Davies and Catherine Elder (eds) *The Handbook of Applied Linguistics*. Oxford: Blackwell.

Giles, Howard and Richard Bourhis (1975) Linguistic assimilation: West Indians in Cardiff. *Language Sciences* 38, 9–12.

Giles, Howard and Richard Bourhis (1976) Black speakers with white speech: A real problem? In Gerhard Nickel (ed.) *Proceedings of the Fourth International Congress on Applied Linguistics: Volume 1*. Stuttgart: Hochschul Verlag.

Giles, Howard, Richard Bourhis and Donald Taylor (1977) Towards a theory of language in ethnic group relations. In Howard Giles (ed.) *Language, Ethnicity and Intergroup Relations*. London: Academic Press.

Giles, Howard and Jane Byrne (1982) An intergroup approach to second-language acquisition. *Journal of Multilingual and Multicultural Development* 3, 17–40.

Giles, Howard and John Edwards (2010) Attitudes to language: Past, present and future. In Kirsten Malmkjær (ed.) *Linguistics Encyclopedia*. Oxford: Routledge. [3rd edition]

Giles, Howard and Patricia Johnson (1981) The role of language in ethnic-group relations. In John Turner and Howard Giles (eds) *Intergroup Behaviour*. Oxford: Blackwell.

Giles, Howard, Vikki Katz and Paul Myers (2006) Language attitudes and the role of community infrastructure. *Moderna Språk* 100, 38–54.

Giles, Howard and Peter Powesland (1975) *Speech Style and Social Evaluation*. London: Academic Press.

Giles, Howard and Ellen Bouchard Ryan (1982) Prolegomena for developing a social psychological theory of language attitudes. In Ellen Bouchard Ryan and Howard Giles (eds) *Attitudes Towards Language Variation: Social and Applied Contexts*. London: Edward Arnold.

Gill, Rosalind (2007) *Gender and the Media*. Cambridge: Polity.

Gill, Rosalind (2008) Empowerment/sexism: Figuring female sexual agency in contemporary advertising. *Feminism and Psychology* 18, 35–60.

Gill, Rosalind (2009) Beyond the 'sexualization of culture' thesis: An intersectional analysis of 'sixpacks', 'midriffs' and 'hot lesbians' in advertising. *Sexualities* 12, 137–160.

Gimson, A. C. (Alfred Charles) (1980) *An Introduction to the Pronunciation of English*. London: Edward Arnold. [3rd edition]

Gleitman, Lila and Henry Gleitman (1970) *Phrase and Paraphrase*. New York: Norton.

Goffin, Richard and Allison Boyd (2009) Faking and personality assessment in personnel selection: advancing models of faking. *Canadian Psychology* 50, 151–160.

Goffman, Erving (1959) *The Presentation of Self in Everyday Life*. New York: Doubleday.

Goffman, Erving (1979) *Gender Advertisements*. New York: Harper & Row. [originally published as the autumn 1976 number (3:2) of *Studies in the Anthropology of Visual Communication*]

Goldberg, David and Elizabeth Welles (2001) Successful college and university programs, 1995-1999: Part 1. *Profession* (Annual of the Modern Language Association), 171–210.

Goodman, Bridget (2009) The ecology of language in Ukraine. *Working Papers in Educational Linguistics* (University of Pennsylvania) 24(2), 19–39.

Goot, Murray (1993) Multiculturalists, monoculturalists and the many in between: Attitudes to cultural diversity and their correlates. *Australian and New Zealand Journal of Sociology* 29, 226–253.

Gornick, Vivian (1979) Introduction. In Erving Goffman, *Gender Advertisements*. New York: Harper & Row.

Gottfredson, Linda and Donald Saklofske (2009) Intelligence: foundations and issues in assessment. *Canadian Psychology* 50, 183–195.

Graddol, David (1997) *The Future of English? A Guide to Forecasting the Popularity of English in the Twenty-First Century*. London: British Council.

Graddol, David (1998) Will English be enough? In Alan Moys (ed.) *Where are We Going with Languages?* London: Nuffield Foundation.

Graddol, David (2006) *English Next: Why Global English may mean the End of 'English as a Foreign Language'*. London: British Council.

Graddol, David and Ulrike Meinhof (eds) (1999) *English in a Changing World*. Oxford: The English Company. [= *AILA* (Association Internationale de Linguistique Appliquée) *Review* 13]

Gramsci, Antonio (1985) *Selections from Cultural Writings*. London: Lawrence & Wishart. [edited by David Forgacs and Geoffrey Nowell-Smith]

Green, Jonathon (1996) *Words Apart: The Language of Prejudice*. London: Kyle Cathie.

Greenberg, Robert (2004) *Language and Identity in the Balkans: Serbo-Croatian and its Disintegration*. Oxford: Oxford University Press.

Grenoble, Lenore and Lindsay Whaley (eds) (1998) *Endangered Languages*. Cambridge: Cambridge University Press.

Grenoble, Lenore and Lindsay Whaley (2006) *Saving Languages: An Introduction to Language Revitalization*. Cambridge: Cambridge University Press.

Grin, François (2004) L'anglais comme *lingua franca*: questions de coût et d'équité. *Économie publique* 15, 1–11. [a commentary on van Parijs (2004b), involving – as readers will note – some pagination errors]

Guest, Edwin (1838) *A History of English Rhythms*. London: Pickering.

Haarmann, Harald (1989) *Symbolic Values of Foreign Language Use: From the Japanese Case to a General Sociolinguistic Perspective*. Berlin: Mouton de Gruyter.

Hall, Geoff (2003) Review of *World English* (Janina Brutt-Griffler). *Journal of Sociolinguistics* 7, 443–447.

Hall, Robert (1974) *External History of the Romance Languages*. New York: Elsevier.

Halliday, Michael (1968) The users and uses of language. In Joshua Fishman (ed.) *Readings in the Sociology of Language*. The Hague: Mouton.

Haney, Craig, William Banks, and Philip Zimbardo (1973). Interpersonal dynamics in a simulated prison. *International Journal of Criminology and Penology* 1, 69–97.

Harbert, Wayne, Sally McConnell-Ginet, Amanda Miller and John Whitman (eds) (2009) *Language and Poverty*. Bristol: Multilingual Matters.

Harder, Peter (ed.) (2009) *English in Denmark: Language Policy, Internationalization and University Teaching*. Copenhagen: Museum Tusculanum.

Harrington, Jonathan, Sallyanne Palethorpe and Catherine Watson (2000) Does the Queen speak the Queen's English? *Nature* 408(6815), 27–28.

Hart, John (1569) *An Orthographie, Conteyning the Due Order and Reason Howe to Write or Paint Thimage [sic] of Mannes Voice, Most Like to the Life or Nature*. London: William Ser(r)es.

Haugen, Einar (1972) The ecology of language. In Anwar Dil (ed.) *The Ecology of Language: Essays by Einar Haugen*. Stanford: Stanford University Press.

Haugen, Einar (1985) The language of imperialism. In Nessa Wolfson and Joan Manes (eds) *Language of Inequality*. The Hague: Mouton.

Havel, Václav (1993) Short-sighted stumbling toward a new Europe. *The Globe and Mail* [Toronto], 30 November.

Hayward, Tim (1995). *Ecological Thought: An Introduction*. Cambridge: Polity.

Healy, Thomas (2007) A new tongue. *Times Literary Supplement*, 8 June.

Hellinger, Marlis and Anne Pauwels (2007) Language and sexism. In Marlis Hellinger and Anne Pauwels (eds) *Handbook of Language and Communication*. Berlin: Mouton de Gruyter.

Hendry, Leah (2000) Want to be bilingual? Try Spanish. *The Globe and Mail* [Toronto], 22 June.

Henry, Frances and Carol Tator (eds) (2009) *Racism in the Canadian University*. Toronto: University of Toronto Press.

Herder, Johann Gottfried (1772) *Abhandlung über den Ursprung der Sprache*. Berlin: Voss.

Herman, Simon (1961) Explorations in the social psychology of language choice. *Human Relations* 14, 149–164.

Hertzler, Joyce (1953) Toward a sociology of language. *Social Forces* 32, 109–119.

Hertzler, Joyce (1965) *The Sociology of Language*. New York: Random House.

Higginson, Edward (1864) *An English Grammar: Specially Intended for Classical Schools and Private Students*. London: Longman, Green, Longman, Roberts & Green.

Hinde, Wendy (1974) *George Canning*. New York: St Martin's.

Hiraga, Yuko (2005) British attitudes towards six varieties of English in the USA and Britain. *World Englishes* 24, 289–308.

Hirdman, Anja (2000) Male norms and female forms. In Karin Becker, Jan Ekecrantz and Tom Olsson (eds) *Picturing Politics: Visual and Textual Formations of Modernity in the Swedish Press*. Stockholm: Stockholm University, Department of Journalism, Media and Communication.

Hogg, Michael and Dominic Abrams (1988) *Social Identification*. London: Routledge.

Hoggart, Richard (1993) Mysteries of mass appeal. *Times Literary Supplement*, 9 July.

Hohenhaus, Peter (2005) Elements of traditional and 'reverse' purism in relation to computer-mediated communication. In Nils Langer and Winifred Davies (eds) *Linguistic Purism in the Germanic Languages*. Berlin: Walter de Gruyter.

Holborow, Marnie (1999) *The Politics of English: A Marxist View of Language*. Thousand Oaks, California: Sage.

Holden, Ronald and Talia Troister (2009) Developments in the self-report assessment of personality and psychopathology in adults. *Canadian Psychology* 50, 120–130.

Hollander, Anne (1979) How we believe we behave. *New York Times Book Review*, 29 April.

Holmes, Janet (1995) *Women, Men and Politeness*. London: Longman.

Holmes, Janet (1998) Women talk too much. In Laurie Bauer and Peter Trudgill (eds) *Language Myths*. London: Penguin.

Holmes, Janet (2001) A corpus-based view of gender in New Zealand English. In Marlis Hellinger and Hadumod Bussmann (eds) *Gender Across Languages: The Linguistic Representation of Women and Men* (Volume 1). Amsterdam: John Benjamins.

Holmes, Janet and Miriam Meyerhoff (eds) (2003) *Handbook of Language and Gender*. Oxford: Blackwell.

Homans, George (1961) *Social Behavior*. New York: Harcourt, Brace & World.

Honna, Nobuyuki (2008) *English as a Multicultural Language in Asian Contexts*. Tokyo: Kuroshio Shuppan.

Hovland, Roxanne, Carolynn McMahan, Guiohk Lee, Jang-Sun Hwang and Juran Kim (2005) Gender role portrayals in American and Korean advertisements. *Sex Roles* 53, 887–899.

Hughes, Geoffrey (2010) *Political Correctness: A History of Semantics and Culture*. Oxford: Wiley-Blackwell.

Hughes, Robert (1993) *Culture of Complaint: The Fraying of America*. Oxford: Oxford University Press.

Hunsley, John (ed.) (2009a) *Developments in Psychological Measurement and Assessment / Développements en mesure et évaluation psychologiques*. Ottawa: Canadian Psychological Association. [= *Canadian Psychology* 50(3)]

Hunsley, John (2009b) Introduction to the special issue on developments in psychological measurement and assessment. *Canadian Psychology* 50, 117–119.

Huygens, Ingrid and Graham Vaughan (1983) Language attitudes, social class and ethnicity in New Zealand. *Journal of Multilingual and Multicultural Development* 4, 207–223.

The Independent (2008) Dramatic decline in foreign languages studied at university. 19 August.

Ives, Peter (2004) Managing or celebrating linguistic diversity in the EU? *Note de recherche 03/04* (Institut d'études européennes, Montréal).

Ives, Peter (2006) 'Global English': Linguistic imperialism or practical lingua franca? *Studies in Language and Capitalism* 1, 121–141.

Ives, Peter (2009a) Cosmopolitanism and global English: Language politics in globalisation debates. *Political Studies* (online no. 1467-9248.2009.00781.x) http://www3.interscience.wiley.com/journal/120121142/issue

Ives, Peter (2009b) Global English, hegemony and education: Lessons from Gramsci. *Educational Philosophy and Theory* 41, 661–683.

Jaccard, James (1981) Attitudes and behavior: Implications of attitudes toward behavioral alternatives. *Journal of Experimental Social Psychology* 17, 286–307.

Jackman, Philip (2008) Accent envy. *The Globe and Mail* [Toronto], 31 July.

Jacobs, Roderick (2002) The role of foreign languages at university. *Modern Language Journal* 86, 251–252. [part of a forum in this issue on 'Language curricula in universities': see Larivière, 2002]

Jeffrey, David (1993) English literature. In Bruce Metzger and Michael Coogan (eds) *The Oxford Companion to the Bible*. Oxford: Oxford University Press.

Jenkins, Jennifer (2007) *English as a Lingua Franca: Attitude and Identity*. Oxford: Oxford University Press.

Jespersen, Otto (1922) *Language: Its Nature, Development and Origin*. London: Allen & Unwin.

Jin-Kyu Park (2009) 'English Fever' in South Korea. *English Today* 97 (25:1), 50–57.

Johnson, Patricia, Howard Giles and Richard Bourhis (1983) The viability of ethnolinguistic vitality: A reply. *Journal of Multilingual and Multicultural Development* 4, 255–269.

Johnson, Sally and Ulrike Meinhof (eds) (1997) *Language and Masculinity*. Oxford: Blackwell.

Jones, Edward and Harold Sigall (1971) The bogus pipeline: A new paradigm for measuring affect and attitude. *Psychological Bulletin* 76, 349–364.

Jones, Katharine (2001) *Accent on Privilege: English Identities and Anglophilia in the U.S.* Philadelphia: Temple University Press.

Joos, Martin (1967) *The Five Clocks*. New York: Harcourt, Brace & World.

Joseph, John (2001) Review of *The Politics of English: A Marxist View of Language* (Marnie Holborow). *Journal of Sociolinguistics* 5, 283–287.

Joseph, John (2004) *Language and Identity: National, Ethnic, Religious*. Basingstoke: Palgrave-Macmillan.

Joseph, John (2006) *Language and Politics*. Edinburgh: Edinburgh University Press.

Kachru, Braj (1985) Standards, codification and sociolinguistic realism: The English language in the 'outer circle'. In Randolph Quirk and Henry Widdowson (eds) *English in the World*. Cambridge: Cambridge University Press.

Kachru, Braj (1986) *The Alchemy of English*. Oxford: Pergamon.

Kachru, Braj (1988) The sacred cows of English. *English Today* 16 (4:4), 3–8.

Kang, Mee-Eun (1997) The portrayal of women's images in magazine advertisements: Goffman's gender analysis revisited. *Sex Roles* 37, 979–996.

Kang, Okim and Donald Rubin (2009) Reverse linguistic stereotyping: Measuring the effect of listener expectations on speech evaluation. *Journal of Language and Social Psychology* 28, 441–456.

Kedourie, Elie (1961) *Nationalism*. New York: Praeger.

Kenner, Hugh (1971) *The Pound Era*. Berkeley: University of California Press.

Kiesling, Scott (2007) Men, masculinities and language. *Language and Linguistics Compass* 1, 653–673.

Kindell, Gloria (1997) Summer Institute of Linguistics: What does SIL have to do with sociolinguistics? In Christina Bratt Paulston and G. Richard Tucker (eds) *The Early Days of Sociolinguistics*. Dallas: Summer Institute of Linguistics.

King, Lid (2001) The European Year of Languages: Taking forward the languages debate. *Language Teaching* 34, 21–29.

Kissau, Scott (2006) Gender differences in motivation to learn French. *Canadian Modern Language Review* 62, 401–422.

Klee, Carol (2002) Perspectives from Spanish. *Modern Language Journal* 86, 248–249. [part of a forum in this issue on 'Language curricula in universities': see Larivière, 2002]

Klee, Carol (2009) Internationalization and foreign languages: The resurgence of interest in languages across the curriculum. *Modern Language Journal* 93, 618–621. [part of a forum on 'The role of foreign language departments in internationalizing the curriculum': see Byrnes, 2009]

Kondro, Wayne (2000) Welcome to the dead language society. *The Globe and Mail* [Toronto], 24 July.

Krauss, Michael (1992) The world's languages in crisis. *Language* 68, 4–10.

Kreindler, Isabelle (1993) A second missed opportunity: Russian in retreat as a global language. *International Political Science Review* 14, 257–274.

Kristiansen, Tore (2001) Two standards: One for the media and one for school. *Language Awareness* 10, 9–24.

Kubota, Ryuko (2009) Internationalization of universities: paradoxes and responsibilities. *Modern Language Journal* 93, 612–616. [part of a forum on 'The role of foreign language departments in internationalizing the curriculum': see Byrnes, 2009]

Kuter, Lois (1989) Breton vs French. In Nancy Dorian (ed.) *Investigating Obsolescence: Studies in Language Contraction and Death.* Cambridge: Cambridge University Press.

Kutner, Bernard, Carol Wilkins and Penny Yarrow (1952) Verbal attitudes and overt behavior involving racial prejudice. *Journal of Abnormal and Social Psychology* 47, 649–652.

Labov, William (1976) *Language in the Inner City.* Philadelphia: University of Pennsylvania Press.

Labov, William (1977) *Sociolinguistic Patterns.* Philadelphia: University of Pennsylvania Press.

Labov, William (1994) *Principles of Linguistic Change.* Oxford: Blackwell. [Volume 1: *Internal Factors*; Volume 2: *Social Factors*]

Labov, William (2006) *The Social Stratification of English in New York City.* Cambridge: Cambridge University Press. [2nd edition: originally published in Washington by the Center for Applied Linguistics, 1966]

Lacordaire, Henri-Dominique (1872) *Conférences de Notre-Dame de Paris.* Paris: Poussielgue Frères. [in 5 volumes; the citation is from the third volume, covering the years 1846–1848]

Ladefoged, Peter (1992) Another view of endangered languages. *Language* 68, 809–811.

Ladegaard, Hans (1998a) Assessing national stereotypes in language attitude studies: The case of class-consciousness in Denmark. *Journal of Multilingual and Multicultural Development* 19, 182–198.

Ladegaard, Hans (1998b) National stereotyopes and language attitudes: The perception of British, American and Australian language and culture in Denmark. *Language and Communication* 18, 251–274.

Ladegaard, Hans (2000) Language attitudes and sociolinguistic behaviour: Exploring attitude-behaviour relations in language. *Journal of Sociolinguistics* 4, 214–233.

Ladegaard, Hans (2001) Popular perceptions of standard language: Attitudes to 'regional standards' in Denmark. *Language Awareness* 10, 25–40.

Ladegaard, Hans (2006) 'I like the Americans... but I certainly don't aim for an American accent': Language attitudes, vitality and foreign language learning in Denmark. *Journal of Multilingual and Multicultural Development* 27, 91–108.

de Laine, Michael (2001) Diversity or lingua franca for Europe? *Times Higher Education Supplement*, 23 February.

Laitin, David (1993) The game theory of language regimes. *International Political Science Review* 14, 227–239.

Lakoff, Robin (1990) *Talking Power: The Politics of Language in our Lives.* New York: Basic Books.

Lakoff, Robin (2004) *Language and Woman's Place: Text and Commentaries.* New York: Oxford University Press. [this revised and expanded edition of Lakoff's 1975 classic includes two dozen commentaries, under the editorship of Mary Bucholtz]

Lambert, Wallace, Robert Hodgson, Robert Gardner and Steven Fillenbaum (1960) Evaluational reactions to spoken languages. *Journal of Abnormal and Social Psychology* 60, 44–51.

Lambert-Drache, Marilyn (2001) Francophonie et cyberespace. *University Affairs*, May (42:5), 30.

Lane, Bernard (2009) Threatening blot on the polyglot. *The Australian*, 10 July.

LaPiere, Richard (1928) Race prejudice: France and England. *Social Forces* 7, 102–111.

LaPiere, Richard (1934) Attitudes versus actions. *Social Forces* 13, 230–237.

Larivière, Richard (2002) Language curricula in universities: What and how. *Modern Language Journal* 86, 244–246.

Lawrence, Jason (2006) *'Who the Devil Taught thee so much Italian?': Italian Language Learning and Literary Imitation in Early Modern England.* Manchester: Manchester University Press.

Lazar, Michelle (2005) *Feminist Critical Discourse Analysis.* London: Palgrave Macmillan.

Leaper, Campbell and Melanie Ayres (2007) A meta-analytic review of gender variations in adults' language use. *Personality and Social Psychology Review* 11, 328–363.

Leavis, Q. D. (Queenie) (1932) *Fiction and the Reading Public.* London: Chatto & Windus.

LeBon, Gustave (1895) *Psychologie des foules.* Paris: Félix Alcan.

Leet-Pellegrini, Helena (1980) Conversational dominance as a function of gender and expertise. In Howard Giles, Peter Robinson and Philip Smith (eds) *Language: Social Psychological Perspectives.* Oxford: Pergamon.

Lemon, George (1783) *English Etymology.* London: Robinson.

Lenneberg, Eric (1967) *Biological Foundations of Language.* New York: Wiley.

Leon, Pat (2002) Languages come under threat as demand falls. *Times Higher Education Supplement*, 12 July.

Leoussi, Athena (ed.) (2001) *Encyclopaedia of Nationalism.* New Brunswick, New Jersey: Transaction Publishers.

Leoussi, Athena and Steven Grosby (eds) (2007) *Nationalism and Ethnosymbolism.* Edinburgh: Edinburgh University Press.
Levin, Saul (1986) Can an artificial language be more than a hobby? In Humphrey Tonkin and Karen Johnson-Weiner (eds) *The Idea of a Universal Language.* New York: Center for Documentation on World Language Problems.
Levy, Leonard (1993) *Blasphemy.* Chapel Hill: University of North Carolina Press.
Lewis, Amanda (2005) *Race in the Schoolyard.* Piscataway, New Jersey: Rutgers University Press.
Lewis, E. Glyn (1976) Bilingualism and bilingual education: The ancient world to the Renaissance. In Joshua Fishman (ed.) *Bilingual Education.* Rowley, Massachusetts: Newbury House.
Li, David (2003) Between English and Esperanto. *International Journal of the Sociology of Language* 164, 33–63.
Linard, Jacques (1919) A French directive. *The Crisis* 18, 16–18.
Lindner, Katharina (2004) Images of women in general interest fashion magazine advertisements from 1955 to 2002. *Sex Roles* 51, 409–421.
Linn, Lawrence (1965) Verbal attitudes and overt behavior: A study of racial discrimination. *Social Forces* 44, 353–364.
Lippi-Green, Rosina (1997) *English with an Accent: Language, Ideology and Discrimination in the United States.* London: Routledge.
Livy (1971 [c. 25 B.C.]) *The Early History of Rome.* Harmondsworth, Middlesex: Penguin. [edited by Aubrey de Sélincourt]
Long, Daniel and Young-Cheol Yim (2000) Perceptions of regional variation in Korean. *Journal of the Linguistic Society of Japan* 117, 37–69
Macaulay, Thomas (1920 [1835]) Minute on education. In Henry Sharp (ed.) *Selections from Educational Records* (Part 1). Calcutta: Government Printing Office.
Machiavelli, Niccolò (1950 [1532]). *Il principe.* Rome: Antonio Blado. [a good modern edition is Max Lerner's 1950 version for the Modern Library, New York]
Mackey, William (1980) The ecology of language shift. In Peter Nelde (ed.) *Languages in Contact and Conflict.* Wiesbaden: Steiner.
MacLaughlin, Jim (1995) *Travellers and Ireland: Whose Country, Whose History?* Cork: Cork University Press.
Macnamara, John (1973) Attitudes and learning a second language. In Roger Shuy and Ralph Fasold (eds) *Language Attitudes: Current Trends and Prospects.* Washington: Georgetown University Press.
Maffi, Luisa (2000a) Language preservation vs. language maintenance and revitalization: Assessing concepts, approaches and implications for the language sciences. *International Journal of the Sociology of Language* 142, 175–190.
Maffi, Luisa (2000b) Linguistic and biological diversity: The inextricable link. In Robert Phillipson (ed.) *Rights to Language.* Mahwah, New Jersey: Erlbaum.
Maffi, Luisa (ed.) (2001) *On Biocultural Diversity: Linking Language, Knowledge and the Environment.* Washington: Smithsonian Institute Press.
Maffi, Luisa (2005) Linguistic, cultural and biological diversity. *Annual Review of Anthropology* 34, 599–617.
Mair, Christian (ed.) (2003a) *The Politics of English as a World Language.* Amsterdam: Rodopi.

Mair, Christian (2003b) Linguistics, literature and the postcolonial Englishes. In Christian Mair (ed.) *The Politics of English as a World Language*. Amsterdam: Rodopi.

Mair, Christian (2006) *Twentieth-Century English: History, Variation and Standardization*. Cambridge: Cambridge University Press.

Maiworm, Friedhelm and Bernd Wächter (2002) *English-Language-Taught Degree Programmes in European Higher Education*. Bonn: Lemmens.

Mallinson, Christine (2009) Sociolinguistics and sociology: Current directions, future partnerships. *Language and Linguistics Compass* 3/4, 1034–1051.

Mandela, Nelson (1995) *Long Walk to Freedom*. London: Abacus.

Marlow, Mikaela and Howard Giles (2010). 'We won't get ahead speaking like that! Expressing and managing language criticism in Hawai'i. *Journal of Multilingual and Multicultural Development* 31, 237–251.

Marsh, George (1860) *Lectures on the English Language*. New York: Scribner.

Marsh, Joss (1998) *Word Crimes*. Chicago: University of Chicago Press.

Martin, Bernice (2009) Review of *What Do You Want from Me?* (Terri Apter). *Times Literary Supplement*, 20 November, 27.

Maurais, Jacques and Michael Morris (eds) (2003) *Languages in a Globalising World*. Cambridge: Cambridge University Press.

de Mauro, Tullio (1963) *Storia linguistica dell'Italia*. Bari: Laterza.

Mayall, David (1995) *English Gypsies and State Policies*. Hatfield: University of Hertfordshire Press.

Mazrui, Alamin (2003) Review of *Words of the World: The Global Language System* (Abram de Swaan). *Journal of Multilingual and Multicultural Development* 24, 462–464.

Mazrui, Alamin (2004) *English in Africa: After the Cold War*. Clevedon: Multilingual Matters.

Mazrui, Alamin and Ali Mazrui (1993) Dominant languages in a plural society: English and Kiswahili in post-colonial East Africa. *International Political Science Review* 14, 275–292.

Mazzaferro, Gerardo (ed.) (2002) *The English Language and Power*. Alessandria: Edizioni dell'Orso.

McAleer, Joseph (1992) *Popular Reading and Publishing in Britain, 1914-1950*. Oxford: Clarendon.

McArthur, Tom (1998) *The English Languages*. Cambridge: Cambridge University Press.

McArthur, Tom (2001) World English and world Englishes: Trends, tensions, varieties and standards. *Language Teaching* 34, 1–20.

McArthur, Tom (2006) English world-wide in the twentieth century. In Lynda Mugglestone (ed.) *The Oxford History of English*. Oxford: Oxford University Press.

McCracken, Scott (1998) *Pulp: Reading Popular Fiction*. Manchester: Manchester University Press.

McCrum, Robert (1986) Tongue-tied to next year's words. *Times Higher Education Supplement*, 17 October.

McCrum, Robert, William Cran and Robert MacNeil (1986) *The Story of English*. New York: Viking.

McLean, Daryl and Kay McCormick (1996) English in South Africa, 1940-1996. In Joshua Fishman, Andrew Conrad and Alma Rubal-Lopez (eds) *Post-imperial*

English: Status Change in Former British and American Colonies, 1940-1990. Berlin: Mouton de Gruyter.

Melchers, Gunnel and Philip Shaw (2003) *World Englishes.* London: Edward Arnold.

Mencken, H. L. (Henry Louis) (1919–1948) *The American Language.* New York: Knopf. [the first edition appeared in 1919, the fourth in 1936; it had grown from about 400 pages to almost 800. Two supplements were published (in 1945 and 1948), of about 700 and 900 pages, respectively. In 1963, Raven McDavid presented a one-volume abridgement of the fourth edition and the two supplements]

Mencken, H. L. (Henry Louis) (1999 [1935]) The future of English. *Harper's* (September), 86–90. [an edited reprint of an article that first appeared in the April 1935 issue of *Harper's*]

Merton, Robert (1940) Fact and factitiousness in ethnic opinionnaires. *American Sociological Review* 5, 13–28.

Mesthrie, Rajend and Rakesh Bhatt (2008) *World Englishes.* Cambridge: Cambridge University Press.

Michaels, Leonard (1990) Prefatory note. In Christopher Ricks and Leonard Michaels (eds) *The State of the Language: 1990 Edition.* London: Faber & Faber.

Milgram, Stanley (1963) Behavioral study of obedience. *Journal of Abnormal and Social Psychology* 67, 371–378.

Milgram, Stanley (1974) *Obedience to Authority: An Experimental View.* New York: Harper & Row.

Miller, Katherine (2005) *Communication Theories.* New York: McGraw Hill.

Mills, Jean (2006) Talking about silence. *International Journal of Bilingualism* 10, 1–16.

Mills, Sara (2003) *Gender and Politeness.* Cambridge: Cambridge University Press.

Mills, Sara (2008) *Language and Sexism.* Cambridge: Cambridge University Press.

Milroy, Lesley and Paul McClenaghan (1977) Stereotyped reactions to four educated accents in Ulster. *Belfast Working Papers in Language and Linguistics* 2(4).

Milroy, Lesley and Dennis Preston (eds) (1999) *Attitudes, Perceptions, and Linguistic Features.* Los Angeles: Sage. [= *Journal of Language and Social Psychology* 18(1)]

Mok, Ka Ho (2007) Questing for internationalization of universities in Asia. *Journal of Studies in International Education* 11, 433–454.

Monck Mason, Henry (1846) *History of the Origin and Progress of the Irish Society, Established for Promoting the Education of the Native Irish, through the Medium of their own Language.* Dublin: Goodwin, Son & Nethercott.

Morry, Marian (2007) Relationship satisfaction as a predictor of perceived similarity among cross-sex friends: A test of the attraction-similarity model. *Journal of Social and Personal Relationships* 24, 117–138.

Moss, Howard (2000) Language and Italian national identity. In Gino Bedani and Bruce Haddock (eds) *Politics of Italian National Identity.* Cardiff: University of Wales Press.

Mufwene, Salikoko (2008) *Language Evolution: Contact, Competition and Change.* London: Continuum.

Mugglestone, Lynda (1995) *'Talking Proper': The Rise of Accent as Social Symbol.* Oxford: Clarendon Press. [a revised and enlarged second edition appeared in 2003]

Mugglestone, Lynda (ed.) (2006) *The Oxford History of English*. Oxford: Oxford University Press.

Mühleisen, Susanne (2003) Towards global diglossia? English in the sciences and the humanities. In Christian Mair (ed.) *The Politics of English as a World Language*. Amsterdam: Rodopi.

Mühleisen, Susanne (2007) Language and religion. In Marlis Hellinger and Anne Pauwels (eds) *Handbook of Language and Communication: Diversity and Change*. Berlin: Mouton de Gruyter.

Mühlhäusler, Peter (1996) *Linguistic Ecology*. London: Routledge.

Mühlhäusler, Peter (2000) Language planning and language ecology. *Current Issues in Language Planning* 1, 306–367.

Mulcaster, Richard (1582) *The First Part of the Elementarie*...London: Vautroullier.

Müller, Max (1862) *Lectures on the Science of Language*. London: Longman, Green, Longman & Roberts.

Mulvey, Laura (1975) Visual pleasure and narrative cinema. *Screen* 16(3), 6–18.

Mulvey, Laura (2009) *Visual and Other Pleasures*. Basingstoke: Palgrave Macmillan. [2nd edition]

Murray, Heather (2003) The status of English in Switzerland. In Joy Charnley and Malcolm Pender (eds) *Living with Languages: The Contemporary Swiss Model*. Berne: Lang.

Myers, David, Steven Spencer and Christian Jordan (2009) *Social Psychology*. Toronto: McGraw-Hill Ryerson. [4th Canadian edition]

Myhill, Debra and Frances Dunkin (2005) Questioning learning. *Language and Education* 19, 415–427.

Nahir, Moshe (1977) The five aspects of language planning. *Language Problems and Language Planning* 1, 107–123.

National Center for [Japanese] University Entrance Examinations (2008) Past center examination information. http://www.dnc.ac.jp/index.htm.

Nelson, Raymond (1999) Babylonian frolics: H. L. Mencken and *The American Language*. *American Literary History* 11, 668–698.

Nettelbeck, Colin (2009) *Beginners' LOTE (Languages other than English) in Australian Universities: An Audit Survey and Analysis*. Canberra: Australian Academy of the Humanities. [Nettelbeck was the Chief Investigator here, but was assisted by several others – including such well-known scholars as Michael Clyne and Joseph Lo Bianco]

Nettle, Daniel (1999) *Linguistic Diversity*. Oxford: Oxford University Press.

Nettle, Daniel and Suzanne Romaine (2002) *Vanishing Voices*. Oxford: Oxford University Press.

Nevalainen, Terttu and Ingrid Tieken-Boon van Ostade (2006) Standardisation. In Richard Hogg and David Denison (eds) *A History of the English Language*. Cambridge: Cambridge University Press.

Ngũgĩ wa Thiong'o (1981) *Detained: A Writer's Prison Diary*. London: Heinemann.

Ngũgĩ wa Thiong'o (1985) On writing in Gikuyu. *Research in African Literatures* 16(2), 151–155.

Ngũgĩ wa Thiong'o (1986) *Decolonising the Mind: The Politics of Language in African Literature*. London: Currey.

Ngũgĩ wa Thiong'o (1993) *Moving the Centre: The Struggle for Cultural Freedoms*. London: Currey.

Niedzielski, Nancy (2005) Linguistic purism from several perspectives: Views from the 'secure' and 'insecure'. In Nils Langer and Winifred Davies (eds) *Linguistic Purism in the Germanic Languages*. Berlin: Walter de Gruyter.

Noels, Kimberly and Richard Clément (1998) Language in education. In John Edwards (ed.) *Language in Canada*. Cambridge: Cambridge University Press.

Oakes, Leigh (2001) *Language and National Identity: Comparing France and Sweden*. Amsterdam: John Benjamins.

O'Donoghue, Daniel (1947) Nationality and language. In Columban League (ed.) *Irish Man – Irish Nation*. Cork: Mercier.

Ogbu, John (1999) Beyond language: Ebonics, proper English and identity in a Black-American speech community. *American Educational Research Journal 36*, 147–184.

O'Leary, Brendan (2001) Instrumentalist theories of nationalism. In Athena Leoussi (ed.) *Encyclopedia of Nationalism*. New Brunswick, New Jersey: Transaction Publishers.

Omoniyi, Tope and Joshua Fishman (eds) (2006) *Explorations in the Sociology of Language and Religion*. Amsterdam: Benjamins.

Onysko, Alexander (2004) Anglicisms in German: From iniquitous to ubiquitous? *English Today* 77(20:1), 59–64.

Oppenheim, A. N. (Abraham) (1992) *Questionnaire Design, Interviewing and Attitude Measurement*. London: Pinter. [2nd edition]

Orne, Martin (1962) On the social psychology of the psychological experiment: With particular reference to demand characteristics and their implications. *American Psychologist 17*, 776–783.

Orwell, George (1970 [1941]) The lion and the unicorn: Socialism and the English genius. In Sonia Orwell and Ian Angus (eds) *The Collected Essays, Journalism and Letters of George Orwell, Volume II*. Harmondsworth: Penguin. [this essay was first published by Secker and Warburg in 1941]

Orwell, George (1970 [1944]) As I please. In Sonia Orwell and Ian Angus (eds) *The Collected Essays, Journalism and Letters of George Orwell, Volume III*. Harmondsworth: Penguin. [this essay first appeared in *Tribune*, 21 April 1944]

Orwell, George (1970 [1947]) The English people. In Sonia Orwell and Ian Angus (eds) *The Collected Essays, Journalism and Letters of George Orwell, Volume III*. Harmondsworth: Penguin. [this essay, written in 1944, first appeared in an illustrated edition published three years later by Collins as part of their *Britain in Pictures* series]

Ostler, Nicholas (2005) *Empires of the Word: A Language History of the World*. London: HarperCollins.

Oulton, Nick (2000) Letter. *Times Literary Supplement*, 17 March.

van Parijs, Philippe (2000a) The ground floor of the world: On the socio-economic consequences of linguistic globalization. *International Political Scienc Review 21*, 217–233.

van Parijs, Philippe (2000b) Must Europe be Belgian? On democratic citizenship in multilingual polities. In Catriona McKinnon and Iain Hampsher-Monk (eds) *The Demands of Citizenship*. London: Continuum.

van Parijs, Philippe (2003) Linguistic justice. In Will Kymlicka and Alan Patten (eds) *Language Rights and Political Theory*. Oxford: Oxford University Press.

van Parijs, Philippe (2004a) Europe's linguistic challenge. *Archives européennes de Sociologie / European Journal of Sociology / Europäisches Archiv für Soziologie*

44, 113–154. [a revised edition of a 2001 paper, 'Europe's three language problem']

van Parijs, Philippe (2004b) L'anglais lingua franca de l'Union européenne: impératif de solidarité, source d'injustice, ferment de déclin? *Économie publique* 15, 1–21.

van Parijs, Philippe (2007) Tackling the Anglophones' free ride: Fair linguistic cooperation with a global lingua franca. *AILA* (Association Internationale de Linguistique Appliquée) *Review* 20, 72–86.

Park, Joseph Sung-Yul (2009) *The Local Construction of a Global Language: Ideologies of English in South Korea.* Berlin: Mouton de Gruyter.

Partridge, Eric (1963) *Swift's Polite Conversation.* London: André Deutsch.

Pečujlić, Miroslav, Gregory Blue and Anouar Abdel-Malek (eds) (1982) *Science and Technology in the Transformation of the World.* London: Macmillan.

Pennycook, Alastair (1994) *The Cultural Politics of English as an International Language.* London: Longman.

Pennycook, Alastair (1998) *English and the Discourses of Colonialism.* London: Routledge.

Pennycook, Alastair (2001) *Critical Applied Linguistics.* Mahwah, New Jersey: Erlbaum.

Phillipson, Robert (1992) *Linguistic Imperialism.* Oxford: Oxford University Press.

Phillipson, Robert (1994) English language spread policy. *International Journal of the Sociology of Language* 107, 7–24.

Phillipson, Robert (1997) Realities and myths of linguistic imperialism. *Journal of Multilingual and Multicultural Development* 18, 238–247.

Phillipson, Robert (2000) English in the new world order: Variations on a theme of linguistic imperialism and 'world' English. In Thomas Ricento (ed.) *Ideology, Politics and Language Policies.* Amsterdam: Benjamins.

Phillipson, Robert (2001) English in the new world order. Paper to the Nigerian Millennium Sociolinguistics Conference, Lagos.

Phillipson, Robert (2003a) Point-counterpoint: Perspective 2. *World Englishes* 22, 324–326.

Phillipson, Robert (2003b) *English-Only Europe?* London: Routledge.

Phillipson, Robert (2004) English in globalization: Three approaches. *Journal of Language, Identity and Education* 31, 73–84.

Phillipson, Robert (2007) Linguistic imperialism: A conspiracy, or a conspiracy of silence? *Language Policy* 6, 377–383.

Phillipson, Robert (2008) *Lingua franca* or *lingua frankensteinia*? English in European integration and globalisation. *World Englishes* 27, 250–267. [this article opens a 'forum' section (pp. 268–284) in which seven scholars make brief comments on Phillipson's thesis, followed by a final response from the author]

Pierce, A. H. (Arthur Henry) (1908) The subconscious again. *Journal of Philosophy, Psychology and Scientific Methods* 5, 264–271.

Plant, E. Ashby, Patricia Devine and Paige Brazey (2003) The bogus pipeline and motivations to respond without prejudice: Revisiting the fading and faking of racial prejudice. *Group Processes and Intergroup Relations* 6, 187–200.

Polzenhagen, Frank and René Dirven (2004) Rationalist or romantic model in language policy and globalisation. Paper presented at the LAUD (Linguistic Agency, University of Duisburg) Conference, Landau.

Pool, Jonathan (1991) The official language problem. *American Political Science Review* 85, 495–514

Porter, Bernard (2004) *The Absent-Minded Imperialists*. Oxford: Oxford University Press.

Poser, William (2006) The names of the First Nations languages of British Columbia. www.billposer.org/Papers/bclgnames.pdf

Puttenham, George (1589) *The Arte of English Poesie*. London: Richard Field.

Quirk, Randolph (1982) *Style and Communication in the English Language*. London: Edward Arnold.

Quirk, Randolph (1985) The English language in a global context. In Randolph Quirk and Henry Widdowson (eds) *English in the World*. Cambridge: Cambridge University Press.

Radway, Janice (1984) *Reading the Romance*. Chapel Hill: University of North Carolina Press.

Rahman, Tariq (1996) British language policies and imperialism in India. *Language Problems and Language Planning* 20, 91–115.

Ratzinger, Joseph (2005a) Cardinal Ratzinger on Europe's crisis of culture. (www.zenit.org/article-13705?l=english) [Ratzinger's lecture was given in Subiaco, on 1 April, the day before the death of John Paul II]

Ratzinger, Joseph (2005b) *L'Europa di Benedetto nella crisi delle culture*. Siena: Cantagalli.

Reagan, Timothy (2005) Review of *English as a Global Language* (David Crystal) and *The Local Politics of Global English* (Selma Sonntag). *Language Problems and Language Planning* 29, 289–291.

Réaume, Denise (2003) Beyond *personality*: The territorial and personal principles of language policy reconsidered. In Will Kymlicka and Alan Patten (eds) *Language Rights and Political Theory*. Oxford: Oxford University Press.

Réaume, Denise (2009) Lingua franca fever: Sceptical remarks. Unpublished paper, Nuffield College (Oxford), March.

Reicher, Stephen (2004) The psychology of crowd dynamics. In Marilynn Brewer and Miles Hewstone (eds) *Self and Social Identity*. Oxford: Blackwell.

Reisz, Matthew (2009) Mind your languages. *Times Higher Education Supplement*, 2 July, 30–35.

Rhodes, Nancy and Ingrid Pufahl (2009) *Foreign Language Teaching in U.S. Schools: Results of a National Survey (Executive Summary)*. Washington: Center for Applied Linguistics.

Ricento, Thomas (ed.) (2000) *Ideology, Politics and Language Policies*. Amsterdam: Benjamins.

Rich, Frank (1997) The Ebonic plague. *The Globe and Mail* [Toronto], 9 January.

Rist, Ray (1970) Student social class and teacher expectations: The self-fulfilling prophecy in ghetto education. *Harvard Educational Review* 40, 411–451.

Ritzer, George (1992) *The McDonaldization of Society*. Newbury Park, California: Pine Forge Press.

de Rivarol, Antoine (1797) *De l'universalité de la langue française.*. Paris: Cocheris.

Robins, Robert and Eugenius Uhlenbeck (eds) (1991) *Endangered Languages*. Oxford: Berg.

Robinson, John (1870) The future of the British Empire. *Westminster Review,* July (38), 47–74.

Rodd, Laurel (2002) Language curricula in universities: The case of Japanese, a 'more commonly taught less commonly taught language'. *Modern Language Journal* 86, 249–251. [part of a forum in this issue on 'Language curricula in universities': see Larivière, 2002]

Romaine, Suzanne (1999) *Communicating Gender*. Mahwah, New Jersey: Erlbaum.

Rosewarne, David (1984) Estuary English. *Times Educational Supplement*, 19 October.

Rosewarne, David (1994) Estuary English: Tomorrow's RP? *English Today* 37, 3–8.

Rothkopf, David (1997) Impraise of cultural imperialism. *Foreign Policy* 107, 38–53.

Rubin, Milka (1998) The language of creation or the primordial language: A case of cultural polemics in antiquity. *Journal of Jewish Studies* 49, 306–333.

Ryan, Alan (1993) Review of *Culture of Complaint* (Robert Hughes). *Times Literary Supplement*, 21 May.

Ryan, Ellen Bouchard (1979) Why do low-prestige varieties persist? In Howard Giles and Robert St Clair (eds) *Language and Social Psychology*. Oxford: Blackwell.

Ryan, Ellen Bouchard and Miguel Carranza (1975) Evaluative reactions of adolescents toward speakers of standard English and Mexican American accented English. *Journal of Personality and Social Psychology* 31, 855–863.

Ryan, Ellen Bouchard, Miguel Carranza and Robert Moffie (1977) Reactions toward varying degrees of accentedness in the speech of Spanish–English bilinguals. *Language and Speech* 20, 267–273.

Safran, William (2008) Language, ethnicity and religion: A complex and persistent linkage. *Nations and Nationalism* 14, 171–190.

Sahlins, Peter (1989) *Boundaries: The Making of France and Spain in the Pyrenees*. Berkeley: University of California Press.

Salminen, Tapani (1998) Minority languages in a society in turmoil: The case of the northern languages of the Russian Federation. In Nicholas Ostler (ed.) *Endangered Languages*. Bath: Foundation for Endangered Languages.

Samuels, David (2006) Bible translation and medecine man talk: Missionaries, indexicality, and the 'language expert' on the San Carlos Apache Reservation. *Language in Society* 35, 529–557.

Sapir, Edward (1921) *Language*. New York: Harcourt Brace.

Saraceni, Marion (2008) Comment 7. *World Englishes* 27, 280–281.

de Saussure, Ferdinand (1980 [1916]) *Cours de linguistique générale* [publié par Charles Bally et Albert Sechehaye, avec la collaboration de Albert Riedlinger]. Paris: Payot.

Sawyer, John (2001) Religion and language. In Rajend Mesthrie (ed.) *Concise Encyclopedia of Sociolinguistics*. Amsterdam: Elsevier.

Schiffman, Harold (1996) *Linguistic Culture and Language Policy*. London: Routledge.

Schlosser, Eric (2001) *Fast Food Nation*. Boston: Houghton Mifflin

de Schutter, Helder and Lea Ypi (2009) Language and luck. Unpublished paper, Nuffield College (Oxford), March.

Scollon, Ron (2001) Review of *The Politics of English: A Marxist View of Language* (Marnie Holborow). *Language in Society* 30, 323–324.

Seeley, J. R. (John Robert) (1883) *The Expansion of England*. London: Macmillan.

Séguin, Rhéal (2000) France not French enough, PQ says. *The Globe and Mail* [Toronto], 29 March.

Sharifian, Farzad (ed.) (2009) *English as an International Language*. Bristol: Multilingual Matters.

Sharifian, Farzad and Michael Clyne (eds) (2008) *International Forum on English as an International Language*. Melbourne: Monash University Press. [= *Australian Review of Applied Linguistics* 31(3)]

Shaw, John (1977) A devotion to the language. *West Highland Free Press*, 16 and 23 September. [Part 1: 'A widespread devotion to the language'; Part 2: '*Bithidh iad a'moladh na Gàidhlig, ach 'sann anns a'Bheurla*' – which translates as 'They praise Gaelic all right, but in English'; written under the pseudonym '*An ciaran siùbhlach*' – the 'dark wanderer']

Sherif, Muzafer (1956) Experiments in group conflict. *Scientific American*, 195(5), 54–58.

Sherif, Muzafer, O. J. Harvey, Jack White, William Hood and Carolyn Sherif (1961) *Intergroup Conflict and Cooperation: The Robber's Cave Experiment*. Norman, Oklahoma: University of Oklahoma Institute of Group Relations. [reprinted as *The Robber's Cave Experiment* by Wesleyan University Press (Middletown, Connecticut) in 1988]

Shuy, Roger and Ralph Fasold (eds) (1973) *Language Attitudes: Current Trends and Prospects*. Washington: Georgetown University Press.

Sidney, Philip (1973 [1595]) *An Apology for Poetry* [*The Defence of Poesie*]. Manchester: Manchester University Press. [both titles appeared on 1595 editions, published in London by William Ponsonby]

Sigall, Harold and Richard Page (1971) Current stereotypes: A little fading, a little faking. *Journal of Personality and Social Psychology* 18, 247–255.

Sillitoe, Alan (1995) *Leading the Blind: A Century of Guide Book Travel, 1815-1915*. London: Macmillan.

Simon, Paul (2001) Beef up the country's foreign language skills. *Washington Post*, 22 October.

Skutnabb-Kangas, Tove (2000) *Linguistic Genocide in Education or Worldwide Diversity and Human Rights*. Mahwah, New Jersey: Erlbaum.

Slotkin, Richard (2005) *Lost Battalions: The Great War and the Crisis of American Nationality*. New York: Henry Holt.

Smith, Anthony (1986) *The Ethnic Origins of Nations*. Oxford: Blackwell.

Smith, Gregory (2006) *Erving Goffman*. London: Routledge.

Smith, Hayley-Jane and Lance Workman (2008) The effect of accent on perceived intelligence and attractiveness. Paper presented at the Annual Conference of the British Psychological Society, Dublin (April).

Smith, Ross (2005) Global English: Gift or curse? *English Today* 82(21:2), 56–62.

Smith, Russell (2007) Who knew 'nooz' was about morality? *The Globe and Mail* [Toronto], 20 December.

Smitherman, Geneva (2006) *Word From the Mother: Language and African Americans*. London: Routledge.

Sonntag, Selma (2003) *The Local Politics of Global English*. Lanham, Maryland: Lexington.

Spencer, John (1985) Language and development in Africa. In Nessa Wolfson and Joan (eds) *Language of Inequality*. The Hague: Mouton.

Spolsky, Bernard (1989) Review of *Key Issues in Bilingualism and Bilingual Education* (Colin Baker). *Applied Linguistics* 10, 449–451.

Spolsky, Bernard (1996) English in Israel after independence. In Joshua Fishman, Andrew Conrad and Alma Rubal-Lopez (eds) *Post-imperial English: Status Change in Former British and American Colonies, 1940-1990*. Berlin: Mouton de Gruyter.

Spolsky, Bernard (1998) *Sociolinguistics*. Oxford: Oxford University Press.

Spolsky, Bernard (2003) Religion as a site of language contact. *Annual Review of Applied Linguistics* 23, 81–94.

Spolsky, Bernard (2004) *Language Policy*. Cambridge: Cambridge University Press.

Spurlock, Morgan (2004) *Super Size Me*. New York: Kathbur Pictures.

Stanyhurst, Richard (1582) *Thee First Fovre Bookes of Virgil his Aeneis translated intoo English heroical verse by Richard Stanyhurst*. Leiden: Iohn Pates.

Staples, Brent (1997) The last train from Oakland. *The New York Times*, 24 January.

Steiner, George (1992) *After Babel: Aspects of Language and Translation*. Oxford: Oxford University Press. [2nd edition]

Stewart, George (1975) *Names on the Globe*. New York: Oxford University Press.

Stewart, Mark, Ellen Bouchard Ryan and Howard Giles (1985) Accent and social class effects on status and solidarity evaluations. *Personality and Social Psychology Bulletin* 11, 98–105.

Stoll, David (1990) *Is Latin America Turning Protestant? The Politics of Evangelical Growth*. Berkeley: University of California Press

Stone, John (2004) Deconstructing rational choice: Or why we shouldn't over-rationalise the non-rational. *Journal of Ethnic and Migration Studies* 30, 841–843.

Straight, Stephen (2009) The role of FL departments: Enabling and fostering ubiquitous use of languages. *Modern Language Journal* 93, 624–627. [part of a forum on 'The role of foreign language departments in internationalizing the curriculum': see Byrnes, 2009]

Strong, Tracy (2009) Language learning and the social sciences. *Modern Language Journal* 93, 621–624. [part of a forum on 'The role of foreign language departments in internationalizing the curriculum': see Byrnes, 2009]

Sturgis, Patrick and Patten Smith (2009) Fictitious issues revisited: Political interest, knowledge and the generation of non-attitudes. *Political Studies* 58, 66–84.

Sussex, Roland (1999) Review of *English as a Global Language* (David Crystal). *Language in Society* 28, 120–124.

Sutherland, William (2003) Parallel extinction risk and global distribution of languages and species. *Nature* 423, 276–279.

de Swaan, Abram (1993a) The emergent world language system: An introduction. *International Political Science Review* 14, 219–226.

de Swaan, Abram (1993b) The evolving European language system: A theory of communication potential and language competition. *International Political Science Review* 14, 241–255.

de Swaan, Abram (1998a) A political sociology of the world language system (1): The dynamics of language spread. *Language Problems and Language Planning* 22, 63–75.

de Swaan, Abram (1998b) A political sociology of the world language system (2): The unequal exchange of texts. *Language Problems and Language Planning* 22, 109–128.

de Swaan, Abram (2001) *Words of the World: The Global Language System.* Cambridge: Polity.

de Swaan, Abram (2004) Endangered languages, sociolinguistics, and linguistic sentimentalism. *European Review* 12, 567–580.

Swaffar, Janet (1999) The case for foreign languages as a discipline. *ADFL* [Association of Departments of Foreign Languages] *Bulletin* 30(3), 6–12.

Swain, Harriet (2004) Anglo-Saxon 'weed' choking European flowers? *Times Higher Education Supplement*, 17 September.

Swann, Joan, Ana Deumert, Theresa Lillis and Rajend Mesthrie (2004) *A Dictionary of Sociolinguistics.* Edinburgh: Edinburgh University Press.

Swift, Jonathan (1712) *A Proposal for Correcting, Improving, and Ascertaining the English Tongue.* London: Tooke.

Swift, Jonathan (1738) *A Complete Collection of Genteel and Ingenious Conversation...* London: Motte and Bathurst. [Swift used the pseudonym 'Simon Wagstaff' here]

Tacitus (1964 [*c.* 110]) *The Annals and the Histories.* New York: Twayne. [edited and abridged by Hugh Lloyd-Jones]

Tajfel, Henri (ed.) (1978) *Differentiation Between Social Groups.* London: Academic Press.

Tajfel, Henri (ed.) (1982) *Social Identity and Intergroup Relations.* Cambridge: Cambridge University Press.

Talbot, Mary (2003) Gender stereotypes. In Janet Holmes and Miriam Meyerhoff (eds) *Handbook of Language and Gender.* Oxford: Blackwell.

Tannen, Deborah (1986) *That's Not What I Meant.* New York: Morrow.

Tannen, Deborah (1990) *You Just Don't Understand.* New York: Morrow.

Tannen, Deborah (1994) *Talking from 9 to 5.* New York: Morrow.

Teachout, Terry (2003) *The Skeptic: A Life of H. L. Mencken.* New York: Perennial (HarperCollins).

Teagle Foundation Working Group (Modern Language Association) (2009) Report to the Teagle Foundation on the undergraduate major in language and literature. *Profession* (Annual of the *Modern Language Association*), 285–312.

Terralingua (1999) *Statement of Purpose.* Hancock, Michigan: Terralingua.

TESOL (Teachers of English to Speakers of Other Languages) (2000) *TESOL Board of Directors Reaffirms Position on Language Rights.* Alexandria, Virginia: TESOL.

Thomas, George (1991) *Linguistic Purism.* London: Longman.

Todd, Loreto (1997) Ebonics: An evaluation. *English Today* 13(3), 13–17.

Tonkin, Humphrey and Timothy Reagan (eds) (2003) *Language in the Twenty-First Century.* Amsterdam: John Benjamins.

Tönnies, Ferdinand (1887) *Gemeinschaft und Gesellschaft.* Leipzig: Fues.

Townend, Matthew (2006) Contacts and conflicts: Latin, Norse and French. In Lynda Mugglestone (ed.) *The Oxford History of English.* Oxford: Oxford University Press.

Troyna, Barry and Richard Hatcher (1992) *Racism in Children's Lives.* London: Routledge.

Trudgill, Peter (1972) Sex, covert prestige and linguistic change in the urban British English of Norwich. *Language in Society* 1, 179–195.

Trudgill, Peter (2000) *Sociolinguistics: An Introduction to Language and Society.* London: Penguin. [4th edition]

Trudgill, Peter (2002) *Sociolinguistic Variation and Change.* Washington: Georgetown University Press.

Tsitsipis, Lukas (2005) Review of *Languages in a Globalising World* (Jacques Maurais and Michael Morris). *Language in Society* 34, 649–652.

Tsunoda, Minoru (1983) Les langues internationales dans les publications scientifiques et techniques. *Sophia Linguistica* 13, 144–155.

Tucker, G. Richard and Wallace Lambert (1969) White and Negro listeners' reactions to various American-English dialects. *Social Forces* 47, 463–468.

Turgeon, Mathieu (2009) 'Just thinking': attitude development, public opinion, and political representation. *Political Behavior* 31, 353–378.

Turner, John and Howard Giles (eds) (1981) *Intergroup Behaviour.* Oxford: Blackwell.

Twain, Mark (1882) Concerning the American language. In *The Stolen White Elephant, etc.* Boston: Osgood.

Utley, Alison (2002) Opt-out sounds 'death-knell' for languages. *Times Higher Education Supplement,* 21 June.

Walsh, Catherine (1991) *Pedagogy and the Struggle for Voice.* New York: Bergin & Garvey.

Wardhaugh, Ronald (1987) *Languages in Competition.* Oxford: Blackwell.

Wardhaugh, Ronald (2006) *An Introduction to Sociolinguistics.* Oxford: Blackwell. [5th edition]

Waterman, John (1966) *A History of the German Language.* Seattle: University of Washington Press.

Watson, James (ed.) (1997) *Golden Arches East: McDonald's in East Asia.* Stanford: Stanford University Press.

Watson, James (2000) China's Big Mac attack. *Foreign Affairs* 79(3), 120–134.

Welles, Elizabeth (2002) Foreign language enrollment numbers: Some (mis)interpretations explained. *Modern Language Journal* 86, 253–255. [part of a forum in this issue on 'Language curricula in universities': see Larivière, 2002]

Welles, Elizabeth (2004) Foreign language enrollments in United States institutions of higher education, Fall 2002. *ADFL* [Association of Departments of Foreign Languages] *Bulletin* 35(2/3), 7–26.

Wells, J. C. (John Christopher) (1982) *Accents of English.* Cambridge: Cambridge University Press.

Westoff, Charles and Tomas Frejka (2007) Religiousness and fertility among European Muslims. *Population and Development Review* 33: 785–809.

Wicker, Alan (1969) Attitudes versus actions: The relationship of verbal and overt behavioral responses to attitude objects. *Journal of Social Issues* 25(4), 41–78.

Wicker, Alan (1971) An examination of the 'other variables' explanation of attitude-behavior inconsistency. *Journal of Personality and Social Psychology* 19, 18–30.

Widen, Sherri and James Russell (2002) Gender and preschoolers' perception of emotion. *Merrill-Palmer Quarterly* 48, 248–262.

Wiggan, Greg (2007) Race, school achievement and educational inequality: Toward a student-based inquiry perspective. *Review of Educational Research* 77, 310–333.

Wiley, Terrence (2000) Continuity and change in the function of language ideologies in the United States. In Thomas Ricento (ed.) *Ideology, Politics and Language Policies.* Amsterdam: Benjamins.

Williams, Frederick (1974) The identification of linguistic attitudes. *Linguistics* 136, 21–32.

Williams, Frederick (1976) *Explorations of the Linguistic Attitudes of Teachers.* Rowley, Massachusetts: Newbury.

Williams, Glyn (1992) *Sociolinguistics: A Sociological Critique.* London: Routledge.

Williams, John, Susan Bennett and Deborah Best (1975) Awareness and expression of sex stereotypes in young children. *Developmental Psychology* 11, 635–642.

Williams, John, Howard Giles and John Edwards (1977) Comparative analyses of sex-trait stereotypes in the United States, England and Ireland. In Ype Poortinga (ed.) *Basic Problems in Cross-Cultural Psychology.* Amsterdam: Swets & Zeitlinger.

Williams, Robert (ed.) (1975) *Ebonics: The True Language of Black Folks.* St Louis: Institute of Black Studies.

Wilson, James (1998) *The Earth Shall Weep: A History of Native America.* New York: Grove.

de Wit, Hans (2002) *Internationalization of Higher Education in the United States of America and Europe.* Westport, Connecticut: Greenwood.

Wolfram, Walt (1998) Black children are verbally deprived. In Laurie Bauer and Peter Trudgill (eds) *Language Myths.* London: Penguin.

Woods, Roger (2005) Speaking in tongues. *Times Higher Education Supplement,* 2 September.

Wright, Sue (2004) *Language Policy and Language Planning: From Nationalism to Globalisation.* Basingstoke: Palgrave Macmillan.

Wright, Wayne (2005) Scholarly references and news titles. In J. David Ramirez, Terrence Wiley, Gerda de Klerk, Enid Lee and Wayne Wright (eds) *Ebonics: The Urban Education Debate.* Clevedon: Multilingual Matters. [2nd edition]

Wyatt, Michael (2005) *The Italian Encounter with Tudor England: A Cultural Politics of Translation.* Cambridge: Cambridge University Press.

Wyld, Henry (1934) *The Best English.* Oxford: Clarendon.

Yates, Frances (1934) *John Florio.* Cambridge: Cambridge University Press.

Ziff, Bruce and Pratima Rao (eds) (1997) *Borrowed Power: Essays on Cultural Appropriation.* New Brunswick, New Jersey: Rutgers University Press.

Zimbardo, Philip (2007) *The Lucifer Effect.* New York: Random House.

Zimbardo, Philip, William Banks, Craig Haney and David Jaffe (1973) The mind is a formidable jailer: A Pirandellian prison. *New York Times Magazine,* 8 April.

Index

Although there is some overlap, this index generally omits entries for material that can readily be found under a heading or sub-heading shown in the table of contents. Space constraints have meant that not all personal names have been listed here.